MW01039684

Romantic Readers

Romantic Readers

THE EVIDENCE OF MARGINALIA

H. J. Jackson

Yale University Press New Haven and London

Published with assistance from the Annie Burr Lewis Fund and the Louis Stern Memorial Fund.

Set in Fournier type by Keystone Typesetting, Inc.
Printed in the United States of America by Sheridan Books, Ann Arbor, Michigan.

Library of Congress Cataloging-in-Publication Data
Jackson, H. J.
Romantic readers : the evidence of marginalia / H. J. Jackson.
p. cm.
Includes bibliographical references and index.
ISBN 0-300-10785-4 (cloth : alk. paper)
1. Books and reading—Great Britain—History—19th century. 2. Marginalia.
3. Publishers and publishing—Great Britain—History—19th century.
4. Romanticism—Great Britain. 5. Great Britain—Intellectual life—19th century.
I. Title.
Z1003.5.G7J33 2005
028′.9′094109034—dc22 2004024638

A catalogue record for this book is available from the British Library.

The paper in this book meets the guidelines for permanence and durability of the Committee on Production Guidelines for Book Longevity of the Council on Library Resources.

10 9 8 7 6 5 4 3 2 1

For

Margaret Elizabeth Murphy

and in memory of

Colman Harrold Murphy

Contents

List of Illustrations

Preface

This book was written in response to two challenges. The first came from Robert Darnton, pondering the difficulties presented by the history of reading. Though some had argued that it was futile to attempt to reconstruct reading experiences from the past, Darnton thought there might be a way. "How can we recapture the mental processes by which readers appropriated texts?" he asks in "Seven Bad Reasons Not to Study Manuscripts" (40). "How can we avoid anachronism, the fatal sin of most historical research? One of the best strategies lies through marginalia." The second challenge was my own. In a survey of readers' notes from the last three centuries, I made historical claims the proof of which lay outside the scope of that preliminary study, declaring that since reading is a social art (everyone is *taught* to read), and since writing of all kinds is designed for communication, the notes that readers wrote in books in a given period might reveal quite a lot about the common codes of reading of that time as well as about the experience of the individual reader (*Marginalia*, 252–58). To test Darnton's hypothesis and verify or correct my own observations, I chose Britain in the Romantic period for close study, in part because I already knew it fairly well but more importantly because at that time the press was extraordinarily busy, "bibliomania" took off in Britain, extended literacy became a matter of public concern, and—perhaps not coincidentally—marginalia came out into the open. For reasons that will become apparent in the course of this book, the period presents, through marginalia, a particularly rich record of readers' engagement with their books.

Romantic Readers is therefore in the first place an empirical study, an account of manuscript notes written in books by readers between 1790 and about 1830. At the core of it is a set of roughly 400 books in the British Library and 200 in other collections, all published during the period and containing notes by unidentified contemporary readers. These books I consider especially valuable precisely because they were *not* acquired by the libraries they are now in on account of the notes; they just came with them. (The books were traced through online library catalogues and, in the case of the British Library, by reference to R. C. Alston's invaluable *Books with Manuscript*. As it turned out, names could often be put to the notes by comparing the hand of the notes with an ownership inscription; but as far as the library and its cataloguers were concerned, the identity of the writer was of no importance.) Where the annotator is named and famous, the notes are less likely to be accepted as normal or typical or run-of-the-mill than in the case of the unidentified reader (though in fact they may be quite ordinary), and I hoped to be able to describe ordinary use. The first 600 books thus helped to establish conventional practice, something I had skated over previously. To them I added about 500 with notes by named but minor figures, many of them antiquarians, collectors, scholars, and editors who had been influential in their time and were considered important for some time after, people like the Duke of Sussex, the lawyer Francis Hargrave, the antiquary Francis Douce, the classicist Charles Burney, the poet Anna Seward, the botanist James Edward Smith, and the clergyman and literary editor John Mitford. The great advantage of this group, besides contributing to the profile of normal use, was that it brought in older books and books in other languages, most of the contemporary titles belonging to the first group being in English—so it increased the range of kinds of work and thereby kinds of marginalia included. Finally I added about 700 books annotated by celebrities, people whose names guaranteed attention to their relics, whether they were recognized during their lifetimes or not. The scale and impressiveness of this group may be diminished by the fact that 400 of the books were Coleridge's, but it still contains a healthy number of examples of work by the likes of Horace Walpole, Hester Piozzi, William Blake, Leigh Hunt, John Thelwall, and John Keats. These gifted writers might be expected to prove themselves exceptional readers and to raise the standard in whatever they wrote, even if only marginalia, but the previous groups of books provide a context for assessing the alleged adept or genius. The anonymous, the minor, and the major figures are therefore mingled in the account that follows. The resulting gallery of characters and publications (for the annotated books themselves are not all well known), which I thought of at first as a by-product of the survey, now seems to me of interest in its own right as a display of the richness and variety of the book world at the time. Since most of the materials of this study—the marginalia themselves—existed only in an unpublished manuscript form, my first goal has been simply to *exhibit* them, to describe and quote from them in a way that may recreate for my readers the experience of direct contact, and as far as possible to let the voluble readers of the Romantic age speak for themselves. For the same reason, in establishing a context I have tried to get back behind the standard secondary studies to their sources in the letters, diaries, memoirs, and journalism of the period, so that there too Romantic readers can have their own say, individually and collectively.

From its empirical core, *Romantic Readers* expands to take up a number of related issues. Our own assumptions about (not to say prejudices against) the practice of writing in books have tended to blind us to the value that marginalia once had and to unfit us for interpreting documents of this order. A study of such documents, historically focused, ought to go some way toward correcting that tendency. But interpretation requires context and in this case the most appropriate context seemed to me to be provided not by conventional political history, still less by notions of a swelling spirit of Romanticism, but by history of the book and print culture. I therefore endeavor to set the scene for the investigation of Romantic-period marginalia by describing the commercial and social environment of reading: the availability of books, developments in publishing and marketing, and attitudes toward books and reading. The Romantics feel like us in so many ways that it is salutary to be reminded sometimes of the differences between their world and ours, especially the subtle inward differences of attitude or mentality.

This work is addressed to Romanticists, or rather to students of the Romantic period in Britain; to literary scholars interested in reception and reader response; to historians of the book; and to owners or custodians of annotated books who might want help in figuring out what's going on in them. Following a broad survey of the reader's world in the Introduction, three chapters examine marginalia of various kinds from a grassroots level. The first kind is found in books connected with the professional work of educators, lawyers, and publishers; in the first chapter, therefore, while stopping short of actual professional paperwork, I confront the sort of workaday routine use that is usually taken for granted and ignored. This evidence of ordinary "common-sense" use is included because it represents a part of the continuum of the practice of readers writing in books—it's part of the whole picture—and because there are some surprises in the midst of dull routine. The second chapter shows books being treated as companions, whether as substitutes for or as contributions to human socializing. The third has to do with showpieces, books got up to display their owners' taste or knowledge. Though the method of categorization is not perfect, something had to be done to bring a vast, miscellaneous crowd of examples into order, and function offered more common ground than genre or chronology. Under different circumstances, readers wrote different kinds of notes in books of the same kind: a classical author, for example, might inspire one reader to collect textual variants while another might take issue with the argument, assess the quality of the writing, or compare it with contemporary English literature.

The contents of all three chapters are mustered in a fourth to address the central question: what can we learn or infer about reading in the Romantic period—"the mental processes by which readers appropriated texts," as Darnton puts it—from marginalia of that time? Which question leads to others, in the Conclusion. Why should we care? What do we mean by "history of reading" anyway, and why does it matter?

DEFINITIONS OF TERMS

It is customary to say that in this period the roles of bookseller and publisher were indistinct. I'm not convinced that is so: it might be more accurate to say that some individuals or firms filled both roles, some only one or the other. In this book in defiance of tradition I use "publisher" freely to mean the one who pays the costs of publishing (printing, advertising, distribution). The author may be, often was, the publisher. "Bookseller" is reserved for the one from whom readers bought books and other typeset matter, such as newspapers and periodicals. "Marginalia" I use inclusively, as in the earlier book, for all manuscript additions made by readers to a printed text, whether or not they are in the margins proper. For all their limitations I prefer "annotator" and "annotate" to the antique-sounding "marginator" and "marginate," however, and have used them throughout to describe the various roles and activities of readers writing in books.

CONVENTIONS

A few conventions of presentation and reference have been slightly adapted for this volume. All references, whether they are included in parentheses in the text or given in notes, are keyed to two bibliographies at the back of the book. In a variation of the standard MLA system, very brief references are incorporated in the text but longer ones as well as discursive additions are presented in notes. Context provides the name of the author or, in the case of anonymous works, the title. If the reference is to an annotated book where the marginalia exist only in manuscript form, it will be found in the Bibliography of Books with Manuscript Notes. Otherwise it will appear in the Bibliography of Secondary Sources, which includes published marginalia. In the transcription of marginalia spelling, punctuation, and capitalization are faithfully recorded but cancellations are silently omitted. Underlining represents the annotator's underlining both in excerpts from the printed, commented-on text and in marginalia; italic is used where the printed text is italic and when marginalia are quoted from a published version that employs this convention. In numbering flyleaves I count back from the first printed page and forward from the last, so −3 means the third blank page before the first printed page, +1 the first blank page after the last printed one.

ACKNOWLEDGMENTS

This book would not have been written without a lot of outside help. I am most grateful to the Killam Foundation of the Canada Council for the Arts, which awarded me two precious years of freedom from other academic responsibilities, and to the Social Sciences and Humanities Council of Canada, which provided funding to support research travel and expenses, including graduate assistants. Those assistants—Andrea England, Susan Brown, and Nicola Hessell—contributed largely to the book, especially to the backdrop of the reading environment, and by giving me sympathizers to talk to, they preserved me from total isolation. (Nicola Hessell, who was completing a dissertation on Coleridge's journalism at the time, was the source of all the newspaper evidence and many of the illustrations from periodicals, correspondence, and memoirs.) To several friends, students, and colleagues I am indebted for generous advice and encouragement, particularly to Donna Andrew, Sharon Howe, Brad Inwood, Paul Magnuson, James McConica, Andrew Nicholson, and Carol Percy. Jane Millgate and Robin Jackson read drafts of the whole book. Historians of the law, Allyson May and Sir John Baker kindly read and commented on the section that deals with Francis Hargrave. In every library visited on behalf of this project the staff assisted me in professional and super-professional ways, but I must single out a few individuals who were exceptionally helpful: John Hopson, Archivist at the British Library; Richard Landon, in the Thomas Fisher Rare Book Library at the University of Toronto; Guy Holborn, Librarian of Lincoln's Inn; Robert Brandeis and Carmen Socknat at

Victoria College in Toronto; Stephen Wagner at the Pforzheimer Collection in the New York Public Library; Gina Douglas, at the Linnean Society; and Maggie Powell at the Lewis Walpole Library in Farmington, Connecticut. And for cheerful, expert support in the final stages, my thanks to Larisa Heimert, Phillip King, and Kay Scheuer of Yale University Press.

POSTSCRIPT

William St. Clair's *The Reading Nation in the Romantic Period* was published by Cambridge University Press in 2004 while *Romantic Readers* was in the press. Though I could have enriched this book, particularly in the Introduction, with scores of references to it, I was pleased to find that the two studies, relying on different kinds of documentary evidence, were broadly compatible and complementary in their results. Where St. Clair's version of the history of publishing and reception varies from other accounts, including mine, he should have the credit of new discoveries and interpretations. I decided not to alter my work, but I heartily recommend his independent and thorough survey.

The Reading Environment

What did the reading environment feel like to Romantic readers? Exciting. Unstable. The period is so routinely portrayed as an age of revolution that it is hardly surprising that even the peaceful occupation of reading is sometimes said to have been revolutionized during those turbulent years.[1] At the time, commentators in the press alerted their readers to the remarkable upheavals they were experiencing. These days, historians like to quote the memoirs of the rags-to-riches bookseller James Lackington, published in 1791, which claimed that the poorest country laborers "now shorten the nights by hearing their sons and daughters read tales, romances, &c. and on entering their houses you may see Tom Jones, Roderick Random, and other entertaining books stuck up in their bacon-racks, &c. and if *John* goes to town with a load of hay, he is charged to be sure not to forget to bring home 'Peregrine Pickle's adventures;' and when *Dolly* is sent to the market to sell her eggs she is commissioned to purchase 'The History of Pamela Andrews.' In short all ranks and degrees now READ."[2] Writers of the period made the same point as Lackington again and again, only differing as to whether the central matter of fact—"all ranks and degrees now read"—was reason for rejoicing or for regret. In 1793 Horace Walpole deplored the "herd of idle readers"—here there is no explicit social distinction—generated by the periodicals, which, as he said, "must make rapid impression, or are shoved aside by their own tribe" (*Correspondence,* 15:239). A sour reviewer of Robert Southey's collection of new poetry, the *Annual Anthology,* in the *Monthly Review* of April 1800, also thought that the judgment of the marketplace had been affected for the worse: "the art of printing has rendered the beauties of poetry accessible to persons of all degrees of information, and has increased the number of bad judges still more than that of bad writers" (13:352). A few months later, though, in the *Monthly Magazine* of August 1800, Mary Robinson took a more positive position, observing that "Every man, nay, almost every woman, now reads, thinks, projects, and accomplishes," with the result that "the poorest peasant is now enabled to trace the language of truth, in pages calculated by the plainest doctrines and the most rational reasonings to awaken, enlighten, harmonize, regulate, and refine the human understanding" (10:35).

The political debate about the value of extended literacy that is implied in these contrary opinions continued throughout the period, but the huge increase of readership was a given, just as it was understood that most of the increase came from social groups with little formal education, not only servants and laborers but also the families of shopkeepers and artisans, and most women. While intellectuals like Godwin and Coleridge merely grumbled about the dumbing-down of literature and the decline of studious reading, fears of a working-class rebellion fueled by the likes of Tom Paine and William Cobbett led the government to respond with taxes and prosecutions aimed at reining in the radical press.[3] And of course almost everyone made fun of the silly women—ladies, ladies' maids, cooks, and kitchen-maids, according to the standard mythology—who glutted themselves on novels and romances (Fig. 1).[4] But neither ridicule nor legislation could stop them. By 1820, according to the *Quarterly Review,* newspapers, novels, and the improving literature promoted by Dissenters had entirely driven out the chapbooks that used to keep the old stories alive. John and Dolly are revisited: "The kitchen wench, who thumbs the Mysteries of Udolpho, or the Rose of Raby, *won't grieve at all* for the death of Fair Rosamond. . . . The old broadside-ballads have given way to the red stamp

FIG. 1 "Luxury, or the Comforts of a Rum p ford" (1801)—the title alluding to Gillray's earlier "Comforts of a Rumford Stove." The publishers offer "Folios of Caracatures lent out for the Evening." The books depicted are *The Oeconomy of Love, The Kisses,* and *The Monk.* © The Trustees of The British Museum.

of the newspaper; and pedlars burn their ungodly story-books like sorcerers of old, and fill their baskets with the productions sanctified by the Imprimatur of the Tabernacle" (21:91–92). The *Retrospective Review,* starting up in the same year, took a more cheerful view of the spectacle of "a whole nation employing nearly all its leisure hours from the highest to the lowest ranks in *reading*—we have been truly called a READING PUBLIC" (1:iv). In a private letter also of 1820, Sydney Smith judiciously assessed the situation and correctly forecast its political and commercial consequences. Middle-class publishers, he said, should and would take over the cause of parliamentary reform from the radical press (1:343):

> There are four or five hundred thousand readers more than there were thirty years ago, among the lower orders. A market is open to the democrat writers, by which they gain money and distinction. Government cannot prevent the commerce. A man, if he know his business, can write enough for mischief, without writing enough for the Attorney-General. The attack upon the present order of things will go on; and, unfortunately, the gentlemen of the people have a strong case against the House of Commons and the borough-mongers, as they call them. I think all wise men should begin to turn their faces reform-wards. We shall do it better than Mr. Hunt or Mr. Cobbett. Done it *must* and *will* be.

A downturn in the economy after 1825 seemed only to accelerate the production of books. A package review of some of the season's new novels, most of them produced by the firm of Colburn and Bentley, in the *Monthly Review* for March 1830, marveled that in times of "ruined agriculturalists" and "woeful crisis" readers could still be found for the hundreds of novels coming off the presses, yet conceded that the readers must exist, "For, if there were no readers, there would be no circulating libraries; if no circulating libraries, no novels, no contract authors, no Colburn and Bentleys. It is now in literature as in other trades; great consumption is followed by great supply" (n.s. 13:462).

From the point of view of eyewitnesses like these—and it would be easy to multiply them many times over—the supposed reading revolution of 1790–1830 consisted in an expansion of the market followed by a transformation of the products of the press, specifically, a switch to periodicals and novels. It was frequently noted that households that might once have owned only a Bible, with perhaps a few broadsides and chapbooks, now enjoyed a more varied reading diet and demanded novelty. The census-taker John Rickman complained in 1812 that "Every one who reads at all reads a Sunday newspaper, not the Bible" (Williams, 160). Robert Southey in 1822 coolly described to a correspondent a dynamic of social unrest and market forces, with a dash each of opportunism and luck: "One effect of general education (such as that education is) is beginning to manifest itself. The twopenny journals of sedition and blasphemy lost their attraction when they no longer found hunger and discontent to work upon. But they had produced an appetite for reading. Some journeymen printers who were out of work tried what a weekly twopenny-worth of miscellaneous extracts would do; it answered so well, that there were presently between twenty and thirty of these weekly publications, the sale of which is from 1000 to 15,000 each" (5:116–17). What Southey describes is essentially the process later documented by historians: general education (fostered by the churches) leading to widespread basic literacy and a demand for print which in turn brought about increased profits and competition in the publishing business. Whether these developments add up to a revolution of any kind is another question.

Historians find support for the idea of a new mass market in population statistics and literacy rates.

> Between 1780 and 1830 the population of Great Britain had doubled, from approximately 7 to 14 millions, with the greatest national rate of increase between 1811 and 1821. Between 1801 and 1821 the population of Greater London expanded by over 40 per cent, while Liverpool and Manchester each grew by over 40 per cent in one decade 1821 to 1831. The reading public, it is estimated, quintupled in the whole period 1780 to 1830, from 1½ to 7 millions.[5]

But the fact that many people believe and say a thing does not make it so; contemporary witnesses could be echoing one another, indulging in wishful thinking, or just reiterating the gossip and alarms of the day. And solid statistical data for pre-Victorian Britain are hard to come by. Kathryn Sutherland's well-documented survey, just quoted, refers guardedly to an "estimated" reading public, in the absence of reliable overall numbers and bypassing the notoriously flawed figures available for lower-class literacy. There is some disagreement about population statistics. Whatever the details, however, the general pattern is plain. A doubling of the population coinciding with the rapid growth of cities, and the success of the Sunday School movement (from 1780) increased the number of readers and purchasers of printed matter. The presses and all their dependent industries were busy. To writers it seemed a time of great and rapid change, and they both welcomed and feared the emergence of a mass audience, that is, very large numbers of people all calling for the same product, at a time when large numbers could be found only by admitting lower-class readers.

Literacy was not in itself the prime agent of change. Studies of literacy are bedeviled by problems of definition at least as much as by problems of evidence. What constitutes literacy, and what proofs are sufficient and available? Does it mean the ability to sign one's name in a marriage register? But boys and girls in church schools and charity schools were often taught to read but not to write, as a matter of policy. Lackington himself, who was self-taught, had been reading at an advanced level for some time before he decided that he needed to be able to write.[6] Does it mean the ability to sound out words, to read aloud, which was the basic goal of elementary schooling; or does it also entail the ability to follow and understand a text? And in either of these cases, what criteria can be applied? What reports could be fitted together to produce a credible general estimate of the strength of the reading public? Historians are resourceful but the records are sketchy. An analysis of the number of books published based on the online records of the *Eighteenth-Century Short-Title Catalogue* and the *Nineteenth-Century Short-Title Catalogue* indicates a fairly steady rise in the number of titles produced annually, but the two catalogues were formed on different bases and are hard to join up. Furthermore they do not allow for lost titles, especially from earlier years; and the number of titles would have to be correlated with print runs to demonstrate growth decisively.[7] We tend to have to rely on figures occasionally reported by publishers, booksellers, or authors, but these are in the nature of things exceptional cases, and the figures are often unsubstantiated. Lackington is the only authority for the claim that he once had in stock 10,000 copies of Watts's hymns (*Memoirs*, 230). Did Paine really sell 200,000 copies of the second part of *The Rights of Man* (1792) in a year? This spectacular number, constantly repeated, rests on what the *Dictionary of National Biography* (*DNB*) refers to as "a sixpenny tract, adding little." Did the Cheap Repository for Religious and Moral Tracts, established by

Hannah More and others, really print and distribute two *million* of their little chapbooks within a year of their founding in 1795, "besides great numbers in Ireland," as their Treasurer declared?[8] The estimate of seven million readers in 1830 might be right, but it is hardly secure.

More damaging to the notion that an increase in literacy rates effected a reading revolution during the Romantic period is the fact that the widespread ability to read seems to have existed before the period began. Lackington's memoirs describe as the status quo of 1791 a situation in which "all ranks and degrees now read," and his representative laborers already read novels. Back in the 1770s, Hester Thrale had won a bet with Johnson by proving that five of the Thrales' eighteen servants had read *Don Quixote* (though it has to be said, first, that Johnson was surprised by this result, and, second, that it is not clear that the household staff could not have passed his test by having heard it read rather than by having read it themselves).[9] If the second part of Paine's *Rights of Man* did sell 200,000 copies in a year, the mass audience so much wooed and dreaded by the end of the period must have been already latent at the beginning of it. John Rule believes that literacy rates were in fact relatively stable during the Romantic era (140). The difference after 1790 seems to lie not in literacy rates per se but in increased population (greater absolute numbers) and in the spread of the desire to exercise the ability to read, or in Southey's words the growth of an "appetite for reading." Where did *that* come from, then, and why did it peter out in the late 1820s? Some of the commentators who attribute the expansion of the reading audience to excitement about the Revolution and the French wars blamed the subsequent loss of interest to the public debate about parliamentary reform that was to culminate in the Reform Bill of 1832.[10] (The point is that only newspapers and topical pamphlets were selling by then, as we tune in to 24-hour news stations at times of crisis now.) But the argument that political events should arouse interest in the first place and kill it off later does not make much sense, and we have to consider other possibilities.

A second approach to the alleged reading revolution starts from the business or supply end of things rather than from the demand end. It emphasizes the effect of the industrial revolution on publishing and argues that the introduction of important technology in the Romantic period—notably the Stanhope Press, Fourdrinier paper-making machinery, Church's letter-founding machine, lithography, stereotype, steam printing, and cloth bindings—swept away traditional artisanal methods and brought in mass production, making possible lower prices and larger sales. This argument suffers from the opposite of the flaw in the mass-market case: the possibility of a mass market existed even before 1790, but mass production of printed matter did not take hold until after 1830. Most of the technological innovations listed should properly be said to have been under development between 1790 and 1830, along with many other projects that fell by the wayside. Their value at this time therefore was largely potential. The iron Stanhope Press first constructed in 1800 did not significantly increase the rate of production, which awaited the application of steam-power—the pioneering example being that of *The Times* in 1814, with improvements in 1828.[11] The paper-making patents acquired by the Fourdrinier family firm in 1804 led them to bankruptcy and protracted litigation, and although other manufacturers took up the idea, taxes together with the steep cost of raw materials during the war years kept paper prices high until the mid-1820s, and they did not really tumble until after the successful production of wood-pulp paper in the 1840s. The first English patent for what is now known as lithography was taken out in 1801 but as Michael Twyman reports, "In Paris and London it was not until the early to mid 1820s that the [lithographic] trade began to emerge."[12] Church's letter-founding machine, which could cast up to 20,000 letters in a day as opposed to the maximum of 7,000 cast by hand, was not invented till 1822, and uniform cloth publishers' bindings were likewise a phenomenon of the 1820s and not yet a threat to the norm of leather bindings made to order. In 1805 the Clarendon Press at Oxford acquired Stanhope's system for stereotyping, which meant that casts taken from formes of type could be kept for making reprints; but the system was not perfected, nor widely employed, before 1829. In any case these and other improvements in the printing industry took time to prove their worth and before 1830 were not so widely adopted as to produce radical change either in working methods or in the quantities of printed matter available.[13]

If "revolution" is the wrong word to apply to the reading environment of Britain in the Romantic period, how should we think of it? If it was not until after 1830 that the mass audience and mass production came together, what was going on in the meantime? It seems to me that between 1790 and 1830 we can see the beginning and end of a reading boom, a boom activated not so much by social, political, or technological changes (though partly by them) as by competitive commercial activity, especially advertising and reviewing; and that when the boom was over, a somewhat chastened industry started up a new path, courting the mass market that it had previously been inclined to spurn. The eighteenth century as a whole had seen steady growth in printing and publishing and related trades.[14] After 1790 the trend continued; it was business as usual, only more so. All readers benefited from the boom; the same cannot be said for all authors and publishers. The remainder of this chapter describes the multifaceted publishing system of the time, both its stable elements and its occasional convulsions and innovations, from the reader's point of view, dealing with basic facts about the book trade, with common economic calculations, with the availability of reading matter, and with customs and fashions related to reading. The goal is to sketch out a complex but familiar system in which readers played an active role and neither were perceived nor saw themselves merely as the final stage of delivery and consumption.

THE BASICS: DISTRIBUTION, THE ECONOMY, COPYRIGHT

At the end of the eighteenth century, to state the obvious, print media monopolized education and communications and had a dominant share of what we now call the entertainment industry. Though exhibitions, outdoor activities, and live performances of various kinds were occasionally available, for everyday recreation in the absence of radio, television, CDs, movies, and the Internet, people of all classes read or were read to or looked at prints together. Poverty and illiteracy were not insurmountable obstacles, as anti-Jacobin hand-wringers were quick to point out: if you could not read or possess reading matter, you could still listen and talk about what you had heard. The daily newspapers were on the front lines, and to the existence of the dailies readers owed many direct and indirect benefits: the fostering of the habit of reading itself; notice of new publications; above all, an enviable distribution network. Altick points out that the daily sales of the *Morning Chronicle* in 1803 amounted to 3,000 copies and of the *Morning Post* to 4,500; by 1822 *The Times* and its evening edition, the *Evening Mail*, together reached 5,730, the *Morning Chronicle* 3,180, and the *Morning Post* (now thrice-weekly) 2,000 (392). Though these figures are very small by today's standards, we have to allow for the smaller population and for the resourcefulness of readers who coped with the punitive taxes on newspapers by renting and sharing. Every paper had multiple readers and passed, by Altick's estimate, "through a dozen or even scores of hands" (322).[15]

The owners of provincial newspapers used local agents to distribute papers in their districts. The tax-paid stamped paper that they were obliged to use had to come from London, however, so they needed metropolitan agents as well. They therefore obtained paper through contacts in London, carried advertising for London publishers, and made their networks available for the distribution of printed materials from all over the country. It was a well-established, mutually advantageous system.[16] The title pages of books published in the period often say simply, "Sold by all booksellers." Advertisers conventionally but accurately used the formula "printed for X and sold by all other booksellers, stationers, and news-carriers, in town or country" or "Sold by Booksellers and Newsmen" (Figs. 2, 3).[17] So the metropolitan and provincial newspapers, the periodical reviews, and the book trade tended to reinforce one another. In Wales in 1796, Hester Piozzi and her friends were impatient to see Edmund Burke's latest book, of which they had had a foretaste from advertisements or reviews; as Piozzi shrewdly observed, "the News Papers tantalize one with extracts which increase one's Appetite without gratifying it" (*Letters*, 2:319). Once the

The Newcastle Chronicle.

[Price Fourpence.] SATURDAY, July 1, 1797. [Ready Money with Advertisements.] No. 1728.

FIG. 2 Front page of *The Newcastle Chronicle*, 1 July, 1797. By permission of Newcastle Libraries and Information Service.

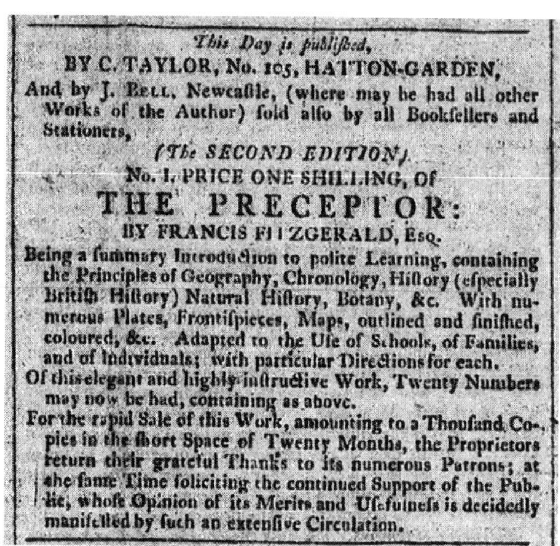

This Day is publifhed,
BY C. TAYLOR, No. 105, HATTON-GARDEN,
And by J. Bell, Newcaftle, (where may be had all other Works of the Author) fold alfo by all Bookfellers and Stationers,
(The SECOND EDITION)
No. I. PRICE ONE SHILLING, OF
THE PRECEPTOR:
BY FRANCIS FITZGERALD, Esq.
Being a fummary Introduction to polite Learning, containing the Principles of Geography, Chronology, Hiftory (efpecially Britifh Hiftory) Natural Hiftory, Botany, &c. With numerous Plates, Frontifpieces, Maps, outlined and finifhed, coloured, &c. Adapted to the Ufe of Schools, of Families, and of Individuals; with particular Directions for each.
Of this elegant and highly inftructive Work, Twenty Numbers may now be had, containing as above.
For the rapid Sale of this Work, amounting to a Thoufand Copies in the fhort Space of Twenty Months, the Proprietors return their grateful Thanks to its numerous Patrons; at the fame Time foliciting the continued Support of the Public, whofe Opinion of its Merits and Ufefulnefs is decidedly manifefted by fuch an extenfive Circulation.

FIG. 3 Close-up of publisher's advertisement from Fig. 2.

book came out, it would be efficiently distributed around the country but if for some reason it did not appear in a local bookshop or circulating library it could be ordered from the publisher, directly by post or through the newsagent, to be delivered within a week.[18] A secondary effect of this excellent commercial arrangement was that it created a nationwide network of *readers* more or less on a par with one another as far as access was concerned and more or less conscious, as television viewers are today, of their common experience and their collective power.

Close on the heels of the newspapers and beneficiaries of the same distribution network were the periodical reviews, with smaller circulation figures but a longer shelf-life. Taken in by book clubs and subscription libraries, or passed from hand to hand, "these journals carried news into the quietest villages and to persons of modest means and education."[19] Individuals might subscribe to one or two periodicals, but reading clubs, libraries, and literary societies had to carry several. Their numbers—both the reading groups and the periodicals—grew rapidly and fed the burgeoning trade. Jon Klancher maintains that the *Monthly* and *Critical* between them "stimulated a fourfold increase in British book publication by the end of the century."[20] By 1817 Southey was able to boast that the print run of the *Quarterly Review* to which he was a major contributor was 10,000 "and fifty times ten thousand read its contents" (4:240).

Readers compulsively consulting and discussing the papers of the day were affected in the routines and habits of their daily lives by developments in publishing as well as by the events that make up official history. From the reader's perspective, the peace treaty signed between France and Germany in 1797 and the naval mutinies of early summer in that year probably mattered less than the increase of the stamp tax on newspapers, and 1802 was more likely to be remembered for the founding of the audacious *Edinburgh Review* than for the short-lived Peace of Amiens. Sometimes the concerns of the two worlds coincided, as when the Act of Union with Ireland (1801) brought Dublin printers under the jurisdiction of British copyright law, or when a major public event, such as the trial of Queen Caroline in 1820, created a press frenzy. But an alternative history of readers and reading would tend to dwell on characters and events that are not usually considered part of the public record and cast a different light on ones that are. In a period for which the official history is generally grim, the history of reading is a bright, if untidy, area—and that seemingly *because* rather than in spite of widespread hardship.

Economic histories leave no doubt about the dire state of Britain, which was in an almost constant state of war—in India, in America, and on the Continent—until 1815, and then in a postwar slump for years after. A time of increasing trade (especially with the United States) and general prosperity came to an end in 1792, to be followed by a decade of bad harvests, government overspending, and labor unrest. Wages rose during the war years, when able-bodied men were needed in the army and navy, but wages did not keep pace with prices. Periods of respite and recovery such as 1809–10 and 1817–18 seem to have been short-lived, and the longer hopeful period of 1822–24 led to inflation, financial panic, severe unemployment, and a general depression in 1826.[21] Trends in publishing are consistent with this overall economic pattern, but only up to a point. The period of expansion and prosperity had included substantial investment in the infrastructures of publishing.

Twyman notes that toward the end of the eighteenth century, the number of printing shops in London began to increase, with 124 of them recorded in 1785, 216 in 1808, 316 in 1824, and around 500 by 1850; at the same time, printing spread all over the country, no longer restricted to cities and the larger towns.[22] By 1814 an itinerant bookseller, David Love, could *reprint* the most popular items in his stock as he went from place to place (Harris, 96): "We rested three times on our return, first at Berwick-upon-Tweed, where I reprinted one of my books, and called the town; I got as many books before-hand, as carried me to Newcastle-upon-Tyne; there again I reprinted, called the town, and got books to bring up to Leeds in Yorkshire. I did the same at Leeds, which enabled us, by the Lord's blessing, to come to Nottingham." Production of books, measured in published titles, grew as we have seen; some years saw an abrupt rise because of an event of great public interest, but the trend is an even upward incline. Production of newspapers and periodicals, measured by the number of newcomers every year, also climbed steadily, with a peak in 1824–5; and though it is not clear how many of the newcomers—like dot-coms today—survived their first year, there was evidently no shortage of investors ready to take a chance.[23] The crash that hit the economy as a whole at the end of 1825 and beginning of 1826 took some publishers with it, notably Constable (and with him, Scott), but after a careful study of the available figures, Simon Eliot concludes that the crisis of 1826 "can be seen as no more than a little local difficulty, a somewhat exaggerated version of the 'dip' which almost always followed a year of exceptionally high production" (24). John Sutherland also demonstrates that the statistics do not bear out the publishers' sense of apocalypse: "the British book trade as a whole," he says, "seems to have weathered the 1826 storm quite serenely" (161).

British publishing appears to have been one of those "exceptional groups," as Rule calls them, that profited from the state of war (185). The hunger for news engendered by foreign and domestic crises created a great demand for newspapers and everything that went with them, from reporters and editors to reading rooms and debating clubs. If the loss of French sources of paper and of fine rags for paper-making pushed prices up, at the same time it meant new opportunities for

British industry. The high import duties on foreign books that Southey bitterly complained of must have been good for domestic sales. The British print industry enjoyed the double advantage of skilled émigré workers and the elimination of French competition. Though book prices on average were high, still there were bargains to be had and the stimulus and comfort of the printed word were in one form or another available to every income. Books were for a time both highly prized and *obtainable* luxuries. So the presses prospered, and readers too.

The year 1774 is a crucial date for the history of publishing in Britain. The major London publishers had previously exercised control over the book market by claiming perpetual copyright in the works they owned, by purchasing copyrights or sharing them only within their own group, and by engaging in informal partnerships to prevent other dealers from selling their books. When the case of Donaldson *v.* Becket was decided on appeal to the House of Lords in February 1774, however, perpetual copyright was declared invalid in common law.[24] Copyright practice thus fell back on the provisions of the Act of 1710, which gave the author of a new work copyright for fourteen years, renewable once. A severe blow to the London cartels, this decision had two immediate and long-lasting effects, both with happy consequences for readers: it improved the status of the author, and it opened the door—some would say, the floodgates—to other publishers, especially for works now officially out of copyright.

Under the new dispensation, authors gained important powers. They could, and in many cases still did, choose to sell their work outright to the publisher, but the copyright would revert to them after fourteen years, and if the book had done well, they could negotiate anew. Or they could keep the copyright and publish for themselves, taking both the risk and the profits. As a compromise, they might sell the copyright of a single edition or a limited number of editions. Authors who had already had some success could hold out for a higher price for the copyright of a new work. Publishing history records some legendary sums highly encouraging to aspiring writers in this period. Constable paid Scott an advance of 1,000 guineas for a poem in 1807 and, once he had proved himself as a novelist, gave him £12,000 for his existing copyrights. Hannah More on the other hand kept her copyright, paid her own printing costs, and sold her two-volume novel *Coelebs in Search of a Wife* (1808) for only twelve shillings but still cleared £2,000 in a year. Murray offered Byron £2,000 for Canto 3 of *Childe Harold* in 1816, and in 1822 offered Washington Irving 1,000 guineas for a new work sight unseen.[25] The profits that could be made from writing were reflected at less starry levels by the fees paid to anonymous reviewers. In 1796, for example, the *Monthly Magazine* was paying Southey five guineas a sheet, but before long he was getting seven pounds from the *Annual Review.* In 1807 he heard from Scott that the *Edinburgh* was paying ten guineas a sheet. As the number of reviews multiplied and competition for reviewers became fiercer, the *Edinburgh* doubled that rate.[26] During the vogue for the pretty gift-books known as "annuals" in the late 1820s, John Clare earned twenty guineas a sheet writing for the *Forget-Me-Not* (*Letters,* 121).

But these new powers inevitably brought new burdens for authors as well: since there were no literary agents, they had to negotiate and take business decisions on their own behalf. Judging by their correspondence, the small talk of writers must for years have been dominated by the question of what to do about copyright. The old system was gone; the giddy confusions of free enterprise took over. If you could not afford to publish for yourself and had to bargain with a publisher, how much protection did copyright really provide? Southey sought always to keep his copyrights, but as late as 1812 he was not sure that he could bequeath them to his heirs (*Life,* 3:331). Lackington thought authors were ill advised to hold onto their copyrights, partly because of the inconvenience to buyers, who might have to order specially from the author rather than dealing with their regular bookseller; and partly because the trade could be lukewarm or actually hostile in handling such a book.[27] The maverick John Trusler, who dabbled in just about everything from divinity to table-setting, took a similar position for different reasons. He kept his copyrights only because he could not get what he considered a fair price from another publisher. He thought copyrights were more trouble than they were worth: "if a Writer cannot sell his first manuscript as soon as he has completed it, he had better burn it & employ himself any other way than attempt a second. . . . if an Author can get but 300£ for a two guinea volume in manuscript it is better to sell it outright than have the trouble (if it be attended with success) of printing & reprinting, binding advertizing & vending it."[28]

Coleridge was perhaps typical of his kind in not knowing quite what to do but being ready to try almost anything, as his correspondence with successive publishers shows. In 1796, for instance, he was taken with a scheme of Count Rumford's (probably his ideas about poor relief in Bavaria) and offered his publisher Joseph Cottle a pamphlet adapting that scheme as an urban project for Bristol. With a few changes to the text, he pointed out, the same plan could be put to Birmingham and Manchester, thus tripling the sale with very little effort. They could print 750 copies at a shilling apiece. "Now will you undertake this—either to print it & divide the profits with me—or (which indeed I should prefer) would you give me three guineas for the Copy-right?"[29] Cottle sent him the money—the equivalent of a guinea a sheet, much less than Southey was getting for his reviews—though he declined to publish. In the long run, outright sale of copyright came to be less common than the alternative arrangement Coleridge put forward: the publisher paying expenses and then having an equal share of the profits once the expenses were recovered. (Scott complained that even under this sensible compromise the publisher generally contrived "to take the lion's share of the booty" [*Letters*, 6:45]. And yet he invariably recommended shared profits as the best available arrangement.[30]) Copyright continued to be a contentious issue, however, with authors vigorously campaigning for a longer term. In 1814 it was extended to 28 years in the first instance and then, if the author were still alive, for the remainder of his or her life; in 1842 to 42 years or the life of the author plus seven years, whichever was longer.

PRINT BARONS AND PRINT SERFS

The copyright ruling of 1774 that enhanced the position of writers diminished that of publishers and obliged them to try new devices to keep ahead of their competitors. By 1790 it was already clear that even with little capital investment fortunes could be made through authorship, bookselling, and publishing. Blake noted with approval in 1800, "There are now I believe as many Booksellers as there are Butchers."[31] Crabb Robinson recorded the rumor that Joseph Johnson had made at least £10,000 as the publisher of Cowper (1:381). The early nineteenth century produced ever more spectacular examples both of triumph and of failure. Lackington, for instance, had started out as a shoemaker with a sideline in books; John Nichols's father was a baker, Joseph Johnson's a farmer; William Chambers in Scotland earned only four shillings a week as a bookseller's apprentice in 1814; but all of them achieved wealth and respectability through publishing. Rudolph Ackermann, the son of a German coach-builder and himself at first a drawing-teacher in London, built up a lucrative business in fine-art publishing, with its headquarters in the Repository of the Arts in the Strand. Even the disasters were inspiringly ambitious. John Boydell, an engraver and print publisher, became Lord Mayor of London in 1790, but his Shakespeare Gallery fell foul of the war economy and had to be sold by lottery with his other assets in 1805 to pay off his debts. Archibald Constable began humbly but enjoyed a spectacular career before the crash of 1826. In a self-conscious trade with built-in opportunities for self-promotion, these stories were well known.

The period 1790–1830 offers an impressive display of enterprise and ingenuity in the book trade from top to bottom. It also exhibits complex interdependencies through patterns of ownership and combinations of roles. At the high end of the business, the major publishing firms of London and Edinburgh saw to it that they kept their grip on the trade by involvement in other print media.[32] In 1800 Southey complained of the advantage that a publisher like Richard Phillips had over someone like himself, hoping to avoid the middleman: Phillips owned the *Monthly Magazine*, and therefore "can afford to pay [an author] a good price, because he can advertize and puff his own property every month" (*Life*, 2:121). It was part of a regular pattern. Publishers like Phillips all had their bookshops and their vehicles for advertising and reviewing. John Bell, who specialized in cheap editions of standard authors, was one of the proprietors of the *Morning Post*. Joseph Johnson was cofounder of the *Analytical Review* of 1788–99. Nichols was from 1792 to 1826 part-owner and editor of the *Gentleman's Magazine*. Longman and Constable each had a half-share of the *Edinburgh Review*, while Murray owned the *Quarterly*. These great publishers followed the traditions of liberality established by their eighteenth-century precedessors, supporting their stables of writers and winning their loyalty with breakfasts, dinners, soirées, and salons that created and cemented literary alliances. Godwin and Wollstonecraft met at one of Joseph Johnson's dinners in 1791: in his *Memoirs* Godwin fondly recalled that he hadn't liked her very much because he had been obliged to pay attention to her when he wanted to listen to Paine (Wollstonecraft, 235–36).[33] Murray's drawing-room receptions were legendary.[34] Scott's printer Ballantyne, ordinarily a modest host, rose to "aldermanic" feasts on special occasions such as book-launches (Lockhart, 5:129–32). In 1804 Southey urged Coleridge to give Longman a chance: "Go to one of his Saturday evenings; you will see a coxcomb or two, and a dull fellow or two; but you will, perhaps, meet Turner or Duppa, and Duppa is worth knowing" (*Life*, 2:268). What we now refer to as corporate hospitality was a routine part of the business of the successful publishing houses.

At the other end of the economic scale, too, members of the trade were likely to fill several roles at once. Taking his cue from commercial directories, Maxted distinguishes between primary and secondary trades: in London in 1817, for example, he counts 176 printers of whom 31 also counted themselves publishers, and 335 booksellers doubling as stationers (xxv). The printer John Abraham in London published and sold *A Tour from London to the Lake . . . in the Summer of 1791. By a Gentleman* from his circulating library in Lombard Street, where customers could also purchase his exclusive American Salve, good for corns, sprains, and breast cancer.[35] In smaller places the combination of tasks was likely to be even more pronounced. In Bromley in Kent, about 1797, the bookseller Thomas Wilson like many of his provincial colleagues sold stationery and ran a circulating library. He probably carried newspapers and periodicals. He may have had a sideline in tobacco.[36] And he was the author of a pamphlet about circulating libraries, a poem for children called *The Battle of the Boys and the Flies*, a

(119)

A CATALOGUE OF BOOKS

Sold by THOMAS WILSON,

BROMLEY, KENT,

At the following remarkable low Prices.

1 APPLEGARTH's Theological Survey of the Human Underſtanding — 1s. 6d.
2 Art of living in London — 6d.
3 Anecdotes (Wilſon's) — — 1s.
4 Battle of the Boys and Flies — 6d.
5 Botanical Prints from Bailey's Botany, by J. F. Miller, exquiſitely coloured from Nature — 9s.
6 Belcher's Literary, and Critical Remarks 2s. 6d.
7 Britiſh Songſter — — 2s.
8 Concubine (Apſem) — — 6d.
9 Cook's Voyages, 3 vols. complete — 15s.
10 Cooper's Complete Diſtiller — 6s.
11 Dr. Watſon's Anſwer to the Age of Reaſon 1s.
12 Dickſon's Catalogue of Plants — 5s.
13 Dixon's Voyage round the World, fine plates, 15s.
14 Davis's Diary — — 1s. 9d.
15 Encyclopedia Brittanica, 36 half volumes 18l. 18s.
16 Emma Dorville — — 1s. 3d.
17 Feſtival of Love — 3s. 6d.
18 Fortune Teller — — 1s.
19 Fairfax's Sportſman — 2s. 6d.
20 Gibſon's Pocket Atlas — 2s. 6d.
21 Glaſs's Cookery Abridged — 8d
22 Gay's Fables — — 2s. 6d.
23 Hervey's Meditations — 2s. 6d.
24 Hill's Herbal — — 4s.
25 Junius's Letters, 2 vols. — 5s. 6d.

(120)

26 Lavater on Phyſiognomy, upwards of 300 plates, 4 vols. handſomely bound — 2l. 10s.
27 Life of the Counteſs De la Motte, with the Tranſaction of the Diamond Necklace, 2 vols. 8vo. 5s.
28 Modern Pariſh Officer — 1s. 6d.
29 Mouſe Trap, 2 vols. — 2s. 6d.
30 Myſterious Mother — — 1s.
31 Memoirs of Miſs Bellamy — 2s.
32 Memoirs and Life of Miſs Bellamy, 6 vols. 9s.
33 Newgate Callendar, 6 vols. — 20s.
34 New Gardener's Callendar — 1s.
35 Nature ſtudied — — 2s.
36 Patterſon's Travels, 4to. — 3s. 6d.
37 Pratt's Gleanings, 3 vols. 8vo. — 19s.
38 Porney's Romances — 2s. 6d.
39 Philips's Voyage to Botany Bay, fine plates 1l. 1s.
40 Prior's Nut Brown Maid, — 6d.
41 Rowe's (Mrs.) Letters — 2s.
42 Sir John Thorold on the Trinity — 1s.
43 Supplement to the Life of D. Hume — — 6d.
44 Sportſman, Farrier, and Shoeing Smith's Guide 3s.
45 Tryal of Lord Baltimore, — 1s. 3d.
46 Ten Minutes Advice in the Purchaſe of a Horſe 6d.
47 Vernon's Songſter — — 1s.
48 Vicar of Wakefield and Peruvian Princeſs 3s.
49 Virtuous Orphan, with plates, 4 vols. 5s.
50 Wright's Bible, handſomely bound — 2l.
51 World Diſplayed, 10 vols. — 1l.
52 Wilſon's Uſe of Circulating Libraries - - 1s.
53 Wondreful Magazine, 5 vols. — 1l.
54 Wonders of Nature and Art, 6 vols. 15s.
55 Watt's Pſalms and Hymns — 1s. 6d.
56 Wright's Every Man his Own Chaplain 8d.
57 Zeluco, 2 vols. 8vo. — — 10s.
58 Zelia in the Deſart, 3 vols. 4s — — 4s.

BOOKS AND STATIONARY, OF ALL KINDS,

WHOLESALE AND RETAIL.

FIG. 4 "A Catalogue of Books" from Thomas Wilson, *An Accurate Description of Bromley, in Kent* (1797). By permission of the British Library.

short history of Bromley, *Anecdotes, Moral . . . and Amusing,* and a fiction entitled *A Village Tale*—all of which of course he sold in his shop (Fig. 4). The one thing he did not do was run a jobbing press. John Soulby of Ulverston in Lancashire, about 1807, advertised as "printer, book-binder, book-seller, and stationer"; he carried patent medicines, supplied periodical publications, and kept a circulating library. His stationer's stock included gold and silver toothpicks, wallpapers, and (because he sold music) violin strings.[37] By diversifying more or less within the bounds of the printing trades, small businesses like these contrived to make a living.

Writers themselves often became publishers in a minor way. With printers as thick on the ground, it seems, as dry cleaners today, it was not difficult.[38] If money was no object, you made your own arrangements and disposed of the product as you pleased. If your means were modest, you could yet print—with or without publishing—documents important to you. The *Gentleman's Magazine* in October 1790 (928) reviewed a 400-page "Geography and History, selected by a Lady, for the Use of her own Children": when she found her children could not read her handwriting, she had the work printed, and once it was printed, she published it. (The reviewer doubted this story and damned the work anyway as "shamefully deficient and inaccurate.") There is a rather wretched subgenre of defensive pamphlets such as Nicholas Tomlinson's *Vindication of the Conduct of an Old Injured Naval Officer* (1800) and Mrs. M.W.'s *Narrative of Insidious Transactions practised towards a Gentleman in the Army* (1806).

If you were penniless, you could still see your work in print, for all the newspapers and magazines printed contributions from readers, though usually anonymously and without pay. Southey's advice to a young poet in 1808 was to start with the newspapers and gauge the response: if the work did well he would be able to ask for a fee another time, and so work up to a volume of his own with his name on it (*Life*, 3:174). The handsome *Poetical Magazine* of 1809–11, published by Ackermann, solicited original work by "poets of every denomination and character," some of whom published under their own names, some anonymously or under pseudonyms. (It appears to have survived mainly by sales to its contributors and their friends, but it did include the first Dr. Syntax poems by William Combe, written to accompany Rowlandson engravings.) Anyone who could raise the printing costs through friends or by subscription could publish a book or start up a journal; copies sold over and above those reserved for subscribers would profit the author, and at least the work would get a hearing. Coleridge tried with limited success to run his own periodicals, *The Watchman* in 1796 and *The Friend* in 1809–10. The numbers of new journals every year show that he was one of many.

Another option available to those who could not afford to print or to buy books, or who did not intend to publish indiscriminately, was the circulation of work in manuscript—a practice of obvious relevance to the writers of marginalia. The advent of print did not mean the end of handwritten texts, and private libraries continued to contain manuscript material. Coleridge's "Christabel" acquired a reputation years before it was printed, thanks to Coleridge's recitations and to the "wide circulation" of copies in manuscript.[39] As a schoolboy, Coleridge by his own account made "more than forty transcriptions" of the complete text of the *Sonnets* of William Lisle Bowles "as the best presents I could offer to those, who had in any way won my regard."[40] For the cost of paper, ink, and one's own labor, any reader could make copies of unaffordable books, or of the best parts of them.

ENTERPRISING BOOKMEN: LEMOINE AND TRUSLER

In the world of publishing itself there are some fascinating figures in the middle distance, independent of the major firms by choice or necessity, and so presenting alternative models. There must have been swarms of men and women of this order investing capital and energy in the growth area of publishing. Henry Lemoine (1756–1812) is a good example. He is usually described as a London eccentric; that was certainly the way his contemporaries saw him (Fig. 5). But the Dickensian ups and downs of his career only reflect the realities of the publishing system, its opportunities on the one hand and severities on the other. The London-born son of a French immigrant, he was apprenticed to a stationer-cum-rag-merchant and then to a baker-bookseller.[41] When he came of age he inherited some money with which he set up a stall selling books and medicines. He began to write for the magazines—prose and verse, biography, bibliography, medicine, pornography. Hack writing of one kind or another sustained him for most of his life. He edited books on boxing (1788?), ghosts (1791), and medicinal plants (1793), which he published himself. He started up the popular *Conjuror's Magazine* in 1792 and the *Wonderful Magazine*—one of a succession of cheap magazines with "wonderful" in the title, dating back to the 1760s—in 1793.[42] After failing in a copperplate printing venture and being imprisoned for debt, he had to give up his bookstand and become an itinerant hawker or colporteur. But he continued to write for hire, and it was after his failure that he produced the one work for which he is still

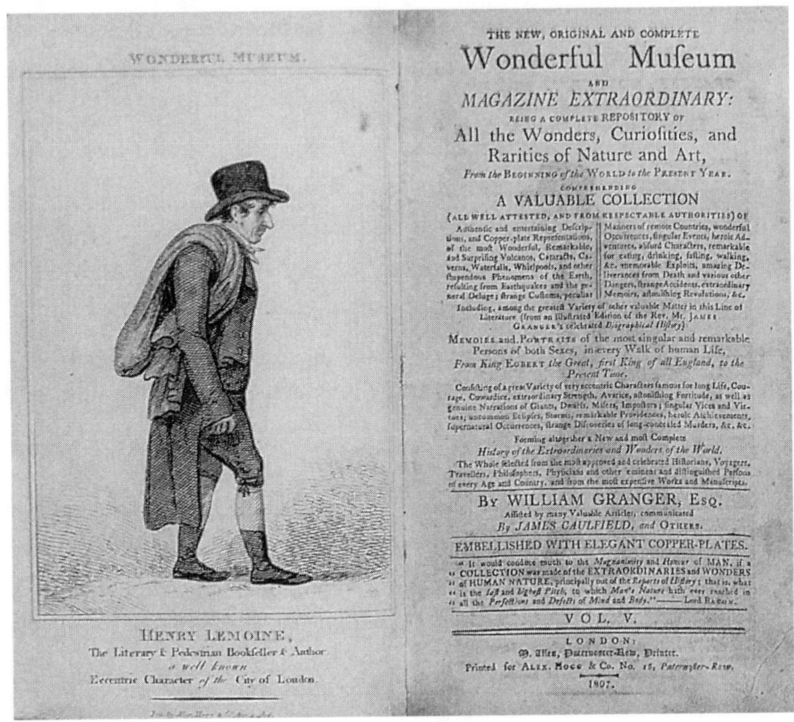

WONDERFUL MUSEUM.

HENRY LEMOINE,
The Literary & Pedestrian Bookseller & Author
a well known
Eccentric Character of the City of London.

THE NEW, ORIGINAL AND COMPLETE
Wonderful Museum
AND
MAGAZINE EXTRAORDINARY:
BEING A COMPLETE REPOSITORY OF
All the Wonders, Curiosities, and
Rarities of Nature and Art,
From the BEGINNING *of the* WORLD *to the* PRESENT YEAR.
COMPREHENDING
A VALUABLE COLLECTION
(ALL WELL ATTESTED, AND FROM RESPECTABLE AUTHORITIES) OF

Authentic and entertaining Descriptions, and Copper-plate Representations, of the most Wonderful, Remarkable, and Surprising Volcanos, Cataracts, Caverns, Waterfalls, Whirlpools, and other stupendous Phenomena of the Earth, resulting from Earthquakes and the general Deluge; strange Customs, peculiar Manners of remote Countries, wonderful Occurrences, singular Events, heroic Adventures, absurd Characters, remarkable for eating, drinking, fasting, walking, &c. memorable Exploits, amazing Deliverances from Death and various other Dangers, strange Accidents, extraordinary Memoirs, astonishing Revolutions, &c.

Including, among the greatest Variety of other valuable Matter in this Line of Literature (from an illustrated Edition of the Rev. Mr. JAMES GRANGER's celebrated *Biographical History*)

MEMOIRS and PORTRAITS of the most singular and remarkable Persons of both Sexes, in every Walk of human Life,
From King EGBERT *the Great, first King of all England, to the Present Time.*

Consisting of a great Variety of very eccentric Characters famous for long Life, Courage, Cowardice, extraordinary Strength, Avarice, astonishing Fortitude, as well as genuine Narrations of Giants, Dwarfs, Misers, Impostors; singular Vices and Virtues; uncommon Eclipses, Storms, remarkable Providences, heroic Atchievements, supernatural Occurrences, strange Discoveries of long-concealed Murders, &c. &c.

Forming altogether a New and most Complete
History of the Extraordinaries and Wonders of the World.

The Whole selected from the most approved and celebrated Historians, Voyagers, Travellers, Philosophers, Physicians and other eminent and distinguished Persons of every Age and Country, and from the most expensive Works and Manuscripts.

BY WILLIAM GRANGER, ESQ.
Assisted by many Valuable Articles, communicated
By JAMES CAULFIELD, and OTHERS.

EMBELLISHED WITH ELEGANT COPPER-PLATES.

"It would conduce much to the *Magnanimity* and *Honour* of MAN, if a "COLLECTION was made of the EXTRAORDINARIES and WONDERS "of HUMAN NATURE, principally out of the *Reports of History*; that is, what "is the *last* and *highest Pitch*, to which *Man's Nature* hath ever reached in "all the *Perfections* and *Defects* of *Mind* and *Body*."——Lord BACON.

VOL. V.

LONDON:
[illegible], Paternoster-Row, Printer.
Printed for ALEX. HOGG & Co. No. 16, *Paternoster-Row*.
1807.

FIG. 5 Henry Lemoine: frontispiece to the *Wonderful Museum*, vol. 5 (1807). Courtesy of the Lewis Walpole Library, Yale University.

known, *Typographical Antiquities* (1797), a study in the history of printing that anticipates Bibliomania by more than a decade. The happy ending of Lemoine's story is that he was able to go back to his bookstand in 1807 and kept it the rest of his life.

A more commanding figure than Lemoine, but at least as versatile, is John Trusler (1735–1820), who did so well as a rogue publisher that he was able like Lackington to buy an estate and publish a volume of his autobiography. His *Memoirs of the Life of the Rev. Dr. Trusler, with his Opinions on a Variety of Interesting Subjects, and his Remarks . . . on Men and Manners, written by Himself. Replete with Humour, Useful Information and Entertaining Anecdote* (1806) is unconventional in content and form—rambling, maddening, full of stale jokes. Trusler presents his as "a life of error" (4) and a warning to others, but he also offers a how-to guide to worldly success and longevity. The first volume did not get as far as the establishment of the publishing business that made Trusler his money, and it was not well received. Trusler, undaunted, started the second volume, presumably in 1806 or 1807, with a response to the critics; wrote twenty chapters; tinkered with it to the end of his life; but never published it. The unfinished manuscript, which breaks off in mid-sentence, is in the Lewis Walpole Library associated with Yale University. It has a lot to say about the publishing system which Trusler fought for many years, and incidentally about topical issues like literacy; self-interested and polemical, it is nevertheless valuable for its hard facts as well as for its forceful style.

Trusler made a better start than Lemoine, taking a Cambridge B.A. in 1757 and serving for a time as a clergyman in several country and city parishes. He must have been a man of restless energy. He tried teaching public speaking. He studied law for a while, and then medicine more seriously, though it is doubtful that he had a legitimate claim to the title of "Dr. Trusler" through any of his professional interests. In the course of a long career he wrote and published dozens of volumes of abridgments, from Chesterfield on manners through Blackstone on law to Captain Cook on travel, besides some original compositions. His great successes, to judge by numbers of editions, were the Chesterfield, *Hogarth Moralized* (text to accompany a set of Hogarth's engravings, published with the cooperation of Hogarth's widow), *The Way to be Rich and Respectable*, and *The Honours of the Table*, a book of household management. In publishing the Hogarth he found himself in competition with Boydell, and lost. But Trusler stands out among his contemporaries for his resourcefulness and vision, as well as for his rugged independence. He was what an earlier age might have called a projector, a man of projects. One of his original ideas, dating from 1769, was to print sermons in a large font that looked like handwriting, to save clergymen the trouble of writing their own: his circulars promised discretion and offered the sermons either individually or in numbers, by post.[43] These sermons were still being sold in 1796 (Fig. 6). In 1793 he made an unsuccessful bid to the government to distribute anti-

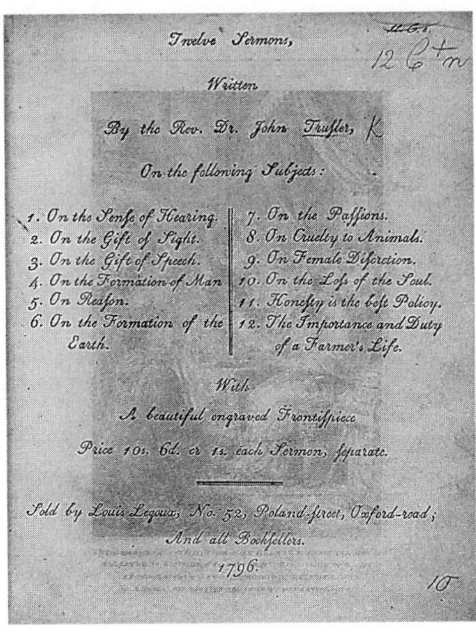

Twelve Sermons,

Written

By the Rev. Dr. John Truſler,

On the following Subjects:

1. On the Senſe of Hearing.
2. On the Gift of Sight.
3. On the Gift of Speech.
4. On the Formation of Man
5. On Reaſon.
6. On the Formation of the Earth.
7. On the Paſſions.
8. On Cruelty to Animals.
9. On Female Diſcretion.
10. On the Loſs of the Soul.
11. Honeſty is the beſt Policy.
12. The Importance and Duty of a Farmer's Life.

With

A beautiful engraved Frontiſpiece

Price 10s. 6d. or 1s. each Sermon, ſeparate.

Sold by Louis Legoux, No. 52, Poland-ſtreet, Oxford-road;
And all Bookſellers.
1796.

FIG. 6 The title page of John Trusler's *Twelve Sermons* (1796). By permission of the British Library.

Jacobin pamphlets *by mail* to every household in Britain, arguing that it was better to change people's minds by print than by bayonets.[44]

In 1765 Trusler devised a scheme for a Literary Society that would enable authors to publish for themselves, free of the London "trade." Each member was to pay at least a guinea a year for membership and to purchase one copy of every book published by the society. The society would buy paper direct from the mill, hire printers or run its own press, determine by committee the works suitable for publication, and run an impartial periodical review. Authors would keep their copyright and any profits after the costs of printing, advertising, sales and distribution had been covered. Retail booksellers would be "allowed their Customary profits on what they sell of books recommended by the Society."[45] If the Society prospered, there were hopes that it might build up a fund to help authors in distress. The scheme attracted some authors and had the approval of a few influential public figures, but according to Trusler no eminent politician would agree to chair the Society and the opposition of the regular publishers killed it. Nevertheless the Literary Society still existed, at least in name, in 1790. John Trusler ran it single-handed. It published as The Literary Press, out of addresses in Clerkenwell and then Soho. Its catalogue of 1790 consists largely but not entirely of Trusler's own compositions and compilations.

In retrospect, though it made him rich, Trusler thought publishing as he had been obliged to do it was hardly worth the trouble. He provides figures to back up this contention.

> Let a Publisher be ever so circumspect and cautious one Publication in five will scarce reimburse the Expences and those that pay him best produce only a profit of 40 per cent which many a trader gains with half the risk & half the trouble. Of every 100£ received at the trade price[,] doing up the books, advertizements & agency cost 32£, the print & paper 27; the gains then in this hundred are 40£ out of which is to be deducted ware-house, ware-house-men—Interest of the Stock[,] Insurance & occasiona[l] loss allow ten per Cent for this & the net profits are but 30 pr. Cent for all the Understanding, the talents & the Study of a man of Education & learning whilst an Ignorant Taylor is clearing more than 35 pr. Cent on all the business he transacts.[46]

Trusler is particularly eloquent on the burden—literally—of the back-list, pointing out that it might take eight to ten years to sell off an edition of 500 or 1,000 copies—"& if the Copy-right owners do not print a large impression [i.e., 500–1,000], they cannot afford to sell the book at a moderate price & would then be subject to rivalry & piracy." He claims that his own stock weighed six or seven tons, "more than three waggon loads of Books," all of it vulnerable to damp and insects if his warehouse-man were incompetent or dishonest; and he points out that the independent author-publisher does not have the benefit of professional support. "The Wholesale booksellers have a mode of circulating their books & lessening their Stock from time to time by exchanging them for other books among one another, which Authors have not an opportunity of doing; of course they can only retail *their* copies by means of an agent & making them public" (210).

Nevertheless, Trusler was proud of his achievements. The mandate of the Literary Press, he said, was utility. He saw himself and all his endeavors as promoting education: the child's book of proverbs with woodblock engravings, the grammar, the math book, the volumes of travels, the law books, the seaman's manual, the farmer's guide, and even the novels (Trusler's own) which "cautioned [young people] against the deceptions and villainies of the world."[47] Perhaps his way of presenting his list of publications as an integrated system of education was driven by the demands of marketing, but by the time he wrote his memoirs, Trusler does seem to have come to believe in this vision of himself as an educator and public benefactor. He was by no means a democrat, though. His support for the anti-Jacobin cause has been noted. His manuscript memoirs argue passionately against universal literacy on the grounds that it only makes the poor dissatisfied and lowers literary standards.[48] More to the point, perhaps, for Trusler—and a more original argument than generally accompanied this point of view—was the fact that the poor could buy only cheap books, and cheap books diminished the profits and prestige of the respectable author: "whilst cheap books find a Consumption there will ever be poor ignorant authors to write them and low mercenary booksellers to publish them." Though he made an exception for Hannah More's Cheap Repository Tracts, as a rule he equated cheap with scurrilous, and observed that More's morality and good reasoning sold nowhere near so well as "libel scandal obscenity and such trash as disgrace the Press" (346). He claimed to be writing from experience, looking back to his own shameful involvement in a fourpenny paper of the 1770s that sold 1,500 copies on the day of issue and made its owner £75 a time.

FINANCIAL CALCULATIONS

When he produced the catalogue of 1790 Trusler was in the midst of one of his most ambitious ventures, *The Habitable World Described*, which consists of a set of translated, reprinted travel narratives arranged geographically, the first group being about lands around the North Pole. Begun in 1788 under the patronage of the Duke of York, the work came out in monthly numbers, each with specially commissioned copperplate engravings or maps, selling at two shillings; five or six numbers would make up a volume. The series ran for nine years and when complete amounted to twenty volumes, so the total cost was £12. Trusler was a strong advocate of the kind of exclusive marketing that it represented:

> Could we restrain then that Inundation of books of which printing is the origin cou[l]d we by a tax on every sheet make them so difficult to come at nothing but a heart felt predilection for science an irrisistable impulse to literature would induce a man to provide himself with a library. The learned then would possibly sink in number, but learning would rise in their defeat; their paucity would add a Lustre to their reputation and as there would be few Competitors to share the rewards of literature these rewards would be more advantageous and Authors would stand higher in the Estimation and regard of the world.[49]

In Trusler's view the book trade was at a crossroads in the early nineteenth century: it would have to decide whether to serve the few or the many, the well-to-do or the poor. It might be said that that had been the situation at least since 1774, and that Trusler had after all only chosen the same safe route as the majority of publishers and booksellers of his generation. On commercial grounds alone, setting aside class politics, it is easy to see why they would prefer the smaller market. A large print run means a proportionally larger capital investment and a greater risk than a small one. A small run selling briskly at a high price would finance reprints with less risk. When the first flurry of sales was over, it would be time to consider cheaper reprints in smaller formats. Such was the received wisdom, well into the 1820s. And experience seemed to prove it right. Low prices increased sales but not necessarily profits. Hannah More's volunteers, buying tracts in bulk to give away, were not looking for a financial return. Paine and Cobbett, successfully courting large numbers, were in constant financial distress as well as in trouble with the law. Lemoine's and Trusler's efforts at cheap periodical publication (Trusler launched his *Monthly Communications* in 1793) were as short-lived as most of their ilk.[50]

On the other hand, an expensive book that broke even with a small sale could make a fortune if it caught on. When Southey was weighing the pros and cons of various arrangements for his poem *Madoc* in 1803, he first considered publishing by subscription, ideally in a luxury quarto format that would sell for a guinea like his ill-fated *Joan of Arc* of 1796; or, failing that, in three small volumes. But then he would have to canvass his friends and ask them to canvass *their* friends, to raise the money for printing. In the end, he went to a London publisher: "Longman shall risk all expenses, and share the eventual profits; printing it in quarto, and with engravings, for I am sure the book will sell the better for being made expensive" (*Life*, 3:115). *Madoc* eventually appeared in 1805, in quarto, at the price of two guineas, obviously aimed at an affluent readership—the same set that paid two guineas for the quarto first edition of Boswell's life of Johnson in two volumes in 1791, twenty-five shillings for Scott's *Lay of the Last Minstrel* in 1805, thirty shillings for two cantos of Byron's *Childe Harold's Pilgrimage* in 1812, two guineas for Thomas Moore's *Lalla Rookh* (2 vols.) in 1817, and a guinea and a half for the first volume of *Don Juan* in 1819. Scott thought that the admission of books to drawing-rooms, where they could be read aloud from at evening parties, had driven prices up by making it necessary for them to live up to handsome furniture.[51] ("I detest a quarto," says Jane Austen in a letter.[52])

As a rough-and-ready way of gauging the relative value of books in the period, it is instructive to look at newspaper advertisements for new books alongside advertisements for other commodities and entertainments. It is a very crude measure. Books were offered at all kinds of prices depending on size and quality and marketing methods, as were other goods. But the newspapers give an official price and make it possible to see what a customer could have had for the same money. A sampling of advertisements in two newspapers, *The Times* and the *Morning Chronicle*, taken at five-year intervals and starting with a standard sort of nonfiction octavo and fiction duodecimo in multiple volumes (to make sure they are of a certain length), without plates, produces some thought-provoking results. The newspapers themselves almost doubled in price from fourpence in 1790–91 (the *Chronicle* was founded in 1791) to sevenpence during this period. The price of books rose in the early years of the war with France and stayed high until 1830. Of course these are only books *advertised*, and we know that there were cheaper alternatives; still it is noteworthy that Blair's sermons, Adam Smith's lectures, and Gibbon's history could be had when first published for five or six shillings a volume (1790) but that the price of comparable productions rose to seven or eight shillings in 1795 and did not go down again. New fiction, starting at five shillings a volume in 1790, seems more variable: 1795, three shillings; 1800, four shillings; 1805, four shillings; 1810, five-and-threepence; 1815, six shillings; 1820, five-and-threepence; 1825, seven shillings.[53] Supposing an average price of six shillings for one volume of a new work, therefore twelve or eighteen for the whole thing, what else could a buyer have? Throughout the period, an elegant entertainment: a seat in the pit at the opera, a ticket for a masquerade at the Pantheon in Oxford Street (with supper), or a place at a benefit concert, for ten-and-six. Several bottles of wine: in 1795, port was advertised at 28 shillings a dozen, or two-and-fourpence a bottle; in 1805 and 1810 it had gone up to 44 shillings a dozen and was still there in 1830. Not quite enough muslin for a dress: the going rate in the papers was about two-and-six a yard. And some oddments: in 1790 the smallest-sized bottle of medicine for venereal disease cost five shillings; in 1795 "female pills" for menstrual disorders cost two-and-nine per box; in 1805 coals from Newcastle came at 54 shillings per chaldron, or 12 sacks, at four-and-six per sack. Waistcoats were on offer in 1815 for 16 or 18 shillings, and for 26 shillings silk hats "combining every requisite a Hat ought to possess." In 1820, mattresses were advertised starting at ten shillings, and beaver hats at 28 shillings; in 1825 kitchen candles cost sixpence-halfpenny a pound and the best wax candles three shillings and twopence. In the context of goods in general, new books were luxuries but not out-of-reach luxuries. And the high cost combined with the cultural worth of new books no doubt helped to sustain the value of older and cheaper ones. Unlike wax candles and fine muslin they were not used up, but could be resold; they were durable consumer goods.[54]

The taxes and production costs that kept prices high—even the modest, pocket-sized *Lyrical Ballads* cost five shillings in 1798 and the daily four pages of *The Times*, though underwritten by advertising, cost sevenpence from 1815 to 1836—might seem for most of the period to have had the effect of polarizing the trade. While small fry like Lemoine struggled to make ends meet, the most successful publishers catered to the rich or to the assured sales of the circulating libraries. They were the ones who produced the poems of Byron and Scott and the *Waverley* novels. Right through the war years they advertised de luxe features such as copperplate engravings and expensive paper, promoting their books as long-term investments. T. J. Mathias, satirizing the trade in his *Pursuits of Literature* (1794–97), observed that even law books were being printed on hot-pressed paper.[55] In 1795 there had evidently been a market even for such ephemera—anti-establishment ephemera at that—as an eleventh edition of the shorthand transcript of the trial of Thomas Hardy printed on "superfine Wove Paper" at seven shillings a volume, in boards.[56] So when he looked back on the recent past in his novel *Vivian Grey* (1826), Disraeli had his protagonist attribute the fashion for reading, by then over, to middle-class prosperity: "Every body being very rich, has afforded to be very literary—books being considered a luxury almost as elegant and necessary as Ottomans, bonbons, and pier-glasses. Consols at 100 were the origin of all book-societies. The Stockbrokers' ladies took off the quarto travels, and the hot-pressed poetry. They were the patronesses of your patent ink, and your wire wove paper. That is all passed" (214).

But Trusler's articulation of stark alternatives and the efforts of genteel publishers to distance themselves from the lower reaches of the trade are unreliable guides to the experience of readers in the period. Trusler's business was selling new books, whereas new books occupy only a small part of the experience of most readers. Furthermore, the trade was not so much polarized as diversified, a spectrum of strategies and practices, a free-for-all; and it had been so for some time. The 1774 copyright decision had given publishers access to the work of most dead authors. There followed endless reprints of plays, poems, novels, and the most popular of the older periodicals, many of these reprints published on the installment plan, in parts—a staple device of the time, of which more later. But publishers had no exclusive legal claim to the texts themselves and had to find other ways of making their reprint editions more desirable than anyone else's. So when a consortium of London publishers commissioned lives of the best English poets of the past century from Samuel Johnson for the series that came to be known as "Johnson's Poets," published in 68 octavo volumes in 1779–81, they were challenged by John Bell's rival series in 109 volumes (1777–82). Bell's edition appeared in a small format (cheaper and also more convenient to carry around), covered a longer timespan, and included engraved frontispieces by contemporary artists. Its success encouraged followers with enticements of their own. Cooke's pocket edition of British poets (1794–1804) was offered in fortnightly numbers at sixpence apiece, but readers could also buy individual poets (Gray for sixpence, Swift for three shillings, and so on) or choose the "superior edition," published simultaneously, on better paper and with more engravings. In his autobiography, published in 1850, Leigh Hunt paid tribute to the sixpenny edition which he had bought as a schoolboy:

> In those times, Cooke's edition of the British poets came up. I had got an odd volume of Spenser; and I fell passionately in love with Collins and Gray. How I loved those little sixpenny numbers containing whole poets! I doated on their size; I doated on their type, on their ornaments, on their wrappers containing lists of other poets, and on the engravings from Kirk. I bought them over and over again, and used to get up select sets, which disappeared like buttered crumpets; for I could resist neither giving them away, nor possessing them. When the master tormented me, when I used to hate and loathe the sight of Homer, and Demosthenes, and Cicero, I would comfort myself with thinking of the sixpence in my pocket, with which I should go out to Paternoster-row, when school was over, and buy another number of an English poet. (*Autobiography*, 1:132–33)

Novels were available on the same terms, *The Castle of Otranto,* being short, to be had for sixpence, *Tom Jones* for four-and-six.[57] In an essay of 1821, "On Reading Old Books," Hazlitt nostalgically recalled the *Tom Jones,* "embellished with cuts," that came in the mailcoach every two weeks (12:222–23). Other competitors in this market were old editions and cheap reprints of individual writers, and alternatively fat anthologies like Anderson's *British Poets* in 13 volumes (1792–95) which Coleridge, Wordsworth, and Southey read, and Chalmers's set in 21 volumes (1810). The point is that new versions were constantly appearing and finding a market, without entirely displacing the old. The quantity of printed matter in circulation grew—and grows—all the time. Books are durable portable property. By 1790 they were already plentiful and not necessarily costly.

With annotating readers in mind it may be worth pointing out one practical way in which the market accommodated them—by providing space to write in. Here we have usually to do with traditions maintained, not with innovations. Some kinds of books were routinely printed with space between the lines of the text (Greek and Latin classics, for example) or with wide margins (as in law books) to take the reader's glosses. Course outlines could be bought interleaved with blank pages for lecture notes. Most luxury books, quartos especially, paraded wide margins, not perhaps with the intent of encouraging the annotator, but with that effect. Though not normally thought of as books at all, some printed items came in the shape of books with very little printed text and were meant to be filled up by the owner: pocket diaries belong to this category, as do naturalists' journals, printed commonplace books, and some travel guides. These had boxes or columns with headings to guide the writer, but they often also included pages of printed matter of one kind or another, and they were not always reserved to the purpose for which they had been intended.[58] Paper was precious and owners could be creative. Stationers, who were often retail booksellers too, sold blank books for use as commonplace books or albums: Mary Shelley wrote to Percy, who was in London in 1817, asking him to "Remember dearest to bring me a good thick book to write extracts in—ruled" (*Letters,* 1:51). And bookbinders would readily incorporate extra blank pages at the front or back at a customer's request. One travel book so bound, a copy of *Letters from Holland* that must have been bought in anticipation of a journey, has a manuscript phrase-book at the front ("How late is it landlord? waiter? chambermaid?") and lists of prices and distances at the back, but it appears not to have been put to use, for the interleaved pages, where the traveler should have written in observations about the places described in the text, are still almost entirely blank.

CHEAP AND FREE BOOKS

I have been describing a system of interconnected parts, a great self-sustaining print-generating machine with an economy of its own. It was not a wasteful system. New publications entered the market. If they sold rapidly, they could be reprinted in the same format or upgraded or downgraded according to demand. If they sold slowly, they could be kept in storage until the edition was exhausted. If they did not sell at all, they would be shunted down the food chain to specialists in remainders like Lackington, or further down still to dealers like Lemoine with his stall and, later, his sack. As a last resort they would still fetch a price as waste paper. The traditional joke or threat in literary circles was that pages of a book could end up as curl-papers for hairdressing, lining for luggage, wrapping for food, or toilet paper—serving "the culinary or post-culinary conveniences," as Coleridge waggishly put it, of the owner.[59]

Old books were also provided for—through retail booksellers and hawkers, who carried secondhand goods along with the new; through auctions and library sales, which were advertised in the newspapers; through book clubs, which distributed books among their members, sometimes by drawing lots, when the group was finished with them; and through the circulating libraries, which traded among themselves but would eventually sell off used copies from their stock. Some of the cheapest items in Lackington's lists were odd volumes and broken sets like the two volumes of a 1787 *Arabian Nights* offered for a shilling apiece in 1804–5; he also sold odd prints at twopence or threepence

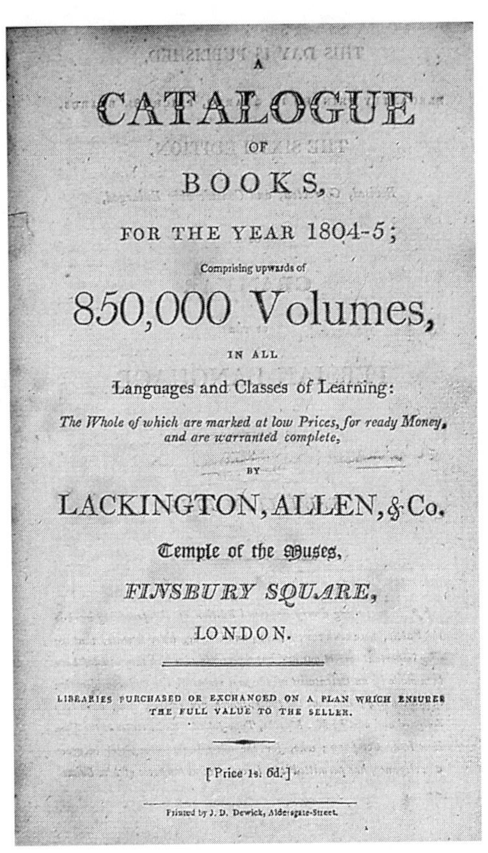

A

CATALOGUE

OF

BOOKS,

FOR THE YEAR 1804-5;

Comprising upwards of

850,000 Volumes,

IN ALL

Languages and Classes of Learning:

The Whole of which are marked at low Prices, for ready Money, and are warranted complete,

BY

LACKINGTON, ALLEN, & Co.

Temple of the Muses,

FINSBURY SQUARE,

LONDON.

LIBRARIES PURCHASED OR EXCHANGED ON A PLAN WHICH ENSURES THE FULL VALUE TO THE SELLER.

[Price 1s. 6d.]

Printed by J. D. Dewick, Aldersgate-Street.

FIG. 7 Lackington, Allen, and Co., *A Catalogue of Books, for the year 1804–5*. By permission of the British Library.

(Fig. 7). But Lackington had a handsome shop to maintain. The real bargains were to be had on the streets. Lamb and Southey wrote about "stall-hunting"; Lamb even has an essay that describes reading for free by taking in a few pages a day while pretending to browse.[60] With characteristic bravado, he says he knew one "street-reader" who got through two volumes of *Clarissa*, one of the longest novels in the language, that way. And there were the philanthropists' freebies. The Cheap Repository Tracts sold for as little as a halfpenny, depending on length (Fig. 8). Attractively produced chapbooks with woodcut illustrations, they were commonly bought at a discount, by sympathizers,

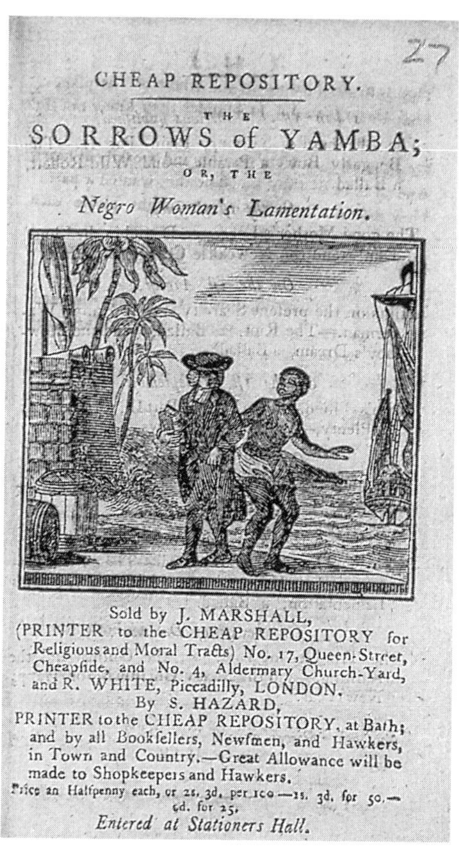
CHEAP REPOSITORY.

THE

SORROWS of YAMBA;

OR, THE

Negro Woman's Lamentation.

Sold by J. MARSHALL,
(PRINTER to the CHEAP REPOSITORY for Religious and Moral Tracts) No. 17, Queen-Street, Cheapſide, and No. 4, Aldermary Church-Yard, and R. WHITE, Piccadilly, LONDON.
By S. HAZARD,
PRINTER to the CHEAP REPOSITORY, at Bath; and by all Bookſellers, Newſmen, and Hawkers, in Town and Country.—Great Allowance will be made to Shopkeepers and Hawkers.
Price an Halfpenny each, or 2s. 3d. per 100—1s. 3d. for 50.—9d. for 25.

Entered at Stationers Hall.

FIG. 8 Title page of Hannah More's *The Sorrows of Yamba* (1795), published for the Cheap Repository. By permission of the British Library.

for free distribution. (Hester Piozzi paid to have More's *Village Politics* translated into Welsh and printed for distribution among local laborers, but her husband objected that the workers would only be put to the expense of candles for reading, so they gave soup instead.[61]) *An Apology for the Bible,* the Bishop of Llandaff's rebuttal of Paine's *Age of Reason,* went through seven editions in its year of publication (1796), the fourth and following editions being published cheaply to ensure wide distribution. It cost only one shilling, for a work of about 200 pages, and was even cheaper in bulk: for two pounds supporters could have fifty to give away. And free books were not necessarily cheaply produced or distributed to the uneducated: the Duke of Grafton, to support the Unitarian cause, gave away 700 copies of Griesbach's scholarly edition of the New Testament in Greek.[62]

In an interesting self-help manual addressed to young apprentices, *Advice to the Teens* (1818), Isaac Taylor discusses management of finances, relations with women, and ways of keeping the mind active. He urges his readers to keep up the best parts of their schooling, especially reading and drawing, reminding them that books can be had for pennies at a stall and that "An author is a silent tutor; one of the cheapest, most important, convenient, and efficient, in the grand work of instruction" (13).[63] He gives a vivid if idealized image of working-class self-improvement, encouraging young men to develop disciplined habits by "always having a book in reading" (27) and setting up some private space to read it in, with a book shelf, writing materials, a table if possible, and "a folio to keep your drawings in, if it were only to hide them" (48).

> Secure some place, however small, which you may call your study. I have known a separation made in a corner of a room, by a few sheets of brown paper hung as curtains from top to bottom, answer the end quite well. The object of this sacred inclosure is retirement. He that has nowhere to be alone will scarcely be able to think, will hardly pursue any distinct plan of reading; he must take his chance in the bustle of a family, and be at the mercy of accidents, dunces, and purposed interruptions. (45–46)

Taylor's apprentice class were likely customers for periodical publications—Taylor specifically recommends reviews—and perhaps even more so for publications that came out in weekly or monthly parts, selling at about the price of a newspaper. This was a publishing practice of long standing, but because the bound products look like conventionally published books, it is more or less invisible today.[64] It operated at both ends of the publishing spectrum, being used for lavish or complicated projects such as the *Encyclopedia Britannica* and D'Oyly and Mant's *Family Bible,* and for reprint series like Bell's, with projects like

Trusler's *Habitable World* somewhere in the middle. New ventures were advertised in the press and through publishers' advertisements in other books; the parts were distributed by retail booksellers and newsagents. Southey claims, credibly, that as a schoolboy, a merchant's son in the West Country, he bought the whole works of Josephus in sixty sixpenny parts with his pocket money (*Life*, 1:117). (Dorothy Wordsworth in 1802 calculated that with £60 a year and frugal habits, she would not have to work for anyone and would be able to indulge in some charity, some books, and some travel.[65] Taking $40,000 as the modern equivalent and thinking about proportion of income, a sixpenny number would have about the impact of a movie ticket.) Part-publication offered flexibility and limited financial risk. Publishers could test the waters with a few numbers and let the early ones pay for their successors, or stop the series if it did not pay. Even a small establishment could print one number at a time and break up the type from it to print the next. Their customers could subscribe to the series or buy just the numbers they wanted. When the series was finished, unsold numbers were gathered and sold as books. For a relatively low unit cost buyers regularly received something new to read, built up their libraries, and developed a habit of collecting.[66] They were thus buying *and reading* on an installment plan—the last point perhaps marking a significant difference between their ways and ours. Another is the marked prevalence of sharing.

LIBRARIES

Although books can be said to have been plentiful in the Romantic period, they were also in a sense scarce, so everyone shared. This is not to say, of course, that books circulated freely, but that it was customary to lend, borrow, and split costs. There can have been few personal libraries that met the owner's every need, there were no free nonsectarian public libraries (in the modern sense of publicly funded collections open to everyone), and there were no comprehensive centralized collections. The Library of the British Museum was not yet forty years old in 1790, and although it had been established on the solid footing of the Sloane, Harleian, and Cottonian collections and the library of George III would be added in 1823, the trustees were still in the process of building up a national collection through purchases and bequests. Institutional libraries had specialized collections intended for members of the institution. Even the largest and most splendid of the university libraries, the Bodleian Library in Oxford, catered to fairly narrowly conceived academic needs. People who worked with books—scholars, writers, and booksellers—seem to have been able to count on access to such libraries, however, wherever they went. So Southey, who lived in the country and accumulated 14,000 books of his own, still visited other collections when he could, "gutting the libraries" of Exeter while he was there in 1799 (*Life*, 2:25), and gaining admission to the King's old chronicles (*Life*, 2:25, 216). When Wordsworth and Coleridge were trying to decide whether to stay in the West Country or move north to the Lakes, books were the main point of contention:

> His [Wordsworth's] chief objection to Stowey is the want of Books—the Bristol Library is a *hum* & will do us little service, & he thinks that he can procure a house near Sir [Gilfrid] Lawson's by the Lakes, & have access to his immense Library.—I think it is better once in a year to walk to Cambridge, in the summer vacation—perhaps, I may be able to get rooms for nothing—& there for a couple of months read like a Turk on a given plan, & return home with a mass of materials which with dear *independent* Poetry will fully employ the remaining year.[67]

In literary circles everyone occasionally had to call on colleagues for assistance, and it appears from letters and published acknowledgments that books and transcriptions from books and manuscripts were readily made available. (Annotated volumes circulated as enhanced copies, and borrowers sometimes asked permission to copy the notes into their own books; the flyleaf note recording such a source is quite common—for instance in Kemble's copy of John Horne Tooke's notorious *Diversions of Purley*, where suppressed passages in the text are filled in on the authority of Kemble's friend Boaden's copy, itself corrected from Tooke's original manuscript.) So Coleridge's panic, when he found he had acquired the reputation of being a bad person to lend books to, is understandable. He called on his acquaintances to counteract the calumny, citing several lost opportunities: "on the strength of this Slander Mr Rogers . . . prevented Mr Rose from lending me Carl Gozzi's Works, which he was previously most ready to do, and which I had in vain endeavoured to obtain from Leghorn" (*Letters*, 4:656).

The relative scarcity of books, that is, the fact that almost no one could acquire all the books he or she might want or need, or have access to them all in one place, and that there were no reliable sources for rare and out-of-print materials, may in part account for the rampant book-making that is one of the least appealing features of publishing in the period. Anthologies, extracts, anecdotes, anas, beauties, readers, collections, epitomes, miscellanies, and compilations on topics of current interest offered ready-made digests of information copied from other books, usually without much evidence of authorial or editorial effort. They were cheap to produce. They came in all shapes and sizes. There were the best-selling "Elegant Extracts" of Vicesimus Knox—poetry (1784), prose (1784), and letters (1790), in many editions. There was the earnest *Manual of Liberty* (1795), an anthology of "testimonies in behalf of the rights of mankind . . . selected from the best authorities, in prose and verse" and organized alphabetically under such headings as "Equity or Justice" and "Liberty of Conscience." And there was Coleridge and Southey's *Omniana* (1812), translatable as "something about everything," but mostly a container for scraps from Southey's commonplace books. "Literary" magazines, obliged to find new matter every month, were perhaps the most desperate and least scrupulous of all. (Readers' notes incidentally achieved some exposure this way, as when the *European Magazine* of May 1790 described Bishop Warburton's bescribbled margins and when *Blackwood's* printed Coleridge's "marginalia" on Sir Thomas Browne in 1819.[68]) As Mary Russell Mitford observed, it was "an age fertile in abridgments and selections" (2:230). A Continental writer, C. A. G. Goede, was shocked by the book-making "*compilations*" of British booksellers, and called them "a nuisance to the world of letters" (130). The trend affected the composition of textbooks so noticeably that Hester Piozzi, writing about 1815, also complained of "selectae" as enemies to literature: "In former days you asked a boy what Book he was in and he told you: he's in no Book now; he learns the Bible in the same volume that he reads about Regulus; And a Boy once told me he had been learning that Day how Jesus Christ tamed an Elephant. The miracles of our Saviour were bound up in some book of instruction with Eastern Stories & Travels & to be confounded one Strange Tale with another not unnatural."[69] The good side of this sort of anthologizing is that it must have spread the knowledge of the existence of some authors and works that would otherwise have been lost altogether. People who could not afford many books would find samples in the one they had. But it was not good for authors and holders of copyright, who were not paid for the use of their material and had no control over context or cutting, and it induced a piecemeal approach in readers by giving them just a little of this and a little of that.

Outside professional circles, too, the possession of printed matter seems to have been understood to entail an obligation, or rather an opportunity, to share. Newspapers and periodicals passed from hand to hand; poetry, plays, and novels went from household to household; friends exchanged enthusiasms. Coleridge referred to a set of Scott that made the rounds of families in Highgate as his "ever circulating Copy of Scott's Novels" (*Marginalia*, 4:612). Lamb told Wordsworth that he generally waited to have his books bound (they would have come in paper or board covers) until they were no longer in demand by borrowers.[70] Where the local circles were too small or had been exhausted, however, or where a keen reader was unwilling to depend on private generosity, readers banded together on a commercial basis. Apart from informal arrangements—say, two apprentices agreeing to buy something together so as to halve the cost to each—there existed various more regular kinds of association. The periodicals, with a commercial interest in such associations, publicized new organizations at all levels and encouraged readers to send in letters describing their local arrangements, such as the survey of fifty-one societies of "working people" in Scotland, published in the *Monthly Magazine* (4:275–77). Though these articles and letters were preeminently practical, political considerations were never far from the surface, as witness the quarrel about suitable titles for the servants' hall in the same magazine in 1814 (37:225, 310).

"A Traveller" in the book trade reported on some of these associations in the *Monthly Magazine* of June 1821 (397–98). He is interestingly dismissive of church-related organizations—"tract societies, vestry libraries, chapel libraries, school libraries, parish libraries, &c." whose influence, he says, is slight because it is widely understood that their purpose is to "hoodwink" their users into "submission to the doctrine or principles" of their party. But he is pleased to report the rapid growth of what he calls "free" societies—independent of sect or party—of various kinds. At the bottom of the scale he describes "newspaper societies"—5,000 of them, he reckons, in "every parish and hamlet"—in which the poorest families in groups of twelve or so pay one penny a week to take one or two of the local papers, and the better off in groups of seven or eight pay sixpence a week for a London daily and one or more provincial papers. In "magazine societies" ten or twelve members pay a pound or guinea a year for a set of monthly periodicals. Book clubs, sometimes also called societies, worked the same way: the members drew up a set of rules, agreed on what to buy or nominated a committee for that purpose, circulated the books among themselves, and either sold the books off when everyone had read them (reinvesting the proceeds) or distributed them among the members. A note in a copy of Rousseau's *Social Compact* (1791) indicates that the owner had acquired the book by lot in 1798 when the Shrewsbury Library decided by a majority vote at its general meeting of subscribers that a group of Jacobin books should be "expelled from the Society."[71] Some but not all of these clubs had a social aspect, members meeting over food and drink at regular intervals. In 1796 Henry Crabb Robinson attended a tea-party and debate sponsored by the Royston book club in "the largest room the little town afforded" (1:36). The topic was, "Is private affection inconsistent with universal benevolence?" The meeting was attended by 44 men and 42 women. Thomas Moore, elected a member of the Book Club at Chippenham in 1819, gave a speech after dinner praising these societies of the "middling classes" for their choice of "solid, useful, & enlightening" books including the best contemporary fiction (1:205). "Traveller" believed that the first book society was formed at Leicester in 1740 and that by 1821 there were more than 500 in the United Kingdom; modern research suggests that the phenomenon may go back to the late seventeenth century.[72]

Circulating libraries, subscription libraries, and literary institutions were larger and more permanent establishments with physical premises where readers might meet; all but the humblest had space set aside for reading. Their features overlap a bit and the names are not applied quite consistently, but a general picture emerges.[73] The circulating libraries were the oldest and most common, having started up in the late seventeenth century as an offshoot of the bookseller's business. A hundred years later big booksellers had substantial collections available for borrowing, and small-scale operations were everywhere, ubiquitous as Starbucks and less uniform. These were commercial operations renting out books. They strove to provide what their neighborhoods wanted. Thomas Wilson in Bromley, for example, advertised for sale novels, songs, encyclopedias, volumes of travels, almanacs, magazines, children's stories, practical guides, and mildly erotic fictions in prose and verse; it is likely that the circulating library in his bookshop likewise carried something for everyone. Newspapers included advertisements from investors seeking to buy established libraries in particular locations and from owners seeking to sell lock, stock, and barrel. A country shop, "the business of a Stationer, Bookseller, and Circulating Library, eligibly situated in a genteel and populous Village, 3 miles from London," was offered in 1800 for something less than £140, including stock and fixtures.[74] A library advertised in *The Times* on 9 May 1825 consisted of 2,700 volumes (2,350 of them duodecimo, the standard format for novels) at one-and-six a volume.

Robert Southey's engaging account of how he embarked on a career of chain-reading indicates the sort of influence the smallest local collection might have (*Life*, 1:82–85). A reference in a chance volume of letters in his parents' small set of books made him wish to read Hoole's translation of Tasso. By miracle he found it one day when his mother took him to a shop "one side of which was fitted up with a circulating library, containing not more than three or four hundred volumes, almost all novels." Hoole's notes mentioned Ariosto's *Orlando Furioso*, which became the next object of the boy's quest. That took him to Bull's Circulating Library, "which was to me then what the Bodleian would be now." A copy on the counter turned out to be in Italian, "but the shopman, Mr. Cruett (a most obliging man he was), immediately put the translation into my hand," and the same Mr. Cruett later found him the *Faerie Queene*, referred to in the notes to Ariosto (1:84–85). Southey's experience reveals a hierarchy of circulating libraries. Or rather it describes a hierarchy of libraries—growing need being met by ever larger resources—from the Southey family collection, contained in a "small cupboard over the desk in the back parlour" along with the wine glasses, to the august Bodleian.

From the novels of Austen and an extensive academic literature, we know that commercial circulating libraries were a prominent part of social life in the late eighteenth and early nineteenth centuries, and that they were generally denounced as frivolous or immoral.[75] The stereotype proposed that they carried nothing but novels, thereby catering to women and their romantic fantasies, and that because they were socially indiscriminate, young women might meet unsuitable men in them. Austen herself spoke up warmly both for novels and for circulating libraries, but it is true that in *Pride and Prejudice* the circulating libraries appear to be places for pick-ups: Lydia Bennet goes to Clarke's Library in Meryton and later to its counterpart in Brighton to meet officers.[76] Though the stereotype is demonstrably unfair—Kaufman for instance proves that a very small part of the stock of most of these places consisted of escapist fiction—and probably tells us more about middle-class anxiety than anything else, it does seem to have played a part in the development of the circulating library open only to subscribers, which imposed a membership fee and in theory kept riffraff out. The fees were not prohibitive, though. A Lydia Bennet of the 1780s could have met unsuitable men even at a subscription library, for William Cobbett joined one while he was a young recruit insatiable for "novels, plays, history, poetry."[77] "Traveller" estimates that by 1821 there were at least 1,500 circulating libraries of this sort, "supported on the average by 70 subscribers, and supplying with books at least another 100,000 regularly; and another 100,000 occasionally." Their collective purchasing power spread its influence throughout the trade. As the reviewer of 1830 wearily observed, without them there would be no novels, no contract authors, no Colburn and Bentleys. "No novels" is an exaggeration, but certainly less encouragement to novelists, less enthusiasm from publishers. Because they *could* be had from the circulating library, and because they were unlikely to be read more than once by a single reader, novels and other entertaining books sold mainly to the libraries, prudent readers saving their shillings for less ephemeral publications. Southey no doubt spoke for many unhappy authors when he grumbled that thousands read his books without buying them—"even those persons who know that I live by these books, never buy them themselves, and then wonder that they do not sell" (*Life*, 3:134).

The regulations of Fellows's subscription library in Salisbury in 1800 are standard for the time (Fig. 9). The libraries published catalogues of their holdings and sent books by post or wagon to subscribers in the country, the borrowers paying carriage (until 1840 the cost of sending letters too was paid by the recipient). Fellows's charges represent a middle ground, annual fees for the services of these establishments varying from about twelve shillings to five guineas; he allows short-term membership and even permits nonsubscribers to borrow books. At twopence a week for reviews and magazines, his library would have been competitive with the magazine societies. The monthly reviews were good value—book-length publications with leisurely articles containing long extracts from the latest publications.[78] Fellows's regulations incidentally indicate some of the frustrations of the owner's job: borrowers are requested not to pass books on to other subscribers themselves, but to respect the waiting list; and not to lose or damage library property, specifically not by writing in the books. But prohibitions exist to counteract existing behavior, and while it was generally accepted that writing notes was a prerogative of ownership, occasionally we see a reader's anger or public spirit or confirmed habit win out over propriety. A subscription-library copy of A. G. Sinclair's privately printed *The Critic Philosopher; or Truth Discovered* (1789), for instance,

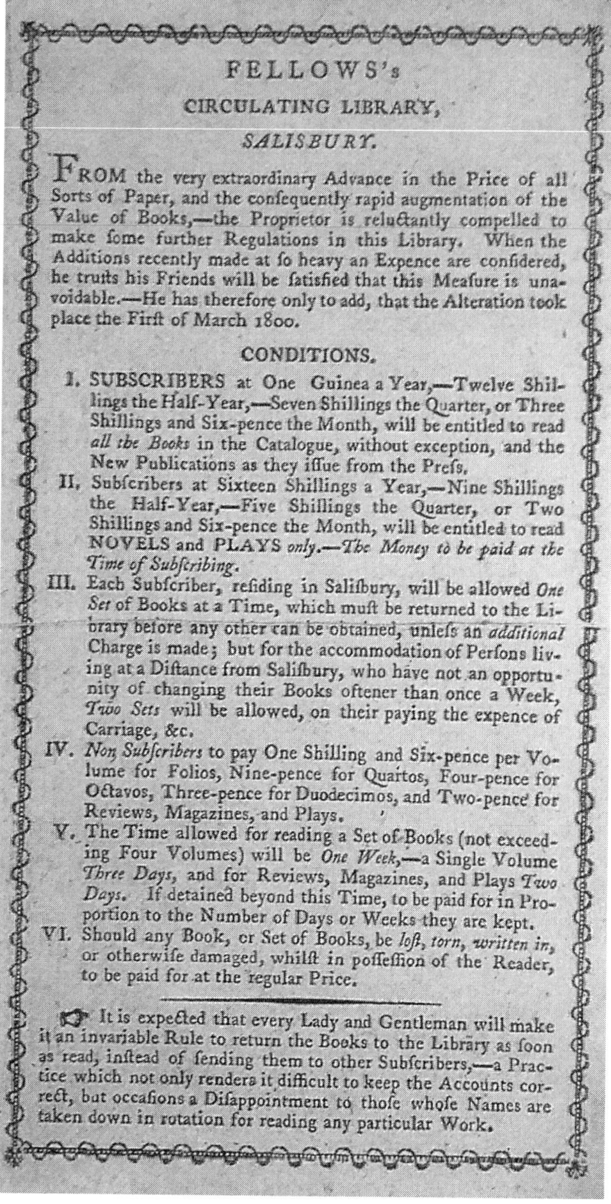

FELLOWS's

CIRCULATING LIBRARY,

SALISBURY.

FROM the very extraordinary Advance in the Price of all Sorts of Paper, and the conſequently rapid augmentation of the Value of Books,—the Proprietor is reluctantly compelled to make ſome further Regulations in this Library. When the Additions recently made at ſo heavy an Expence are conſidered, he truſts his Friends will be ſatisfied that this Meaſure is unavoidable.—He has therefore only to add, that the Alteration took place the Firſt of March 1800.

CONDITIONS.

I. SUBSCRIBERS at One Guinea a Year,—Twelve Shillings the Half-Year,—Seven Shillings the Quarter, or Three Shillings and Six-pence the Month, will be entitled to read *all the Books* in the Catalogue, without exception, and the New Publications as they iſſue from the Preſs.

II. Subſcribers at Sixteen Shillings a Year,—Nine Shillings the Half-Year,—Five Shillings the Quarter, or Two Shillings and Six-pence the Month, will be entitled to read NOVELS and PLAYS *only.—The Money to be paid at the Time of Subſcribing.*

III. Each Subſcriber, reſiding in Saliſbury, will be allowed *One Set* of Books at a Time, which muſt be returned to the Library before any other can be obtained, unleſs an *additional* Charge is made; but for the accommodation of Perſons living at a Diſtance from Saliſbury, who have not an opportunity of changing their Books oftener than once a Week, *Two Sets* will be allowed, on their paying the expence of Carriage, &c.

IV. *Non Subſcribers* to pay One Shilling and Six-pence per Volume for Folios, Nine-pence for Quartos, Four-pence for Octavos, Three-pence for Duodecimos, and Two-pence for Reviews, Magazines, and Plays.

V. The Time allowed for reading a Set of Books (not exceeding Four Volumes) will be *One Week*,—a Single Volume *Three Days*, and for Reviews, Magazines, and Plays *Two Days*. If detained beyond this Time, to be paid for in Proportion to the Number of Days or Weeks they are kept.

VI. Should any Book, or Set of Books, be *loſt, torn, written in*, or otherwiſe damaged, whilſt in poſſeſſion of the Reader, to be paid for at the regular Price.

☞ It is expected that every Lady and Gentleman will make it an invariable Rule to return the Books to the Library as ſoon as read, inſtead of ſending them to other Subſcribers,—a Practice which not only renders it difficult to keep the Accounts correct, but occaſions a Diſappointment to thoſe whoſe Names are taken down in rotation for reading any particular Work.

FIG. 9 Regulations of Fellows's Circulating Library, Salisbury, 1800. In Thomas Wilson, *A Village Tale* (1798). By permission of the British Library.

contains a reader's warning, in ink, ahead of the first page of text: "A profane Book, unworthy of being read—The Author tho' professing a belief in the Scriptures, holds up human reason (particularly his own) as superior to them." This renegade reader, however, was soon contradicted by another, and I wonder whether the second recognized the handwriting of the first: "A very sensible book well worth reading. The Author without professing any sanctity expresses his ideas fearlessly and they are extremely clever, true, and quite original—too true indeed to be acceptable to parsons."

A step up from the commercial circulating libraries were what are sometimes called "general" subscription libraries, in which subscribers were shareholders: they owned the property, hired the librarian, and determined the policies governing book orders. With their large stock and handsome facilities, the grander subscription libraries blended with the literary and scientific institutions and endowed libraries that had grown up, a matter of civic pride, in cities and growing towns (Fig. 10). Like the libraries, some of these institutions were special-interest clubs (antiquarian societies, for instance, being analogous to the foreign-language libraries), but others served broader interests. Founded by wealthy citizens and supported by annual subscriptions, they provided genteel meeting places in their well-supplied reading rooms. The periodicals naturally cheered them on. The *Gentleman's Magazine* of October 1800 reported the opening of an Athenaeum at Liverpool, with a newsroom for papers and conversation on the ground floor and a presumably quieter library above, and in November described a more modest version of that arrangement recently opened, at less expense to its supporters, in High Wycomb.[79] For those who were not willing or able to sign on, coffeehouses also served as newsrooms. Charles Lamb provocatively declared that such public spaces did more for higher education than conventional scholarly isolation—and incidentally made up a punning new etymology for the word "college": "I think public reading rooms the best mode of educating young men. Solitary reading is apt to give the headach. Besides who knows that you *do* read? There are ten thousand institutions similar to the Royal Institution which have sprung up from it. There is the London Institution, The Southwark

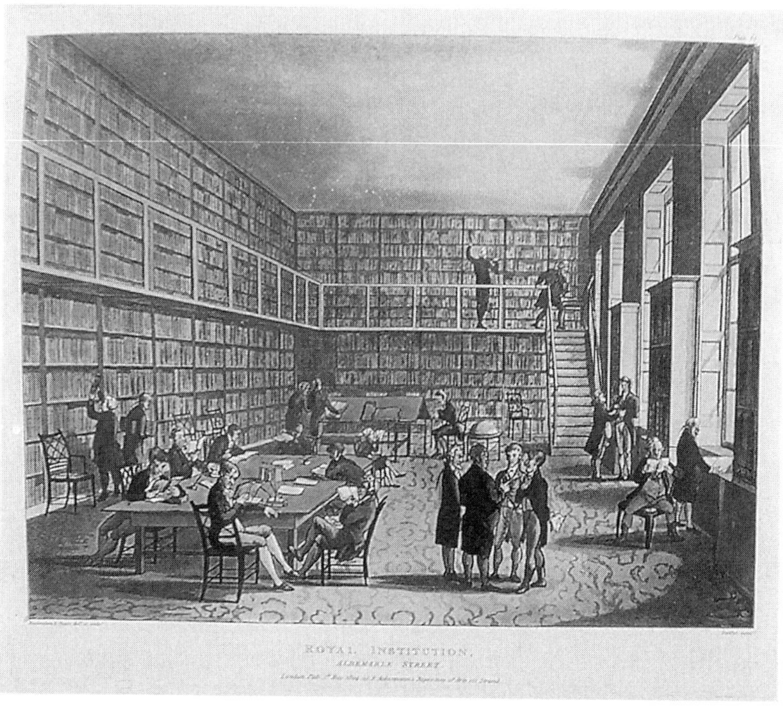

FIG. 10 "The Library of the Royal Institution," from Rudolph Ackermann's *Microcosm of London* (1808–10), facing 3:32. Courtesy of the Lewis Walpole Library, Yale University.

Institution, The Russell Square Rooms Institution &c—**College** quasi **Con-lege,** a place where people read together" (*Letters*, 2:274).

The ideal, however, was a library of one's own. As books and printed matter became more generally available in the course of the eighteenth century, private ownership extended the full length of the social scale. We have, on Lackington's authority, *Tom Jones* in the bacon racks. The agricultural day-laborer and poet John Clare wrote fondly of his "snug cupboard of Books" (105). Southey's merchant father might have read only *Felix Farley's Bristol Journal* but he and his wife had a glass-fronted cupboard with what sounds like a score of volumes of old periodical essays and some miscellaneous literature (*Life*, 1:83–84). Jane Austen's father, a country clergyman, had a library of over

500 volumes to dispose of in 1801.[80] Coleridge in 1805 aspired to wholesome poverty with his wife, children, "two or three friends, and a thousand Books" (*Letters,* 2:1162). The campaigner Granville Sharp, who lived on a clerk's salary and some support from his brothers, amassed a collection that was sold at auction after his death in 1812, compassing 1,875 lots in a sale that lasted eight days and realized almost £800.[81] The King's library contained at his death approximately 65,000 books (counting by volumes, not titles), 19,000 pamphlets, and 50,000 maps and charts; the Queen's collection as sold by auction in 1819 consisted of 4,636 lots of books and 563 of prints, and brought almost £6000.[82]

Many who did not depend on books for their livelihood cherished them and made special provision for them where they lived. In *Confessions of an English Opium-Eater,* De Quincey writes about book treasures washed up in family libraries in the provinces, or drowned in shipwrecks (a "vast submarine Bodleian").[83] Young apprentices, as we have seen, were urged to curtain off a space that they could call a study. Isaac Taylor's *Advice to the Teens* itself has a place in a new genre of books offering advice about the fitting up of a library, including T. F. Dibdin's *Library Companion* (1824) and Goodhugh's *English Gentleman's Library Manual* (1827). (Goodhugh was a bookseller who offered for sale all the books he wrote about, so his work is a glorified catalogue.) Though they are related to the tradition of educationists' advice about what to read and perhaps grew out of it, these works are based on the assumption that the reader will be buying and keeping books. Dibdin also contributed to the literature of libraries that stirred up emulation among the well-to-do with luscious descriptions of great collections, Clarke's *Repertorium Bibliographicum: or Some Account of the Most Celebrated British Libraries* (1819) being an important model for his—Dibdin's—bibliographical tours of Great Britain and the Continent (Fig. 11). Guides like these reflect the interests of prosperous parts of society, especially newly emerging industrial wealth, for a library was among other things a status symbol. Possession of a library showed that the owner had time, space, leisure, and taste. Raven notes that an "unprecedented number of private libraries were built in the last two-

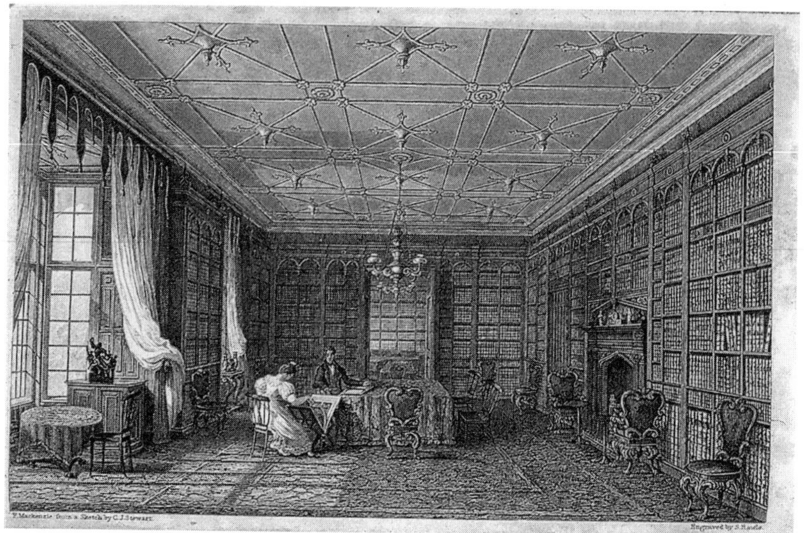

FIG. 11 The drawing-room of Miss Richardson Currer of Yorkshire, from T. F. Dibdin, *Reminiscences* (1836). By permission of the Thomas Fisher Rare Book Library, University of Toronto.

thirds of the eighteenth century"—and great quantities of books and other library furniture purchased too. Pearson points out that the gentleman's library, at first a sign of male power, in this period was increasingly represented as and in reality did become a place for the whole family, "an image of domesticity" (158).

THE FASHION OF READING

The fact that people *can* read does not mean that they do. Between 1790 and 1830, however, it appears that people did, and furthermore that they wanted to own the works they read. (When the price was low enough, large numbers chose to buy.) What created this widespread desire? Some credit must go to the work of publishers during the eighteenth century, when they built up business networks and worked out what was most likely to sell and what were the most effective ways of promoting their wares; when a period of high demand occurred, they were ready for it. Educators, too, had laid foundations, providing an outlet for working-class aspirations. Hazlitt, Southey, and other commentators of the time thought that the French Revolution, first with its promise of a new order and then with its threats of invasion, made newspapers exciting and that reading newspapers had led to a taste for reading in general. This theory, with eyewitness backing, has much to recommend it, not least its neat accounting for start and finish. With advertisements for new books and periodicals, book auctions, and sales of manuscripts, copyrights, and libraries on the front and back pages, and with poetry, reviews, and sometimes serialized fiction on the inside, the newspapers fostered book culture. On the other hand, readers did not stop taking newspapers after Waterloo; the reading boom seems to have lasted until the general economic depression of 1826. Halfway between the daily press and the world of books, periodical reviews certainly also exercised an influence, training up readers in the ways of critical analysis and bringing particular publications to their notice. But at a certain point we have to invoke the wild card of fashion which—its restless dependence on novelty coinciding with a failing economy—may be enouogh to account for the end of the boom after 1826.

In an essay of 1825, "Readers Against the Grain," Charles Lamb celebrated the "enlargement of the reading public" that had multiplied the quantity of cheap publications, "not blasphemy and sedition—nor altogether flimsy periodicals, though the latter abound to a surfeit—but I mean fair re-prints of good old books. Fielding, Smollett, the Poets, Historians, are daily becoming accessible to the purses of poor people."[84] That was all to the good, he thought, but he pitied the poor "readers against the grain," young men of the bank-clerk class who thirty years earlier might have been "play-goers, punch-drinkers, cricketers, &c." in their free time but were now, thanks to peer pressure, readers. "We are all readers; our young men are split up into so many book-clubs, knots of literati; we criticise; we read the *Quarterly* and *Edinburgh*, I assure you; and instead of the old, honest, unpretending illiterature so becoming to our profession—we read and *judge* of every thing. . . . We read to say that we have read. No reading can keep pace with the writing of this age, but we pant and toil after it as fast as we can."

Lamb is not an ideal witness. He loved paradox and hyperbole and projected his own very bookish sensibility onto the world around him. As Elia he adopted an eccentric, unworldly, fogeyish persona. And of course the observations he makes here go back a long way, far more than the thirty years he suggests. From the Old Testament complaint that "Of making many books there is no end" onwards, every age seems to have felt oppressed by the quantity of reading available to it, and yet to have considered itself as exceptional in that regard. In 1760 in his *Citizen of the World* essays, Goldsmith calculated that even if they were keeping up with only an eighth of the books being turned out by British presses, scholars must be reading a thousand books a year, and anticipated his Romantic successors by observing, "In a polite age, almost every person becomes a reader, and receives more instruction from the press than the pulpit" (2:124, 311). Dick Minim the Critic in Samuel Johnson's *Idler* 60 (9 June 1759) is a prototype for Lamb's unhappy bank clerks. And yet Lamb's observation about the fad of reading is echoed in countless essays and letters of the time. Reading was a part of the texture of everyday life, seemingly for everyone, as it had not been a generation before. If this situation had not already existed to be described, constant reiteration would have brought it about; if it had existed in a limited way, the press would have turned it into a full-scale movement. In any case, there it was, and publishers fanned the flames not only by overt advertising but also by the subtler means of self-reflection, bringing out periodical essays like Lamb's, biographies and memoirs like Boswell's, and histories like Nichols's, all about the book trade. The twenty years before Waterloo saw at least a dozen long poems about the press, authors, and authorship, some satirical and some didactic, including T. J. Mathias's *Pursuits of Literature* (1794–97), McCreery's *The Press* (1803, 1827), Dibdin's *Bibliomania* (1809), Byron's *English Bards and Scotch Reviewers* (1809), Leigh Hunt's *Feast of the Poets* (1810), and Ireland's *Scribbleomania* (1815).

"We read to say that we have read. . . . These are your readers against the grain, who yet *must* read or be thought nothing of—who, crawling through a book with tortoise-pace, go creeping to the next Review to learn what they shall say of it." Lamb rightly emphasizes the social value of books and reading in his time. Elia would like to opt out: "I die of new books, or the everlasting talk about them. I faint of Longman's. I sicken of the Constables. Blackwood and Cadell have me by the throat." But he knows that in expressing that wish he himself is acting against the grain. Reading was a common subject of conversation in all kinds of social gatherings from the family circle to the county ball, and not just in "mixed" or what is sometimes dismissively referred to as "feminized" company.[85] When it appeared in 1813, Cobbett said of "The Book"—the previously suppressed depositions of witnesses in the investigation into the conduct of the Princess of Wales—that it "was the subject of conversation in every tavern, in every coffee-house, in every ale-house, and by every fire-side."[86] Safer than direct declarations of one's views on politics or religion, and more various than the weather, books had come to be indispensable tools for establishing and reinforcing social connections. With such rewards at stake, there must have been always an element of competitiveness among readers wanting to maintain or improve their social standing. Read the wrong books or express the wrong opinions about them, and you were marked, as Lamb observes—you must read and have something to say about it "or be thought nothing of." Though the right books and opinions varied from one group to another, a given circle might be expected to show consistency and to some extent to define itself by its standards of literary taste.

The court set an example, the King and Queen, as indicated earlier, both being known to pursue bookish pastimes. George III had been building up a fine collection throughout his reign; the catalogue began to appear after his death in 1820 and was finally completed in five back-breaking folios in 1829. The Queen, who liked to talk about books with Fanny Burney, had her own collections of books and prints, kept a Reader among her personal attendants, had a hobby press, and occupied herself by extra-illustrating some of her favorite volumes.[87] Bibliomania, a brief phase of intense competition for certifiably rare books and manuscripts, was a craze among wealthy collectors, but it too filtered down: when Dibdin, who had led and fed the craze, published *Reminiscences of a Literary Life* in 1836, his list of subscribers included book societies in Chelmsford, Exeter, Melford, Norwich, and other provincial centers. Though collectors are often suspected of not really being readers at all, only fetishizers of books, the record of marginalia in the period shows that they had established practices of their own and that at least some of them—the Duke of Sussex, for example—were capable of intelligent engagement with the contents of the books they owned.

READING HABITS

Discussion of books and conversation in general, in social circles of the time, were often prompted by reading aloud: one person read, talk ensued. There have recently been many salutary reminders of this common practice in critical and historical studies; it cannot be too often stressed that reading aloud was still pervasive in that society.[88] In the family, at school, at church, and at work, some read while others listened. William Chambers, an apprentice in Edinburgh, earned a penny roll for breakfast in the mornings by reading old novels to a baker and his men (*DNB*), a practice akin to the house-painters' radio today, perhaps, except that the bakers very likely exchanged opinions about the story as it unfolded. Lamb has an amusing essay, "Detached Thoughts on Books and Reading," about the right choice of reading for the bank office and the coffeehouse. Southey recalls Sunday evenings at his school when all the boys assembled to hear the headmaster read "a sermon, or a portion of Stackhouse's History of the Bible" (*Life*, 1:57). (Perhaps there was not much conversation after that.) Workingmen's clubs and voluntary societies often made reading aloud a regular part of their program, the famous London Corresponding Society being a case in point. Francis Place, a journeyman tailor when he joined in 1794, later described its pattern of public reading followed by invitations to comment (131). Adam Fergusson, a captain in the British army in Portugal in 1811, read *The Lady of the Lake* aloud to his messmates to "bursts of applause" over the stag-hunting scene, "the favourite among the rough sons of the fighting Third Division" (Lockhart, 3:155). Mary Shelley's and Claire Clairmont's diaries carefully record what they were reading themselves, separately, and what they were reading together, as in, "work [sewing] in the Evening while Shelley reads the Gospel of Mat[t]hew aloud."[89] In a letter of 1796 Anna Seward mentions her success with an English translation of Bürger's *Leonora*, which she had read aloud more than fifty times: "there was scarce a morning in which a knot of eight or ten did not flock to my apartments, to be poetically frightened."[90]

Henry Crabb Robinson, who was in demand as a reader and prided himself on his ability to read aloud—especially to read the poetry of Wordsworth aloud—describes many social occasions on which this sort of performance was a catalyst for conversation. The reader generally chose the text. After dinner on January 22, 1817, for instance, "I read Lord Byron's 'Manfred' to Mrs. Becher and Miss Lewis. I had occupied myself during the forenoon in writing a critique on this painful poem, which nevertheless has passages of great beauty. The ladies would have been greatly delighted with it, I dare say, if I had encouraged their admiration" (2:59). But Robinson was also a willing listener. On 27 February 1818, in an entry that brings home the oral quality of their experience, Robinson records having taken Mrs. Gurney to hear Coleridge lecture in the afternoon, and then bringing her home where they "heard Mr. Gurney read Mrs. Fry's examination before the committee of the House of Commons about Newgate—a very curious examination, and very promising as to the future improvements in prison discipline" (2:88–89). From the point of view of reception—what readers make of books—it is interesting to see evidence of collective reading that resists the guidance of the text, as in the case of a party that Mary Russell Mitford describes, held on a wet afternoon in a country house, where the situation was saved by "a young barrister, who had sufficient courage to confess his indifference to field sports," who proposed to read aloud from a law book and succeeded in entertaining everyone by the zest of his reading and "the humorous manner in which he expounded the mystery of the legal phrase" (1:83). In this case the reading was unexpectedly comical and further enlivened, apparently, by the reader's asides.

It has recently become standard procedure to draw attention to the widespread custom of reading aloud in groups. Habits of reading in pairs or alone have received relatively little attention, though to a modern reader the practices of the time in this regard may also be surprising. The intimacy of reading aloud where there are just two is bound to be qualitatively different from the experience of larger groups. Here too there is evidence in abundance of reading creating common ground in all sorts of social relations. Henry Francis Cary, the translator of Dante, attracted Coleridge's attention when they both happened to be on holiday at Littlehampton by reading the Greek text of Homer on the beach with his son—"in order that the pupil might learn to read *ore rotundo*, having to raise his voice above the noise of the sea that was breaking at his feet." Coleridge himself always remembered the unexpected kindness of his outdoorish, unbookish older brother Frank, who read Pope's translation of Homer to him when he was five or six years old and sick in bed. On the theme of the sick child, Mary Russell Mitford recalls reading a poem about one to her maid "whose fair-haired Saxon boy, her pet and mine, was then fast recovering from a dangerous illness"; they were both so overcome by the experience that the reader could scarcely get the words out and the listener could hardly hear for sobbing.[91] Perhaps it should be noted that the reader's is invariably the superior position, in these cases, just as the father in the family generally got to be the reader. On the other hand, women like Mitford's maid, a "hemmer of flounces," were read to because their hands and eyes were occupied with work, and the sick child because he was too sick to read for himself. We do have plentiful records of women as readers-aloud, Jane Austen among them; so I'm not disposed to make heavy weather of the power relations involved.

Henry Crabb Robinson, the great go-between, has left a particularly abundant and detailed record of his own reading practices, a record that can usefully and safely be taken as representative partly because it is confirmed by other evidence (not, I mean, evidence that he behaved in certain ways but that his contemporaries behaved in the same ways) and partly because of his wonderful social adaptability. Robinson was at least as interested in talking to an old soldier, a bricklayer, or a lunatic ("the insane poet, painter, and engraver, Blake") as to the lawyers, Dissenters, and socialities of his proper sphere.[92] Ever a joiner, he attended many kinds of public-speaking events where he would have been in socially mixed crowds, not only his court work but also plays, forums, debates, lecture series, sermons, conversazioni, and recitations. He mentions having gained some practice in "business speaking by attending the Surrey Institution" in 1808 (1:269). It is not surprising that when he spent leisure time alone with Wordsworth, Coleridge, or Blake, they generally wound up being read to. On 24 May 1812, for example, he had "a very interesting day": "At half-past ten joined Wordsworth in Oxford Road; we then got into the fields, and walked to Hampstead. I read to him a number of Blake's [poems], with some of which he was pleased. He regarded Blake as having in him the elements of poetry much more than either Byron or Scott" (1:385). In the same way, Robinson read some of *Faust* to Coleridge and some Wordsworth to Blake, of whom he reports, "in general Blake loves the poems" (1:395, 2:309, 324). To all of them Robinson also lent books. So while he and his friends could have read these works on their own, they preferred to hear them read and to talk them over on the spot. As second best,when he lent books, Robinson must have encouraged the borrowers to write down their opinions; it is to him that we owe important marginalia by Coleridge and Blake, generally written in pencil but then carefully overtraced or transcribed in ink by Robinson.[93]

A significant amount of both the shared and the solitary reading reported in journals and letters of the period takes place outdoors, and not only in the recreational way that Keats described when he went boating on the Isis in 1817, exploring "all the streams about, which are more in number than your eye lashes," and rested among the rushes where "we have read Wordsworth and talked as may be" (*Letters*, 1:162). Sometime between 1800 and 1807, Wordsworth himself composed an angry little poem "On seeing some Tourists of the Lakes pass by reading; a practise very common" (*Poems*, 535). Perhaps we should not be surprised, knowing that indoor space was liable to be busy with other people, and that foot-journeys might be long and tedious. We still read while traveling in subway cars or planes, as they did in coaches and wagons. (Hannah More reports herself "much amused in my post-chaise with Lord Monboddo's ninth volume on the Origins and Progress of Language, which he sent to me"; Dibdin "strolled abroad, now with Pope, now with Dryden, now with Milton as my companion"; Lady Lyndhurst flatteringly told Thomas Moore that a friend of hers "nearly broke his neck over your book yesterday" by trying to read it while driving; Crabb Robinson read *Don Juan* riding on the outside of a stagecoach while his friends played whist inside.[94]) But Robinson was apparently no more conspicuous then as he walked reading from place to place—from Cambridge to Bury, from Enfield to Hornsey, from London to Blackheath ("After an early dinner walked to Blackheath, reading a very amusing article in the *Edinburgh Review* about ants" [1:398])—than someone with a Walkman would be now. Presumably he passed other readers on the road; Constable was pleased to be able to report to Scott that people were reading his work on the streets of London "as they passed along" (3:219). The weather seems to have made little or no difference to Robinson: "I was employed in looking over law papers all the forenoon; I then walked in the rain to Clapton, reading by the way the *Indicator*" (2:192). Robinson also read privately in his rooms, and in bed, but the point of taking him as an example is that reading was a visible feature of everyday life, indoors and out, alone and in company.

READERS WRITING IN BOOKS

What was the place of the writing reader, the amateur annotator, in such a world, where reading was for the first time a common occupation and where reading matter was abundant? Readers were a vital part of the system I have been describing, and most if not all readers were writing readers on occasion. Writing in books was a recognized privilege of ownership; most forms of note-making were not merely tolerated but valued. As I have already indicated, some books were printed to be written in. Catalogues issued by auction houses and booksellers promoted books with notes, especially but not only when the notes were by famous scholars or celebrities: "enriched by MS. marginal notes" is the standard phrase. Lamb in a letter of 1806 assured Wordsworth that the writing in a Shakespeare that he had acquired for him at second hand was only variant readings "which some careful Gentleman the former Owner was at the pains to insert in a very **neat** hand from 5 Commentators. It is no defacement" (*Letters,* 2:205). Annotated books circulated like others, and the notes were sometimes copied out by borrowers. Book owners sought out the written opinions of people they admired: strangers used to send Coleridge books to annotate, and Byron's friend Hobhouse was thrilled to hear—as who would not be?—that Napoleon had written marginal notes for him in a French translation of Hobhouse's book about his reign.[95] Institutional libraries purchased annotated collections and accepted specific bequests of annotated books. At a personal level, annotated copies were shared by friends and passed down as heirlooms in families. But this high value assumed and depended on conformity with traditional standards of annotation. In the course of the reading boom that I have described, with easier access to books and much more widespread ownership, it seems that those standards were at times ignored or abandoned in the name of freer or more creative use, so that by 1830 the status of marginalia had become more equivocal than it was in 1790. The chapters that follow document the ordinary and the extraordinary practices of actual Romantic readers.

chapter one

Mundane Marginalia

The case for the centrality of print in British culture in the Romantic period does not rest on the impact of a handful of great works or popular best-sellers but on the widespread everyday service of publications of all kinds. It is hard to speak up for the everyday: it seems dull or low or self-evident, therefore uninteresting. It is by definition tedious, if we let definitions go unquestioned. The everyday of two hundred years ago, however, has a degree or two of exotic glamour more than the everyday that we are used to, so I turn first to the witness of readers' notes in books of the most humdrum kinds, those associated with education and working life. What did readers of the day customarily do with the books they worked with all the time? What inferences can we make from routine use? And what can we learn from exceptional cases?

Early Education

Certain forms of writing in books had been immemorially approved as study methods: interlinear glosses, as aids to translation; heads—words indicating topics and changes of topic—for comprehension and rapid review; marginal commentary taken by dictation from the instructor.

The Romantic period, which saw continuing debate about many aspects of education, may have refined these traditional techniques but saw no reason to question them.[1] Many readers therefore acquired the habit of writing in books early and extended it to books not assigned by teachers. It must have felt like a *natural* thing to do. Humanist educational theory encouraged such habits. Erasmus had recommended a system of marks to highlight different kinds of beauties in a work and declared that he preferred a battered book with notes in the margins to the pristine treasure of the bibliophile.[2] Locke spoke out against memory-work and insisted that the point of reading was to improve the mind by exercise of its own powers, not to stuff it with the words of others: "Reading furnishes the mind only with materials of knowledge; it is thinking makes what we read ours" (193). His successor Isaac Watts echoed his words. (Watts was perhaps the most frequently consulted practical writer on education in the late eighteenth century and the early nineteenth, his *Improvement of the Mind* [1741] being regularly reprinted.) "It is meditation and studious thought, it is the exercise of your own reason and judgment upon all you read," he declared, "that gives good sense even to the best genius, and affords your understanding the truest improvement" (6).

Watts specifically advised readers to write in the margins of their books. Their notes, he said, would serve various purposes. Readers should mark passages that contained matter "new or unknown" to them, for a second reading; they should detect the writer's faults, make note of them in the margin, and "endeavour to do it better" (the copy of Watts that I read had a reader's "NB" at this point); they would find it convenient to create a rough-and-ready index, if the book did not come with one; and they might make "remarks" about the faults and beauties observed along the way (74, 78, 80, 81–82).

> Other things also of the like nature may be usefully practised with regard to the authors which you read, viz. If the method of a book be irregular, reduce it into form by a little analysis of your own, or by hints in the margin: if those things are heaped together, which should be separated, you may wisely distinguish and divide them . . . all

> these practices will have a tendency both to advance your skill in logic, and method, to improve your judgment in general, and to give you a fuller survey of that subject in particular. When you have finished the treatise with all your observations upon it, recollect and determine what real improvements you have made by reading that author. (79–80)

Watts's strenuous program of self-discipline through reading was consistent both with academic tradition and, perhaps surprisingly, with the progressive, post-Rousseauian educational theory of the age. Whatever the real-life experience of the schoolroom, the consensus among reforming writers on education was that gentle methods worked best; that the tutor's task was to inculcate good habits, not to enforce strict rules; and that the goal of education was to train the mind, not fill it up. And this was true at all levels, even the most elementary.

Mothers in the home, who were often responsible for early education, were told to ensure that children understood what they were taught and did not just repeat verbatim what they had been told. While offering this advice, Elizabeth Hamilton reminds her reader that were it only for the children's sake she must not neglect her own education, even if she has the misfortune to be married to a man who "despises female intellect" and "merely wishes in his wife to find the qualities of the housekeeper, and the virtues of the spaniel" (2:252). In their advice on the use of books in the family, Maria Edgeworth and her father also stress the importance of understanding over memorization and give practical advice to the parent about building the child's critical self-confidence: "When young people have established their character for truth and exact integrity, they should be entirely trusted with books as with every thing else. A slight pencil line at the side of the page will then be all that is necessary to guide them to the best parts of any book" (2:118).[3] Schoolbooks that have survived from the period naturally contain traces of the sort of parental guidance and purposeful reading that the Edgeworths and their like recommended. The commonest forms of children's marginalia are ownership inscriptions, practice writing, heads, and solutions to problems in mathematics. Parents and teachers often wrote in dates, either to assign a reading or to record progress; and they may have been responsible for marks at passages deserving special attention. Besides such routine use, I note a few special cases in the collections of the British Library, special because they were tailored to individuals and happen to have survived, but probably common enough in their kind at the time.

The first is a well-worn copy of *A Key to Spelling and Introduction to the English Grammar. Designed for the Use of Charity and Sunday-Schools* (1788). Intended for the children of the poor, this little book covers the elements of pronunciation, grammar, and public speaking, and incidentally reminds us that oral and print cultures were not conceived of as being distinct from one another to the extent that they are now. Reading was taught orally, the child or children sounding out letters and words ("spelling") and reading aloud in chorus as well as individually. (Writing about similar methods of instruction in America about this time, William J. Gilmore observes, first, that the process of learning was probably more rapid because they were thus building on oral practice, and, second, that "the substance of oral and print culture were, from the earliest years of an individual's life, indissolubly linked" [38–39].) The children taught from this *Key* might never reach the writing stage, but they would speak well and be able to read aloud when called on. They would not have had their own copies of the primer; it belonged to the teacher and was interleaved to take the teacher's notes, clarifications, and additional illustrations. Where the text explains "ew" sounded as "u" in "*brew, crew, Jew, ewe*" (3), for example, the facing page shows the teacher going through the alphabet to find further instances: "Drew, few, grew, knew, mew, new, pew, screw, two [*sic*], view." Further on, facing p. 17 he or she notes,

> These faults must be corrected.
> All knows you cares not for me.
> All know you care
> I does not mind you.
> I do

And when they reach the stage of putting it all together,

> When you speak in public, or in any Oration, do not clip your Words, but express every Syllable, except in Poetry where the Measure being confined may require it. As, say not, Should'st, for Shouldest. Could'st for Couldest. (facing p. 31)

It's a small point, but the exception made for poetry tends to confirm the social range of poetry in the period, since these children destined most likely to be servants needed nonetheless to be aware of poetic measures.

In 1811 Eliza Hawtrey, whose brother had been an upper master at Eton College, whose husband was a clergyman and fellow of the College, and whose son Edward Craven Hawtrey went on to become headmaster and then provost, gave her daughter Mary a copy of Thomas Gisborne's *Familiar Survey of the Christian Religion* for her birthday. Besides the presentation inscription (with a little paper heart stuck on with sealing-wax to reinforce the hope "May she ever love this Gift; & *Giver*! as she loves her excellent, and affectionate Child!") it has other manuscript elements: a letter tipped in; extracts from other books, copied onto the back flyleaves; reading dates of 1814 and other dates, up to 1817, in connection with occasional notes; heads in the historical section; and some parental advice for further reading, such as "Look to the 221st Essay in the Spectator—Excellently good!" (+5). These notes were written over a period of years; the fact that the donor continued to write in the book after she had given it away says something about family use and the relative absence of possessiveness about such property, though of course we don't know how Mary felt about it. Sharing of books was normal and, as later chapters will show, books with marginalia were common social currency, especially among women.

My final example in this section is another instance of shared use, probably again within a family. The owner having acquired James Lee's *Introduction to Botany* (1806) as a student at Oxford later adapted it for "Betsy," composing lessons in the form of a poem that occupies three and a half closely written flyleaves. Samples: "Can my Betsy repeat those first ten lines, / Which tell of the classes, their names and signs? / How MON meant one Stamen, and DEC ten?—/ Well! we'll borrow these words from the valiant Men. . . . There! don't be afraid, Love! peep down the *Corolla*, / And tell us now—what do you see in the hollow?" Botany is the one subject consistently associated with poetry (and with women) in the period, following the example of Erasmus Darwin's *Botanic Garden*, and where the manual itself did not versify, readers often made their own contributions, as in this clumsy but charming case. The British Library copy of Priscilla Wakefield's *Introduction to Botany* that belonged to Lady Eleanor Fenn, herself an author of books for children, contains eight pages of poetic extracts in manuscript.[4]

THE CLASSICIST: CHARLES BURNEY

Outside the home, the heart of formal education was the study of classical literature, so middle- and upper-class boys, and occasionally girls, spent years locked into the discipline of classical scholarship and the conventions of classical editions, an experience that must have had a profound effect on their approach to literature, to books, and to the writing of notes. The formats are familiar: on each page a few lines of text, scholarly apparatus in double columns below, and at the back a glossary. The glossary translates words and phrases. The editorial notes traditionally reflect the concerns of textual editors by recording variant readings from manuscripts or from other printed editions, by proposing emendations where the text does not make sense, and by introducing parallel passages that show how other classical writers used the same words or phrases, as a way of establishing the meaning of the lines at hand. More daringly, they might venture into other areas of commentary by providing some historical context or identifying literary sources. A textbook Virgil of 1820 advertises all the desirable elements in its title, *Opera, locis parallelis ex antiquis scriptoribus et annotationum delectu illustrata in usum juventutis (Works, illustrated with parallels from the ancient writers and with a selection of annotations, for the use of youth)*: it is designed for "youth" and therefore is "illustrated" with parallel passages and a selection of the best scholarly notes. Students worked with these editions, absorbing their concerns with the minutiae of the text and enriching their own copies with additional evidence when they could get it, whether by noticing parallels in their own further reading or by consulting more comprehensive editions and dictionaries. An extreme but not anomalous example of the result is the copy of Theophrastus that belonged to the classical scholar John Wordsworth, who acquired it in 1825 when he was twenty and must have worked with it till he died in 1839. All the pages of the Greek text are crammed with notes in a tiny neat hand, the results of his trawling through the relevant literature—editions, histories, reference books, and criticism. Such systematic annotation might in due course lead to a new edition of the work in question, or to the separate publication of the scholar's notes, as in the posthumous edition of Richard Porson's *Adversaria* (1812), which was based on his books at Trinity College, Cambridge. Till then they would serve the student and teacher, the best of them being disseminated by way of the academic grapevine. Derwent Coleridge said of his brother Hartley's translations from Greek and Latin that they were so vivid that they circulated privately among classicists, turning up for example in "the Sophocles of a late Tutor at Queen's College, Oxford, who had them from tradition."[5]

One of the best *known* classicists of the time if not one of the best was Charles Burney (1757–1817), son of Johnson's friend of the same name, and brother of Fanny Burney. Though he eventually became "Doctor" Burney himself—a Doctor of Divinity, not of Music like his father—his career got off to a bad start when he was expelled from Cambridge for stealing books from the library (Walker). He redeemed himself, however: took his degree at Aberdeen instead, ran a very successful school, wrote about classical editions and modern Latin literature for popular periodicals, and published some scholarly essays, including an account of the meters of Aeschylus and a critique of Milton's Greek verses. His appetite for books never failing, he bought at auctions and built up an enormous collection consisting chiefly of editions of classical authors but also of important manuscripts, besides the newspaper collection that goes by his name to this day and a set of scrapbooks, extracts, and prints bearing on the history of the English stage. According to the *DNB*, he owned more editions of classical authors than the British Museum, where his collection went in the end.

One of the features that sets Burney apart from other major collectors of his day is that he did not merely catalogue and classify his books, he used them—apparently without making exceptions for age or rarity. Having acquired volumes already annotated by eminent scholars like Casaubon, Bentley, and Porson, who themselves had collated manuscripts and editions to assemble sets of variant readings and commentary, Burney claimed his place in the tradition with contributions of his own. Some authors and titles get more attention than others; some books may have been prepared for the schoolroom (Quintilian), and others have fed into Burney's own literary projects, notably his reviewing (Huntingford, Wakefield) and his edition of scholarly correspondence (Bentley). They are a mixed bag. But the striking pattern overall is the engagingly human one of the keen starter and poor finisher, or perhaps we should say of one whose work was mostly in progress.

Burney had many of his books interleaved to receive notes, collations, and compilations, but the interleaves are not heavily used. He started lists of various kinds—bibliographies, testimonials, tables of contents, Greek indexes—but did not finish them. (The first volume of his copy of Burton's edition of five Greek tragedies, an extreme example, has a list of praise for *Oedipus Rex* consisting of only one entry, and a list of references to the play in later literature, likewise with a single entry.) The very size of his collection may have been a deterrent to him. A less fortunate scholar might make his copy of Longinus into a variorum edition by entering all the variants and references he could find from books and manuscripts to which he had temporary access; but one who had several copies, as Burney did, might never settle on one to be the sole repository of learning on that author.

As far as I can see, Burney's original contribution to his working library, apart, that is, from sporadic efforts to copy materials from one book into another, was his habit of adding to classical texts parallel passages from major *English* writers. This practice is hardly systematic, but fairly frequently his notes include such information. At first I found it a little puzzling and wondered whether it reflected classroom practice. As a schoolmaster, was Burney hoping to make lessons more appealing by linking them to recreational reading? The tradition in classical editing is to use parallels to determine usage, but English would not serve that purpose. Were the English parallels meant to testify to the value of the ideas expressed, or to demonstrate the writers' indebtedness to their Greek and Latin masters? Did they simply reveal Burney's fondness for English literature; was it implied that the English are great in the same way? Burney's Burton and Sophocles record parallels to Sophocles in Shakespeare and Milton. He glosses Cebes with lines expressing similar sentiments from later writers, *hoi polloi* for instance with examples from Xenophon and Shakespeare (18). A typical note in his Virgil, on *Aeneid* 9.491, reads, "Pope on an Unfortunate Lady. Horace. Epode II. Gray El. Country C. Yard. Thompson—Georg. II" (495). There may indeed have been a deliberate pedagogical motive behind Burney's recording of English parallels, but the more examples of contemporary annotation I examined, the more I came to see the conventionality of his way of registering likenesses. His contemporaries were doing it too, sometimes under the commodious umbrella of "illustration," which will be considered later in this chapter. Many of us do it still without really considering to what end we might be writing "cf. Sons and Lovers" in *Oedipus Rex*, or vice versa. The process is largely subjective and of personal value, though it also implicitly affirms the continuity of literary tradition. Linking one work to another strengthens memory and consolidates knowledge by creating bonds of association, reminding us of what we already know and fitting the newcomer into an established structure.

ADULT EDUCATION

At the universities, dissenting academies, and medical schools, it was standard procedure to take notes in an interleaved copy of the course syllabus. It is often possible to identify the note-taker by matching the ownership inscription to the notes. The syllabi are themselves extensive, varying from about fifty pages to about two hundred, but they lack the details—proofs, illustrations, complications—that were supplied at the lecture. In their annotated form, therefore, these books are potentially valuable for the history of education and of scholarship: they flesh out the syllabus with notes taken on the spot. In practice they often prove disappointing, as they reveal how little of the course the student actually attended, or attended to. There must have been diligent students who kept complete records, but the fifty or so exemplars that I have seen appear mostly to have belonged to idlers. I wonder about the fate of women looked after by the student in midwifery who took notes only at an introductory lecture on "Classes, and Orders of Labors" and at one later one on treatment for diseases of the labiae (*Syllabus* 1799). Even so, these student records provide some insight into what went on in the lecture hall and display different methods of note-taking, from the seemingly verbatim report to the distanced critical appraisal.

A British Library copy of the *Syllabus of Lectures on Mineralogy* (1794) by G. Schmeisser, for instance, contains detailed notes, including diagrams, from the beginning of the course when the lecturer described the apparatus necessary for the chemical analysis of minerals, and again from lectures toward the end when he spoke about particular minerals; perhaps the student switched to another method of note-taking in between, or perhaps he was present at only two or three lectures. These notes appear to be a neutral record of what was said in the lecture theater, the student writing, on the subject of "Magnetic Iron Stone,"

> Steel differs from Iron in specific Gravity & Solidity
> More elastic
> Not so easily affected by Acids
> Higher Polish
> Iron containing Manganese best for Steel

and so forth (facing 116). But Thomas Barber, at Cambridge in 1800, whether on Watts's principle of mental exercise or by irresistible need, introduced his own thoughts as well as the lessons of the lecturer, the astronomer Samuel Vince: "Query How is the latter Part of this Article (46) to be reconciled with the former?" (facing 15). Barber stopped taking notes about a quarter of the way through the course. Another

Cambridge student, Robert Smith, appears to have taken rough notes in pencil on the margins of the pages and then later to have copied what he wanted to preserve onto the interleaves in ink as a more permanent record. His notes on Harwood Busick's lectures on natural history and comparative anatomy in 1812 indicate the lecturer's eclectic approach to the subject, for they include a quotation from Pliny, references to recent scientific publications, and the series of examples that Busick used to illustrate his remarks about instinct ("Muscovy duck when he leaves the nest pulls off his feathers to keep the young warm"), but once again the notes cover only a small part of the whole, being confined to the lecture "Of Animals in General" (16–20).

The habit of annotation stayed with medical men. Though their notes in books are usually technical, they also occasionally express personal reasons for professional opinions, as in John Sherwen's views about avoiding contagion, written in Joshua Dixon's life of Dr. Brownrigg. Dixon recommends that the attending physician wash his hands, rinse out his mouth, and in extreme cases change his clothes after attending a contagious patient, but in a footnote he expresses the belief that "fortitude of mind" arising "from the consciousness of performing a duty" may also help to protect him. Sherwen comments, "Fortitude of Mind with a consciousness of acting well together with a Life of Sobriety and Temperance always preserved me from the Effect of Contagion. The bilious remitting Fever of Bengal alone excepted which was contracted by a Night Excursion in a Budgerow on the River Ganges" (211). This sort of personal testimony is valuable both for the incidental disclosure of the physician's working conditions and for the revelation of common attitudes.

PHILIP MACDERMOTT

Much the most interesting case of an annotating physician is Philip MacDermott, whose only claim to fame appears to have been two contributions to the study of Irish history published in Dublin in 1846: some of the footnotes in Connellan's translation of *The Annals of Ireland*, and *A Typographical and Historical Map of Ancient Ireland*. He is described on the title pages as Philip Mac Dermott, Esq., M.D." MacDermott's was so far from being a name to conjure with that he was not identified as the author of the "ms notes" when his books were catalogued, though his name usually appears clearly at the front, with a date and place of acquisition. It was only after noticing the recurrence of the name that I enquired about the provenance of the books and hit it lucky: the British Library had kept a record of the original purchase. In December 1862 the Trustees of the British Museum were sent a handwritten list of 502 books, most of them unimportant editions and many of *those* Dublin editions, from which they chose to buy just under 200 (rejected titles are crossed through on the list) for a total of £11. Though MacDermott's name is not given on the list, a sampling of the titles purchased produced a 100 percent match: every one had either an ownership inscription or notes in his distinctive hand and manner; therefore it seems likely that the list consisted entirely of books from his library. (It may not represent the whole collection, though: some standard English authors, such as Shakespeare and Milton, are missing, and there are very few medical books.) Paradoxically, the volumes thus acquired are especially attractive to researchers today precisely because they are such poor things, most of them cheap duodecimos or sixteenmos, many of them acquired secondhand by MacDermott, and nearly all scribbled in more or less heavily. They were not the cossetted possessions of a wealthy collector or bookman but the companions and comforts of a working physician who could not afford the biggest, best, and newest editions, and who hung on to books he had had as a schoolboy.

Though I have not made a complete survey, the set examined is enough to flesh out the profile of MacDermott and to establish the general features of a habit he exercised for half a century. He must have been born about 1797 and died about 1860, perhaps in 1862 when his library—or a substantial portion of it—was offered for sale. The earliest annotated book is a school textbook of rhetoric by John Stirling published in Dublin in 1806, with an ownership inscription of 1811, and the latest a copy of Goldsmith's essays and poems published in London in 1826 that found its way into MacDermott's hands in 1858. The latest date of publication is 1859. MacDermott was still in Dublin and presumably still at school in 1817 when he acquired a new copy of the anonymous *Elements of Logic*, but from 1825 to 1827 his books were inscribed from London and in 1828 from Edinburgh, where he must have done his medical training before going back to Dublin to establish his practice. The main strengths of MacDermott's eclectic collection are history, the Latin classics, English and French literature, and Ireland, with an unusual minor interest in American history and poetry. There is a sizable set of travel books and guides, especially for France. A "Lady's Encyclopedia" (not purchased by the Museum) suggests the presence of a woman in the household, a wife or sister.

MacDermott started by marking his books in a fairly conservative way (heads, glosses, indexes) but quickly evolved a freer, more flexible style suited to his needs, allowing him to combine assimilation of the text with corrections and expressions of opinion of his own, and to treat special cases in a special way. On the whole his technique seems to have been consistent from about 1825 onwards, so even if his notes were made at various readings over a period of years, they would have been the same *kind* of notes. The copy of Magendie's *Elementary Compendium of Physiology; for the Use of Students* that he bought in 1828 contains the record of thoughtful study: some heads, some cross-references to other writers, but also (exceptionally, for him) on the front flyleaves a draft essay "on the Nature and Connexion of Life—Soul—Mind and Matter" that does not appear to have been taken down at a lecture but composed in the book, with revisions and cancellations. The notes in the margins characteristically show MacDermott reflecting on and developing ideas from the text. Magendie, for example, explains that all animal bodies "contain a considerable portion of azote" or nitrogen, but that authorities disagree about whether the nitrogen gets there through food or respiration (470). In his first penciled note, MacDermott is disposed to agree with Magendie, who is of the food party: "The Irish peasantry live principally on <u>potatoes</u>, but this vegetable consists chiefly of <u>Starch</u>, and Starch contains some <u>Nitrogen</u>." On second thought, however, he wonders whether there is not some middle ground to be found between the two parties in the debate. Another note, in ink this time, begins, "I think it very probable that part of the Nitrogen, which enters into the composition of the body; (being one of the chief constituents of the muscular fibre) is derived from the atmospheric air in the process of Respiration, and as a proof of this it might be adduced, that we find no vigorous healthy, Strong individuals, with their muscular system well developed; except those whose organs of Respiration are in a sound State." MacDermott typically spells out his reasons for adopting one position rather than another. When he consulted his books again he would find the original reasoning as well as the conclusion.

Alongside his professional reading, MacDermott enjoyed literary recreations and annotated copies of Latin, English, and French authors in much the same spirit as he brought to Magendie. In 1827 he bought a tiny but complete copy of Byron's *Childe Harold's Pilgrimage* and proceeded to squeeze into its limited blank spaces various conventional marks, heads, and index entries; explanatory footnotes identifying persons, places, and events when Byron had neglected to do so; and a few appreciative comments. Though the last are commonplace enough, they show the enthusiasm of the reader and the kind of thing that excited him. At the front of the book he notes, "Byron is the greatest Poet on Greece since Homer," and makes a list of Byron's "Greek" poems. At the end of "To Ianthe," he rhapsodizes, "The Address to Ianthe is of surpassing beauty. She was Lady Charlotte Harley—daughter to the Earl of Oxford, a beautiful girl then in the 11th year of her age" (4). He may have been on the lookout for passages to share through reading aloud or recitation: at the beginning of Canto Four he observes, "Passages of surpassing beauty Quote—Stanzas 1—2—3 11—12—13—14—15—16—17" ([105]).

MacDermott continued throughout his life to subject his books to the same critical treatment. A copy of Johnson's *Poetical Works* acquired in 1848 gave him an opportunity to bring his love of Latin to bear, as he commented on Johnson's Latin models and Latin verse. Of the translation of Johnson's epitaph for Goldsmith, he growls, "This translation is damned nonsense done by some Jackass" (191). His unsurprising general assessment is that "Johnson was a first rate prose writer but only a

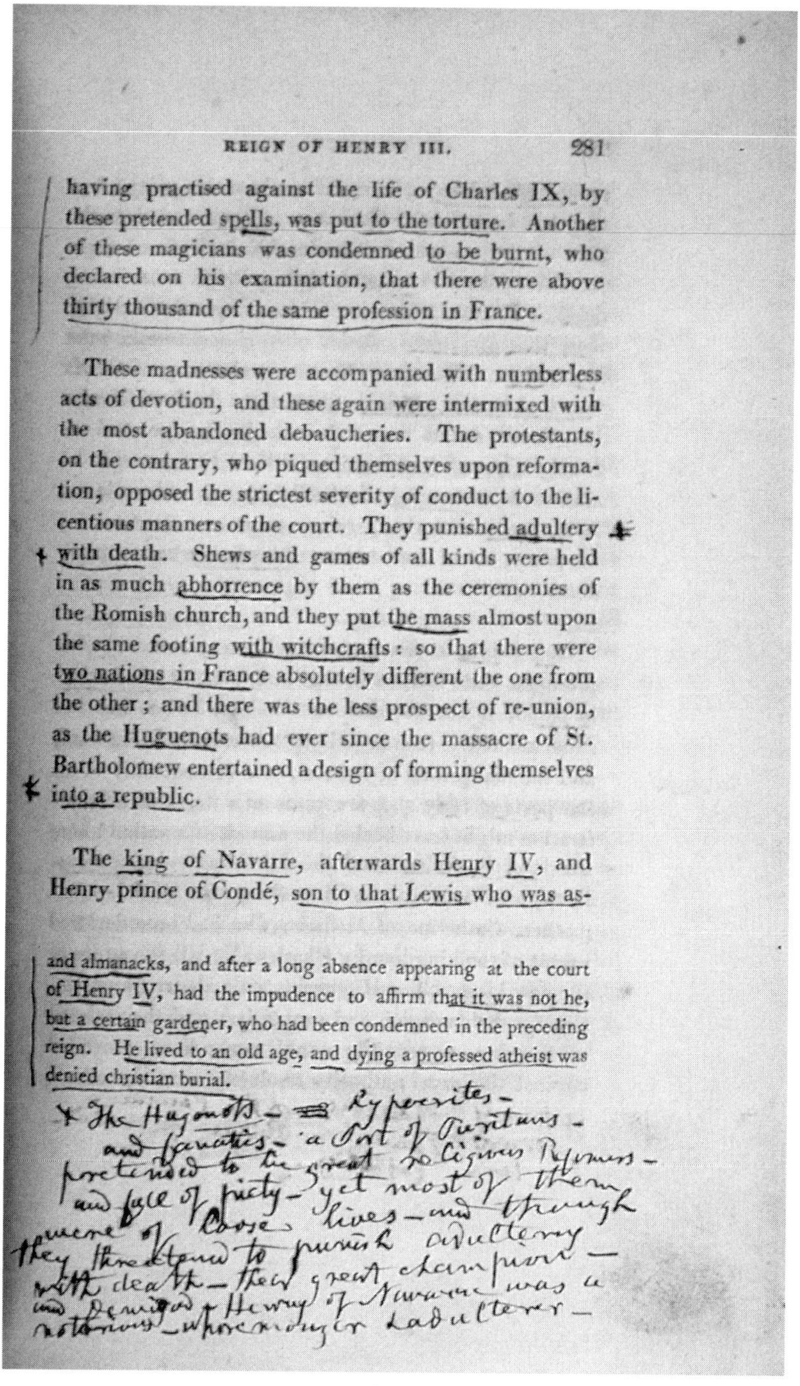

REIGN OF HENRY III. 281

having practised against the life of Charles IX, by these pretended spells, was put to the torture. Another of these magicians was condemned to be burnt, who declared on his examination, that there were above thirty thousand of the same profession in France.

These madnesses were accompanied with numberless acts of devotion, and these again were intermixed with the most abandoned debaucheries. The protestants, on the contrary, who piqued themselves upon reformation, opposed the strictest severity of conduct to the licentious manners of the court. They punished adultery with death. Shews and games of all kinds were held in as much abhorrence by them as the ceremonies of the Romish church, and they put the mass almost upon the same footing with witchcrafts: so that there were two nations in France absolutely different the one from the other; and there was the less prospect of re-union, as the Huguenots had ever since the massacre of St. Bartholomew entertained a design of forming themselves into a republic.

The king of Navarre, afterwards Henry IV, and Henry prince of Condé, son to that Lewis who was as-

and almanacks, and after a long absence appearing at the court of Henry IV, had the impudence to affirm that it was not he, but a certain gardener, who had been condemned in the preceding reign. He lived to an old age, and dying a professed atheist was denied christian burial.

✝ The Hugonots — hypocrites — and fanatics — a Sort of Puritans — pretended to be great religious Reformers — and full of piety — yet most of them were of loose lives — and through they threatened to punish adultery with death — their great champion and Demigod Henry of Navarre was a notorious — whoremonger & adulterer —

FIG. 12 Notes by Philip MacDermott in Voltaire's *Henriade* (1807). By permission of the British Library.

third rate poet—yet still he wrote pleasing & polished verses" ([154]). In Voltaire's *Henriade,* which for once he did not inscribe with his name and a date, but in which the hand and manner of annotation are unmistakable, he gave most of his attention not to the poem (though again he ventures to improve on the translation) but to the accompanying historical essay, where he wrote notes to summarize and supplement the text, such as in the case of the Huguenots, whom he seems to have thought Voltaire took too much at face value for the sake of their opposition to the Roman Catholic Church and the political establishment. Voltaire points out that they were strict in their conduct and "punished adultery with death" (281; Fig. 12). MacDermott responds: "The Hugonots—hypocrites and fanatics—a Sort of Puritans—pretended to be great religious Reformers—and full of piety—yet most of them were of loose lives—and though they threatened to punish adultery with death—their great champion—and Demigod—Henry of Navarre was a notorious whoremonger & adulterer—" There is no sign that MacDermott marked and annotated his books with a view to later publication: he was simply taking notes and recording his approval or disagreement, being careful, usually, to give specific reasons for both.

THE NATURALIST: JAMES EDWARD SMITH

Beyond the schoolroom, botany and natural history provided the most respectable recreational pursuits of the time and had their own multitiered literature, from children's books to the exhaustive catalogues of the experts. As noted earlier, publishers brought out blank journals with columns for daily information about weather and observations of flora and fauna. Presses vied with one another to produce the beautiful, expensive volumes of prints representing shells, fossils, insects, birds, and flowers that were prized both by the fashionable world and by serious amateur collectors. But even readers who could not afford the prints could play a role in the collective enterprise. In the realm of natural history the vital unit of information was the firsthand observation, preferably taken from the wild or from preserved specimens in a collection or, as second best, from an authoritative written record. Any enthusiast could hope to contribute a unit or two and the work proceeded by accumulation, so it is not surprising that many books on these subjects contain readers' notes.

Leaders of the movement set the tone. Gilbert White's *Natural History and Antiquities of Selborne*, a naturalist's diary in epistolary form, was first published in 1789 in a handsome quarto with engraved plates and occasional footnotes. In the natural history section, the footnotes identify quotations, provide learned references, and add illustrative examples, such as a correspondent's testimony about respiration in the antelope (41n) or White's own record of the seasonal appearance of the little bat (75n). Readers working with this instant classic followed suit, so that by 1833 it could be issued in the form of a variorum edition "with notes by several eminent naturalists."[6] Their printed notes, like White's, range from bookish cross-references to expansive anecdotes with a very personal flavor, such as the one by W. H. Herbert about an injured swift that he had taken in and kept by an open window, fenced in with "quarto books." Eventually the bird recovered and flew away. Herbert comments, "I make little doubt that in less than a week after its vain attempts to surmount Johnson's Dictionary, my young friend was flying sky high in the heart of Africa" (218n–19n). If these published notes were not originally marginalia, as I am inclined to suppose they were (probably in interleaved copies), still they were closely tied to the text of White's work and were written in the same spirit.

The same is true of the less lovable but more practical catalogues produced in the period. Though the term "field guide," meaning a portable version, was not yet available, the thing itself existed. The new systems of classification introduced by Linnaeus and Jussieu rationalized the study of natural history, botany in particular, making it more accessible to the lay person. An important landmark for such studies in Britain was the arrival of the collections of Linnaeus in London, including the bulk of his library—roughly 1,600 books, about a quarter of them with manuscript annotations by Linnaeus or his contemporaries—in 1784. This acquisition was the great coup of an English botanist, James Edward Smith, who went on to found the Linnean Society in 1788.[7] Smith's own books remain in the library of the Society. Though many were presentation copies from their authors and many of those have no marks of ownership beyond the presentation inscription, several of the books that Smith put to use in the field or in preparing publications of his own show that he followed Linnaeus (and occupational tradition) in his modus operandi.

Smith's copy of William Hudson's *Flora Anglica* (1778), for example, has several layers of notes made over a period of at least twenty-five years. Catalogues of plants were created at the time by one or both of two methods, as catalogues of books are in bibliography today, either by combing through and synthesizing previous catalogues or by examining actual specimens. Hudson's book, a major source for Smith's standard *English Botany* (1790–1814), was chiefly of the first kind: Hudson surveyed existing catalogues and reorganized the data they produced to conform to the Linnaean system. Smith's heavily used copy adds references from authorities not included by Hudson, names and details for plants unrecorded by him, cross-references to the entry-numbers of *English Botany* as it came out, new observations of Smith's own, and occasionally a pressed sample (e.g., 292). The entry for a stonecrop (*sedum*) typically has several concise additions, two cross-references and a sighting: "Curt. Lond. fasc. 3. t. 26," "Engl. Bot. t. 656," and "On a wall by the 1½ Mile Stone near Chelsea Hospital. JES" (197). In the case of a rare *cyperus,* a species of sedge, Smith rejects a sighting reported in Hudson and replaces it with a better, though unpublished, authority: "By a little rivulet y[t] runs into Whitsand bay, between S[t] David's town & S[t] David's head, the only certain hab[t] of this plant. July 25 1775. S[r] J. Cullum bar[t] Mss" (17).

As this last example suggests, when printed authorities, manuscript records, and their own range of observation failed, naturalists networked, sharing information through correspondence. One of Smith's copies of William Withering's *Arrangement of British Plants* (3rd ed., 1796), less heavily used than his copy of Hudson, includes evidence from correspondents, as when Withering notes of a lichen that it had been "Found by Mr. Griffith upon oaks in the dingle at Garn near Denbigh," but Smith introduces the contradictory testimony of Dawson Turner, who knew the area—" 'unknown to us.' D. Turner" (2:20).

This painstaking method of confirmation and correction was an essential part of the routine, collaborative, cumulative work of naturalists. Some but not all of Smith's records found their way into his own publications, which in turn he annotated for future editions, as for example the interleaved copy of *Flora Britannica* (1800) in the Linnean Society library.

Though he was exceptionally punctilious and thorough, Smith used his books in a perfectly conventional way. The same practices can be seen in any number of catalogues and handbooks of the period annotated by professional and nonprofessional readers. An unidentified owner of Eleazar Albin's catalogue of insects (1731) used the plates in that heavy quarto as a place to record local sightings, noting for instance of a handsome black-and-burgundy moth, "This Moth was taken on the Leaves of Parsley—Maize Hill June 22nd: 1827. The larva has not yet been found by me." In 1808–9, before he became director of Kew Gardens, William Jackson Hooker kept dated records in a copy of Haworth's *Miscellanea Naturalia* (1803) that is still on the open shelves at Kew (58). William and Dorothy Wordsworth took a copy of Withering out on their walks in 1802 to record places and dates of their own sightings of the plants it describes, and occasionally to make up deficiencies in Withering's descriptions. Of common butterwort, *pinguicula vulgaris,* Dorothy observes,

> In great abundance all round the Grasmere fells. This plant is here very ill described, a remarkable circumstance belonging to it is the manner in which its leaves grow, lying close to the ground, and diverging from the stalk so as exactly to resemble a starfish, the tall slender stalk surrounded by the blue flower and rising from the middle of the starfish renders the appearance of this plant very beautiful especially as it is always found in the most comfortless and barren places, upon moist rocks for instance.[8]

Dorothy Wordsworth's attention to aesthetic effect sets her annotation subtly apart from that of the average user, reminding us of her special purpose in observations of nature; and yet she was only vying with the similarly detailed description given by the author. Working within the bounds of accepted use, she was at the same time, probably unconsciously, adapting its conventions to meet her own needs.

Smith's own works often survive in annotated versions. Richard Dreyer, a clergyman in Norfolk, both annotated and most beautifully illustrated his copy of *Flora Britannica,* with a combination of drawings from nature and watercolor copies of the prints of *English Botany* (Fig. 13).[9] Two British Library books, a copy of *Flora Britannica* in three volumes and one of the little one-volume *Compendium Florae Britannicae,* were brought up to date by their unidentified owners with systematic cross-references to *English Botany* but little evidence of field use. A copy of Smith's handy *Compendium of the English Flora* (1829), on the other hand, became a family project: John Tatham, born in 1793, assembled a herbarium and used the book as a field guide for local flora, recording in it places where the plants were found; forty years after him his grandson revisited the sites and verified Tatham's findings before presenting the book to the Library at Kew.

Pictorial illustrations are a distinctive feature of natural history books of this period, some of them being supplied by readers from their own field observations or preserved collections, or copied from other books, as in the case of Dreyer's Smith. Often they are coupled with written notes. One unusual case involving such illustrations is a New York Public Library copy of Richard Salisbury's *Paradisus Londinensis* (1806–8), a guide to plants "cultivated in the vicinity of the metropolis," as the title page has it, designed to capitalize upon the "present taste for botany, so general among all ranks" (Preface). The handsome quarto plates, all described as "Drawn & Published by William Hooker" (Hooker the artist, not the future director of Kew), are bound in alphabetical order along with their accompanying but subordinate text, and the unidentified owner, probably a man, has written a few notes on them. He supplies drawings for some plants described but not illustrated and corrects or questions Salisbury's descriptions as other readers might have done. He cites other authorities and records a few apparently original observations. But this reader was in a special position, having been a silent collaborator in the publication. He can

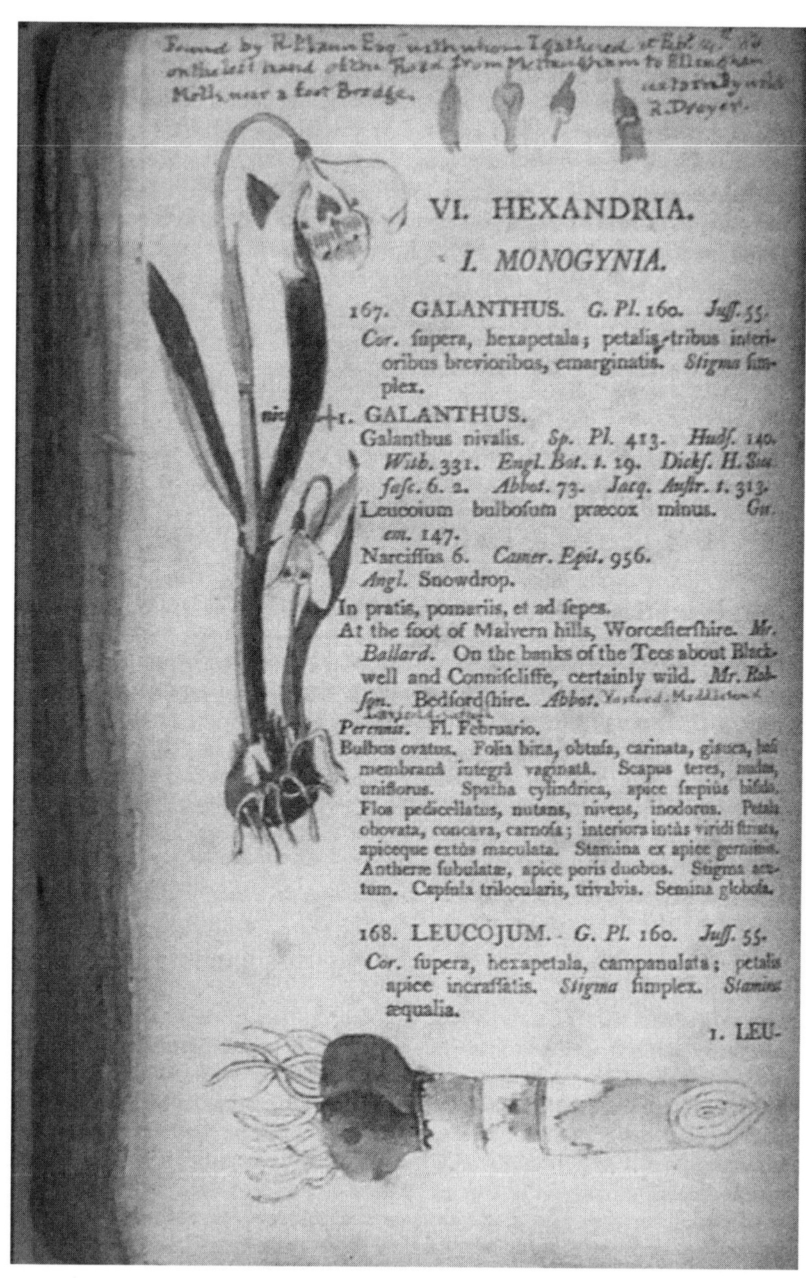

VI. HEXANDRIA.

I. MONOGYNIA.

167. GALANTHUS. *G. Pl.* 160. *Juſſ.* 55.
Cor. ſupera, hexapetala; petalis tribus interioribus brevioribus, emarginatis. *Stigma* ſimplex.

1. GALANTHUS.
Galanthus nivalis. *Sp. Pl.* 413. *Hudſ.* 140. *With.* 331. *Engl. Bot. t.* 19. *Dickſ. H. Sicc. faſc.* 6. 2. *Abbot.* 73. *Jacq. Auſtr. t.* 313.
Leucoium bulboſum præcox minus. *Ger. em.* 147.
Narciſſus 6. *Camer. Epit.* 956.
Angl. Snowdrop.
In pratis, pomariis, et ad ſepes.
At the foot of Malvern hills, Worceſterſhire. *Mr. Ballard.* On the banks of the Tees about Blackwell and Conniſcliffe, certainly wild. *Mr. Robſon.* Bedfordſhire. *Abbot.*
Perennis. Fl. Februario.
Bulbus ovatus. Folia bina, obtuſa, carinata, glauca, baſi membranâ integrâ vaginatâ. Scapus teres, nudus, uniflorus. Spatha cylindrica, apice ſæpiùs bifida. Flos pedicellatus, nutans, niveus, inodorus. Petala obovata, concava, carnoſa; interiora intùs viridi ſtriata, apiceque extùs maculata. Stamina ex apice germinis. Antheræ ſubulatæ, apice poris duobus. Stigma acutum. Capſula trilocularis, trivalvis. Semina globoſa.

168. LEUCOJUM. *G. Pl.* 160. *Juſſ.* 55.
Cor. ſupera, hexapetala, campanulata; petalis apice incraſſatis. *Stigma* ſimplex. *Stamina* æqualia.

1. LEU-

FIG. 13 Richard Dreyer's notes and illustrations in James Edward Smith's *Flora Britannica* (1800–1804). By permission of the Linnean Society.

consequently be seen adapting the conventions of note-making to suit his own purposes and complaining here and there that "Hooker has not copied my drawing at all faithfully" (Plate CIV) or "I suppose Hooker has blundered or else myself in the drawing" (Plate LXIII).

A more typical case is the copy of a third edition of Pennant's *History of Quadrupeds* (1793), now in the National Library of Wales, which belonged to Pennant's friend, the ornithologist John Latham. For at least thirty-five years, he added to it relevant bits of information clipped or copied from books and periodicals, or sent to him by friends. In the entry on the ox, for instance, of which Pennant remarks that "by cultivation, many parts of *England* rival in their cattle many parts of the continent" (1:22), he notes,

> At a Sale in Leicester on Tuesday, a Bull was sold to Mr Grasley of Worcestersh$^{re.}$ for y^{e} enormous Sum of 400 Guineas, & a 2 Year old Heifer for 84 Guineas, St James's Chron. Nov$^{r.}$ 19–21, 1793

There are also many drawings and watercolors, more often than not also copied from printed sources, inserted on extra leaves, including one of a deer dated 1754, when Latham had been fourteen, and on the other hand a picture of a platypus taken from the *Transactions* of the Linnean Society in 1829. At some point after 1800 he explained his role in a note on the title page: "The additional MS. Drawings & Plates by J. Latham M.D. Winchester." In all these cases we find original and secondhand observations combined indiscriminately, usually without comment.

REFERENCE BOOKS

Reference books, essential to students and serious readers at all levels and on all subjects, were the staples of the personal library. They are often found with readers' notes, usually just a few, where the reader has been able to correct or supplement the book from another source. Dictionaries, genealogies, biographical dictionaries, bibliographies, chronologies, and lists of all kinds are kept up to date this way. On a small scale, Elizabeth Ross was able to add a few names to the "List of British Female Literary Characters Living in the Eighteenth Century" at the back of Randall's *Letter to the Women of England*, including the name of Randall herself. The owners of two dictionaries of foreign-language quotations not only added a few good new quotations but also commented on the ones they found, sometimes rather cynically. Of "*Ne tentes, aut perfice*. Lat.—'Attempt not, or accomplish.'—Motto of the Ir. Marquis of DOWNSHIRE," one remarks, "no doubt a highwayman repeats this Sentence on his going to Ounslow h[ea]th." The other, adding his or her own entry, builds the comment in: "Fugere est triumphus. Lat. 'Flight is triumph.' Applied to temptations to which youth is exposed."[10] These impersonal reference books are personalized in a small way by their readers' additions.

Now and again, reference books seem to have become projects in themselves, the owner laboring over a period of years to improve them and increase their usefulness. They come to express the reader's growing expertise. If shared with other specialists they might eventually be acknowledged in print, but in the meantime the owner had the satisfaction of having an improved copy. Normally the reader begins with a book that is a regular resource, reliable in itself but perhaps not comprehensive. A good example is Richard Pulteney's *Historical and Biographical Sketches of the Progress of Botany in England* (1790), which an unidentified reader worked on from the time of publication to the 1820s, pasting in relevant extracts (including a transcription of a manuscript note to another book by the botanist Peter Collinson), correcting errors, and adding bibliographical and biographical evidence piece by piece, usually with scrupulous recording of sources:

> D^r. Pulteney was born 1730 died 1801[.] See Maton's "Memoirs of Dr Pulteney" prefixed to the 2nd Edit of "The General View of the Writings of Linnaeus"—1805 4to—also Nichols "Literary Anecdotes" Vol. 8 p 196. & Gent. Mag. 1801 V. 71 p 1058, 1207[.] Elizabeth, his Widow died at Lymington in Hants April 1820 aged 81 Gent. Mag. May 1820 p 476 (1:+1).

Where basically reliable work was not available, however, readers might make an inadequate book do by adding labor of their own. One had a copy of Ralph Wewitzer's *Theatrical Pocket Book, or Brief Dramatic Chronology* (1814) interleaved to take many additions and corrections, but recorded his or her exasperation with the original on a page facing the publisher's Advertisement which declares that the book, "though brief, is in several respects more comprehensive than any extant." The owner comments, "and more incorrect should also have been added for very few of the dates are correct, and it is in other respects the most incomplete work I ever saw—". Similarly, the numismatist who had to work with *The Virtuoso's Guide, in Collecting Provincial Copper Coins* (1795) copiously and expertly annotated his interleaved copy, but prefaced it with a warning that begins, "Notwithstanding the Assertions of the author in the foregoing Preface, it is pretty certain he has inserted some coins which he has not seen, as some are only named, & not described."

A particularly splendid case of the enriched reference book is a copy of a compendium on farming and horticulture, *Gleanings from Books, on Agriculture, and Gardening* (1802), that the owner worked on for at least thirty years. Itself a sort of ready-made commonplace book on gardening subjects, with entries starting at "acre" and proceeding to "zeugometer," with a few extra pages of topics "omitted" from the original alphabetical series, it was interleaved and then packed tight with supplementary information. The anonymous author had been inclined to be careless about citing sources, so the owner added the appropriate references where possible. But for the most part the reader built on the foundation provided by going to sources the writer had overlooked, or by turning to current publications, all properly documented. The sources are eclectic: the *British Farmer's Magazine*, Smith's *English Botany*, Young's *Annals of Agriculture*, but also the *Gentleman's Magazine* and Steevens's notes to Shakespeare. The only section not crammed with new information is the entry on "Cheese." In this case, the book provided an outline for the reader to work with as a sort of post-publication collaborator.

As the examples of MacDermott and the naturalists demonstrate, schoolroom methods of note-taking and annotation carried over easily to reading of other kinds, especially when the reader was in study mode. Interleaving was most often used for reference books and for special projects. Of the several kinds of notes written on the printed pages, heads are especially common, ranging from the systematic practice of R. Sarel Junior, who wrote heads in in pencil and then selectively copied them in ink so as to make a neat summary parallel to the text in his copy of Joseph Walker's *Historical Memoir on Italian Tragedy* (1799), to the hasty scribbles of a busy man like Bentham, found in several British Library pamphlets.[11] Sarel took the simple route of picking out words from the text; Bentham summarized in his own words—"plea of antiquity combated," for instance, to stand for a page in Burke's *Speech . . . on the 11th of February, 1780* (12–13). An outstanding example of this second, superior system is the volume of Plotinus in Thomas Taylor's translation written in by an unknown reader, probably in the mid-1790s. These ink notes, carefully composed and certainly not copied from another source, summarize the argument step by step so as to produce, in the end, a parallel reader's version of the content. The reader has to provide a digest of one phase of the argument before going on to the next, and the process of assimilation is clearly laid out (Fig. 14). On a later reading the summary might stand in for the original text, but the original would still be there as a check on it.

Sometimes heads were written at the front or back instead of in the text, forming a personalized index. J. Dyer Hewitt's copy of Johnson's *Lives* (1794), acquired while he was at Cambridge, is a typical example, with a list that informally registers the topics that interested him: "Def. of Poetry. p. 222. | Genius p. 2. | See pp. 27, 28. Wit. | Sublimity p. 30," etc. (2:-2). The Bishop of Limerick used the back endpapers of his copy of Robert Keith's *Historical Catalogue of the Scottish Bishops* (1824) for lists assembled from the book itself—"Archdeacons of St Andrews promoted to Bishopricks" and the like. A well-organized reader might manage to get the index into alphabetical order, as did the owner of a

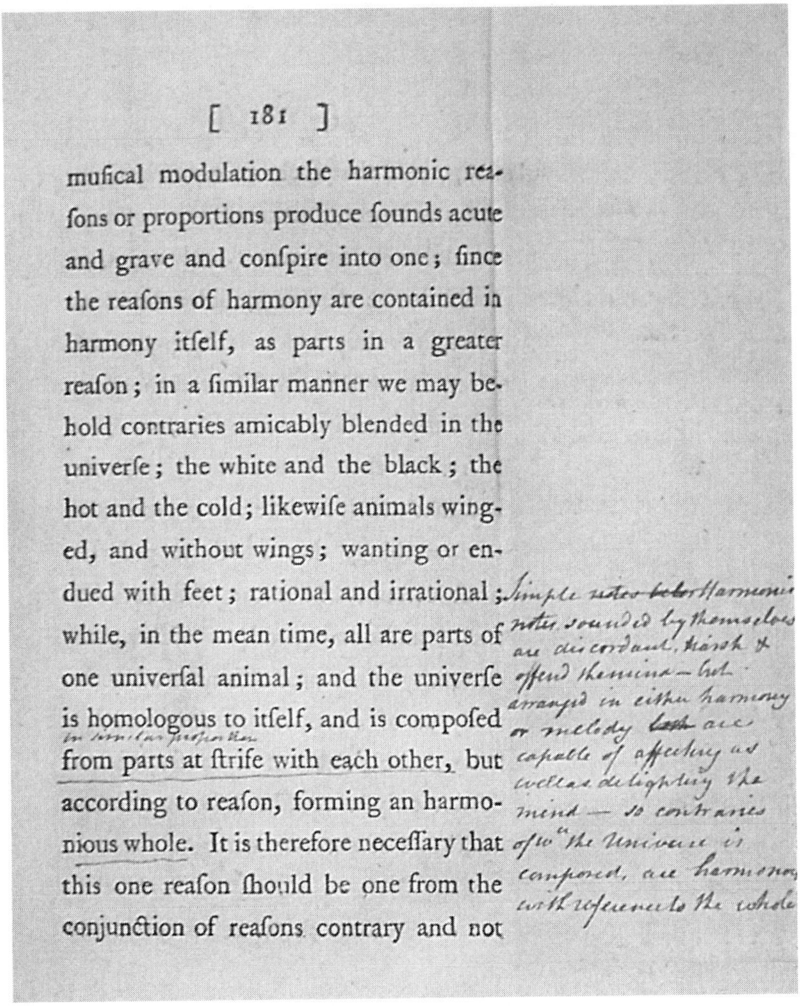

[181]

muſical modulation the harmonic reaſons or proportions produce ſounds acute and grave and conſpire into one; ſince the reaſons of harmony are contained in harmony itſelf, as parts in a greater reaſon; in a ſimilar manner we may behold contraries amicably blended in the univerſe; the white and the black; the hot and the cold; likewiſe animals winged, and without wings; wanting or endued with feet; rational and irrational; while, in the mean time, all are parts of one univerſal animal; and the univerſe is homologous to itſelf, and is compoſed from parts at ſtrife with each other, but according to reaſon, forming an harmonious whole. It is therefore neceſſary that this one reaſon ſhould be one from the conjunction of reaſons contrary and not

Simple notes Harmonic notes sounded by themselves are discordant, harsh & offend the sense—but arranged in either harmony or melody are capable of affecting as well as delighting the mind—so contraries of w[ch] the Universe is composed, are harmonious with reference to the whole

FIG. 14 Notes by an unknown reader in *Five Books of Plotinus* (1794). By permission of the British Library.

copy of Richard Watson's *Apology for the Bible* (1820), where the manuscript index begins "Angel approaching to Joshua, 63" and ends, "Writers of Scripture 52-54" (+1–+3).

Reading dates are also very common, a boon to future biographers if the reader happens to become famous, as in the case of the exceptionally punctilious Sir James Mackintosh, who recorded both place and date when he read his presentation copy of Bentham's *Plan of Parliamentary Reform:* "Read in the Hall at Haileybury Saturday 16 May 1818 from 10 A.M. to 3 P.M." One of the very few books from the library of Count Rumford, now in the Royal Institution, that contain more than ownership inscriptions is a presentation copy of Luigi Castiglioni's account of his travels in the United States. Rumford's pencil notes translate words and phrases throughout, and reading dates show his rate of progress through the Italian text: on Thursday he read 35 pages of the first volume; on Saturday he had got to page 74, and on Sunday to 136. Even the record of a reader such as Henrietta Harrison, with no known claims to fame, may be of interest for the evidence of dates that shows that she did not read Hannah More's *Practical Piety* (1821) right through, but dipped into it, rereading portions of it at various dates between 1828 and 1845, the chapter on "True and False Zeal" four times, that on the "Cultivation of a Devotional Spirit" seven.

Akin to the writing of heads and composing of indexes, but a hybrid of his own cultivation, was William Beckford's routine of taking extracts from a book and writing them in pencil on the flyleaves, starting at the front and continuing at the back if necessary. Hundreds of his books survive so marked, most of them belonging to the category of light reading (especially travels and memoirs, in French or English) purchased new and read before the books went to the binder.[12] It is a good system, providing occupation and pleasure while reading as well as a ready précis for future reference, and it does not spoil the pages of the text itself. The sequence of page references indicates that Beckford read these books straight through and apparently only once. The selection of passages is naturally subjective (as the entries in a reader's index are), and though Beckford usually copies the wording of the text faithfully, the selection implicitly involves a critical point of view; occasionally, too, he makes an overt comment, praising or mocking the writer. Copying out a passage from the first volume of Captain Basil Hall's travels in Chile, Peru, and Mexico, for example, he observes, "168 Visit to the Lake of Aculéo, which lay placidly in the midst of the mountains—perhaps (says Captn Hall or the polisher of these pleasing & brilliantly written volumes for him)—perhaps it is the smoothness and delicacy of finish, as it were, of a mountain Lake together with its unassuming solitude, compared with the bold & rugged majesty of the surrounding scenery which give it so much grace & beauty—".

It is worth stressing that Beckford does occasionally approve of the book he is reading, because his far more usual mode is mockery. He particularly relished being able to turn a writer's own words against him or her, to expose prudery or affectation by clever sampling. His gathering of choice passages highlighted absurdity, making ludicrous applications of serious statements. In Robert Proctor's *Narrative of a Journey*, for instance, he added a title to a short extract so as to make fun of the author's sense of propriety:

> Decent arrangements
>
> "Finding (writes the author) that I must expect only one apartment for my family during the whole journey, I made up my mind that the two female servants must sleep in the room with us—I arranged for this very purpose thus: the females always went to bed first & on a concerted signal the candle was extinguished and I used to come & undress; in the morning I rose before the room was light."—

In Lackington's *Confessions* of 1804, Beckford had little more to do than to put in a sardonic phrase, "the poor Author," and change from first person to third, to turn conventional piety on its head. Lackington laments, "For I was so destitute of knowledge and abilities, as not to be able to answer the witty and artful objections of that arch infidel Voltaire, and others whose works soon after I read" (6). Beckford's transcription begins, "6 The poor Author being destitute of knowledge & abilities is unable to answer the witty & artful objections of the arch infidel Voltaire." More often than not no editing was necessary. Mawman's *Excursion to the Highlands of Scotland* really does contain these lines that Beckford gleefully copied out, among others: "201 The sleek Herd with their brawny Male murmuring in his mighty strength" and "291 The Travellers return to London & hide their heads in the midst of smoke, toil & heart-rending jealousies—". He treated his French books just the same way, incorporating his own comments in French with the transcriptions, an interesting case being the rhapsodic description of the beauty of Byron in Stendhal's *Rome, Naples, et Florence, en 1817*, of which Beckford wonders whether Stendhal himself, described on the title page as a cavalry officer, could have been the author, since "la tirade est absolument Androgyne." In 1834, when he was seventy-five, Beckford told his bookseller that he was thinking of publishing some of his extracts though he feared that they were "so incredibly absurd, so loftily conceited, and so arabesquely florid" that readers would hardly believe they were authentic; nevertheless, he says, while he might have abridged, he "never amplified."[13] Eccentric as it seems now, a collection of the kind Beckford envisages would have readily found a market among the ephemeral anas and beauties and elegant extracts of the day.

EXTRACTS, ILLUSTRATION, AND RECORD-KEEPING

Beckford's method of copying passages from the book onto its own flyleaves was an exception to the general rule of supplementary extracts. Eliza Hawtrey's additions to Gisborne's *Survey*, the extracts from poems in the *Introduction to Botany*, and the transcriptions pasted into Pulteney's history represent one of the simplest and most popular forms of manuscript supplement practiced by adult readers, that is the use of books on the shelf as a primitive filing system. When readers had books on loan they would take advantage of the occasion to copy out and preserve interesting passages. But where to put them? Mary Shelley, as we have seen, kept separate books of extracts, like the dull, industrious Mary Bennet of *Pride and Prejudice*. She (the real Mary) may or may not have organized her extracts by topic, in the commonplace-book tradition. Readers who chose instead to copy extracts into their books accepted the value of extracts but rejected the discipline of the commonplace-book, seen as a rather antiquated and laborious method of note-taking by this time. (Coleridge kept a commonplace-book as a young man but switched to notebooks early on.) Transcriptions stored in books probably stood a better chance of being read again, the books themselves providing an appropriate context. So the owner of David Rivers's *Sermon* on "the perfect law of liberty" of James 1.25 copied out another sermon on the same biblical text on the back flyleaves, partly in shorthand to fit it all in; the anonymous *Letters from a Father to His Son, a Student of Divinity* has an added extract from William Gurnall's *The Christian in Compleat Armour;* and Hannah Hutton's copy of Doddridge's *Rise and Progress of Religion in the Soul* includes passages from a prayer by Henry Kirke White and a New Year's sermon by Charles Bondin.

Recipe books attracted recipes, at home and abroad. A British Library copy of Eliza Rundell's fascinating book of household management is an obvious instance, but recipes of a sort appear also in medical, veterinary, and agricultural books—Townsend's *Physician's Vade Mecum* now comes with manuscript additions such as Dr. Godfrey's Cordial and a "Metal to fill diseased Teeth with"; Samuel Drinkwater's *Every Man His Own Farrier* with charms and lists of ingredients for salves and ointments; Roger Treffry's *Dissertation on Smut-Balls* with an extract outlining a rival method of cleaning wheat, proposed by the Board of Agriculture in 1798. In such cases it is apparent that the reader is assembling materials under the guidance of the original book but with an element of personal choice and judgment, even as listeners nowadays download music from the Internet, making up the equivalent of anthologies to suit their own tastes.

Books like these, thoughtfully supplemented with extracts and transcriptions, shade into what might be considered "office copies"—real working books—on the one hand, and decorative "extra-illustrated books" (ornamented with prints and drawings assembled by the owner) on the other. In the eighteenth century the concept of illustration included and in the publishing world might even be said to have been dominated by *verbal* illustration. Commentators "illustrated" the Bible, editors "illustrated" Virgil and Shakespeare, by means of extracts from other works intended to clarify the meaning of obscure passages.[14] In Britain it seems to have been in the Romantic period that the emphasis began to shift to the pictorial—*Shakespeare Illustrated,* a set of prints, dates from 1793—but for a long time the two meanings continued to coexist. Francis Douce's *Illustrations of Shakespeare,* meaning verbal, historical illustrations, appeared in 1807. When Scott wrote to Croker in 1829 about his plan for an expanded version of Boswell's *Life of Johnson*, he offered him "some curious illustrations" for the section on the journey to the Hebrides (*Letters*, 11:111). Extracts copied into books could function in the same way as illustrative quotations, that is, not merely as an extension of the text but as a point of comparison to elucidate it. The informal filing system may thus include an element of interpretation and commentary.

One version of this practice is found in books owned by John Horseman, a follower of Godwin in his youth and a fellow of an Oxford college later. Into a copy of Maria Edgeworth's *Letters for Literary Ladies*, a supposed correspondence between two gentlemen about the education of women, Horseman over a period of at least forty years copied passages from other works having to do with Maria Edgeworth or female education or Ireland, where Edgeworth lived. These extracts are for the most part written on extra pages bound in at the front and back of the volume, but some found their way into the text, notably quotations from Catharine Macaulay's work on the same subject. Horseman's copy of Godwin's memoirs of Mary Wollstonecraft follows the same pattern but includes far more of the extracts on the text pages, suggesting that for Horseman these annotated books served a double purpose, both "illustrating" the text and serving, like commonplace-books, as a means of filing extracts by topic.[15] But he cannot have given many books this kind of attention, or else the commonplace function was the less important one, because once extracts went into the body of the text he would have had to be able to rely on good recall of the work in order to find his extracts—say, the collection on suicide—again.

A still more extraordinary case of methodical long-term "illustration" appears in Edmund Ferrers's copies of Laurence Sterne's *Tristram Shandy* and *A Sentimental Journey*. Ferrers, who became a clergyman and antiquary, acquired these volumes as a student and worked with them for many years, filling them with supplementary information: biographical details about Sterne, identifications of the characters with their real-life models, cross-references to Sterne's works as a whole, and vast quantities of parallel passages. He died in July 1825 and his books were sold at auction a little less than a year later, the sale catalogue including about a dozen books described as containing notes by him and many others with notes by unidentified readers. Ferrers may have been inspired, and was certainly spurred on, by the example of John Ferriar's well-meant *Illustrations of Sterne* (1798). In magazine articles of the 1790s, culminating in the *Illustrations,* Ferriar aimed to explain the context of Sterne's learned wit, particularly by reference to French literature of the sixteenth century. As he said, "It was not the business of Sterne to undeceive those, who considered his Tristram as a work of unfathomable knowledge" (5). Less friendly critics uncovering Sterne's recycling of old books bluntly called it theft and ignited charges of plagiarism. Ferrers includes discoveries by Ferriar, duly credited, and by William Jackson of Exeter, whose essay "On Literary Thievery" also appeared, from the same publisher, in 1798. But he adds dozens of parallels that appear to be his own, of which two samples will suffice. When "Yorick" in the *Sentimental Journey* says, "and God is my record, (before whose tribunal I must one day come and give an account of this work)—that I do not speak it vauntingly—" (1:33), Ferrers underlines the last words and and observes that this kind of disclaimer had been made before by Fielding in *Joseph Andrews* and Burnet in his *History:* " 'I do not produce this out of ostentation,' says Parson Adams of his half-Guinea—see Vol 2^{d} and the Conclusion of the Preface to B^{p} Burnets History of his own Times." And in *Tristram Shandy,* he sees a resemblance between Mr. Shandy's remark about the significance of gestures—that "a man of sense does not lay down his hat in coming into a room,—or take it up in going out of it, but something escapes, which discovers him" (6:303–4)—and Johnson's dictum about Burke, reported by Boswell in the *Life* in 1791: "If says Johnson, you had been driven into a Shed where Chance had thrown Burke you could not have come away without feeling that he was a most Extraordinary Man."

Modern readers, myself among them, are liable to be puzzled by this kind of readerly activity, noted earlier also with the example of Charles Burney. What *is* the point of it? Ferriar had aimed to supply the obscured literary context of Sterne's comedy. Jackson of Exeter was engaged in critical polemic. Charles Wentworth Dilke knew what he was aiming at when he recorded parallel passages in a copy of Milton and knew, too, that some readers did it more blindly than he: "I do not drag into these notes every passage that hath a distant & obscure similitude to some other," he declared in a marginal note (Lau, 22). He recorded sources in order to explore Milton's creative use of other writers, the "food & nurture" of his mind. But Ferrers was not primarily exploring sources or working up a case against the author. Like Horseman and other devoted readers, he seems to have been doing two things. For himself, he was making associative connections between one book and another and thereby fixing both of them more securely in the private databank of memory: Yorick's modesty brings to mind Fielding and Burnet, Mr. Shandy's faith in gesture is associated with Johnson's notion about Burke. He exercised his reading skills and kept his knowledge of books fresh by *registering* the links, so that whenever he came on that passage, with his note, again, he would have the same thought anew. For the beloved work itself, it appears that he was seeking a form of legitimation by proving that it was not as anomalous as it appears, that in fact its ideas, down to the most pedestrian, had been invoked by well-known writers before and since. The implication is that greater value inheres in the work that confirms received wisdom, as it is expressed by acknowledged authorities, than in the one that is singular, *sui generis*. Ferrers tacitly accepted Johnson's remark that "Nothing odd will do long. 'Tristram Shandy' did not last," for his parallels show that *Tristram Shandy* was not all that odd and might therefore deserve a lasting reputation.[16]

Unlike the books illustrated by readers, office copies seldom aspired to interpretation; they had more obvious practical functions. Playtexts as marked up by prompters, actors, stage managers, and directors rather than by readers in their closets, for example, were immediately useful and have become historically invaluable for the insight they provide into the details of performances. They are often one-sided—the actor's copy with the cuts only to the actor's own part, for instance. A copy of Thomas Morton's *A Roland for an Oliver* (1819) that belonged to John Byrne of the Theatre Royal in Glasgow at various points notes the need for a gun, a written letter, a purse and money, and so on: Byrne must have been responsible for props. In spite of hard use and built-in obsolescence, many copies of these interesting little books survive. Perhaps they were valued as souvenirs. They certainly served to sustain theatrical traditions. One interleaved copy of Shakespeare's *Henry the Fourth Part 1* with some very detailed manuscript stage directions ("Soldiers enter when Falstaff gets himself seated between Hotspurs leggs fanning himself with his Cloak," etc.) turns out to be a transcription of notes passed on from one theater to another: the final entry indicates that the script is "Marked according to the prompt Book Theatre Royal Bow Street."[17] Play-texts were also annotated by play-goers and collectors: the British Library contains several untidy but precious volumes under the general titles "Songs Sung at Covent Garden" and "Songs Sung at Drury Lane," collections of little pamphlets, like programs, that give the texts (not music) of songs sung at different performances. For most of them the collector, apparently William Tapsell, supplies the name of the author of the piece, for some the date of the first performance, and for several the names of the singers and indications of changes made at particular performances—presumably, performances he attended.

Outside the world of entertainment, too, the documentation of daily business can be found in books with readers' additions. It was perhaps an employee of the East India Company who owned two manuals bound together, Pitman's *Young Merchant's Key to a Knowledge of Marine Insurance* and Conyers's *Tables of Weights*. On about 200 extra blank pages he created a compendium of useful documents: rates for painting, instructions for placing a ship's masts, a cure for ringworm, a recipe for glue, form letters for official services, conversion tables, and so on. It became a personal business encyclopedia. Similarly, the Treasurer's copy of the *Report of the Committee for the Relief of the Distressed Districts in Ireland* (1823) contains various manuscripts connected with the appeal, such as a list of subscribers, draft minutes from a meeting, letters, invitations, and receipts for donations. Occasionally these kinds of documents are unexpectedly lively. A collection described on the spine as "Poll Books" for Hull does indeed contain records of elections in Kingston-upon-Hull between 1802 and 1820 (who were the candidates, who won, by how many votes), but since those elections were close-run it also includes annotated satires, songs, and voters' lists. After a particularly bitter fight in 1818, a subscription was started to compensate those who had lost their jobs for not voting in accordance with the wishes of their employers, and the manuscript record specifies their names and circumstances in form:

> Ellerker Edw$^{d.}$ Weaver. This man had 5.6.0. given him from the Subscription he having been discharged from M$^{r.}$ Whitakers Factory—for voting Mitchell & Graham.
>
> McDouglas Walter—this mans Mother had 5.6.0. given her from the subscription she having been discharged from working for M$^{rs.}$ Wimble &c. in consequence of her Son, coming from Wisbeach to vote a Plumper for Graham—

In this case as in the records of performance we are probably indebted to a history-conscious collector, rather than to an actual scrutineer, for the context supplied for contemporary ephemera.

Many readers, it seems increasingly as time went on, dropped other kinds of materials into their books, not just extracts but notes and memoranda made on separate slips of paper, letters and drafts of letters, prints and drawings, and above all clippings from newspapers and periodicals—reviews of the book or references to it, for example, or the obituary of the author.[18] (If the practice did become increasingly common it may have been because of the growing availability and cheapness of periodical publications, which could be cut up for these purposes and save the trouble of copying by hand.) These materials often complement marginalia, reminding us that notes in books are likely to have been part of a larger system of note-taking and record-keeping. Readers' notes themselves sometimes point to the presence of such systems. An unnamed traveler who made notes about the sites described in guidebooks also kept travel diaries, so comments in the margins of his books go with and may be keyed to diary entries. In *The Kentish Traveller's Companion*, he combines such firsthand observations as that the gravestone of William Payne is now "hid by the flooring of new seats" (108) with information from other published works ("in the Ambulator p 83 it is named Severndroog Castle," [27]) and his own manuscript diaries (Shipwray appears also "near Hythe in my Thanet tour"). Coleridge's notes occasionally cross-reference not only other books but also notebooks and other marginalia of his own, for instance, in a copy of Luther, "See the MSS Note written in the blank leaf at the end of a small Volume translated from Fenelon, belonging to my *all-dear-and-holy-names-in-the-name-of* Friend, M[rs] Gillman" (*Marginalia*, 3:750).

When readers had a cross-referencing system of however rough-and-ready a kind, their books show traces of it. Passages may be marked for copying into commonplace-books; notes may be written in to link one book with another in the same collection. Dibdin recalled marking books as he strolled through meadows, around 1805, "taking with me one day a volume of the letters of *Erasmus, Scaliger, Casaubon,* and *Lipsius*—another day, a volume of old *English Divinity*, scoring the more striking passages—to be afterwards inserted in a common-place book" (*Reminscences*, 1:221–22). The modest marks in Southey's books are explained by his son Cuthbert in his account of his father's efficient manner of dealing with new books. He would scan them page by page. If he found anything he thought he could use, he marked the passage with a small penciled "S" and put a paper marker at the place with a brief note of the topic. The topics, with page references, would then be transferred to notebooks and the markers removed. Passages that Southey wanted to extract "he would transcribe himself at odds and ends of times, or employ one of his family to transcribe for him" into commonplace-books which he eventually published (*Life*, 6:18). These techniques are conventional and effective; students today use post-it notes and computer files in a similar way.

Some owners who, fastidious like Southey, did not want to leave permanent marks in their books might make reading notes on loose pieces of paper and leave them in the book; or write some notes in the text and others on loose leaves, especially where there was not enough room in the margins. Then the marginalia and the reading notes become part of the same enterprise. Occasionally loose notes come to be bound in, whether by the original owner or a later one. Such is the case with a copy of Paine's *Rights of Man* and a set of pamphlets about Fox in the British Library, and with a remarkable copy of Boswell's *Life of Johnson* in the National Library of Scotland.[19] These are displaced marginalia, written in the course of reading and matched to the pages of the book, having the advantages over marginalia of not defacing the book and not being restricted in length. The Paine notes are signed, so perhaps the book was not the property of the person who made the notes but was being shared with a friend or friends who might be expected to take an interest in his opinions about it.

THE LAWYER

All the learned professions of the time had their own traditional practices, among them traditional ways of handling books and writing marginalia. Perhaps the most striking records of the practical everyday kind of reading that is the subject of this chapter have been left to us by lawyers who, alive to the value of precedent, routinely enriched their books with annotations useful to their profession. A general introduction and series of examples of standard legal practice lead in the following pages to a detailed case study, the remarkable example of Francis Hargrave.

The legal profession as a whole seems to have lost ground in the eighteenth century. David Lemmings calls it "a watershed in the history of law in English society; a critical moment when the culture of common law began to move to the margins of national life" (328). There was a falling-off of litigation and in consequence, increased competition for such business as remained. Regulations and procedures were byzantine, time-consuming, and mysterious; calls for reform became increasingly urgent. The literature associated with law was chaotic and increasingly so, since new cases were being tried and judgments made session after session, year after year, without a standardized official system of reporting. There was also no regular program of education. Until 1758 when the Vinerian professorship was created, university lectures in law dealt with civil or canon law, not common law. The lawyer's training was primarily practical, a matter of seeking a place in an established law office, attending in court, and eventually being called to the bar through the Inns of Court. In Lemmings's words, again, "the essence of legal education in Georgian England was private reading in chambers" (136) or, as Baker more bluntly puts it, "self-help" (195). Books being scarce and works of reference unavoidably incomplete and expensive, the student would spend a lot of time tracking down the important works, purchasing them when he could but otherwise copying out what he needed in order to form his own working library.

Henry Crabb Robinson, foreign correspondent for *The Times* in 1807–9 and after that a not very happy or successful barrister, later recalled the attorney's office at Colchester where he had been an articled clerk from 1790 to 1795. He experienced a liberating but, he thought, professionally damaging moment of rebellion in 1794.

> When I went to Colchester I was very desirous of studying but I had no one to direct me, and therefore followed the routine practice and advice given to all clerks. I bought a large folio volume to be filled with precedents, and copied therein my articles of clerkship. One evening I was writing very industriously in this volume when Ben Strutt came in. "I'm sorry to see you so lazy, young gentleman!" "Lazy! I think I'm very industrious." "You do? Well, whatever you think, let me tell you that your writing in that book is sheer laziness. You are too lazy to work as you ought with your head, and so you set your fingers at work to give your head a holiday. You know it is your duty to do something, and try to become a lawyer, and just to ease your conscience you do that. Had you been really industrious you would have studied the principles of law and carried the precedents in your head. And then you might make precedents, not follow them." I shut up the book, and never wrote another line; it is still in existence, a memorial of Strutt.

Robinson's editor confirms the survival of the book, Robinson's work breaking off at page 120 "in the middle of a precedent" (1:21–22).

Though Robinson in Colchester might not have felt the benefit, the situation of the law student had improved toward the end of the eighteenth century, one great milestone being the publication of William Blackstone's *Commentaries on the Laws of England* in four quarto volumes (1765–69). The *Commentaries,* based on Blackstone's Oxford lectures, presented the English common law as a coherent whole, consistent in its basic principles since the days of the Anglo-Saxons. Blackstone's systematic presentation of the law must have been a lifesaver to clerks like Crabb Robinson floundering in the ocean of legal literature. Furthermore it was agreeable to read. (It may even have been responsible for Strutt's emphasis on principles over precedents—though it has to be admitted that the high ground of "principles" was claimed by all parties, including those who attacked Blackstone's conservatism and campaigned for reforms in legal practice, as in Bentham's title *Principles of Morals and Legislation.*) Originally addressed to the gentlemen of Oxford, the *Commentaries* became a textbook for students of the law. T. F. Dibdin, who went from Oxford to Lincoln's Inn in the late 1790s, complained that the law student was supposed "to grapple with Coke upon Littleton—to have Blackstone at his fingers'ends—to know Buller and Tidd by heart—to make Viner, and Bacon, and Comyns his very pillow, mattress, and coverlid" (*Reminiscences* 1:127).

Blackstone seems even to have been read in schools: in 1811 while he himself was still a student in the Inner Temple, Barron Field published what he called a "catechism" to this "Bible" of the law, intending it as a study guide for schoolboys (vi, viii). His *Analysis of Blackstone's Commentaries* is a workbook designed to guide the student to create his own "analysis" by requiring him to answer questions on each chapter. Although it is not so much an illustration of standard legal practice as of pedagogical technique, it may be seen as a primer in legal education. The questions follow the order of the text, and page references indicate where in Blackstone the answers are to be found; the first question, for example, is "What is *law,* in its most general and comprehensive sense? 38." The British Library copy is interleaved to take answers to Field's questions. The original student owner dutifully answered questions for 127 pages but then stopped dead, and the book appears to have been abandoned for seventy or eighty years until a younger child took it up and used some of the nice blank pages remaining for his own purposes, putting in his name, Thomas something, and a date in 1886 (facing 138); a list of the names of counties (facing 144); and a pencil drawing of a "Four Masted ship in Lyme Docks Dec[r] 1890" (facing 133). Field's experiment in this instance was one of many casualties of the well-meant but oppressive device of interleaving in schoolbooks.

In conjunction with conscientious or ambitious members of the bar, the resourceful publishers of the period did much to make the law student's life easier. It was not the courts but private enterprise that began regular, reliable periodical series of law reports in 1785 (Baker, 211). As a service to the profession and to raise their own standing, some scholars brought out editions of historically important documents; Blackstone for example edited *Tracts, chiefly relating to the Antiquities and Laws of England* (1762). Others contributed pamphlets or monographs on specific subjects, such as copyhold or divorce. Still others, less original but at least as welcome, produced reference books. Instead of copying out precedents himself or trawling the uneven and sometimes contradictory judges' notes and anonymous records of old cases to make extracts for his commonplace-books, the student could buy a set ready-made, organized alphabetically by topic, and be left with the responsibility only for making additions to keep the set current. Charles Viner's standard *General Abridgment of Law and Equity*, issued in parts between 1742 and 1758, a useful base, might have been hard to find by 1790 and the 24 folio volumes would certainly have been expensive, but in 1791 the publishers proposed a new octavo edition, cheaper and brought up to date, which duly appeared over the next three years. The market could be lucrative. As time passed, competitors appeared: Richard Wooddeson's *Systematical View of the Laws of England* (1792–93), another set of Oxford lectures, represented an alternative to Blackstone; and a consortium cleverly brought out a handy six-volume supplement to Viner, *An Abridgment of the Modern Determinations in the Courts of Law and Equity* (1799–1806). There were even cribs to Blackstone, such as Trusler's *Summary* of 1788 (with a duodecimo edition in 1796), and Field's 1811 *Analysis*, previously mentioned.

Law books had traditionally been printed with wide margins to allow for manuscript annotation; in this period they might also be issued in an interleaved form or be bound up that way at the owner's direction. In this as in other subjects, different sorts of books invited different sorts of readerly annotation, with the structure and content of the books themselves serving as guides. It is reasonable to expect that new information should be added to a reference book; confirming or contradicting authorities to a treatise on a particular topic; and signs of agreement, disagreement, or incomprehension to a connected discourse like Blackstone's. Actual readers' notes in law books follow well-established conventions, but they also prove that there was room for individual variations to the system. Since the readers were not writing formal commentary for publication, private interests and concerns find their way in.

In order to explain common practice before turning to the special case of Hargrave, I am going to describe just three books annotated in this period by unidentified owners. Thomas Peake's *Compendium of the Law of Evidence* (2nd ed., 1804–6) includes a conventional apparatus of four kinds of *printed* marginal note, and footnotes as well. Much the most common form of marginal note is the reference, with sources, to cases that illustrate the rules and practices that Peake explains, such as "Hanson v. Tomlin, Peake's Cas. 193" (243), meaning the case of Hanson v. Tomlin in Peake's own reports of five years of King's Bench cases, *Cases Determined at Nisi Prius* (1795). The margins also provide references to other books ("Vide Wood's Inst. 594"), internal cross-references ("Ante, 5"), and heads or what the profession calls "titles" ("Of Interest acquired since the fact to be proved," 157). The reader of one British Library copy responds in kind, adding a few references to relevant books or to cases that had escaped Peake's attention; at "Depositions," for instance, where Peake has no cases to cite, the reader puts one in: "See the King & Lord Hunsden v. Countess Dowager of Arundel &c. Hob. 109" (58). The method of citation is standard. This reader also made a few discursive notes. For instance, where Peake in a footnote in the section on depositions comments on the problem of a witness's having fallen ill, saying, "Though a good ground for postponing the trial, this would hardly now be considered as sufficient to make the deposition evidence," the reader cites a practical exception: "But I understand that on the circuits, depositions are sometimes admitted, where enough appears to shew, that from age or infirmity there is not any reasonable prospect of being able ever to produce the witness in a court of justice" (59). The reader is still following the format of the text, arguing footnote-style with a footnote just as he had added references in the margins to match the ones he found there.

A British Library copy of Richard Preston's *Succinct View of the Rule in Shelley's Case* (1794) appears to have had two contemporary readers, each using the pamphlet in a distinct way, although neither made very many notes. The first reader takes the author up on technical details, occasionally adding a reference to confirm or question the interpretation of this long-standing rule of law in the inheritance of estates. On p. 65, he both confirms and questions. Preston affirms that "though the estate does not vest in the ancestor, and though it cannot by any *possibility* become a vested interest in him, he will have the same as a *contingent* interest." The reader cites appropriately remote authorities: "See acc. Co. Litt. 378.b. But yet quaere, & see Litt. Rep. 258."—referring to "Coke upon Littleton," the Bible of property law; and to a set of reports of cases from the reign of Charles I published in 1683, which were attributed to a later Littleton. In contrast to the first reader, who sticks close to the text and meets it on its own ground, the second reader stands back from the text to express his opinion of the style and content of the treatise. Is the great seventeenth-century judge Sir Matthew Hale "a character of the first respectability" (18)? The reader objects to the phrase: "oddly expressed whether in relation to his character as a judge or as a lawyer." His final position is that Preston's work is superfluous after Charles Fearne's *Essay* of 1772: "I find in this work nothing which is not contained in Mr Fearne's observations of the same topic in his Essay" (152).

My final example is the *Concise View of the Common and Statute Law of England* (1784?) by the multifaceted John Trusler. One British Library copy contains extensive notes of the early nineteenth century: some supplementary references (for example, on p. 86, a reference to

William Selwyn's 1806–8 *Abridgment of the Law of Nisi Prius*); some heads ("Malus Usus abolendus est"—the maxim that "a bad custom ought to be abolished," 5); and much thoughtful commentary, such as a long note on the history of the office of the sheriff (56), or this casual reflection (136; Fig. 15): "It has always appeared to me as very strange that our Laws, which seem to have taken such especial care to provide Owners for all sorts of Property (in order to prevent disputes & confusion) should ever have tolerated General Occupancy."

From these and other examples of the period we can see the basic conventions governing the reader's additions to law books and begin to develop an impression of the frame of mind in which such notes were written. Heads or "titles" are reference aids that make it possible to find a passage quickly by scanning the margins, or to follow the main points of an argument without attending once again to all the detail. These reflect the reader's training: sometimes they simply echo a few words from the page, sometimes they are in the reader's own words and show a rudimentary process of assimilation. They require close analytical attention to the text, section by section, on the first reading but have the effect of turning it subsequently into a reference book for dipping into piecemeal. They can, as a further stage of information management, be copied out in the form of an index or as entries in a commonplace-book.

New references to cases, statutes, and treatises enable the reader to trace the further history of the issue or to explore complications, such as contrary decisions. For these the reader must have been working with at least two books, getting up to consult the second and entering the reference exactly: no one is likely to have had perfect recall in such matters, and an imperfect reference to a set of reports would be almost as useless as an inaccurate URL on the Internet today. The most efficient practice would be to add a note to the other book at the same time: by this method the reader of Peake's *Compendium* could start either with that book or with the report of the Countess of Arundel's case and then quickly assemble everything he needed to know about depositions. The process implies further that in making such notes the reader would, over time, be creating a system of cross-references for his own library

156 THE RIGHTS OF THINGS. BOOK II.

the original proprietor or his heirs; but it muſt be remembered, that no eſtates, eſcheat, but entire fees-ſimple.

II. Occupancy is another claim to lands under the title of purchaſe; which is, taking poſſeſſion of things which before belonged to no one, as we have ſeen at the beginning of Chap. I. Book II.

The right of occupancy, ſo far as it relates to real property or eſtates, our laws have confined to one ſingle inſtance, *viz.* where a man has lands granted to himſelf only, not his heirs, for the life of another perſon, and dies during that life, by which he held them. In this caſe, he that could firſt enter on the eſtate, might lawfully retain poſſeſſion during that life, by which the deceaſed perſon held it, unleſs the reverſion of ſuch eſtate was in the crown. Had ſuch eſtate been granted to the man and his heirs; the heir would have enjoyed it during the life by which it was held, and would have been called a *ſpecial occupant*: to curtail, however, the claim of occupancy, it is enacted, by 29 Car. II. c. 3. That where there is no ſpecial occupant, in whom the eſtate may veſt, the tenant for the life of another may deviſe it by will, or it ſhall go to the executors or adminiſtrators, and be aſſets in their hands for payment of debts; alſo by 14 Geo. II. c. 20. that the ſurplus of ſuch eſtate for another man's life, after payment of debts, ſhall go in a courſe of diſtribution like a chattel intereſt. But notwithſtanding theſe ſtatute clauſes; as, before they were enacted, no one could claim a right, by common occupancy, to incorporeal hereditaments, ſuch as rents, tithes, or the like; becauſe of theſe there could be no corporal poſſeſſion had, or any entry made, and, of courſe, a grant of ſuch hereditaments for the life of another determined or ended with the death of the grantee: and as theſe clauſes cannot be conſtrued ſo as to create a new eſtate, or keep that alive, which by Common Law was determined, it is apprehended, that ſuch eſtate granted to one man for the life of another, muſt revert to the grantor, after the death of the grantee. When there is a reſidue left, the ſtatutes give it to the executors or adminiſtrators, inſtead of the firſt occupant; but they will not *create* a reſidue to give it to either.

In other caſes where a landholder dies inteſtate, and no heir or owner can be found in the common courſe of deſcent, the law gives the eſtate to the King, or to lord of the fee, by eſcheat.

If an iſland ariſes in the middle of a river, it belongs to the owner of the land on that ſide, to which the ſaid iſland is neareſt; but if an

iſland

It has always appeared to me so very strange that our Laws, which seem to have taken such especial care to provide owners for all sorts of Property (in order to prevent disputes & confusion) should ever have tolerated General Occupancy—

FIG. 15 Comment by an unidentified reader made after 1808 in John Trusler's *Concise View of the Common and Statute Law of England* (1784). By permission of the British Library.

or, if the books were not all his own property, for the virtual library to which he had access.

Longer remarks reflect personal opinion or expertise. Precisely because they are not done methodically as heads and references are, they are relatively speaking more intimate and confiding. They reveal individual interests: what the reader knows or cares little about he will not usually take the trouble to comment on. Where such comments exist, therefore, it is worth considering for whom or for what purpose they can have been written. Extended notes like the ones in Trusler about sheriffs and general occupancy seem to record a passing idea that could be made use of later, if the lawyer-owner ever had to speak or write on those topics. It could be taken for granted that they would go with the book when it left its owner's hands; he would want them to be viewed as valuable or at least useful supplements to it. They are not likely to have been instances of wanton self-expression.

As a professional skill, marginal annotation was a necessary part of the lawyer's tool kit, and in the ordinary course of business it paid to be good at it. Adept practitioners might seek further recognition through publication, for reference books were often compiled by a process of supplement and accretion as well as by digest, and the common law historically depended on annotated editions of key works, Coke upon Littleton being the most obvious model. A resourceful publisher presented the marginalia of two seventeenth-century judges, Wyndham and Hale, as gloss and commentary respectively to an English translation of Fitzherbert's classic manual of procedure, the *New Natura Brevium* (1730, reprinted in 1755 and 1794). Blackstone's lectures themselves, in due course, took on the apparatus of the classic: by 1800, in the thirteenth edition, they had "notes and additions by Edward Christian"; the sixteenth edition of 1825 was annotated by John Taylor Coleridge, a nephew of the poet. What distinguished routine use from annotation worthy of publication were the status of the annotator, the thoroughness and consistency of the notes (in the normal course of business only some parts of a book would be likely to be covered), and more elusively, their quality. Of course new references should be accurate and up to date, but who is to say whether they are well chosen, and who is to determine that one idea or observation is more pertinent than another?

FRANCIS HARGRAVE

In 1813 the House of Commons by a unanimous resolution took the unusual step of requesting that £8,000 be allocated to purchase the library of Francis Hargrave of Lincoln's Inn for the benefit of the nation. The collection of books and manuscripts "selected with the greatest skill and judgment" in the course of a long career was recommended to the House particularly for the notes in the books, said to be "extremely valuable, in the opinion of those who were the most competent judges."[20] The committee responsible for the recommendation and estimate had examined a bookseller, Richard Priestley, who estimated the value of the books at just over £2,000 but had not allowed for the additional value of the notes, not having had time to appraise them. He was asked to speculate:

> Have you not known, in recent instances, a very great additional value given for Books, in consequence of marginal Notes?—Yes; Books worth three guineas I have known produce 200 under these circumstances; and Books worth 4 or 5*s* fetching £40 under the same circumstances; so that it is impossible for a Bookseller to estimate that.[21]

Hargrave had been a hard-working and in many ways exemplary lawyer. The collection became available for purchase when he suffered some sort of breakdown, perhaps a stroke—an "attack," according to his doctor, which left him "considerably deranged" in mind and unable to work and support his family, but aware of his condition and capable of consenting to the proposal. He was by then seventy-one, his wife Diana sixty-one, their daughter Mrs. Curtis thirty-one.[22] There were two sons, the younger also a lawyer.[23] Happily for the Hargraves, their petition was successful, Hargrave lived another eight years in good enough health for him to be able to carry out some parts of his old work, and to judge by dated notes in his hand he kept his library, or at least had privileged access to it, to the end. The Commons vote was partly a reward for long service, partly an investment in legal learning. It incidentally reveals the value attached, at the time, to expert marginalia.[24]

Hargrave was a diligent, respected lawyer if not a great one like his idols Coke and Hale. He seems to have known the law inside and out. He acted as counsel in several prominent cases, served as legal adviser to high-profile people, was consulted especially on property, inheritance, and constitutional issues, and published energetically. A transitional figure in his profession, he mastered the muddle that presented itself to him as a student in the 1760s and contributed substantially to the process of sorting it out for future generations. Whether from lack of ambition or of capital or connections, however, he never rose to public eminence as a judge or statesman, and his grandest ventures in publishing proved in one way or another abortive. His highest office was in legal administration as Recorder of Liverpool, and he was already in his mid-fifties in 1797 when he took up that appointment. He did not become a Bencher at Lincoln's Inn until 1802, nor King's Counsel until 1806—positions some men attained in their thirties.[25]

Hargrave had been a student at Lincoln's Inn from 1760 to 1771, and it was as a student that he published (anonymously) his first work, a pamphlet on receiving stolen goods. The second treatise appeared under his own name and might be said to have *made* his name. He had acted as counsel on behalf of James Sommerset, the slave whose master tried unsuccessfully to reassert his claim to ownership in England. Mansfield's verdict in that case, a critical decision in the debate about the slave trade, is said to have been swayed by the junior counsel's point about medieval villeinage.[26] Hargrave published his views in a pamphlet (*An Argument in the Case of James Sommerset, a Negro*, 1772; 3rd ed., 1788) which may in retrospect be seen as the foundation of his publishing career, as it combines sharp legal reasoning with deep historical understanding.

Hargrave continued to publish his own opinions in significant cases; eventually he began to issue collections of these papers under such titles as *Juridical Arguments and Collections* (1797, 1799) and *Jurisconsult Exercitations* (3 vols., 1811). But his enduring legacy to the profession was a set of editions of historically important texts, and the greatest of these was his edition of Coke upon Littleton. Hargrave could not have embarked on this project without financial backing.[27] By 1775 he had come to an agreement with the publishers: he provided a new preface to the big fourth edition of *State Trials*,[28] and they began to issue the edition of Coke in parts, "with the addition of Various Readings of Littleton, from the more early editions; and a Preface, Notes, and References, by the Editor." As this statement from the title page indicates, Hargrave initially saw his task as the establishing of a reliable text by collation of editions, a labor-intensive scholarly chore. His address to the reader indicates also his plan to simplify the layout of this complicated work and to clarify the import of his new references: rather than simply citing a slew of references, he will have them "so expressed, as clearly to shew whether they tend to confirm, to question, to contradict, or to illustrate the doctrine advanced in the text." (His editorial policy articulates his assumptions about the functions of such references and reflects his practice in his own books.) Like many editors before and since, however, Hargrave underestimated the scale of the task. He must have found it difficult to make time for this work while he was earning a living as a young lawyer with a family. He also gave in to a temptation that emerged after he published his first number, which must have presented itself practically as a duty and therefore irresistible, when the Earl of Hardwicke gave him a transcript of Hale's marginalia to Coke, written in Latin and Law-French, which he then translated and incorporated as a part of the commentary, as had been done with the 1730 Fitzherbert. But what seems to have finished him was the process of historical annotation. In 1785 he surrendered the project, after 190 folio pages, to a colleague who brought it to a conclusion three years later. In his "Address to the Purchasers of the New Edition, Announcing his Relinquishment of the Undertaking, and Mr. Butler's succeeding to it," Hargrave alludes to personal "sacrifices" no longer tolerable, but he also defends himself as having performed more than he had originally contracted to do: "In truth, had he not rashly exceeded the limits first prescribed, by wandering into the wide field of annotation, it is most probable, that the *whole* of the edition would have been finished long ago, and consequently that the editor would not now have to mortify himself by apologizing for executing only *one half* of it."[29]

Hargrave continued to be frustrated in his editorial work. A thick *Collection of Tracts relative to the Law of England, from Manuscripts* (1787), intended to be the first of several, failed to raise enough interest and, presumably, sales to warrant the continuation. Hargrave had to apologize to his readers again in the preface to his edition of Hale's treatise *The Jurisdiction of the Lords House, or Parliament* (1796): the editor had been delayed in writing his introduction, he confessed, "sometimes by professional avocations, sometimes by the pressure of domestic cares and anxieties, sometimes by broken or languid spirits, and not unfrequently by distrust of himself" (ii). Conventional as these sorts of excuses are, the last phrase is disarmingly honest. Hargrave was a perfectionist and perhaps a compulsive. Hale's tract is 208 pages long, Hargrave's introduction 230, although "even as late as six weeks ago," he says, apologizing once more, he thought it would be half that length (ccxxiv). This ingenuous remark obliquely reveals that Hargrave wrote most of his share in less than two months, other commitments notwithstanding; also that publishers could move fast in those days.

Hargrave's personal collection went to the Library of the British Museum, where it was divided between the departments of Manuscripts and Printed Books. Ellis's catalogue of the manuscripts shows that Hargrave had acquired hundreds of volumes of reports and reference aids (indexes, extracts, lists of cases, commonplace-books) made during the eighteenth century by unknown hands as well as more ancient and valuable materials; it does not appear to include Hargrave's own working papers from cases in which he was involved except accidentally, where such records were included among "miscellaneous papers." While the Hargrave manuscripts are still preserved as a collection under his name in the British Library, the books were dispersed among the collections, and it is difficult to be sure how many there are. R. C. Alston lists over 200 works catalogued as containing notes by Hargrave, some merely pamphlets but others, such as the Viner, running to many volumes. He also indicates areas where other Hargrave books, probably also annotated, may be found (xii). Even the set of 200 titles is of interest as constituting the better part of the working collection of a lawyer of moderate means in the period. It has impressive breadth: new titles and old, multiple editions of classic texts (three, for instance, of Blackstone), histories and treatises concerned with civil and canon law as well as common law, and a few books that appear to have nothing to do with law at all. I have examined about half the recorded annotated books, aiming for range in my selection and trying to ascertain what was normal for Hargrave and what exceptional.

Hargrave's habits were established early and appear to have been consistent throughout his career, except that as time passed and the number of books increased he may have spent less time digesting the contents of a particular book and more time integrating it into the collection by cross-references and introductory statements. Some books show evidence of repeated use over forty years, from an ownership inscription of the 1760s to reference to a case of the 1800s. Like the other readers whose notes I have described briefly, Hargrave no doubt behaved somewhat differently when reading a connected treatise or history from the way he did when using a reference book or set of reports, and the mindset of the editor may have produced different results from that of the advocate. But he was a methodical man whose habits tended to override the role of the moment. His additions to his books, besides the frequent ownership inscription on the title page, are of four kinds, all with precedents in the tradition of legal literature: heads (summaries of portions of the text), references (to cases, statutes, and authorities), comments on particular statements (points of interpretation, historical details), and general overview.

While certainly methodical, Hargrave cannot be called systematic. Though all his books display some of these manuscript features, not all include all four, and not all parts of all books are evenly marked; in fact few of his books can be said to be heavily or copiously annotated. The typical Hargrave reference may be illustrated by one example in his first edition of Blackstone, where Blackstone defines a parish: "A parish is that circuit of ground. . . ." Hargrave writes, "Concerning the original of parishes, see Bingh. Orig. Eccles. lib. 9. cap. 8. Florent. op. tom. 2. p. 247 ed. Norimberg. Brett on Church Governm. ch. 7" (1765–69, 1:107). These are, then, punctiliously exact references to two authorities that supply further information on the topic, should Hargrave ever need it. He must have looked out the other books in order to make the note, perhaps not in his own collection (there are occasional acknowledgments to other libraries in his notes). He similarly adds to Viner's explanation of the status of a bankrupt as witness a set of more up-to-date cases: "See Barnes' Notes 315. Buller's Nisi Prius 43. Case in Green's Bank. L. 4th ed. 221. note (3.)" (12:27). On the whole Hargrave observes his own policy as it was articulated in the edition of Coke and tries economically to remind himself what kind of bearing the references have on the topic at hand, using "see" for further confirmation or illustration, "quaere" for doubt, and "but see" for contradiction. There are thousands of entries like these in Hargrave's books, reflecting the accumulation of information in his profession and his attempts to keep on top of it. Once in a while, but rarely, one finds a blank left to be filled in later with a page number or the specification of an edition that never was filled in, as in his Ayliffe (xxxiii) and his Schomberg (66).

Hargrave's longer notes are considerably more interesting to the lay reader. The notes on the title pages of his books tend to be of a strictly bibliographical character. They identify the book: outline its provenance, assess the value of the work relative to other editions or other works of the same kind, and sometimes provide information about the life of the author. In these little acts of bibliographical description, Hargrave conforms to the usage of collectors and antiquarians of his day. (A few titles not connected with the law—Blackburne's essay on Johnson's life of Milton, Bossuet's sermons, the fables of Phaedrus, and Roper's life of More—have *only* notes of this kind.) Besides these, however, there are within the text many reflective notes prompted by the argument at hand: they elaborate objections, correct errors, refine distinctions. They may not be economical of space but they are punctilious. Many of Hargrave's notes take the form of a statement, or a question and answer, followed by references that look like a futile paperchase but in fact represent in brief the rationale for his now considered opinion, as when in a first edition of Blackstone he comments on the seemingly innocuous assertion that "no custom can prevail against an express act of parliament; since the statute itself is proof of a time when such a custom did not exist" (1:76–77):

> A custom may prevail against a statute which is only declaratory of the common law 5. Co. 108. a. for such a statute is no more than the common law reduced into writing by authority of parliament. But if such a statute is expressed in negative words, some hold that then it will toll [i.e., defeat] a custom & therefore cannot be prescribed against. W. Jo. 289: but lord Coke is of another opinion Co. Litt. 115. a. 4. Inst. 297. & both authority & reason seem to be on his side.

Hargrave characteristically spares no pains to get to the root of an error; where he corrects, he wants also to understand how the error could have arisen. In George Booth's *Nature and Practice of Real Actions* (1701), for instance, he objects to the statement that in a writ of right patent the tenant "defends his own Right by saying, Ven' & defend' jus suum quando, &c. in this he defends the right and seisin of the Demandant" (94):

> The author misconceives the import of the world defendit. The technical sense in our law Latin is different from the general sense: for it means, in this instance of proceeding on a writ of right, denial, & not defence. This peculiar sense is derived from the French word defendre, which means to forbid, & from applying the Latin word defendere as a substitute for the French word defendre.

Likewise for a suspected error in translation in his 1730 Fitzherbert, he consulted an earlier edition and was able to correct "the Abbey is disturbed" to "the Abbey is dissolved," for "So it is in the old French ed^{n}" (77).

Typically, Hargrave wrote notes that would enable him to mobilize the knowledge contained in his library by a system of additions and cross-references. This traditional system, deployed over a career of almost fifty years, turned his collection into what we would perhaps now call a database, an essential resource for Hargrave personally and for the colleagues and clients with whom he shared his books. What is exceptional about it is not the fact of annotation but the scale of it, its qualities of precision and reliability, and the size of the collection to which it is attached. That said, there were a few atypical books on Hargrave's shelves. One is his heavily annotated 1656 Coke, but that was a working copy used for his edition, a special case. Another is his copy of Vesey Junior's *Case upon the Will of the Late Peter Thelluson, Esq.*, a gift from the reporter. Hargrave had been part of the team of lawyers acting for the family which contested the will of a fabulously wealthy man. His historical argument about executory devise is published in full in *The Case upon the Will* as an addition to the detailed record of proceedings. One thing lawyers of the period hardly ever did was express personal emotional reactions in their marginalia—sympathy, hostility, anger. But in this case Hargrave responded bitterly, point by point, to the part of the report that recorded the argument of his opponent, Francis Buller. (It may or may not be relevant—in the rough-and-tumble of the courts of the day one could not afford to be thin-skinned—that Buller dismissed Hargrave's historical approach as all very well for "the amusement of a leisure hour" but irrelevant to the case [105] and described his opponent's manner as laborious [110].) Buller, for example, cited as precedent Booth's settlement of the Duke of Norfolk's estate in 1767, praising Booth as the best in the business (109). Hargrave hotly declares that Booth in that case had been on "unknown ground" and scarcely knew what he was doing; but this time his evidence is anecdotal.

> Note that during the last session of parliament I was consulted by the Duke of Norfolk on an estate bill, in which the very settlement here referred to was necessary to be considered; & that at a consultation at my house, in consequence of my adverting to the limitat[n] to a posthumous child for life, his Grace mentioned his having often been with M[r] Booth whilst this settlement & another of the like kind & of the same date were under consideration, & M[r] Booth's having said as

to that limitation & some other parts of the settlements he had gone upon a terra incognita. F. H. 6. Dec. 1802.

The notes in this case report are remarkable both for the element of personal feeling in them and for the glimpses they give of the lawyer's practice at the time.

Another book exceptional in its annotation is a little quarto pamphlet of only 14 pages that Hargrave acquired in 1811. The heavy annotation on several pages of *Facts and Observations relating to the Temple Church, and the Monuments contained in it* eloquently demonstrate Hargrave's enthusiasm for the history of the law and everything associated with it—in this case, the Temple Church, of twelfth-century origin, occupied jointly by lawyers of the Middle and Inner Temples since 1608 (Fig. 16). The notes are vintage Hargrave, from the extensive bibliography of sources on the Templars and their church on the front flyleaf to patient correction and historical detective work inside. Two samples show Hargrave diligently checking references and in effect competing with the author on his own ground so that the text becomes merely the basis for further investigation. The anonymous author mentions in passing that a lost inscription had been preserved by George Holmes "(as Mr. Stow, the learned antiquary, informs us)" (4). Not exactly, says Hargrave:

> Mr Stow dyed in 1605. But Mr George Holmes was living in 1720 when Strype published his ed^n^ of Stow's London. He was Deputy Keeper of the Tower in 1731, as appears by the Report of the Committee of Commons on the Cottonian Library in 1732. The mistake as to Mr Holmes has arisen from not attending to what came from Strype in his addit^ns^ to Stow. F. H.

On one of the pages used as an illustration in Fig. 16, *Facts* claims that Geoffrey de Mandeville, Earl of Essex, was buried in the Temple Church, and cites "*Dugdale's Monasticon, Vol.* 1, page 448" as its authority, while acknowledging a problem in the fact that Geoffrey is believed to have died before 1185 when the Temple Church was consecrated.

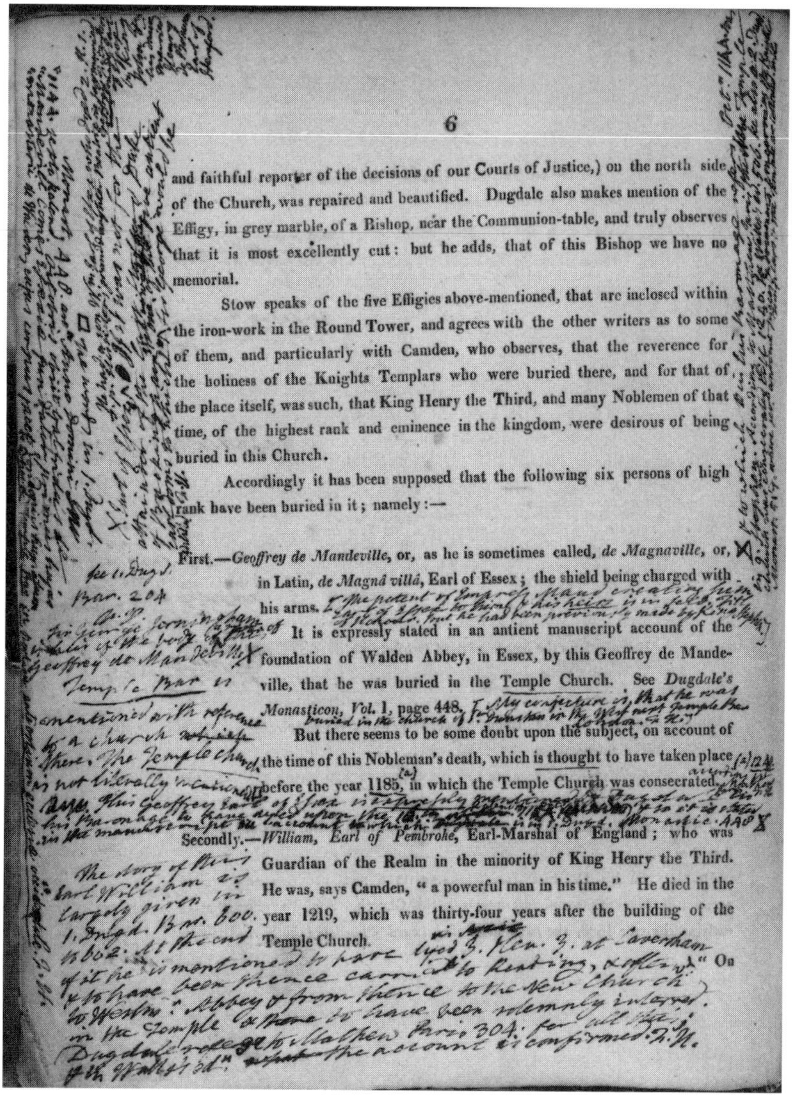

6

and faithful reporter of the decisions of our Courts of Justice,) on the north side of the Church, was repaired and beautified. Dugdale also makes mention of the Effigy, in grey marble, of a Bishop, near the Communion-table, and truly observes that it is most excellently cut: but he adds, that of this Bishop we have no memorial.

Stow speaks of the five Effigies above-mentioned, that are inclosed within the iron-work in the Round Tower, and agrees with the other writers as to some of them, and particularly with Camden, who observes, that the reverence for the holiness of the Knights Templars who were buried there, and for that of the place itself, was such, that King Henry the Third, and many Noblemen of that time, of the highest rank and eminence in the kingdom, were desirous of being buried in this Church.

Accordingly it has been supposed that the following six persons of high rank have been buried in it; namely:—

First.—*Geoffrey de Mandeville*, or, as he is sometimes called, *de Magnaville*, or, in Latin, *de Magnâ villâ*, Earl of Essex; the shield being charged with his arms. It is expressly stated in an antient manuscript account of the foundation of Walden Abbey, in Essex, by this Geoffrey de Mandeville, that he was buried in the Temple Church. See *Dugdale's Monasticon, Vol.* 1, page 448. But there seems to be some doubt upon the subject, on account of the time of this Nobleman's death, which is thought to have taken place before the year 1185, in which the Temple Church was consecrated.

Secondly.—*William, Earl of Pembroke*, Earl-Marshal of England; who was Guardian of the Realm in the minority of King Henry the Third. He was, says Camden, "a powerful man in his time." He died in the year 1219, which was thirty-four years after the building of the Temple Church. On

FIG. 16 An opening of *Facts and Observations relating to the Temple Church, and the Monuments contained in it* (1811), annotated by Francis Hargrave. By permission of the British Library.

"On the tomb of this William," says Camden, "I read, *Comes Pembrochiæ*, and this verse:—

Miles eram Martis; Mars multos viceral armis.

His arms are on his shield.

Thirdly.—*William, Earl of Pembroke*, Earl-Marshall, son of the former William.

He died in the year 1231.

Fourthly.—*Gilbert, Earl of Pembroke,* another son of the first William. He died in the year 1241, being slain in a Tournament at Hertford.

Touching the manner of Gilbert's death, *Weever*, in his *Antient Funeral Monuments*, page 443, observes as follows:—

" *Matthew Paris* recounts, that in the year 1241, Gilbert pro-
" claimed a Tournament in Hertford in scorn of the King's authority,
" by which such sports had been forbidden. It happened that
" himself running was, by the flinging of his horse, cast out of the
" saddle, and the horse gave him such a stroke on the breast that he
" died the same day. His bowels were interred in the Abbey of
" Hertford with the bowels of one *Sir Robert de Say*, a gallant gen-
" tleman slain in the same exercise.

Fifthly.—Here also, say both Stow and Maitland, lies *Robert Rosse*, called *Fursan.*

The arms of Rosse are on his shield.

And Weever, in page 443, speaks more particularly of this person, whom he calls "*Sir Robert Rosse, Knight*," and mentions the following Epitaph on him, as having formerly been seen in the Temple Church.

HIC REQUIESCIT

R . . . I . . . . . EQ . . . . QUONDAM VISITATOR GENERALIS

ORDINIS MILITIÆ TEMPLI IN ANGLIA, FRANCIA, ET IN ITALIA . . .

"This

Here Hargrave lets himself go and challenges the author, suggesting a different site near one of the city gates, in two notes.

> My conjecture is that he was buried in the Church of St Dunstan in the West next Temple Bar London. F. H.
>
> Temple Bar is mentioned with reference to a church there. The Temple Church is not literally mentioned. This Geoffrey Earl of Essex is expressly mentioned by Dugdale in his Baronage to have dyed upon the 16th [?Kalend] of Oct^r & so it is stated in the manuscript account which is in Dugd. Monastic. 448.

The amount of attention and effort expended on a work that was not likely to be of use to him either in his practice or in his editions does suggest that history was Hargrave's real passion and may lend support to Buller's view of him as a pedantic hobbyist. It also illustrates the great hazard of the note-making habit, not knowing where to stop, that got Hargrave into trouble in his edition of Coke. The great swollen variorum editions of the late eighteenth century, the Johnson-Steevens Shakespeare and the Hargrave-Butler Coke upon Littleton among them, eventually generated a publishing backlash in the form of stripped-down alternatives such as Thomas Coventry's *Readable Edition of Coke upon Littleton* (1830), which reversed the trend of steady accretion.[30]

What can the record of annotation of Hargrave and his contemporaries and juniors in the law tell us about the experience of readers in that period that we do not already know, or that is not self-evident? First, that the writing of marginalia was a common practice sanctioned and conditioned by tradition, not a private aberration. All the notes in these books would have been intelligible to any of the other writers of notes by virtue of their shared experience of the conventions of their profession. The books themselves were likely to be lent out to assist other readers (meaning that the notes had to make sense), in a networking process that cut across the generations as notes were copied from one book to another. With characteristic punctilio, Hargrave frequently indicates that a particular note came "from a book lent to me" (*Cases in*

Equity, 52) or that a whole series of notes had been transcribed from somebody else's copy (*General Abridgment,* title page). As the bookseller indicated at the time of the purchase of Hargrave's library, marginalia could greatly increase the resale value of a book. A responsible owner would therefore take care to record provenance, as in the case of Hargrave's Collins, which has this note at the back (+1): "All the Notes that are written in this Book were transcrib'd from the Copy of John Anstis Esqr Garter King of Arms, at the request of the Noble Earl of Oxford, and finish'd the 7th day of Sepr 1739. by me W. Oldys." Hargrave's general note on the title page of this volume alerts the next reader to the different layers of annotation, including his own.

If professional custom were not enough, lawyers of the period were encouraged in the practice of annotation by tributes, such as new editions or high prices in sales, to the great practitioners of the past, and—more practically—by the physical format of the books they acquired, which still came with wide margins and often with an apparatus of printed glosses and annotations. Their attitude toward these books must have been affected by awareness of their own responsibility for an investment of time and mental effort, with results that would sooner or later be judged by their peers. I assume that they felt businesslike about it, but on their mettle. From Hargrave's collection it appears that, naturally enough, the practices of their profession readily crossed over into nonprofessional reading.

These readers were trained to read closely at least the first time, attending to minutiae. Their marginalia would relieve them of the necessity of such attentive reading on another occasion, though they would still have to add new references as the years went by. Most of their books would have been consulted as the need arose, not read through consecutively. Their work involved tracing the subject (hence the heads) and making connections between one book and another (the references). They must have been stopping and starting, frequently getting up to consult other books. For points in which they meant to be particularly thorough, they would check the author's references, evaluate them, correct where necessary, and supplement them with new ones. So the pattern would seem to be brief periods of intense focus interrupted by the assembling of authorities and making of comparisons. Then composing a note—opinion, query, or remark—would call for an independent act of judgment. Some thoughts would form themselves as the note was written. This is the area of license, where individual qualities are most conspicuously displayed. In Hargrave's extended notes the thinking process is most transparent. Here is his response to part of Blackstone's account of property rights in the first edition, where Blackstone observes that writers on natural law differ as to the reason for the general view that property belongs to the first taker. Some insist "that this right of occupancy is founded upon a tacit and implied assent of all mankind" (2:8):

> See this opinion vindicated at large in Rutherford Inst. of Nat. Law. where also the author argues, that labor bestowed by one person on what belongs to him only in common with the rest of mankind cannot gain a just title in exclusion of them, any more than labor bestowed by one man on the sole property of another. The true reason, why occupancy gives a property in immoveables, seems to be the absolute impossibility of enjoying them in common; from which it may be inferred, that mankind was left at liberty by the will of the creator to introduce property by occupancy without having the assent of each other for that purpose.

Here Hargrave seems to be working from memory (he does not cite page references in Rutherford) and to be developing an idea in the process of writing; the book and the note-making together make him think.

The same is true of his reaction to Blackstone's remarks about slavery by contract (1:412–13), a passage that he was moved to comment on more than once, on different occasions. The first, neat note is a reference to a counterargument made by Granville Sharp in 1769: "See Sharp's Representations on the injustice of tolerating slavery in England." But there follow two long untidy notes challenging Blackstone's views, first that the slavery of ancient Rome and modern Barbary is not a matter of sale or contract because "the buyer gives nothing, and the seller receives nothing," and then that "perpetual service" by contrast or mutual agreement is not slavery but a sort of extended apprenticeship. Hargrave's second note, with many cancels and insertions showing the haste of composition, begins, "Another observation which may be made on slavery by contract, is, that if it imports a perpetual obligation of service on the part of the slave, & an entire dependence on the master without any obligation on the master's part to observe his part of the contract, then indeed it may well be deemed a void contract." The arguments registered in the margins here were to be developed in Hargrave's arguments for Sommerset in court and eventually published in his pamphlet on the case. Not only in the making of editions but also in the creative work of making new arguments, Hargrave's working books were his collaborators and his muses.

CONCLUSION

In their everyday lives, readers of the Romantic period were accustomed to work with the books they had as schoolbooks and then in their jobs and avocations. "With" is the operative word; annotators tended to behave as contributors. The written record of their activity is diverse, varying from one kind of book to another and from reader to reader, but patterns do emerge. The evidence of marginalia surveyed in this chapter reveals some of the basic techniques available to readers, and those in turn point to shared assumptions about books and reading. To a modern reader, perhaps the most alien of these techniques is the very common practice of *extracting,* which must have had something to do with methods of education and the (waning) influence of the commonplace-book tradition, but was also made necessary by the relative scarcity of books. Readers were accustomed to making manuscript copies of passages they wanted in works that they might be able to borrow but could not buy. We still do this with photocopies, of course, but the labor of copying dictates informed selection and makes more of an impression on the copyist's memory. In however limited a way, even the humblest readers of the time adopted the attitudes of collectors, personally choosing and arranging the writings they valued.

Extracts, as we have seen, might be filed in other books for convenient reference. A second characteristic of readers who wrote in their books during this period is the impulse to make connections, whether by the shorthand of standard abbreviations and cross-references, or by some other method—physical storage, as in the copying of extracts and dropping of clippings from periodical publications into books, or illustration by direct quotation. These techniques create clusters of information and ideas, enabling readers to define, organize, combine, and recover the knowledge they derived from books. Finally, readers felt free to supplement their books, usually in a spirit of collaboration, as when naturalists recorded sightings and tourists brought their travel guides up to date.

These related habits of note-making and book-building—extracting, linking, supplementing—tend to reinforce a piecemeal approach to reading and composition, an attention to trees rather than to the forest. We observe readers of the period virtually taking a book apart for the sake of good bits they might be able to use themselves by attaching them to other books or by incorporating them in some sort of new writing. And that must mean that they came to their books looking out for short extractable passages. This frame of mind is consistent with the popularity of what we might think of as compilations or "made" books (editions, miscellanies, anas, anthologies, and the like) and with publication in parts throughout the period. There was much more tolerance for compilations than we might expect of the age that we associate with organicism and the celebration of the creative imagination. On the evidence of their marginalia, readers of the period, like their counterparts in earlier generations, conceived of books in general as provisional, not permanent structures, built up from discrete parts and consequently susceptible of similarly piecemeal revision and improvement.

Though it must in the first instance be performed by individual readers for themselves, the conventions of the time and regard for the value of books dictated that writing notes should be done in a responsible way so as to enhance the book for future readers. If this held true for working books, it was even more important for books with a social function, the ones we turn to next.

chapter two

Socializing with Books

We have already noticed some readers referring to books as though they were living friends—Dibdin, for example, walking abroad with Pope, Dryden, or Milton "as my companion" for the day. Hester Piozzi similarly describes "our Leather-coated Friends upon the Shelves; who give good Advice, and yet are never arrogant and assuming" (*Letters,* 4:221). When Coleridge left Southey after an extended visit, Southey registered both loss and consolation: "Coleridge is gone for Devonshire and I was going to say I am alone, but that the sight of Shakspeare, and Spenser, and Milton, and the Bible, on my table, and Castanheda, and Barros, and Osorio at my elbow, tell me I am in the best of all possible company" (2:249). Sydney Smith, writing to his son at school, advised him "always in books keep the best company. Don't read a line of Ovid till you have mastered Virgil; nor a line of Thomson till you have exhausted Pope; nor of Massinger, till you are familiar with Shakespeare" (1:359). This sort of language is far from being peculiar to the Romantic period; it is a topos of Western literature. The early correspondence of Erasmus, for instance, includes a long riddling passage about delightful, loyal, confiding friends who are eventually revealed to be "my books: it is their friendship that has made me perfectly happy, my only misfortune being that I have not had you to share this happiness with me" (1:254).

The idea that books are companions is a commonplace, a sentimental tribute that writers pay to their kind and that readers readily embrace, perhaps in part because of the boost it gives to their own egos by association. Southey does not mention that the house in which he felt so much alone was full of real live women, children, and servants; he was sufficiently self-aware to admit "It is more delightful to me to live with books than with men, even with all the relish that I have for such society as is worth having" (5:333). When we identify books with human companions, it is usually a shortcut for saying that they are *ideal* friends: they provide intellectual stimulation and emotional understanding without asking for anything in return. There never is real reciprocity. A witty writer can play with such entrenched and generally unexamined ideas. So Hazlitt, with characteristic bravado, turned this one around and declared that bookish people are not attached to their friends as persons with the complexities of physical and temporal being, but only to their minds, which they treat as they do their books, "read[ing] them till they are tired" (4:134). Their human companions are substitutes for or are turned into books.

The metaphor of companionship has obvious limitations. Where the history of reading in the Romantic period is considered, however, it usefully reflects real-life circumstances. In isolated situations, books can become substitutes for human contact. Dorothy Wordsworth at the age of nineteen outlined the pattern of her day, beginning thus: "I rise about six every morning and, as I have no companion, walk with a book till half past eight, if the weather permits; if not I read in the house" (46). The implication is that if she had a human companion she would prefer to go out to walk and chat with him or her; the book is chosen by default. On the other hand, the fact that books were read aloud in company every day, for devotion or work or entertainment, has several implications. It seems very likely that readers reading silently on their own associated the words on the page with a human voice and responded accordingly. (This is another truism—the illusion that books speak to us—but one that is especially apt for the period. Accustomed all their lives to hearing other people read aloud, young readers did not need the exhortations of Edward Mangin or his authority, Swift, to remind them that reading was like having the author present in the room [*View*, 79].) Reading furthermore provided the foundation for conversation at many kinds of social events, and thereby fostered actual companionship. In this chapter I shall consider ways in which annotated books provide evidence, first of the one-on-one experience of a reader responding to a book as to a companion, then of the way in which the "conversation" between a book and a reader might prepare the reader for public discussions, and finally of the sociable exchange or sharing of books. In these cases, where reading promotes social engagement or provides a substitute for it, genre proves less important than function. Whatever kind of book it is, whether it treats of travel or politics or dressmaking, it evokes from the reader a response couched in a distinct personal tone that sets it apart from most of the working books of the previous chapter. The model for writing of this kind is not provided by the book itself, nor by the rules of formal critical analysis, but by the conventions of social interaction.

TALKING TO BOOKS

Approaching the end of his life and seeking to make provision for his books, Coleridge in 1825 wrote a note at the front of the first volume of his copy of Southey's *Life of Wesley*, bequeathing it, with his many manuscript comments, to its author and donor. He describes the book as a special favorite, to which he would resort most gratefully "whenever Sickness or Languor made me feel the want of an old friend, of whose company I could never be tired":

> How many and many an hour of Self-oblivion do I owe to this Life of Wesley—how often have I argued with it, questioned, remonstrated, been peevish and asked pardon—then again listened & cried Right! Excellent!—& in yet heavier hours intreated it, as it were, to continue talking to me—for that I heard & listened & was soothed tho' I could make no reply. (*Marginalia*, 5:120–21)

Coleridge may have been an exceptionally self-conscious reader, and the *Life of Wesley*—given the troubled history of Coleridge's relationship with Southey—an exceptional case among his books, but his voluminous notes do bear out this dramatized description of his engagement with it. And the record of readers' notes in the period suggests that he was not alone. In unguarded moments, or under the strong impression that the book was talking to them, readers talked back to their books. All the little gestures of approval, like Coleridge's "Right!" and "Excellent!" could be understood in this way, as could their opposites. Companionship does not mean automatic agreement. An even plainer sign is the direct address "you." John Horne Tooke challenges Locke in this personal way repeatedly in his heavily annotated copy of the *Essay concerning Human Understanding:* "What do you mean by the word All and the Word Matter and the word Is and [the] word Thing?" (2:261).

The telltale "you" may occur under almost any circumstances; it is positively invited by books written in the first person or from a subjective viewpoint. The written "reply," as Coleridge calls it, is not always sympathetic, but in very familiar company or with books that cannot fight back, the restraints of courtesy may be disregarded. When Joseph Stock, the Bishop of Killalla in Ireland, described the hardships of a French invasion, and how he had worn himself out trying to help his people, "till in the evening always, and frequently in the day-time, he was forced to throw himself on a bed, unable to keep his feet," an unidentified reader mockingly commiserated—"Poor Bishop"; and as Stock went on to observe "Yet his health and appetite seemed to be improved by the extraordinary fatigue, nor did he ever in his life sleep better," the reader's riposte was, "What a surprizing fellow you are Bishop" (53–54). The irritated reader of the rather sanctimonious didactic novel *Nubilia,* by William Mudford, talked back in a similar way when challenged with a direct question, "have my readers ever heard an Aeolus's harp? If they have not, surely my rapture will appear extravagant, if not ridiculous" (341): "Why, Nubilia, you are right—one of your readers does really think your 'rapture' extravagant; and to confess a truth, somewhat ridiculous, also!—But it is possible that you are right—which of course, by a parity of reasoning, puts him in the wrong." These notes are not approving, they are inclined to condescension, but they are not unfriendly. Their conversational tone suggests a reader at ease and readily responsive, like an attentive, teasing companion.[1] The notes in the second of these books were written with a clear intent that they should be shared with another reader, while those in the first were not, but in both cases the writing reader takes on the text as though the two of them were alone together, without much thought for the consequences. The quality of focused personal engagement common in readers' notes of the period may be represented by the contrasting examples of two well-known figures, John Horne Tooke and Leigh Hunt.

JOHN HORNE TOOKE

John Horne, third son of a well-to-do London poulterer, born in 1736, well educated, was destined by his family for the Church and duly took orders, though his own inclinations were for the law and politics. He did some preaching, some teaching, some tutoring, and some traveling, but found his métier as a trouble-maker in the 1760s in support of John Wilkes (he later fell out with Wilkes) and on behalf of freedom of the press and parliamentary reform. In 1782 he added the surname of his friend William Tooke to his own, in the expectation—ultimately thwarted—of being Tooke's heir. His criticism of the government took him to prison more than once: he is best known to Romanticists as one of the three acquitted of charges of treason in 1794, along with Thomas Hardy and John Thelwall. In his sixties and seventies, though suffering ill health, he carried on undaunted. He published two volumes of language theory, *The Diversions of Purley*, with disturbingly radical political as well as intellectual implications; briefly held a seat in Parliament; entertained various left-wing thinkers and activists at his home in Wimbledon; and went to law over a legacy. He was evidently a passionate, energetic, quarrelsome man to the end, and a lively companion. After his death his books were sold off, the auctioneers' catalogue highlighting items "With MS. Notes by Mr. Tooke," "With a great number of MS. Notes by Mr. Tooke," "Full of MS. Notes by Mr.

Tooke," and so on.[2] Tooke had been a hero of the people for a time and his books were regarded as relics: the poet Samuel Rogers owned both the copy of Chaucer that Tooke had annotated while being held in the Tower and the transcript of Hardy's trial for treason with Tooke's notes, which to Crabb Robinson's horror Rogers planned to release to auction again when he died.[3]

Most of the volumes described in the sale catalogue as having contained notes by Tooke must have gone to private owners and remain in private hands, though it is likely that their provenance was recorded (in a note by the purchaser) and that they will gradually come to light. I'd very much like to know the whereabouts of Tooke's copies of Blackstone's *Commentaries*, Godwin's *Political Justice*, and Johnson's *Dictionary*. Enough are even now held in public collections to give a vivid impression of his personality and of his reading habits. Nearly all of them are heavily annotated, with the full range of conventional marks (underlining, vertical lines in the margin, braces, fists, crosses, question marks, exclamation marks) as well as discursive comments, some of them quite long. The books fall into three broad categories: working books that he made use of in his philological researches, published transcripts of the trials in which he was involved, and contributions to political debate. The philological works belong mostly to an early phase of his life; the notes to the trials are generally confined to corrections of minor matters of fact. But Tooke's practice was not strictly compartmentalized, so it is not surprising to find a note expressing a personal reaction in the midst of a set of linguistic speculations.[4] It is not possible to be certain of the dating of all of the notes, since some of the books were annotated over the course of many years: his copiously annotated copy of Skinner's etymological English dictionary, for example, published in 1671, contains an ownership inscription of 1774 under the name "John Horne," but also some notes signed "J. H. Tooke" and others dated 1796 and 1802, besides many that might well have been written at the same time but were not thought significant enough to warrant dating.

Tooke's books are worth looking at, aside from their historical and linguistic significance, because his notes are opinionated and challenging, and usually copious. They make bracing company for the text. In Pickbourn's handsome presentation copy of his *Dissertation on the English Verb* (1789), for instance, Tooke trashes most of his rivals: James Beattie is "A reader and a writer, but no thinker, or understander" (xxii); Joseph Priestley "no Linguist" (166); Adam Smith "deplorably superficial, and ignorant" (168). But he also takes the author up over assertions that are not strictly linguistic; he doesn't simply defend his turf. "In the infancy of society," according to Pickbourn, "men's ideas must necessarily have been very few"; not at all, says Tooke, "Just as many as they can ever be" (185). In Burke's *Reflections on the Revolution in France* he had a field day, for Burke brought out Tooke's hatred of the system of rank and privilege. Tooke's proposed heading on the first page is "The Tears of the Priesthood for the loss of their Pudding" (1). He reacts with mocking gaiety to Burke's fears about the lack of incentives under the French scheme of a merely executive monarchy in which the king has no power to reward, "Not in a permanent office; not in a grant of land; no, not in a pension of fifty pounds a year; not in the vainest and most trivial title" (290). Too bad, says Tooke:

> Aye! there is the sting to our author. Under such a king, there would
> be neither
> Office
> Land
> Pension
> nor Title
> for poor Edmund.

A single page defending the nobility provokes a sequence of objections: "Indeed but it has"; "! Ideot"; "Ha! ha! ha!"; "I will not be then of that description"; "sophist" (205). Burke was just the kind of opponent Tooke enjoyed taking on, whether it was in public debate or in amicable private wrangling. The Bewleys' recent biography records several occasions on which Tooke's "outstanding gift for raillery" (119) went too far; it can be seen in action, going with impunity as far as it likes, in the margins of his books.

Why did Tooke consider his friend Priestley, who had a reading knowledge of many languages and published voluminously on the subject of language and grammar, to have been "no Linguist"? It is not likely to have been on account of political difference: politically they were allies. Philosophically, too, their views about language were broadly similar, anti-Lockean and materialist. Tooke's annotated copy of Priestley's *Disquisitions relating to Matter and Spirit*, with a presentation inscription of December 1777 (to John Horne), contains some answers. Although the majority of the notes probably date from early 1778, afterthoughts and second rounds are evidence of there having been more than one reading, and the content of some of the notes suggests a later date for them. Like other books in Tooke's modest but well-used collection, it contains various kinds of marks and notes. Many passages are marked in pencil or ink with underlining, braces, multiple exclamation marks, etc. At some point Tooke put in a series of parallel passages from Baron d'Holbach's *Système de la nature*. On a blank leaf at the end he made a penciled memorandum, summarizing either the position of the book or his own conclusion from it (+1): "Where there is indeed a King, there is no need of a Devil. But unless we were sure of a perpetual good government, there is great need of Xtianity. J. H."

The liveliness of the annotation here arises neither from the effect of any single note nor from a systematic approach to Priestley's work, but rather from the record of fluctuations of response and from the way Tooke can demolish a weak case point by point. In the Preface, Priestley confesses to having ignored his opponents' contributions to the controversy he started: he has their tracts by him, but "I have not looked into [them], and I profess I never intend to" (xx). "Then why keep them by you," asks Tooke teasingly. When Priestley carefully traces the reasons for resistance to the idea that body and soul might be of one substance to the consequence that they must perish together, Tooke underlines key words and comments on the conduct of the argument. (In the extract following, Tooke's remarks are added in square brackets.)

> To avoid this conclusion, of which divines entertained a very unreasonable dread ["I cannot think it unreasonable"], they refined upon the former notion of spirit . . . making it, in the strict metaphysical sense of the term, an immaterial thing ["Consider these terms and see whether they are not incompatible"], without extension. (223)

Tooke writes as though he were addressing the author directly ("you" in the first quotation and the direction "Consider" in the second), but it is hardly likely that he was planning to return this book to Priestley as unsolicited advice; he is just talking back to the book.

Some of Tooke's favorite themes and personal hobby-horses come up in these notes—the distinction between terms and ideas, for instance, and the significance of particular words. Priestley's observation about the first verse of the Gospel of John raises two important issues at once.

> In the beginning, says he, was the λογος [*logos,* Word], as the philosophers also said; but the λογος was with God, that is, it was God's own λογος, or his attribute, so that the λογος was really God himself. (291)

Tooke's reaction: "!!! There is nothing like this But in S[t.] John; but Priestley knows not the great weight of this word But." Further on, as his argument is drawing to a close, Priestley expatiates on the advantages of the Unitarian system, claiming that "it inculcates a degree of devotedness to God, both active and passive, that no other philosophical system can inspire" (354–55). Tooke objects twice, first simply to reject the position: "I cannot think so; but directly the contrary." Then returning to the passage later, he adds, "Nor is it shewn how this happens: it is mere gratis dictum."

This small sample of notes suggests what a full survey would confirm: that the serious differences between Priestley and Tooke were doctrinal, and (a quite separate issue) that Tooke objected to Priestley as a linguist partly because he did not know the Gothic languages as well as Tooke did and did not subscribe to Tooke's (at that point, only just emerging) linguistic theory, but probably also because he did not himself use words with great precision. "Immaterial thing" sounds to Tooke like a contradiction in terms; the Gospel of John is misquoted; and "Priestley knows not the great weight of this word But"—which was to be the subject of 25 pages in the first volume of *The Diversions of Purley* and a cornerstone of Tooke's system. In the notes to Priestley, as he voices disagreement with his friend, Tooke roughs out the contours of his own convictions just as he might have done in conversation.

LEIGH HUNT

Unlike Tooke, Leigh Hunt depended on books and the publishing world for a living—and a precarious living it was. He was in a sense a casualty of successful commercialization. When he first published as a youth at the very beginning of the century, fortunes were being made by writing, especially by writing for periodicals, but as time went on and more newspapers, magazines, miscellanies, monthlies, and quarterlies sprang up, and writers to go with them, the rewards diminished. A member of and advocate for the younger generation of Romantic poets, carrying his causes on well into the Victorian age, Hunt slaved all his life as an essayist, reviewer, anthologist, and editor to make ends meet. He and his brother John, co-founders of the *Examiner*, spent two years in prison for disrespectful remarks about the Prince Regent. He took his whole family to Italy in 1821 on the risky prospect of starting up a new journal with Byron and Shelley. In spite of his long working life and in spite of the fact that his name was regularly before the public in the periodicals, for praise or blame, he is remembered now mainly for some light verse and for a set of impressive bohemian connections—besides having been possibly the model for Dickens's Harold Skimpole in *Bleak House*.

One constant in Hunt's chequered life—rather remarkably under the circumstances—was his enjoyment of books, which he seems always to have annotated freely. At least 155 volumes containing his marginalia are known still to exist (Lau, 10). From about 1820 onwards he capitalized on his experience of reading for pleasure by celebrating it in essays and booksellers' projects such as the *Literary Pocketbook*, a specialist diary that appeared from 1819 to 1822. In a notable essay titled "Pocket Books and Keepsakes," published in one of the popular annuals of the day, *The Keepsake,* in 1828, he explicitly recommends marking up a book that is to be given away. A book makes a good gift, he says, because "like a friend, it can talk with and entertain us." And the gift is enhanced when the donor has taken the trouble to mark "his or her favourite passages throughout (as delicately as need be) and so present, as it were, the author's and the giver's minds at once"—that is, the author's through the text itself, the giver's through the signs of preference, two friendly spirits to be communing with (*Selected Essays,* 226).

Hunt's own practice was not restricted to the marking of favorite passages, though his books often do contain both marked passages and summary criticism. It is better described by his comments in a late anthology, *Imagination and Fancy* (1844), than by the advice in the essay on keepsakes. This selection of English poetry, "with markings of the best passages," as the subtitle indicates, follows on some experiments in the periodicals in which Hunt had presented extracts from the poets "*commented, and marked with italics, on a principle of co-perusal,* as though the Editor were reading the passages in their [the readers'] company" (iii). In this passage from his Preface, Hunt is touching on a social function of annotation that goes beyond the private world of one reader with a text, but he provides for that too. He strongly recommends that young readers should develop the habit of writing in their books: "It is a good practice to read with pen in hand, marking what is liked or doubted. It rivets the attention, realizes the greatest amount of enjoyment, and facilitates reference. It enables the reader also, from time to time, to see what progress he makes with his own mind, and how it grows up towards the stature of its exalter" (61–62). While this statement belongs to a later date than the marginalia that I shall be discussing by Hunt, it describes his own settled custom and incidentally conveys his sunny and optimistic attitude toward books and reading: good books "talk with and entertain us," exalt us, and make us better.

Under the circumstances, it would be churlish to wish that Hunt's marginalia, which so strongly express the comfort he found in the comradeship of books, were other than they are—were less innocuously amiable, had more of the sharp edge that we find in the responses of Tooke. Hunt and his books were kind friends; even when he criticizes, he does it kindly. He was not a methodical annotator. Sometimes he marked a book for the benefit of other readers, but most often he seems to be uttering the thought of the moment, not performing. Sometimes his notes are dated, sometimes not. The discipline of regular study seems not to have been congenial to him—not that he could not do it, but that it interfered with his enjoyment of the book. In the French Horace that he worked on in prison, undertaking an ode a day, the marginalia become progressively fewer (Ristine, 543). Now and again he records repeated readings of a given book, as at the end of his little copy of the *Meditations* of Marcus Aurelius, where, on being dismissed with good wishes, he responds, "Thanks, and love to you, excellent Antoninus. | L. H. Feb. 7th. 1853. | His second regular perusal." In the absence of dates, it is hard to be sure when a particular book was annotated, because Hunt often sold books or gave them away, replacing them from the secondhand stalls. But with one exception, the samples that follow all come from books published before 1830 and contain no evidence that would indicate a later reading.

Hunt normally wrote the notes in his books in ink, as he encouraged other readers to do. He responded to the text as to a speaker, step by step. For example, the Preface to a "Chinese Novel," *Iu-Kiao-Li,* introduces the book by praising it for "a fable simple and well conceived, an easy and agreeable development, characters skilfully introduced and duly sustained to the termination"; Hunt concurs, "All true." The Preface however continues, "It might be better if there were fewer verses, and less of improvisation and poetic description." Here Hunt demurs, "Not for me. I should like more" (1:xxv). This book was passed on to a friend, and it seems that Hunt took the occasion to reread at least the Preface, indicating the extent of his agreement with the judgment of the editor by the rather tedious process of confirming or withholding his assent, statement by statement. In the text there are many marked passages but only a few notes, for example, against a passage describing "the beautiful amethyst colour of the blossoms with which the peach trees were laden," Hunt's appreciative if somewhat fatuous remark, "These people really seem to do justice to the beauties of nature" (1:96).

His role is typically that of cheering the author on. When the younger Pliny in his *Letters* proposes that "a good book, like other good things, is the better in proportion as it is larger," Hunt calls this remark "an excellent contradiction to the proverb; the last word of which may be altered accordingly: μεγα βιβλιον μεγα καλον"—that is, a big book is not a great evil but a great good (1:69). Even where Hunt offers resistance it is generally in the form of an improvement to the author's argument, helping him out. For instance, in his *History of Fiction* (1814), John Dunlop contrasts chivalric romance with the romances of the Greeks and expresses his surprise at the fact that the knight of chivalric romance "is always more interesting than the heroine, which must appear strange when we reflect that these romances were composed in an age when devotion to the ladies formed the essence of chivalry, and that it is quite the reverse in the Greek romances, though, at the time at which they were written, women acted a very inferior part in society" (1:309). Hunt marks the passage and comments, "This seems the very reason,—the books being written in the former instance to please female lovers, & in the latter the lovers of women. But the latter is still singular, & the former additionally accounted for, when we recollect, that the natural tendency of a male author is to exalt his hero rather." Similarly, when John Black in the *Life of Torquato Tasso* speculates about the reasons for the generous criticism of the greatest writers, suggesting that even an "imperfect work may suggest many ideas to a man of genius" and that he will consequently respond as much to his own mental creations prompted by the work as to the work itself, Hunt notes, "This, no doubt, is partly the reason. The rest is the wish to give the pleasure he receives;—the more so as he knows how his praise will be valued" (1:144). And when Black describes how a middle-aged Tasso might have been attracted to a much younger woman, the prospect of death leading him to seek out "some beautiful associate" to attend him "through the wilderness" and "imparadise the way," Hunt sighs, "A true and beautiful remark, and a pitiable fact. Yet middle age ought not to desire to appropriate to itself a young affection; & it might find consolation oftener than it seeks it, in hearts closer to its own season" (1:288).

Hunt was a keen recorder of the process of reading, and the very banality of his responses to his books may make him a more credible representative of the imagined Common Reader than the quick-witted, waspish Tooke. As a rule he approached his books with sympathetic understanding and selected for approval and concord. His best qualities as an annotator are humor and self-revelation. In the Pliny cited earlier, for instance, he reacts wryly, with professional fellow-feeling, when Pliny sends some of his writing to his friend Paternus saying, "How much I value your judgment, you may learn from hence, that I had rather you would give a strict examination to all these performances together, than only to select some few among them for applause" (1:287). "Luckless Paternus," says Hunt. In Black's life of Tasso, he points out—it seems, jocularly—that Tasso's father's asking that his sister and the nuns of her order should pray for the preservation of his wife in her impending confinement, "who in this world is my highest joy," was a "Rather inconsiderate request to the poor nuns" (1:13). And again and again, apparently artlessly, he expresses his gratification at the way in which a book confirms his own experience. In *Iu-Kiao-Li* a character called "examiner Li" is hailed as "Myself! by title & name"—that is, *Leigh* Hunt of the *Examiner* (1:120). A little image of Venus in her chariot, in an edition of Cowley, is "always delightful to me . . . owing to its having been in some of my school-books" (1:lxviii). A late note, probably of 1855–56, in a copy of Montaigne, notes with pleasure the fact that Montaigne is said to have made a memorandum while he was out one day about something he wanted done after his death, "because I was not certain to live till I came home" (30):

> I often do this myself, both abroad and at home, and for the like reason; yet certainly without any fear of death or any belief that I shall that instant die. I only say to myself, "Deaths are often sudden. I had better put this down." And I forget the thought of death, the moment I have done it.

Though it is hardly a profound remark, it serves very well to illustrate the satisfaction that Hunt always took in establishing and reinforcing a personal bond with his books, as though they had been human companions.

OPINION-FORMING

In an age that highly valued conversation and civility, information communicated by print was an asset to a speaker, and the vehicles of print—newspapers, magazines, and books—became topics of conversation in themselves, though strong-minded Elizabeth Bennet, we remember, rejected Darcy's suggestion that they compare opinions about books, saying that she couldn't talk about books in a ballroom (Austen, 2:93). There was no doubt a range of degrees of proximity to the text and of personal application in such talk, from simply discovering that both parties admired the same writers to wrangling about details or using books as a way of raising difficult subjects. (Crabb Robinson describes an occasion on which, when they were ostensibly discussing poems of Wordsworth's, Mrs. Pattison accused him of admiring the work because he—Crabb Robinson—never having been in love would not be likely to mind the lack of passion in it [1:468].) The periodicals painted a rosy picture of the pleasures of such literary conversation. Advising a young lady who complained of being barred from novel-reading in 1810, "at a time when novels are so generally read, that many of our most fashionable people make them the only subjects of bookish conversation," the *European Magazine* agreed that novel-reading was a social necessity and suggested only that she stick to novels approved by a reliable judge, either her Mama or the *Magazine*'s reviewer. When it came to report on the reading rooms of Tunbridge Wells in September 1820, the same magazine rhapsodized:

> The company at these *Libraries* is select, as well as communicative. Here an hour is agreeably passed in the discussion of the events of the day. Out of the miscellaneous contents of a diurnal newspaper

arise topics in abundance, which yield scope to the conversational powers. Different opinions, of course, spring up; but the free expression of them is met by no angry passion. Urbanity is at once the sweetener and ornament of cultivated society.[5]

The general assumption was that reading equipped people for conversation. The owners of books free to write in the margins were therefore in the happy position of preparing themselves for the social circle even as they indulged themselves by talking back to the author. There is seldom a clear line to be drawn between these two functions, and in conversation with books as in conversation proper it is hard to say whether an opinion is being expressed in the conversation or formed by it. Readers annotating books must be forming their opinions *of the books* as they go, but the opinions about various subjects elicited by the text may be one or the other (preformed, ready-made; or made up on the spot) or a bit of both. Jane Austen's spirited defense of Mary, Queen of Scots, in brief notes to a couple of paragraphs about her in the *Elegant Extracts*, is a case in point. In her judgment of Mary she disagreed with the historian quoted, William Robertson. Was Mary violent in her attachments? "No." Was she impatient of contradiction? "No." Was she fond of flattery? "A lie." Did her personal weaknesses betray her into errors and crimes? "[A]nother lie." Can anything justify her attachment to Bothwell? "She was not attached to him." And so on. But in the process Austen develops an opinion on a different figure. Robertson ends by quoting one of his own authorities: "No man, says Brantome, ever beheld her person without admiration and love, or will read her history without sorrow." "No one ought," Austen comments, "but I fear that Mr Brantome has too favourable an opinion of Human Nature, if he makes no exception."[6]

Of many books and pamphlets annotated in Austen's opinionated way, as preliminary to conversation or practice for it, the most common are those that deal with politics and matters of public debate. A small handful of examples of political works annotated by unknown or forgotten figures will pave the way for more extensive accounts of marginalia by the Duke of Sussex and William Blake.

John Prinsep, who went to India as a soldier, made a fortune there trading in indigo and printed cottons and returned to England in 1788. A landowner and occasional writer on Indian subjects, he served as a Member of Parliament for Queensborough from 1802 to 1806. In 1794 he published *Strictures and Observations on the Mocurrery System of Landed Property in Bengal*, which had first appeared as a series of articles in the *Morning Chronicle* under the pseudonym Gurreeb Doss, defending traditional land rights in opposition to a system recently imposed by the British government. To the book version Prinsep added some official publications and letters to the editor prompted by the original articles. His own interleaved copy contains a few notes for a second edition, but not many. (No further edition was called for.) Authorial revisions are normally outside the mandate of this study, and I mention the existence of this copy only to put Prinsep's other marginalia in context. Though he can be seen to have used marginal notes as part of a process of composition, that was not his usual approach to books. When the *Strictures* came out, one of his opponents, Thomas Law, promptly published *An Answer* defending the system as a successful experiment. Prinsep annotated his copy indignantly in ink throughout, challenging statements and interpretations point by point (Fig. 17). Law calls a decision of the Revenue Board "hasty" (12). Prinsep demands more details: "when? by whom? how hasty?" If the Zemindars whom Law supports did restore order by enforcing trials by ordeal, was it really "a most religious & humane use of their Powers" (13)? What is interesting about these marginalia is that they seem to have no relation to the notes in the interleaved copy of his own book: Prinsep was reading as an informed and engaged participant in the debate but not extracting material to further his own case or composing an Answer to the *Answer*.

That this was his normal procedure appears to be confirmed by a volume of pamphlets about policy with regard to neutral nations that he acquired about 1801, all but one of which include his occasional marginal notes. In a pamphlet by the first Earl of Liverpool, Charles Jenkinson, for example, his penciled notes now catch the author out and now support him, in a to-and-fro of agreement and disagreement. (Prinsep

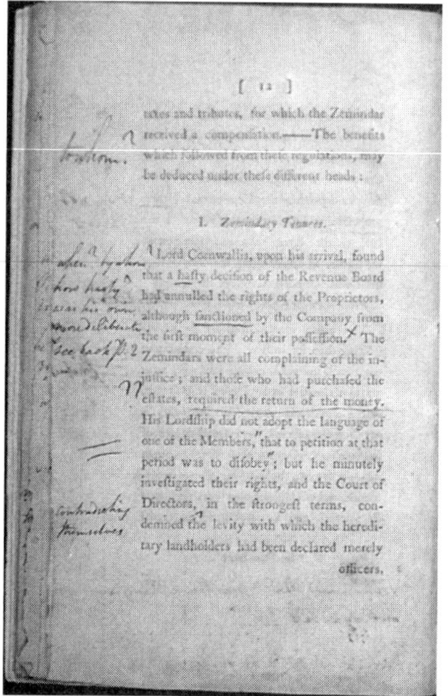

[12]

taxes and tributes, for which the Zemindar received a compenſation.——The benefits which followed from theſe regulations, may be deduced under theſe different heads :

I. *Zemindary Tenures.*

Lord Cornwallis, upon his arrival, found that a haſty deciſion of the Revenue Board had annulled the rights of the Proprietors, although ſanctioned by the Company from the firſt moment of their poſſeſſion. The Zemindars were all complaining of the injuſtice ; and thoſe who had purchaſed the eſtates, required the return of the money. His Lordſhip did not adopt the language of one of the Members, "that to petition at that period was to diſobey" ; but he minutely inveſtigated their rights, and the Court of Directors, in the ſtrongeſt terms, condemned the levity with which the hereditary landholders had been declared merely

officers.

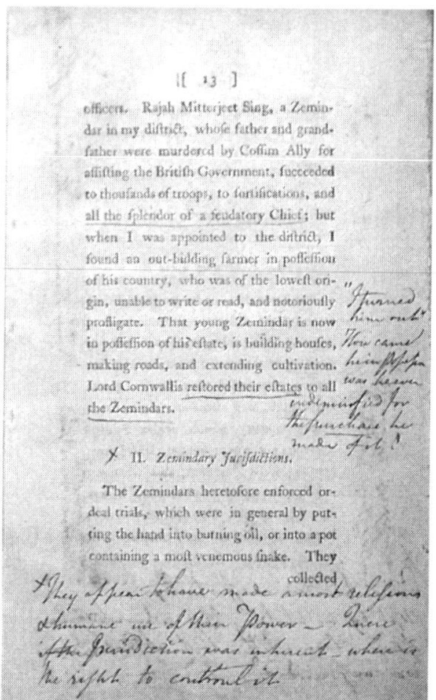

[13]

officers. Rajah Mitterjeet Sing, a Zemindar in my diſtrict, whoſe father and grandfather were murdered by Coſſim Ally for aſſiſting the Britiſh Government, ſucceeded to thouſands of troops, to fortifications, and all the ſplendor of a feudatory Chief ; but when I was appointed to the diſtrict, I found an out-bidding farmer in poſſeſſion of his country, who was of the loweſt origin, unable to write or read, and notoriouſly profligate. That young Zemindar is now in poſſeſſion of his eſtate, is building houſes, making roads, and extending cultivation. Lord Cornwallis reſtored their eſtates to all the Zemindars.

II. *Zemindary Juriſdictions.*

The Zemindars heretofore enforced ordeal trials, which were in general by putting the hand into burning oil, or into a pot containing a moſt venemous ſnake. They

collected

FIG. 17 Notes by John Prinsep in a copy of Thomas Law's *An Answer to Mr. Prinseps's Observations on the Mocurrery System* (1794). By permission of the British Library.

followed the common practice of reading a book—all these pamphlets are over 100 pages long—before it was bound, and in this case the resultant marginalia were damaged in the process of binding; square brackets in the transcriptions fill in losses from cropping.) At one moment he accuses Liverpool of specious reasoning: "Here we have an instance how great men will twist & apply [a] single sentence to support an opinion which the context condemns" (37). But a couple of pages later, he endorses a point about French policy by adding a contemporary illustration: "[F]rance has continued to act on this principle till her last treaty with [A]merica.—Every thing she conceded to America must be conside[red as] having for its object the encouragement of the Northern pow[ers]" (39). Notes like these might in Prinsep's case be the seeds of public pronouncements, but they show no signs of having been written for that purpose or of being anything other than the reader's usual conversation with the text.

One very odd and interesting little volume, playful in spirit in contrast to Prinsep's work, is a copy of the *Letters* of "Junius" copiously annotated over a period of years from 1823 to perhaps 1835 by an alert, witty, combative but appreciative reader—probably a man since he handles Latin confidently. His marks and notes, in pencil or ink, or in pencil overtraced in ink, tend to pick out an idea or phrase from Junius and to respond by improving on it. From Junius's "*caput mortuum* of vitriol" (51), for instance, he evolves "Elixir of Vitriol" (vii). When Junius describes the way in which a jury might be so affronted at the "odious artifices" of the judge attempting to influence their decision as to deliver a verdict against him out of spite, the reader comments, "Such is the quality of 'excess' of Law—the Subversion of Justice & Equity!" (xvii). Pleased with this formulation, he makes it a heading at the top of the page, "Even Excess subverts Success!"—and then repeats it as a motto on the first page of the text. This reader loved mottos, jokes, and wordplay, and he revised the line again to use in a page of epigraphs at the front of the volume: "Hence Zeal in Excess—/ always fails of Success!" He calls Whigs and Tories Prigs and Trogs, and explains why: "Whigs = Privilege or Prigs | Torys = Oratory = Roratower Toroquies or Trogs—" (title page verso). He pretends that the name "Junius" is derived from "'Jugulum' vel juggle 'em" (Latin "throat" punningly translated as "trick them" [title page]). In this unusually playful, high-spirited example, the reader reacts to Junius's invective with political satire and jests.

The problems of Catholics and Dissenters, barred from the universities and from civil or military office, generated public controversy throughout the period. Writers took up their positions in print; readers argued over them on the page and among themselves. Three anonymously published pamphlets with readers' notes register the forming of opinions on different aspects of this perennial problem. *A Letter* of 1807 in support of a bill to extend to Protestant Dissenters certain privileges granted Catholics under the Irish Act is full of irascible penciled notes, challenging the author point by point in an intelligent and knowledgeable way. The writer observes that the King returned without comment some dispatches recommending that restrictions on Catholics in the army and navy should be lifted; what were his aides to conclude from this "but that His Majesty approved of these dispatches?" Not necessarily, says the annotator: "or rather that his Majesty did not approve? did L[d.] Grenville or L[d.] Howick explain, as had been usual to do, the extent of the Measure & its Consequences—No, they left his Majesty's mind to be uninformed by them. They meant to deceive the King & when asked whether they had explained to his Majesty the extent of the Measure they confessed they had not—" (10). We do not know whether or not this reader had a public role, and it does not really matter: disagreement arises in the first instance from a questionable inference that might arouse the suspicions of any alert reader.

John Wilson Croker's *Sketch of the State of Ireland* (1808) also elicited long detailed counterarguments from a reader—R. E. Coote to judge by the ownership inscription. Croker, who is better known today as a pillar of the *Quarterly Review* and the author of the killing review of Keats's *Endymion* than for his politics, argued in favor of Catholic Emancipation but also in favor of more widespread reform. The reader seems to have thought his proposals did not go far enough. Though generally taking the same side as the author, the attentive notes challenge Croker on fine points and matters of emphasis. Croker declares himself apprehensive—but perhaps was boasting—that his scheme will be perceived as "a rash and imprudent novelty," but the reader is able to cite an earlier publication that had made the same suggestion (2). When Croker declares that among the peasantry, "few . . . can read, fewer write," the reader contradicts him, maintaining that "the lower class of Irish are better instructed than is generally imagin'd" (32). Croker makes the familiar point that absentee landlords have been bad for Ireland, but gives an unusual reason: it is "A great evil. Not because the country is drained by remittances, but because she is widowed of her natural protectors" (29). Here the reader responds at length:

> This is not fact the misery of Ireland can be traced to the drain of Capital to England—the residence of Landlords would not remedy this Evil as the Incomes of resident Landlords are remited to England for all Manufactured articles which they consume—they Farm land to raise food for their families consequently they buy nothing their

Tenants sell—It is a middle or a class employ'd in useful manufacture, or as shopkeepers, that is wanted in Ireland.

The idea of the lack of a middle class emerges again when Croker laments the failure of law enforcement, observing that "The body—in England so effective—of mayors, bailiffs, and constables, [is] unknown, or known as a jest" (48). Underlining this sentence, the reader adds, "Where there are but two orders in the Country, the rich and the poor, Magistrates may be found but no bailiffs or Constables or at least none fit to undertake those offices—In Ireland therefore the laws are not nor cannot be properly executed." While it is impossible to tell whether this reader was declaring opinions already formed or finding them in his response to Croker's position, the writing down of his diverging views must at the very least have confirmed and consolidated them.

Then there is the interesting working-class case of the annotator who identifies himself on the title page as "W. Davis the Tinker," contributor of "marginal Notes." He may have been a Methodist: he has warm praise for the Methodist astronomer John Russell (14). The little 14-page pamphlet with his notes is *Reflections on Religious Persecution* by John Lettsom, a Quaker physician—though Davis probably did not know the identity of the author. The pamphlet pleads a liberal, rationalist, optimistic position on the general topic of toleration, arguing that religious oppression has caused endless bloodshed and that it is better for civil society to encourage a variety of religious beliefs, with universal toleration. But Lettsom the relativist encountered vigorous opposition from Davis the absolutist, and the quarrel in the margins is exhilarating. Davis rejects Lettsom's overall position while accepting particular arguments with a word ("agreed" [11]) or a compliment ("this argument shows some finesse" [13]). He rebuts some points and undermines others. When Lettsom, for instance, argues that every sect is made up of individuals convinced of the "rationality and purity" of its beliefs, Davis denies it: "Opinions are too often formed because they favor the commission of some darling lust & are calculated to lull the Conscience asleep in carnal security" (4). Davis writes confidently, his very style a contrast to Lettsom's mildness. Lettsom points out that we may be wrong in thinking ourselves entitled to judge others, since "history proves that the present age knows less than will be known by succeeding ages" (9). But Davis insists that there are some eternal verities: "no more can be known of positive Truths than are now known. the Ideas of Tall short fat lean fire water &c cannot admit of any kind of improvement just so that God Exists. that Virtue is Good. that Vice is Evil. the race of men coming after us can know no more on those subjects than we." And under those circumstances, he maintains that religious persecution may be right and necessary. Though Lettsom suggests that our own weaknesses should lead us to exercise forbearance towards our neighbor, Davis objects (8):

> What has my Character to do with my Belief or with His but is He right Therefore as a Muckletonian when He describes the Heavens 6 Miles high & the Sun to be no bigger than the Eye discovers it to be where is the man that can assert that Nailor was right when he came into Bristol as the Messia. I think they that Pillorid Him did right. Call it Persecution I shall call it Justice.

My last example in this series, one closely resembling Davis's Lettsom, is the British Library copy of a 35-page pamphlet entitled *Harvest: General Weeding of the Earth,* by "A Labourer," published in Dublin in 1799. Following on the Irish Rebellion of 1798 and in the context of debate about the proposed Union of Ireland and Great Britain, this millennial tract cites biblical texts, especially from Revelation, to exhort workers to refuse to take up arms on either side: "Rouse, rouse, my dear Brethren—no longer slumber—shake off the chains of Satan—prove your patience, and support your cross, by suffering death rather than be compelled or seduced to take part with either party of this unhappy, divided, deluded world" (35). A manuscript note on the back of the title page reads, "The Marginal notes by John Lidwill," and the text is indeed accompanied by many notes in a large clear hand (Fig. 18). The book also, oddly, contains a printed slip announcing "Lalor's Revelations,

Price Six Pence, Revised and explained on the Margins by John Lidwill." On the strength of this slip, the Library attributes the work to "Lalor," somebody otherwise unknown. It is possible that the slip has migrated to this book from another but the alternative title is plausible, and there are those notes in the margins. If this is the same work, it is possible that Lidwill meant to have it reprinted with his notes (but no record of any such edition exists), or to make copies each of them with his manuscript notes as a form of publication (but no other copy is known), or to sell off this copy for sixpence (but why have the slip printed?). Whatever the circumstances, the notes are worth looking at.

Lidwill by his own account was born about 1742 of English ancestry, farmed in Ireland, quarreled with his family, considered emigrating to Upper Canada, and began to publish his autobiography in numbers, in Dublin, about 1800. His *History and Memoirs* did not get far, however, presumably for want of purchasers; the British Library copy is incomplete at 63 pages, and I have been unable to locate any other. His notes in *Harvest* are interesting for their attitude toward the text, for their working-class origins and Blakean tone, and for the method of reading that they represent. Lidwill presents himself as a reader who finds much to admire but is distressed to find the author at fault or obscure in his lesson. For the most part he glosses and paraphrases the text, but on the matter of the Sacrament, his notes fulminate against the author, who proposes that it is only upon receiving the Sacrament that "the spirit of God the Holy Ghost" can enter into the worshipper. Lidwill violently disagrees: "none are fit to receive the Sacrament but such as first received the holy Ghost" (8); "These Eight last lines are false, Christ is the Eternal bread, & not the Sacram[t]. The holy Ghost is God, & not the Sacram[t]" (21). His reading method, perhaps because of his religious background, is consistently allegorical: what he finds on the page he translates, in his mind and in his notes, as he goes along, into terms he understands better. Though this is markedly the case with biblical texts, the same method is extended to his interpretation of the author's own words. "To love thy Neighbour as thyself" he parses carefully (4):

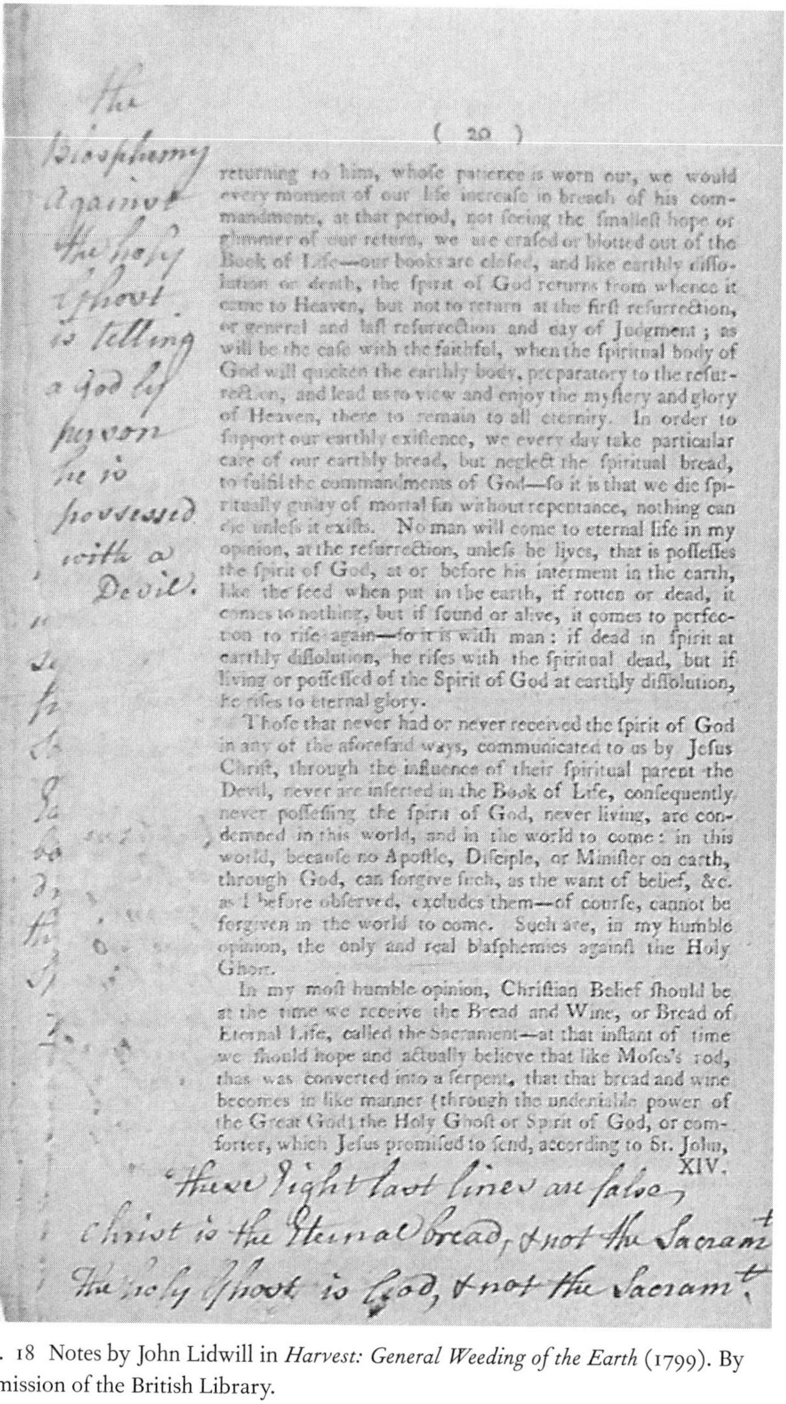

the Blasphemy against the holy Ghost is telling a godly person he is possessed with a Devil.

(20)

returning to him, whose patience is worn out, we would every moment of our life increase in breach of his commandments, at that period, not seeing the smallest hope or glimmer of our return, we are erased or blotted out of the Book of Life—our books are closed, and like earthly dissolution or death, the spirit of God returns from whence it came to Heaven, but not to return at the first resurrection, or general and last resurrection and day of Judgment ; as will be the case with the faithful, when the spiritual body of God will quicken the earthly body, preparatory to the resurrection, and lead us to view and enjoy the mystery and glory of Heaven, there to remain to all eternity. In order to support our earthly existence, we every day take particular care of our earthly bread, but neglect the spiritual bread, to fulfil the commandments of God—so it is that we die spiritually guilty of mortal sin without repentance, nothing can die unless it exists. No man will come to eternal life in my opinion, at the resurrection, unless he lives, that is possesses the spirit of God, at or before his interment in the earth, like the seed when put in the earth, if rotten or dead, it comes to nothing, but if sound or alive, it comes to perfection to rise again—so it is with man: if dead in spirit at earthly dissolution, he rises with the spiritual dead, but if living or possessed of the Spirit of God at earthly dissolution, he rises to eternal glory.

Those that never had or never received the spirit of God in any of the aforesaid ways, communicated to us by Jesus Christ, through the influence of their spiritual parent the Devil, never are inserted in the Book of Life, consequently never possessing the spirit of God, never living, are condemned in this world, and in the world to come: in this world, because no Apostle, Disciple, or Minister on earth, through God, can forgive such, as the want of belief, &c. as I before observed, excludes them—of course, cannot be forgiven in the world to come. Such are, in my humble opinion, the only and real blasphemies against the Holy Ghost.

In my most humble opinion, Christian Belief should be at the time we receive the Bread and Wine, or Bread of Eternal Life, called the Sacrament—at that instant of time we should hope and actually believe that like Moses's rod, that was converted into a serpent, that that bread and wine becomes in like manner (through the undeniable power of the Great God) the Holy Ghost or Spirit of God, or comforter, which Jesus promised to send, according to St. John, XIV.

these eight last lines are false, Christ is the Eternal bread, & not the Sacramt
the holy Ghost is God, & not the Sacramt.

FIG. 18 Notes by John Lidwill in *Harvest: General Weeding of the Earth* (1799). By permission of the British Library.

(21)

XIV. ch. 16 v. And I will pray the Father, and he ſhall give you another Comforter, that he may abide with you for ever. Even the Spirit of Truth, whom the world cannot receive, becauſe it ſeeth him not, neither knoweth him: but ye know him; for he dwelleth with you, and ſhall be in you.—26 v. But the Comforter, which is the Holy Ghoſt, whom the Father will ſend in my name, he ſhall teach you all things, and bring all things to your remembrance, whatſoever I have ſaid unto you.

Our believing that there is a Supreme Being, a great God, is not ſufficient to obtain Heaven without ſtrictly adhering, and obeying one and all God's commandments; fulfilling one and diſobeying another, will not anſwer, neither is it ſufficient that we believe in the Holy Ghoſt or Spirit of God, unleſs we ſtrictly take the Bread and Wine or Sacrament, as I before obſerved, taking it only in commemoration or in any other ſenſe, clearly is without effect, or the words that I have now obſerved are of none effect. The Holy Ghoſt, whom the Father will ſend—by the word ſend it is beyond contradiction it quits the Heavens for the purpoſe of its communication to man, proved by the words "and he ſhall be in you."

these 5 lines are false

Having the belief I obſerve, my humble hope and reliance on the unbounded mercies of God is, that on the top of a mountain or elſewhere, having real and actual ſorrow for our paſt offences, having an unſhaken reſolution never more to break through any of his commandments, he will ſend the Holy Ghoſt to us, and continue it with us to our diſſolution, if we continue with him.

this is fact

Let us, in the name of God, calling for the aid of Jeſus Chriſt, which he promiſes to give us, with the Holy Ghoſt —from this moment be no longer deſerters from ſo good and merciful a God, who is willing to receive us, repenting —let our ſins be as red as ſcarlet; happy and glorious conſolations to the afflicted but penitent ſinner!—Let not my obſervations on the unbounded mercies of God by no means prevent us from having recourſe to the Sacrament; for it is indiſpenſably neceſſary, in my humble opinion, having the opportunity or why the inſtitution? See Chriſt's example in this, by taking it himſelf, and having himſelf baptized; though it's evident he had no occaſion for earthly aid, having an Heavenly and Earthly knowledge of himſelf, which could not be known or communicated to any other, ſave by the Father through him, and the Holy Ghoſt, which are one and the ſame.

Christ never took the sacraint.

O Bre-

Christs baptizm was not for Example: but only fulfilling that part of the Mosaical Law—

This Neighbor Signifies the same disposition
The Godly are the Neibors of the Godly.
The Wicked are Neibors of the Wicked.

The general effect of his glossing, possibly only because of the remorseless X = Y syntax, is dogmatic: "Hephzibah is delightful | Beulah is Married" (17), "Any Object or Idea, meditated on is Spiritually eating & drinking such object" (18), "The Blasphemy against the holy Ghost is telling a Godly person he is possessed with a Devil" (20).

In all these marginalia on public affairs and religious controversy, readers respond familiarly to texts as to a person and an equal, firming up their own ideas in the process.

THE DUKE OF SUSSEX

Augustus Frederick, Duke of Sussex, the ninth child and sixth son of George III, was educated at the University of Göttingen (established by his great-grandfather, George II, in 1737) and remained abroad until he was thirty, in part, it appears, because he was at odds with his family, having contracted an invalid marriage and espoused Whiggish views. After his return to England he proved to be one of the most hardworking of the generally dissolute and unpopular royal dukes: about the worst the Regency satirists could do to him was to call him "wide-mouthed Sussex"—which in that context was practically a tribute of affection.[7] He used his influence and his place in the House of Lords to promote reformist causes; he became president of the Society of Arts and of the Royal Society (Fig. 19). Like his father he was a serious book collector, his library amounting eventually to over 50,000 volumes of manuscript and printed books. A catalogue of the theological holdings alone included 12,000 items.[8] Dibdin frequently mentions this collection and gives a particularly glowing descriptions of it in his *Reminiscences* of 1836 (2:943–48). Crabb Robinson attended one of the Duke's conversazioni at Kensington Palace in 1832 and was favorably impressed: "I was more amused than I expected. There were opened some eight or ten rooms, generally small, and all filled with books. No

FIG. 19 "The Patriotic Dinner": a print by W. Heath commemorating a grand dinner held in support of Spanish Liberals on 7 March 1823. The Duke of Sussex stands at the chairman's right. © The Trustees of The British Museum.

gilding or other finery of a Court, but the air of a gentleman's house,—unostentatious, comfortable, and elegant. There were probably several hundred persons there. The only man I looked for was Schlegel, with whom I had a short chat" (3:3). Robinson had also attended a public dinner, held at the Freemasons' Tavern and chaired by Sussex, to celebrate the repeal of the Test and Corporations Acts in 1828, on which occasion he reported that he was "not a bad chairman, though no orator" (2:394).

After Sussex died in 1843, his books were auctioned in a series of sales for over £14,000.[9] The catalogues occasionally mention marginalia by Sussex as an attractive feature. There is an 1809 copy of Blackstone in four volumes "with MS. Notes by the Duke of Sussex"; a copy of a treatise on the prerogative of kings attributed to Lord Somers "with a MS. Note by the Duke of Sussex, and several Marks"; and a few other titles of similar kinds. But the catalogues do not record many such items, and since the auctioneers attached commercial value to the presence of notes it seems likely that there were not many to record. Although Sussex was relatively uninhibited about writing in his books, he did it only under certain conditions. The British Library now holds sixteen books with his notes, about the same number as we have for Blake and for Keats. Their subjects and languages vary, but the common features are pronounced. With the single exception of the Somers pamphlet (*The Judgment of Whole Kingdoms and Nations, concerning the . . . Prerogative of Kings*—a secondhand copy of the eighth edition of 1713, already annotated by a previous owner, Elizabeth Collins), all were new when Sussex acquired them, the latest with a publication date of 1842. He may have made a distinction between rare books bought for the collection and a closet library that he reserved for personal use, though both groups bore his bookplate and a library shelf-mark. All the annotated books have a political theme or application, including what was presumably his student copy of Cicero, in 20 volumes, which contains his comments and cross-references on Roman history and oratory and on the life of Cicero, rather than the usual textual variants and parallel passages. These books tell of the lives and writings of statesmen or address pressing contemporary issues, testifying to Sussex's passion for politics and his efforts to keep up with current affairs.

Sussex was a systematic annotator who tended to fill books up as he read them with marks of attention and aids to memory, in pencil or ink indiscriminately: there are usually lots of heads, fists, underlinings, lines down the margins, crosses, and question marks. The fact that his handsome three-volume quarto edition of the *Memoirs* of Benjamin Franklin, with nice wide margins, has marks and notes only in the first half of the second volume almost certainly means that he read only the first half of the second volume, which consists of correspondence. Like the contemporary readers whose work is described earlier, he frequently used a word or two to indicate approval or disapproval, with longer interventions when his interest was aroused or he had something specific to contribute. He does not appear to have been performing for any future reader; his notes are not showy or directed to a third party. Sometimes he declares a settled opinion, but more commonly he responds in an open-minded way to ideas offered him as though prepared to discuss them with the author, and agreement on one point does not preclude disagreement later. Benjamin Franklin, wishing to see "the discovery of a plan that would induce and oblige nations to settle their disputes without first cutting one another's throats," asks "When will human reason be sufficiently improved to see the advantage of this?"—and Sussex answers, "When Sovereigns Monarchs & Nations Will discover that honesty is the best Policy & that Reason was given us to [?direct] and follow principle & not to become Slaves to Passion & Private Interest" (2:25). In general he is on Franklin's side, but where they differ he says so: though Franklin argues that statesmen ought to be unpaid, for instance, Sussex believes that all offices should be paid and that the only question should be how much (2:65). In Robert Hall's *Apology for the Freedom of the Press,* a work of 1793 with some notes dated 1815, Sussex likewise backs the author up on some points while declaring on others "This I can not agree to" (59) or "false as Hell" (71). When Hall states that "For private individuals to combine together at all with a view to quicken the vigour of criminal prosecution is

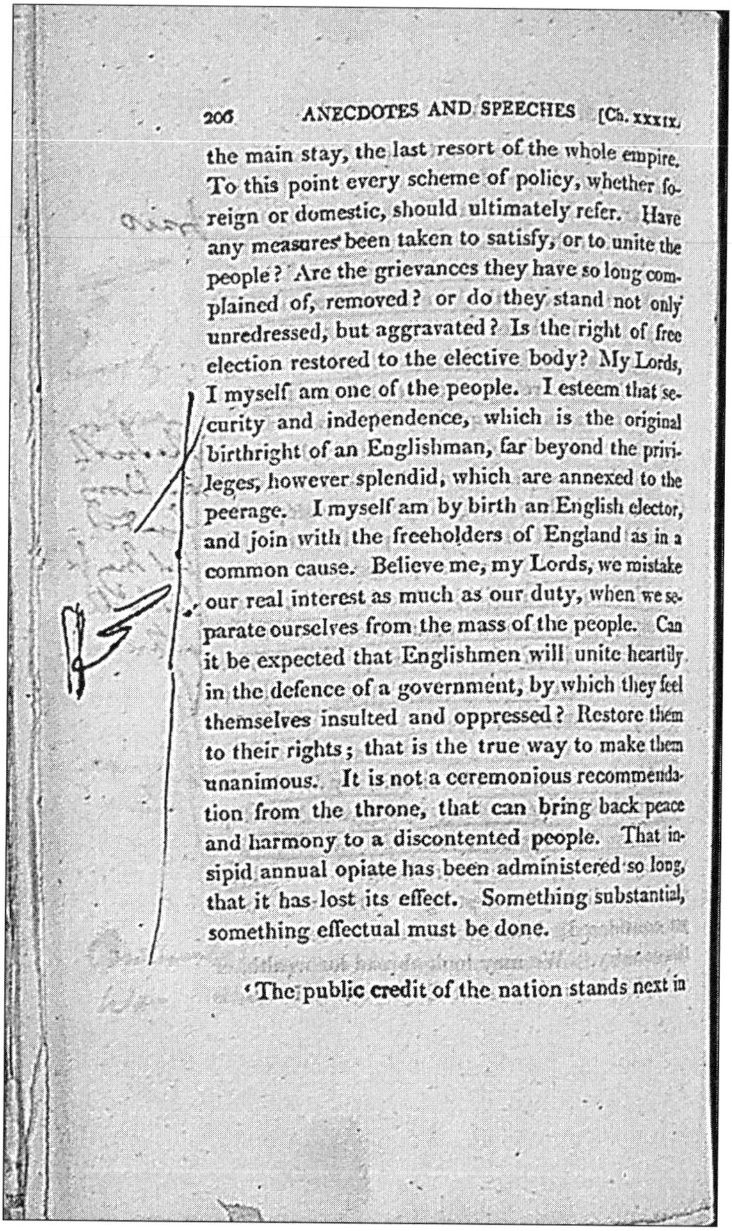

206 ANECDOTES AND SPEECHES [Ch. XXXIX.

the main stay, the last resort of the whole empire. To this point every scheme of policy, whether foreign or domestic, should ultimately refer. Have any measures been taken to satisfy, or to unite the people? Are the grievances they have so long complained of, removed? or do they stand not only unredressed, but aggravated? Is the right of free election restored to the elective body? My Lords, I myself am one of the people. I esteem that security and independence, which is the original birthright of an Englishman, far beyond the privileges, however splendid, which are annexed to the peerage. I myself am by birth an English elector, and join with the freeholders of England as in a common cause. Believe me, my Lords, we mistake our real interest as much as our duty, when we separate ourselves from the mass of the people. Can it be expected that Englishmen will unite heartily in the defence of a government, by which they feel themselves insulted and oppressed? Restore them to their rights; that is the true way to make them unanimous. It is not a ceremonious recommendation from the throne, that can bring back peace and harmony to a discontented people. That insipid annual opiate has been administered so long, that it has lost its effect. Something substantial, something effectual must be done.

'The public credit of the nation stands next in

FIG. 20 Notes by the Duke of Sussex on a speech by Pitt the Elder, in John Almon's *Anecdotes* (1810). By permission of the British Library.

degree to the rights of the constitution; it calls loudly for the interposition of Parliament. There is a set of men, my Lords, in the city of London, who are known to live in riot and luxury, upon the plunder of the ignorant, the innocent, the helpless—upon that part of the community, which stands most in need of, and best deserves the care and protection of legislature. To me, my Lords, whether they be miserable jobbers of 'Change-alley, or the lofty Asiatic plunderers of Leadenhall-street, they are all equally detestable. I care but little whether a man walks on foot, or is drawn by eight horses or six horses; if his luxury be supported by the plunder of his country, I despise and detest him. My Lords, while I had the honour of serving his Majesty, I never ventured to look at the Treasury but at a distance; it is a business I am unfit for, and to which I never could have submitted. The little I know of it has not served to raise my opinion of what is vulgarly called the *monied interest;* I mean that blood-sucker, that muckworm, which calls itself the friend of government—that pretends to serve this or that administration, and may be purchased, on the same terms, by any administration—that advances money to government, and takes special care of its own emoluments. Under this description I include the whole race of commissaries, jobbers, contractors, clothiers, and remitters. Yet I do not deny that, even with these

This is true English British Doctrine

suspicious at least, if not illegal," and declares such combinations "utterly improper" where the liberty of the press is at issue, Sussex proposes as an illustration the Society for the Suppression of Vice, formed in 1802 for just such a purpose: "for instance the Society for the Suppression of Vice is of an inquisitional Nature which might perhaps be prosecuted in various instances upon the principle of a foul conspiracy & which would no Doubt find its warmest Opponents in the Courts" (19). He is not a wholly cerebral reader, however. His notes express irritation, frustration, and pleasure just as others' do. He responds warmly to Franklin's act of lending ten louis to a correspondent with the condition that the loan be "repaid," when the borrower is able, by being lent on to someone else on the same terms ("This is a trick of mine for doing a deal of good with a little money"): "The idea of this Loan is most beautiful & bespeaks a goodness of heart for which one must love the man" (2:54).

Sussex regularly applies historical decisions and situations to the problems of his own day, but he shows an interest in the abstract principles too. The most revealing of his extant annotated books is John Almon's authorized biography of the elder Pitt, which incorporates Pitt's speeches in Parliament from 1736 to 1778. The first two volumes of this three-volume edition, published in 1810, are heavily marked and annotated; the third, an appendix of miscellaneous documents, is not. A four-page draft of a speech on the war with France is tucked into the first volume. Sussex was plainly interested in the example of Pitt's oratory, in the principles articulated in his speeches, and in comparisons between that earlier era of British politics and his own—particularly the relationship between the two Pitts. There are heads, underlinings, and plenty of signs of attention, including stars and exclamation marks. The longer notes make some shrewd observations about court politics and the operations of Parliament; they show that Sussex had a sense of humor, or at least of irony. Lord Bath's advice that "the *official* men ought never to be trusted with information of any measure until it was given them to execute" is, he says, a "Strange principle" (1:197). When Pitt is praised in verse as a man "With sense to counsel, and with wit to please, / A Roman's virtue, with a Courtier's ease," he comments drily, "These

Words would not have done for the Son" (1:14); and when Pitt in a speech confesses that he was unfit for Treasury affairs and attacks the "monied interest" as "that blood-sucker, that muck-worm, which calls itself the friend of government," Sussex remarks, "I completely submit to these principles but Mr Pitt the 2^{d} Son acted upon the direct contrary principle" (2:207; Fig. 20). One very long note, anomalous in that it conveys personal information (though that was probably in the interest of verification and not of self-assertion), has to do with torture in the prisons of Germany: Sussex acknowledges the system to be "horrible" but he corrects the account as he found it, adding details that he learned as a student in Göttingen, with the dates for particular cases and the authority of one of his tutors who had been an eyewitness (1:393–95).

Sussex was always denied powerful positions, and he has not had much attention from historians. The occasional remark suggests that they think he was rather stupid, but his marginalia indicate otherwise, for they show him as a serious reader, opinionated but fair-minded, at work acquiring information and reflecting on ideas relevant to his position.[10]

WILLIAM BLAKE

Of all British writers of all kinds of writing who flourished in the period that we call Romantic, only three have so far come to have their marginalia included among their collected works: Blake, Coleridge, and Keats. Why only three? Why even three? Why *these* three? Marginalia are as vulnerable as other manuscript materials to the indifference of posterity; it takes deliberate action to preserve them for any length of time, and deliberate action in turn calls for motives of affection or financial interest. By the time Keats died in 1821, as we have seen from the auction record, notes in a writer's books might have been expected to have commercial value, whether for their association, as useful supplements to the books, or as unpublished but potentially publishable literary remains. Thousands of books with readers' notes have indeed survived, for one or more of these reasons; but for only three readers has the effort been made to reconstitute a complete set of notes and to present it as part of the body of their written work.

Blake, Coleridge, and Keats expressed themselves vividly in notes to their books, but so did many contemporaries. They were all three, in varying degrees, public figures in their time, but they were not alone in that either. Hunt, Shelley, Piozzi, Thelwall, Walpole, Seward, and Bentham wrote interesting notes in books still extant, were household names for a while, and have their advocates—some their cults—to this day; yet no one so far as I know is proposing to publish their marginalia en masse. The difference between the two groups arises partly from intrinsic merit but mostly from posthumous attention, which is itself mysterious and often accidental. Of course there are important differences as well as resemblances in the three exceptional cases, as I hope to demonstrate in separate accounts of their annotated books. But all of them left devoted followers who treasured their books as relics and saw to it that they were not forgotten. From the point of view of later admirers, Keats and Blake were relatively under-documented, so any new evidence of their powers and their opinions was welcome; and while no one could call Coleridge's ideas under-documented, they took a more accessible form in the marginalia than in most of his published prose. There were already precedents for the occasional publication of writers' marginalia. It had been done for Swift after his death; some of Coleridge's marginalia were published in periodicals before 1820 and a great many more in posthumous editions.[11] Those responsible for the literary reputations of Blake and Keats may therefore also have considered publication as a long-term prospect. But they already valued the marginalia for personal and social reasons, as the writers expected.

Blake's is the most distinctive voice, familiar now after having been in print and under discussion for more than a century.[12] We hear it with relish. It is confident, dogmatic, defiant. "False" he cries in large letters in the margins of Swedenborg (40). "Villain," he says to Bacon, "did Christ seek the Praise of the Rulers" (239). "Presumptuous Murderer," he calls Bishop Watson who thinks the Christian world would be better off if Paine had died young, "dost thou O Priest wish thy brothers death when God has preserved him" (1). His opinion of Sir Joshua Reynolds is, bluntly (large letters again), that "This Man was Hired to Depress Art" (Fig. 21). Blake might appear to fit the classic pattern of a dissident

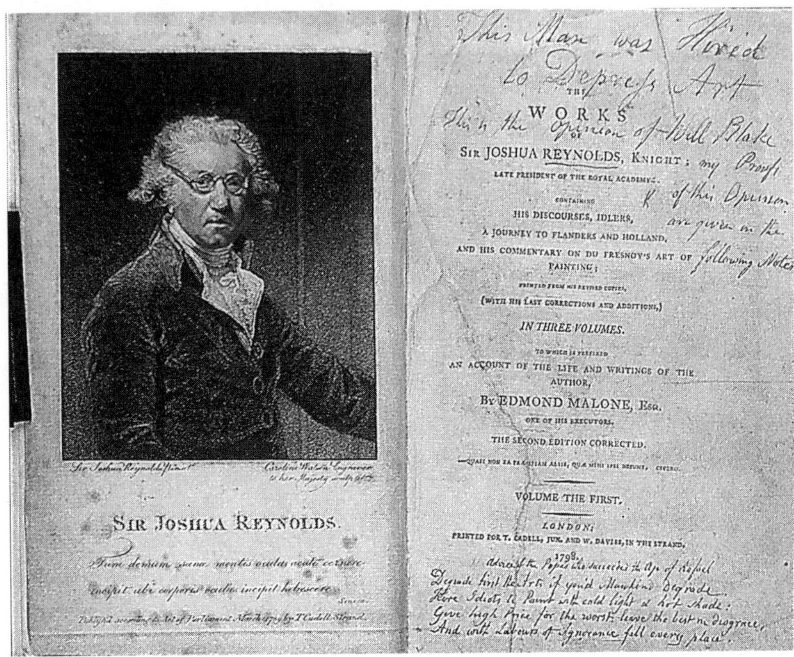

SIR JOSHUA REYNOLDS.

This Man was Hired to Depress Art

THE WORKS OF SIR JOSHUA REYNOLDS, KNIGHT; LATE PRESIDENT OF THE ROYAL ACADEMY:

This is the Opinion of Will Blake my Proofs of this Opinion are given in the following Notes

CONTAINING HIS DISCOURSES, IDLERS, A JOURNEY TO FLANDERS AND HOLLAND, AND HIS COMMENTARY ON DU FRESNOY'S ART OF PAINTING;

PRINTED FROM HIS REVISED COPIES, (WITH HIS LAST CORRECTIONS AND ADDITIONS,)

IN THREE VOLUMES.

TO WHICH IS PREFIXED AN ACCOUNT OF THE LIFE AND WRITINGS OF THE AUTHOR, BY EDMOND MALONE, ESQ. ONE OF HIS EXECUTORS.

THE SECOND EDITION CORRECTED.

VOLUME THE FIRST.

LONDON: PRINTED FOR T. CADELL, JUN. AND W. DAVIES, IN THE STRAND. 1798.

Advice of the Popes who succeeded the Age of Rafael
Degrade first the Arts if you'd Mankind Degrade
Hire Idiots to Paint with cold light & hot shade:
Give high Price for the worst, leave the best in disgrace,
And with Labours of Ignorance fill every place.

FIG. 21 Frontispiece and title page of William Blake's copy of Sir Joshua Reynolds's *Works* (1798). By permission of the British Library.

reader talking back to the book; up to a point, he does fit it. The usual mode of his marginalia is step-by-step refutation, and his attitude is far from respectful. But there is more to it than that. In most of his marginalia he was following a program, a self-imposed discipline with a fixed method and clear goals.

Blake made his living in the publishing world as an engraver and had books around him all the time though he may not have owned many—all the more reason to treat them well.[13] The earliest known instance of his annotation is a copy of Lavater's *Aphorisms on Man* (1788), translated by Blake's friend Fuseli. Blake engraved the frontispiece after a drawing by Fuseli; it highlights the Greek motto ΓΝΩΘΙ ΣΕΑΥΤΟΝ, "Know Thyself." The epigraph on the title page quotes Juvenal's allusion to the same maxim, "e coelo descendit γνωθι σεαυτον" ("From heaven descended Know Thyself"). At the top of the first page of text Blake wrote his own name and a direction to future readers concerning his marginalia: "for the reason of these remarks see the last aphorism." Turn to the last aphorism, numbered 643, and you find this: "If you mean to know yourself, interline such of these aphorisms as affected you agreeably in reading, and set a mark to such as left a sense of uneasiness with you; and then shew your copy to whom you please" (224). Blake must have taken in this final aphorism before embarking on his annotation, which is thus the product not of a first reading but of a later one, and probably of more than one since some of the notes include second thoughts. Being Blake, he adapted the proposed system to meet his own needs. The recommendation calls only for marks, and those of only two kinds. "Interline" Blake understood to mean underline, which he duly did. In some cases he underlined the part of an aphorism that he approved of, without further comment. But most of the time he felt it necessary to add a written comment to explain or qualify his appreciation; and besides the X that he used as a mark of disapprobation he used the word suggested by the final aphorism, "uneasy," or something similar. Therefore many notes consist of a brief written judgment: "A golden sentence" (4), "Bravo" (26), "Would to God that every one would consider this" (102), "the best in the book" (114: "Keep him at three paces distant who hates bread, music, and the laugh of a child"), "True Christian philosophy" (124), "True Experience" (211), or alternatively, "Uneasy" (30), "Rather Uneasy" (35), "Uneasy I do not believe it" (61), "Not always" (70), "This I do not understand" (152), "Very Uneasy indeed but truth" (174). Half a dozen special cases call for an extended explanation of a particular point.

Blake loved this book: only that emotive word will do. He added his own name to the title page next to the author's and drew a heart around the two. At the end of the text he wrote a long note beginning, "I hope no one will call what I have written cavilling . . . For I write from the warmth of my heart, & cannot resist the impulse to rectify what I think wrong in a book I love so much, & approve so generally" (224). Under the circumstances, it is remarkable that he ever let it out of his hands, but the notes were made to be shown to others, and we know that Fuseli saw them. There is some evidence that he did the same for other annotated volumes, his copy of Thornton's translation of the Lord's Prayer having gone to Linnell and probably also to Palmer, and the annotated copies of Wordsworth having belonged to Crabb Robinson, who did not expect Blake to annotate his books but was pleased to find that he had.[14] Once in a while, Blake addresses the unknown reader directly, as when in the first page of notes to Watson he admonishes that person to "Read patiently take not up this Book in an idle hour" (title page verso). In the Reynolds he starts by pointing out that given his years of oppression under Reynolds, "The Reader must expect to Read in all my Remarks on these Books Nothing but Indignation & Resentment" (title page verso).

The essence of Blake's practice of annotation, then, was that he indicated approval or disapproval of parts of the text with a view to exhibiting the results to other people. The procedure itself was quite in keeping with the habits of his contemporaries. What seems unusual about it are first of all the sensational consequences when it was Blake who was thus let loose on books, and second the degree of self-consciousness informing the whole operation. The aphorism recommends the method "if you mean to know yourself." It does not say how marking up books was supposed to contribute to self-knowledge, nor why it should be important to involve others in the process. Presumably the owners would become more aware of their likes and dislikes, and be encouraged to adopt and reinforce a coherent position; but was any more spiritual purpose expected to be served? And why should it be necessary for them to *display* their opinions?

Blake's copy of the Royal Academy *Discourses* of Sir Joshua Reynolds, annotated by the same method as the Lavater but as much as twenty years later, gives an indication of what deliberate annotation did for Blake. On a blank page facing the opening of the eighth Discourse, he made the following declaration (1:244):

> Burkes Treatise on the Sublime & Beautiful is founded on the Opinions of Newton & Locke on this Treatise Reynolds has grounded many of his assertions in all his Discourses I read Burkes Treatise

> when very Young at the same time I read Locke on Human Understanding & Bacons Advancement of Learning on Every one of these Books I wrote my Opinions & on looking them over find that my Notes on Reynolds in this Book are exactly Similar. I felt the Same Contempt & Abhorrence then; that I do now. They mock Inspiration & Vision Inspiration & Vision was then & now is & I hope will always Remain my Element my Eternal Dwelling place how can I then hear it Contemned without returning Scorn for Scorn—

Remembering that this statement was composed for others to see, we may be better equipped to understand the value of the discipline of marginalia for Blake. He says that he wrote his opinions on Burke, Locke, and Bacon's *Advancement* when he was "very Young." These books are now lost, but Blake must have kept them by him because he claims to have been able to compare those early notes with the present copy of Reynolds, and to observe with gratification that his opinion about the position that the whole group represented to him had not changed. If he did indeed annotate those books before the Lavater, then he was already using a version of the system advocated in Lavater before he read about it there; but perhaps he thought of his thirty-two-year-old self as "very Young" by the time he was fifty. It does not really matter whether he learned the system from Lavater's *Aphorisms* or developed it independently. What is interesting is the firm conviction that consistency of opinion over time is a good thing, a sign of personal integrity—and that marginalia could be used to test that integrity.

Whatever the intent of the advice in Lavater was and whatever the psychological benefit of writing marginalia might be for Blake, the *effect* of this way of approaching books is plain enough in the extant annotated books. Blake used his system of annotation to argue in favor of his own convictions, building up and defending a contrary position. He defined himself by opposition in most of his notes to books, even as he spoke up for opposition as a matter of principle in *The Marriage of Heaven and Hell:* "Opposition is True Friendship"; "Without Contraries is no progression" (*Writings,* 1:93, 77). In his copy of Berkeley's *Siris* only one section is annotated (203–41), and that is the part that has to do with the world-view of the ancients, to which Blake contrasts his version of Christianity: "What Jesus came to Remove was the Heathen or Platonic Philosophy which blinds the Eye of Imagination The Real Man" (241). Was it the only section he could find fault with? He did not forget about marks of approval; even his hostile response to Reynolds contains occasional pats on the back: "Here is an Acknowledgment of all that I could wish" (xxix), "Excellent" (16), "These are Fine & Just Notions" (89), etc. But overwhelmingly, his annotations are vigorously critical. This is the quality we cherish in them, and perhaps the quality his friends enjoyed—the exhibition of no-holds-barred antagonism. The best examples are his copies of Bacon's *Essays*, Watson's *Apology for the Bible*, and Reynolds's *Discourses*. All three authors represented positions of worldly power and authority closed to Blake and at odds, he thought, with the precepts of Christianity. They were "The Hirelings of Kings & Courts," as he said in Bacon (xii), and difficult to deal with because as far as he could tell they were all hypocrites. The first two books contain no signs of approval whatever; Blake hated them comprehensively. His marginalia, however, were not, or mostly not, impulsive expressions of exasperation dashed off at first sight, but rather parts of a methodical debate worked out over time and designed to sway an audience. Blake evidently returned to these books with new notes after the first series had been written, and the first series itself, anticipating passages yet to come, shows signs of having been composed after preliminary reconnoitering. The following brief account of these volumes is intended to show the regularity of Blake's method and to convey the characteristic tone of his marginalia.

Bacon's *Essays* was for Blake a fairly straightforward case of a corrupt politician's Machiavellian approach to life. On the title page, Blake inserts a subtitle: these are *Essays Moral, Economical and Political* or "Good Advice for Satan's Kingdom" (according to Blake) by Francis Bacon. A general note on the half-title page introduces the themes of his commentary and invites the reader to choose between Bacon and God:

> Is it true or is it False that the Wisdom of this World is Foolishness with God

> This is Certain If what Bacon says Is True what Christ says Is False If Caesar is right Christ is Wrong both in Politics & Religion, since they will divide them in Two

Throughout the book, brief judgments of particular passages reinforce the ideas of wisdom's seeming folly and truth's seeming falsehood, and vice versa: "False O Satan" (8), "A Lie" (17), "This is Folly Itself" (22), "Nonsense" (62), and so on. What Bacon affirms, Blake contradicts. On p. 85, for example, when Bacon advises the traveler that the acquaintance most profitable to him will be "acquaintance with the secretaries and employed men of ambassadors," Blake scoffs, "Acquaintance with Knaves"; and on the same page the observation—one might think, a truism—that "It is a miserable state of mind to have few things to desire, and many things to fear," meets the retort, "He who has few things to desire cannot have many to fear." And when Bacon, writing about "The True Greatness of Kingdoms and Estates" disparages "sedentary and within-door arts" in favor of "strong and manly arts; as smiths, masons, carpenters, &c. not reckoning professed soldiers," Blake is stung to protest: "Bacon calls Intellectual Arts Unmanly Poetry Painting Music are in his Opinion Useless & so they are for Kings & Wars & shall in the End Annihilate them" (143–44). Blake is predictably hostile to all praise of kings. Is "public envy" directed against officers and ministers, sparing the monarch? "A Lie," says Blake, "Every Body hates a King" (38). To Bacon's advice that princes ought to keep some military power close to them "for the repression of seditions in their beginnings" Blake responds, "Contemptible Knave Let the People look to this" (74; Fig. 22). When Bacon observes that ancient kings and some present ones "were wont to put great trust in eunuchs," Blake asks "because Kings do it is it Wisdom" (203).

As these samples suggest, Blake's more extended remarks demonstrate careful reading and a diametrically opposed way of thinking. We do not look to him for sympathetic exposition or a balanced estimate. Why did he persist with a book that he did not like or trust? Partly, it seems, because it represented an opportunity to develop his own ideas—the self-knowledge associated with Lavater. The important essay "Of Truth" elicits both brief comments and a firm counterstatement that is carefully positioned ahead of Bacon's text. At first sight it seems that Blake is willfully unfair to Bacon, but upon consideration, we can see that there really was a radical difference between them. "What is truth? said jesting Pilate, and would not stay for an answer," is the well-known opening of the essay. Bacon goes on to reflect on why it should be that people avoid the quest for truth: because they don't want to be tied down; because it is difficult to ascertain truth; because of "a natural, though corrupt love of the lie itself." The "masques, and mummeries, and triumphes of the world" show better by candlelight than by the "naked and open daylight" of truth (1). Blake might have been expected to approve of the position and of the metaphor; Bacon appears to be advocating an unworldly simplicity and directness. But Blake says, "What Bacon calls Lies is Truth itself"; and he outlines a contrary position in a counterstatement of his own, picking up some of Bacon's words and ideas (1):

> Self Evident Truth is one Thing and Truth the result of Reasoning is another Thing Rational Truth is not the Truth of Christ but of Pilate It is the Tree of the Knowledge of Good & Evil

The trouble with Bacon's position is that he considers truth only as the product of searching and reasoning. As far as Blake is concerned, self-evident truth is of a different order. It immediately commands belief and, if intuitive, cannot be the love of a lie. Perhaps it was out of prejudice against Bacon's office that Blake opposed him in the first place, but having adopted the role of opposition, he carries it out thoughtfully and not simply by random abuse.

Watson's *Apology for the Bible*, which Blake annotated in 1798 (probably the same year as the Bacon), is a more complicated case. Apprehensive about the spread of revolutionary sentiment in Britain, Watson composed his book in the form of letters addressed to Paine, refuting Part Two of Paine's deistical *Age of Reason*. As he reveals in a

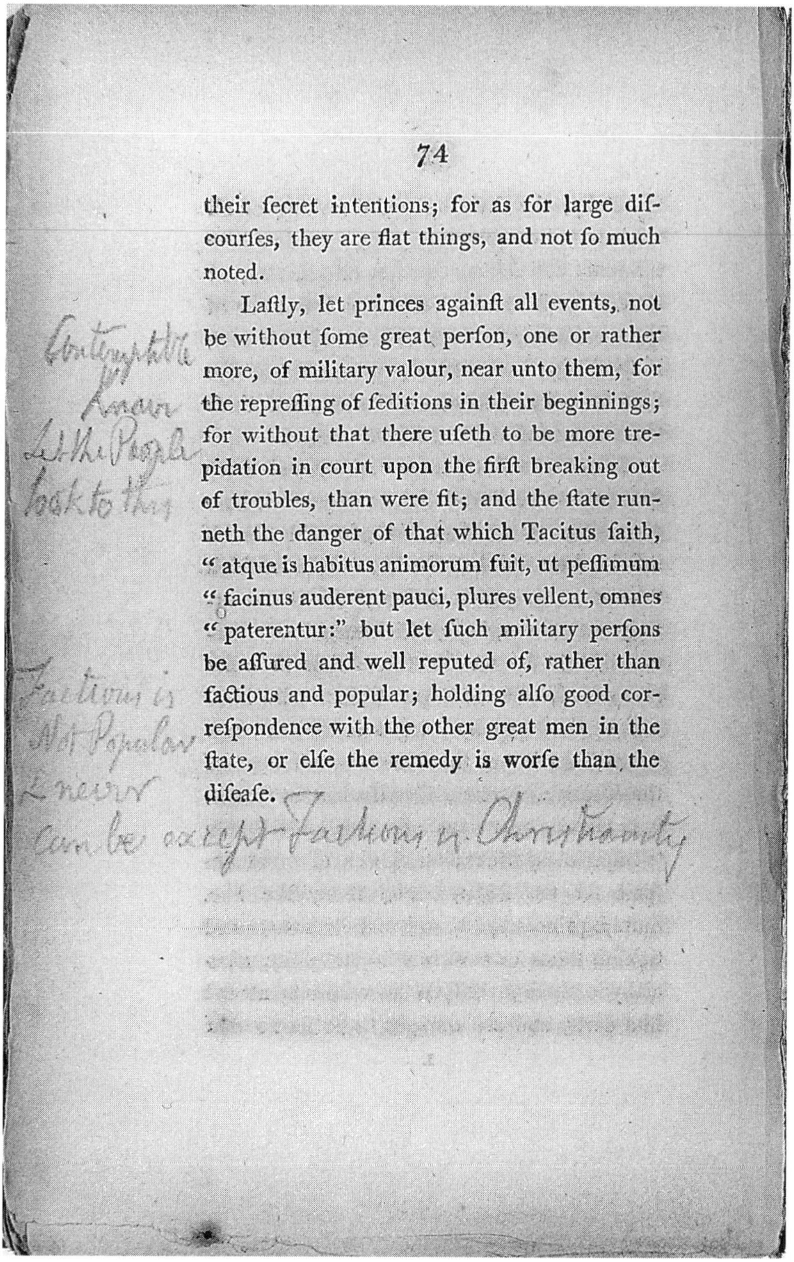
74

their ſecret intentions; for as for large diſcourſes, they are flat things, and not ſo much noted.

Laſtly, let princes againſt all events, not be without ſome great perſon, one or rather more, of military valour, near unto them, for the repreſſing of ſeditions in their beginnings; for without that there uſeth to be more trepidation in court upon the firſt breaking out of troubles, than were fit; and the ſtate runneth the danger of that which Tacitus ſaith, "atque is habitus animorum fuit, ut peſſimum "facinus auderent pauci, plures vellent, omnes "paterentur:" but let ſuch military perſons be aſſured and well reputed of, rather than factious and popular; holding alſo good correſpondence with the other great men in the ſtate, or elſe the remedy is worſe than the diſeaſe.

Contemptible Knave Let the People look to this

Faction is Not Popular & never Can be except Faction in Christianity

FIG. 22 Notes by William Blake in a copy of Francis Bacon's *Essays* (1798). By permission of the Syndics of Cambridge University Library.

OF ATHEISM.

I HAD rather believe all the fables in the legend, and the Talmud, and the Alcoran than that this univerſal frame is without a mind: and, therefore, God never wrought miracle to convince atheiſm, becauſe his ordinary works convince it. It is true that a little philoſophy inclineth man's mind to atheiſm; but depth in philoſophy bringeth men's minds about to religion; for while the mind of man looketh upon ſecond cauſes ſcattered, it may ſometimes reſt in them and go no farther; but when it beholdeth the chain of them confederate and linked together, it muſt needs fly to providence and Deity: nay, even that ſchool which is moſt accuſed of atheiſm, doth moſt demonſtrate religion; that is, the ſchool of Leucippus, and Democritus, and Epicurus: for it is a thouſand times more credible, that four mutable elements and one immutable fifth eſſence, duly and eternally placed, need no God, than that an army of infinite ſmall portions, or ſeeds unplaced, ſhould have produced this order and beauty without a divine marſhal.

passage at the end of the book, Watson's expected audience was "the merchants, manufacturers, and tradesmen of the kingdom" and "such of the youth of both sexes as may have imbibed, from your writings, the poison of infidelity" (119–20). To enlist the sympathy of this middle-class readership Watson relied on an urbanely reasonable tone and coded warnings about the "intemperance," greed, profligacy, and bad behavior of the lower classes ([i]). Blake was furious, and as usual he nailed his colors to the mast. At the beginning of the book he wrote firmly, "Paine has not Attacked Christianity Watson has defended Antichrist" ([i]), and at the end, "I have read this Book with attention & find that the Bishop has only hurt Paines heel while Paine has broken his head the Bishop has not answered one of Paines grand objections" (120). Blake's difficulty was that he could not wholeheartedly support Paine and was therefore obliged to engage in combat with both sides at once, though Watson took the brunt of the attack.

In this case, rather than spreading short notes evenly through the text as he did for Lavater and Bacon, Blake concentrated his campaign in a number of long notes in the first twenty-five pages, with just scattered comments thereafter. This strategy enabled him to address fundamental differences and to establish his contrary position early on, in such a way that it would be impossible for a later reader to accept Watson's subsequent arguments without question. A crucial issue is Watson's honesty. How trustworthy a guide is he? I quote the first notes to the first Letter as representative of Blake's style in general:

> If this first Letter is written without Railing & Illiberality I have never read one that is. To me it is all Daggers & Poison the sting of the serpent is in every Sentence as well as the glittering Dissimulation
>
> Achilles' wrath is blunt abuse Thersites' sly insinuation Such is the Bishops If such is the characteristic of a modern polite gentleman we may hope to see Christs discourses Expung'd
>
> I have not the Charity for the Bishop that he pretends to have for Paine. I believe him to be a State trickster ([1])

Blake comes back several times to proofs of Watson's hypocrisy, effectively discrediting his smooth appearance of civility. In a passage that must have provided Blake with the key terms "Railing & Illiberality" for the note I have just quoted, which appears earlier in the volume, Watson disdains Paine's rough methods:

> A philosopher in search of truth forfeits with me all claim to candour and impartiality, when he introduces railing for reasoning, vulgar and illiberal sarcasm in the room of argument. I will not imitate the example you set me; but examine what you produce, with as much coolness and respect, as if you had given the priests no provocation; as if you were a man of the most unblemished character, subject to no prejudices, actuated by no bad designs, not liable to have abuse retorted upon you with success.

Blake's underlining catches Watson out: coolness and respect could not have produced these insinuations about Paine's character. "Is not this Illiberal" Blake demands of later readers, "has not the Bishop given himself the lie in the moment the first words were out of his mouth Can any man who writes so pretend that he is in a good humour. Is not this the Bishops cloven foot, has he not spoild the hasty pudding" (9).

Watson's credibility disposed of, Blake goes on to address profound differences in outlook between them. What do we mean by "Christianity"? By "the Bible"? By "conscience"? By "miracle"? By "prophet"? Blake challenges Watson's (and in some cases Paine's) conceptions and reasoning on every one of these matters. To take just one example, on the use of miracles as a test of the validity of a religion and specifically as proof of the validity of Christianity—a matter of heated contemporary debate—Blake writes a complicated but under the circumstances a remarkably concise note, pointing out problems of definition and taking on Paine and Watson at once. Paine professed not to believe in miracles; Watson insisted that Christ worked miracles but that other claims to miracle-working were impostures. Blake boldly maintains that Paine himself had worked miracles, indeed that we all do, if we understand the meaning of "miracle" correctly.

> Jesus could not do miracles where unbelief hindered hence we must conclude that the man who holds miracles to be ceased puts it out of his own power to ever witness one The manner of a miracle being performed is in modern times considered as an arbitrary command of the agent upon the patient but this is an impossibility not a miracle neither did Jesus ever do such a miracle. Is it a greater miracle to feed five thousand men with five loaves than to overthrow all the armies of Europe with a small pamphlet. look over the events of your own life & if you do not find that you have both done such miracles & lived by such you do not see as I do True I cannot do a miracle thro experiment & to domineer over & prove to others my superior power as neither could Christ But I can & do work such as both astonish & comfort me & mine How can Paine the worker of miracles ever doubt Christs in the above sense of the word miracle But how can Watson ever believe the above sense of a miracle who considers it as an arbitrary act of the agent upon an unbelieving patient whereas the Gospel says that Christ could not do a miracle because of Unbelief
>
> If Christ could not do miracles because of Unbelief the reason alledged by Priests for miracles is false for those who believe want [i.e., need] not to be confounded by miracles Christ & his Prophets & Apostles were not Ambitious miracle mongers (12–14)

Prompted by Paine and Watson, this note represents Blake's marginalia at their best. It is a serious attempt to reason through an independent position on a question of the greatest public as well as private consequence. Had it been only for his own use, as a means of achieving self-knowledge, it would have been a worthwhile exercise; but as the use of the second person "you" reminds us (for it cannot refer either to Paine or to Watson), the notes were written for the benefit of other people as well.

Reynolds's *Discourses* consists of occasional addresses delivered at the Royal Academy of Arts during Reynolds's term as president (1768–92), which included the period in which Blake studied and exhibited at the Academy (1779–85). An introductory note by Blake, quoted earlier, alerts readers to expect personal hostility in his reactions to "Sr Joshua & his Gang of Cunning Hired Knaves" whose success he believed had been won at the expense of true artists like himself, Barry, Mortimer, and Fuseli (title page verso). And there is hostility aplenty in the crowded pages of this volume. On the one side there are, as Blake sees it, the true artists, individualistic and proud; on the other the hypocrites and sycophants who pander to rich philistines: "Such Artists as Reynolds are at all times Hired by the Satans for the Depression of Art A Pretence of Art: To destroy Art" (Discourses [ii]).[15] When Reynolds praises Blake's deities Michelangelo and Raphael instead of his usual favorites Titian, Rubens, and the Venetians, Blake has to suppose he was lying for some political end (Discourses [ii]). His personal frustration is transparent again and again, as when he observes that "The Enquiry in England is not whether a Man has Talents & Genius But Whether he is Passive & Polite & a Virtuous Ass & obedient to Noblemens Opinions in Art & Science. If he is, he is a Good Man: If Not he must be Starved" ([5]). When Reynolds points out that "To give advice to those who are contending for royal liberality, has been for some years the duty of my station in the Academy," Blake responds indignantly, "Liberality! we want not Liberality We want a Fair Price & Proportionate Value & a General Demand for Art" (Dedication ii). Even when Blake grudgingly expresses admiration for an idea or expression in the text, he tends to turn it into a complaint that Reynolds is contradicting himself, thereby proving that he is weak and wanting in self-knowledge, unlike Blake himself: "The Man Either Painter or Philosopher who Learns or Acquires all he Knows from Others Must be full of Contradictions" (xlii). Or else he supposes that someone else must have written that passage for him (97).

Blake is bitter and amusing about Reynolds, who comes to stand for all his professional enemies. He writes sarcastic headnotes to several of the discourses, for example, "The Purpose of the following discourse is to Prove That Taste & Genius are not of Heavenly Origin & that all who have Supposed that they Are so, are to be Considerd as Weak headed Fanatics" ([188]). But as in the Watson and Bacon, most of the marginalia display a shrewd recognition of important differences of opinion and of the reasons for those differences. They argue principles. The marginalia that take up aesthetic and technical issues are of special interest because we are now inclined to value Blake as an original artist more highly than Reynolds. Therefore we are disposed to take these notes seriously and not to dismiss the writer as a paranoid failure.

The circumstances under which the discourses were delivered more or less obliged Reynolds to promote the teaching of art and consequently to play down the importance of natural genius and "inspiration." The Academy was providing professional training. Reynolds attempted to analyze the elements of commercially successful painting, hence his emphasis on the general and the sublime, and on harmony of coloring. Blake predictably resisted the idea that practically anyone could learn to paint and attacked Reynolds's rhapsodies about color (Blake describes Rubens's shadows as "of a Filthy Brown somewhat of the Colour of Excrement" [135]). His opposition to Reynolds on the issues of the general and the sublime are more surprising, given what we know of Blake's values and of the characteristics of his art. But Blake insists on the importance of the particular as opposed to the general, reversing Reynolds's maxims in a thought-provoking way. To Reynolds's declaration that "the minute accidental discriminations of particular and individual objects" are incompatible with "that grand style of painting, which improves partial representation by the general and invariable ideas of nature," Blake offers a counterposition: "Minute Discrimination is Not Accidental All Sublimity is founded on Minute Discrimination" (9). Reynolds's statement that "instead of endeavouring to amuse mankind with the minute neatness of his imitations, he [the genuine painter] must endeavour to improve them by the grandeur of his ideas" is matched by Blake's "Without Minute Neatness of Execution The Sublime cannot Exist: Grandeur of Ideas is founded on Precision of Ideas" (52). And when Reynolds asserts, "There is a rule, obtained out of general nature, to contradict which is to fall into deformity," Blake asks, "What is General Nature is there Such a Thing what is General Knowledge is there such a Thing Strictly Speaking All Knowledge is Particular" (61). He rejects Reynolds's civilized proposition that disagreement between thinkers might be merely a matter of "inaccuracy of terms," together with the implication that compromise might be possible—"It is not in Terms that Reynolds & I disagree Two Contrary Opinions can never by any Language be made Alike" (198)—and forces the observer to take sides. Here we see a reader disposed to find fault, finding fault and in the process articulating a strong position of his own, partly for his own satisfaction, partly for the correction of error in others, and partly for the enlightenment of a friendly audience.

The effect of Blake's system of annotation was to make manuscript marginalia an integral part of the book and thus to *publish* his quarrel with the author as the book circulated. Though one of Blake's notes to Watson says, "I have been commanded from Hell not to print this as it is what our Enemies wish" (title page verso), limited circulation in manuscript was not incompatible with a prohibition on printing. If Blake could not print, he could nevertheless adopt this alternative form of publication, which is analogous in some ways to his method of controlled distribution for the "illuminated" poems. It is clear that he knew what he was doing. Several title pages or notes preliminary to the text introduce Blake as a participant, like a co-author or approved commentator: "Will. Blake" in these volumes is not just an ownership inscription. The long introductory note in Watson begins, "Notes on the B of L's Apology for the Bible | by William Blake" (title page verso); its counterpart in Bacon reads, "I am astonished how such Contemptible Knavery & Folly as this Book contains can ever have been call'd Wisdom by Men of Sense, but perhaps this was never the Case & all Men of Sense have despised the Book as much as I do | Per William Blake" (i). The first note in Reynolds, on the title page and facing the frontispiece portrait, likewise throws down a gauntlet: "This Man was Hired to Depress Art This is the Opinion of Will Blake my Proofs of this Opinion are given in the following Notes" (Fig. 21). The heart encircling the names of Blake and Lavater on the title page of the *Aphorisms* serves both as a gesture of affection and as a statement of joint authorship.

The idea that Blake designed his marginalia as a form of publication is supported also by the care that he took over the layout and visual effect of his notes. As G. Ingli James observes in his Introduction to the facsimile edition of Watson, conventional letterpress publication would not only have left Blake liable to prosecution but would have required a different kind of composition and entailed various compromises that Blake chose not to make (i–ii). Instead of notes at the front and back of the book and on the side of the page, he would have had to produce a separate tract like Paine's and Watson's and have entered into that sort of public controversy. The composition techniques used for modern editions, including the quotations in this book, distort Blake's notes, especially by running on lines and by making punctuation a problem. His hand is clear and in marginal notes he is able to use line-breaks or capital letters in lieu of punctuation (Fig. 22). Print publication introduces ambiguity and makes Blake's writing appear more eccentric than it actually is. In the context of reading practices of the period, Blake is hardly eccentric at all: he talked back to his books and, like certain other readers, he took steps to disseminate his opinions in a form of manuscript publication.

BOOKS TO SHARE

Though Blake at first sight appears, in his annotated books, to be merely responding to the author and forming his own opinions in opposition, we can see that he also represents another very common use of marginalia during the period, namely, the circulation of manuscript notes as a way of disseminating personal opinions. Lackington himself claimed to have once filled an interleaved Bible with infidel arguments so as to seduce others away from religion. On the other side of the religious fence, William Wilberforce marked a copy of John Swete's *Family Prayers* to indicate prayers that he specifically endorsed and passages that might be better omitted, with a general note to those who would be using it: "Many passages in ye follow^g^ prayers may be profitably used by Individ^ls^. To spare my weak Eyes, I do not alter them—" (21). Though the device may have been especially attractive to Dissenters of various kinds—John Lidwill, William George Thompson, John Lawrence, and W. Davis the Tinker, discussed separately elsewhere in this book, come to mind—it was certainly not confined to those circles. Horace Walpole and Hester Piozzi did it too.

At a time when high prices and relative scarcity meant that there was a regular traffic in books borrowed and lent out among friends (and friends of friends), good manuscript notes were seen as value added to the exchange. Many books with readers' notes therefore reveal either through the content of the notes or through inscriptions that the notes were meant to be shared, usually with someone in particular. Blake is in a minority among these sharing readers in that he seems not to have had a specific recipient in mind as he wrote his notes, only a general idea of controlled circulation. The more typical practice of writing for a special friend was especially common among middle-class women who had the education, money, and leisure to devote to these customized gifts or loans, and who cherished tokens of friendship, though it was certainly not restricted to them. There is also a substantial subset of books exchanged by courting couples.

Though the latter, lower-case "romantic" category includes some of the great names of Romantic literature, there was nothing new or original in lovers' choosing to communicate with one another through the medium of books, and their messages to one another, however personal, follow well-established conventions. It is striking that in all the extant examples I have seen of heterosexual courtship though marginalia, the annotator is the man, offering guidance through his notes to the woman. The pattern is reflected in fiction. When the strong-minded heroine of Mary Brunton's popular *Self-Control* resolved to give up an unworthy suitor, she "banished from her port-folio the designs he had made for her drawings, destroyed the music from which he had accompanied her, and effaced from her books the marks of his pencil" (1:45). While it is possible that the men's notes remain because women were more likely to preserve such gifts, or that the books survived because the men became famous, it is also true that it was socially more acceptable for the man to lead. Jacqueline Pearson documents the dominance of men as readers aloud, in fiction and in nonfiction of the period, with P. B. Shelley as a prime example (98–99, 172–93). On the other hand, she also records some signs of women's challenging the norm by an equal exchange, including Harriet Westgrove's response to Shelley's present of a novel condoning sexual union without marriage—she sent him Opie's *Adeline Mowbray*, a monitory tale said to have been inspired by the sad history of Mary Wollstonecraft (99).[16]

To begin with an everyday example, William Mudford's didactic novel *Nubilia in Search of a Husband*, which I have mentioned before, was annotated by a man, probably A. Urquhart, wooing "a certain fair reader" about 1812 (194). He may have had the book for some time and have read it more than once: a layer of marks and subject-headings probably antedates the longer and more sprightly notes intended for his friend. On her behalf he explains some classical allusions and offers his opinion chapter by chapter in quite extensive critical commentary; he also picks out certain details for her later attention. In the more general remarks he presents himself as a reliable guide and as a companion ready to compare his impressions with hers; for instance, at the end of the first chapter, which deals with the education of Nubilia after the death of her mother, he observes,

> In this chapter there is too much minuteness on the subject of education. It is not possible for any father to present such a front of clock work regulations, as Nubilia's. He is too highly drawn to be natural, and every one knows that the character as above delineated is not very common. As to Nubilia herself, it is not likely that she could be so "all-accomplished" a woman, for this obvious reason, that I do not believe she had so all-accomplished a father. She appears a very good young woman, and well educated. Her father a very clever and elegant man—but not very extraordinary, either father or daughter. (29)

Urquhart's notes reveal growing irritation with the perfections of Nubilia, which he jokes about in the clear expectation of finding common ground with the other reader. Nubilia goes to visit Mary of Buttermere and is disappointed to find that she remains mostly silent and does not utter any "original remark" (326). Just as well, says Urquhart: "And probably if Mary had ventured 'one original remark' she would have incurred the imputation of being a forward young woman. There is no pleasing some people, and Nubilia is one of these fastidious creatures." Finally, he underlines or comments briefly on maxims that may have had particular relevance to their personal connection, such as the idea that there is no true friend to be found in the ranks of social life—a belief "as untrue," he hopes, "as it is illiberal" (365). The reference to the "fair reader" is attached to a passage on the benefits of marriage. In the real-life situation the friend chattily sharing a book is also a lover advancing his cause. All the time that she is reading the book in private, his notes will be before her almost as though she were reading it, thrillingly Paolo-and-Francesca-like, with him.

Coleridge is the most notorious of all writers of marginalia in English; he is sometimes described as incomparable in this genre, though that is generally in the absence of objects of comparison. Since books were always central to his life, he might have been expected to put them to work when he was courting. So he did. At the age of nineteen, he sent Mary Evans love-poems of his own composing and transcriptions of poems by Bowles, along with a volume of Gray's odes. His letters record similar acts of "gallantry" toward other young women about the same time.[17] In the early days of their marriage, he and his wife Sara certainly read together.[18] No annotated books survive as evidence of those early love affairs, however, and it is quite likely that Coleridge did not write in books then, unless it was a presentation inscription or presentation poem. He was rather a slow starter as a mutilator of books.[19] It was not until he was in his thirties that he began to make presents of books with more extensive notes, the first of them to Sara Hutchinson—Bartram's *Travels* with a restrained introductory note on the flyleaf, then works by Sir Thomas Browne from which Coleridge himself (apparently) chose a note to represent his marginalia when he finally published some of them, and finally a Chapman's Homer. His notes in two copies of Ritson's editions of old English songs that belonged to Wordsworth also appear to have been written with Sara Hutchinson—by then part of the Wordsworth household—in mind.[20] These books are very like the annotated *Nubilia*. Like Urquhart, Coleridge presents himself as a genial guide to his lady friend, pointing out good bits and glossing hard ones, and at the same time profiting by the occasion to remind her of his love. Even the innocuous-sounding note to Bartram is a case in point:

> This is not a Book of Travels, properly speaking; but a series of poems, chiefly descriptive, *occasioned* by the Objects, which the Traveller observed.—It is a *delicious* Book; & like all *delicious* things, you must take but a *little* of it at a time.—Was it not about this time of the year, that I read to you parts of the "Introduction" of this Book, when William & Dorothy had gone out to walk?—I remember the evening well, but not what time of the year it was.— (*Marginalia*, 1:227)

Here Coleridge is patently inviting Sara Hutchinson, every time she catches sight of this book on the shelf, to remember an evening they spent alone together and to cherish the memory just as he does: the book is a poignant souvenir.

Though they are often revealing and sometimes intensely personal, Coleridge's notes in books prepared for women to read are among his most conventional. Later recipients include Mary Morgan and her unmarried sister Charlotte Brent, Anne Gillman, and the young ladies of Highgate to whom he lent his Waverley novels.[21] A remarkable feature of the Browne annotated for Sara Hutchinson as also of a Shakespeare annotated for Mary Morgan and Charlotte Brent is Coleridge's censorship of indecent passages in such a way as to protect the ladies while allowing male readers to see what had been concealed. In the case of Browne, he crosses out the offending passage in the text but translates it into Latin in the margin; in the Shakespeare, indecorous suggestions in his own notes are communicated in Latin only.[22] There is no suggestion that any contemporary would have thought this procedure anything other than normal and considerate.

Byron on the other hand did a strange thing—not merely strange but decidedly unconventional—in at least two books associated with his mistress Teresa Guiccioli: the first note in each is in English, a language she could not read at the time.[23] In a copy of Staël's *Corinne*, he writes of his love for her, an intimate message that he did not want others to read. The book was hers, he would be able to translate his own words in person, and the writing itself would remain a memento for her. But the first note in Foscolo's *Ultime lettere di Jacopo Ortis* is different; it describes Byron's state of mind and his general opinion of the novel, but it introduces a series of notes in Italian. Did he do it unthinkingly? Did he do it because it was easier for him to write in English, and he knew that she would value anything in his hand? Did he do it as an incentive to her to learn English? He cannot have been unaware that the book would one day go to another owner, and that notes by him would be handed down to posterity; was this note for posterity? (Byron had already had the disagreeable experience of seeing marginal notes that he meant only friends to see unctuously referred to in print.[24]) The Foscolo is especially interesting because it seems to have been *planned* as a memento. Several notes, including the first one, are dated July 14, 1820—not only the anniversary of the Fall of the Bastille, but also the day on which Teresa was informed by letter that the Pope had granted her a decree of separation from her husband (1116n). All but the first of the notes are in Italian, some of them only brief comments accompanying marked passages, others quite extensive. I quote them here from the *Shelley Circle* translation. The editor expresses surprise that Byron shows so little sign of interest in political aspects of the book, but surely that is because it was being annotated for Teresa on a momentous day in her life. The hero loves "Teresa"—a fact that provides numerous opportunities for Byron to underline expressions of love for Teresa, hunger for her kisses, and so forth. This evidence of romantic attachment is enhanced, if anything, by Byron's sometimes cynical commentary: the novel was too spiritual for him. When the narrator rhapsodizes about kissing Teresa to the usual accompaniment of fragrant flowers, harmonious breezes, the music of distant streams, and the splendor of the moon, for instance, Byron's objection can be translated, "It would have been more natural to have thought more about the *kiss* and less about the '*flowers*' the '*breezes*' the '*streams*' the '*Moon*' &^{c} &^{c} &^{c} true Love does not require an *orchestra* of so many instruments—nor so numerous a chorus—a simple *duet* is enough" (1112).

Women also, on occasion, adopted the role of mentor and fond companion to friends both male and female. Their notes appealed to common interests and aimed to please without invoking the spell of sex. Henry Chorley describes Felicia Hemans's copy of Wordsworth's poems (current whereabouts unknown to me) as her "poetical breviary: there was scarcely a page that had not its mark of admiration or its marginal comment or illustration" (108). But that was a book of her own. He goes on to describe her approach to borrowed books:

> It was a habit with Mrs. Hemans, to illustrate her favourite books with the thoughts excited by their perusal, and with such parallel passages from other writers as bore upon their subject. If one of her intimate friends lent her a book which she chanced to *adopt*, it was sure to return thus enriched. I remember, in particular, that her copy of Mr. Auldjo's "Ascent of Mont Blanc"—which, fortunately, had the amplest of margins—was positively written over with snatches of description, and quotations of poetry, for some of which, I suspect, it would have been no more difficult to find their owner, than it was to assign the delightful fragments from "Old Plays," which headed the chapters of the Waverley novels, to their real source.

Here are brought together some of the activities described elsewhere in this book: the collection and application of "parallel passages," the notion of improvement by verbal "illustration," and the direct connection between reading and new composition. It is worth noting that Chorley places the "thoughts excited" while reading on a par with passages from other writers, and that he assumes that Hemans introduced some of her own verses in the guise of parallel passages, in books that would go from hand to hand in the circle of her acquaintance.

Hemans's annotated books seem not to have survived, but a sample of the work of a poet of an earlier generation suggests that her behavior was not unusual and that she was acting within well-established bounds. Anna Seward's copy of Cowper's *Task* contains many manuscript marks and much underlining and commentary, mostly in ink; one note is dated 1800 (205). They come in spurts, a few pages in a group, and were presumably assembled over time. Some of the notes are so long that they spill over from one page to the next; others deal quickly with "a very inharmonious line" or a confused metaphor—"a strange idea a paved chariot and the pavement Love!" (269). Like Hemans, Seward cites parallel passages from the work of other poets, including herself. Her purpose is critical judgment, both of the style and of the content of Cowper's poem; she is particularly attentive to its politics. Though this book was her own and there is no evidence of the identity of a specific person with whom the notes might have been intended to be shared, the occasional directive to "observe" this or that, and the expansiveness of the notes, implies the existence or at least the future possibility of a sympathetic audience.

Seward put an asterisk next to Cowper's lines "Time as he passes us, has a dove's wing, / Unsoiled and swift and of a silken sound," and commented thus (148–49):

> There is poetic beauty in that remark—but there is more genius in Young's observation—he presents an infinitely grander picture, with that striking & just contrast which Cowper has not given—observe—
>
> "Time, in advance, behind him hides his wings
> "And seems to creep decrepid with his age;
> "Behold him when passed by!—what then is seen
> "But his broad pinions, swifter than the winds!"

This sort of note is an improvement on parallel passages copied without comment, for it explains the point of the parallel (Young had a similar idea but did it better) and is part of a process of appreciation and assessment. Seward is also eloquent on political issues, from the attack on hunting ("I wish our King w[d.] attend to that just & true assertion" [260]) to the general tendency of Cowper's writing. *The Task* was published before the French Revolution but now, Seward says, Cowper would probably be branded a democrat. She makes her own position quite clear, notably in a long note on prisons, prompted by Cowper's reference to the Bastille as a "house of bondage worse than that of old / Which God avenged on Pharoah" (201):

> Cowper did not <u>then</u> foresee, that England w$^{d.}$ adopt, & by palsying her own laws, sanction Bastiles. Every Prison into w$^{h.}$ men are thrust at the arbitrary command of their fellow Creatures & where they may be immured thro' a length of years perhaps thro' life without being brought to trial, is a Bastile, in every respect except the name. The abuse of power w$^{h.}$ immediately succeeded on the suspension of the Habeas Corpus Act, & w$^{h.}$ has been continued thro' the intervening years, proves the sacrilege of that suspension. Miserable Men have languished in our Bastile since that guilty hour—& the just picture the Poet here draws is the lot of Englishmen to whom freedom was a birthright privilege. O worse than murderers are they who have destroyed it
>
> "tho' with <u>necessity</u> the tyrants plea
> "They clothe their Devilish deeds

The lines from Milton that cap Seward's outburst in this case have nothing to do with comparison of styles; they reinforce the idea of a liberal poetic tradition—Milton, Cowper, Seward—opposed to repressive governments. In this case an annotated volume may be a vehicle for sharing strong feelings that—like Coleridge's and Byron's amours—could not be given free public expression.

HESTER PIOZZI

Hester Piozzi is the outstanding representative of all these sociable annotating readers. Many books with her annotations have survived, and though they are scattered, their general style may be sampled through published versions.[25] I therefore offer only a brief account of her activity, with a few examples, before going on to the even more prominent case of Keats. She was born in 1741 to a well-established family in Wales. Something of a prodigy, she learned French, Spanish, Italian, and Latin as a child and picked up some Greek and Hebrew later. She always had books about her; Johnson advised her and her first husband on their library. In her second marriage she became an author, publishing poems, travels, memoirs of Johnson and an edition of her correspondence with him, and a world history. Though she is best known for her reminiscences of Johnson and his circle, her most characteristic (and independent) work is *British Synonymy: or an Attempt at Regulating the Choice of Words in Familiar Conversation* (1794), which conveys her delight in colloquial language and is full of jokes and anecdotes. The reviewers tended to make fun of her as a blue-stocking; London society shunned her after she married her daughters' music-master; she carried on regardless.

Piozzi seems to have written in her books all her life, though for a long time she thought she ought not to: in a diary entry of 1790 she wrote, "I have a Trick of writing in the Margins of my Books, it is not a good Trick, but one longs to say something . . . " (*Thraliana*, 780). A lively mind—apparently to the end, and she lived to be eighty, having outlived her first husband by forty years—and a renowned hostess, she cultivated friendship by sharing books, as women of her class often did. At some point after 1790, she ceased to be squeamish about writing marginalia. She gave away some of her annotated books as gifts and began deliberately to make up annotated copies for particular friends: both Sir James Fellowes and William Augustus Conway, for example, were given annotated copies of three of her own books and Nathaniel Wraxall's *Historical Memoirs of My Own Time* (1815), besides other books appropriate to them individually.[26] Her change of attitude may have had something to do with having become a published writer and celebrity herself, for she could then be confident that notes in her hand would be prized by association. She certainly valued the marginalia of others: John Broster of Chester, to whom she gave an annotated copy of Samuel Pegge's *Anecdotes of the English Language*, records being shown a copy of the Johnson-Steevens edition of Shakespeare with manuscript notes by "Johnson Garrick Kemble Piozzi &c" when he first paid a visit to Piozzi in Wales (Pegge, −2). The sale catalogue of her library, which was auctioned off by Broster in 1823, records dozens of books with "MS. notes," "MS. notes by Mrs. Piozzi," or "Enriched by MS. Marginal Notes." There were still more to be picked up in 1836 when the collection of her adopted son followed: "Many of the Books are illustrated with curious Notes, by the late Mrs. Piozzi" (*Brynbella*).

Piozzi in the first instance talked back to the book when she was reading or else indulged in her own reflections—that is, talked to herself. (This appears to be true whether or not she was writing with a specific future reader in mind, though when she was, she added personal notes for that reader: "Coptic Mythology at last comes in as an Auxiliary you see—will it help me to endure the Absence of Mr. Conway?"[27]) She chats with books, seeming to prompt them with little signs of attention—"yes, certainly," "so he always said," "a beautiful letter," and so on—and from time to time becomes more expansive. The commonest kinds of notes are linguistic speculation, reminiscence, and anecdote; the mental process they reveal is not logical but associative progression—again, like conversation. She is fond of puns and bons mots. In Pegge, a book about Cockney English that must have appealed to her in several ways, she provides an example to substantiate the author's account of the pronunciation "curous" for "curious" and "curosity" for "curiosity" (53):

> Yes, a Cockney giving his evidence against a Prisoner in a Case of Murder and pronouncing so; The adverse Council says, my Lords we must not mind this Man he is murdering the Kings English himself—No No replied the Judge it does not amount to Murder he has only knocked an I / eye out.—

And given the substitution of "regiment" for "regimen," she notes, "I remember a Friend who talking of the Regimen prescribed to him by Heberden, said he was advised to drink only Water. That is my true Regiment said he—Yes replied I—the Coldstream" (60).

Piozzi's books, like Walpole's, convey an impression of the age through gossip and anecdote. Her notes seem to me more various, more surprising, and better natured than his; there is really no telling what might catch her attention. Sir William Forbes's *Account of the Life and Writings of James Beattie . . . Including Many of his Original Letters*, which she annotated in 1807, refers to many people whom she had known, so she writes notes agreeing or disagreeing with Beattie's opinions: Beattie for instance thinks Boswell meant no harm, but Piozzi writes, "I am not convinc'd of any such Thing. Boswell meant to gain Attention; whether by giving Pain or Pleasure he car'd not. Like the Children Rousseau tells of who speak & act all from y[e] Motive of Pourvu qu'on s'occupe d'eux" (2:382). She deals mildly with the views Beattie held, now publicly revealed, about her and her first husband. In a letter of 1781 Beattie claimed that everybody said Thrale should have left Johnson two hundred pounds a year, not just two hundred pounds, but Piozzi observes, "I did not know, till I read this, that any body said so" (2:267). And when, in reference to her second marriage, Beattie says, "I thought her indeed one of the most agreeable women I ever saw; and could not have imagined her capable of acting so unwise a part as she afterwards did," she replies with detached restraint, "no less likely to be unwise sure, for having been pretty and agreeable" (3:49). But her notes in this book also identify figures who are not named in the text, express views on literary matters, and comment expertly on word usage. Her reactions are by no means predictable.

A marvelous example of Piozzi's activity is the *Imperial Family Bible* that she annotated in 1819–21, as the inscription tells us, for the mother of her friend Conway, Susanna Rudd, who was sometimes her landlady at Clifton. This huge folio Bible, over 1,200 pages of double-columned text with only perfunctory commentary, exercised most of Piozzi's skills, including her talent for friendship. To make up the deficiencies of the printed notes, she sought explanations in other editions and commentaries that could be incorporated into this one. Like the annotators discussed in Chapter 1, she copied and transferred materials from one book to the other. She did not proceed systematically, however: some sections are quite heavily annotated, others not at all. In almost every case, she personalized the information as she conveyed it, putting her own stamp on it. She loved to show off her languages, so she often comments on Greek and Hebrew sources, but will temper the display of learning with topical references and anecdotes. Jacob's vision in Genesis 28, for instance, prompts a complicated note on "the Stone Deities Betylia, mention'd by Sanconiathon in his Fragment, & known to the Learned World," and going on through "Bethel Stones, βαιτυλος [*baitylos*] quae nigrae sunt, et rotundae [which are black and round]—says Pliny & there was a black Stone at Strawberry Hill in M^r. Walpole's Time, wch. I have heard Lysons—& Lloyd of Wygfair say—possess'd some extraordinary Qualities—but everybody is dead now 1820 except poor H: L: P." Though she may be pursuing her own train of thought she is also mindful of her audience, the reader who will be reading this Bible with her even after she is gone.

JOHN KEATS

Like Blake, Keats had not many books of his own. Those he had, he cherished and wrote in and bequeathed to his friends.[28] Like Blake again, he followed a basic method of annotation that he could adapt for particular cases. (In fact it is the same method that Blake found recommended by Lavater, a system of marking in which passages that give pleasure are underlined or set off with a vertical line in the margin, while those that make the reader uneasy are marked with a cross.) Like Byron and Coleridge, Keats enlisted marginalia to assist him in a love affair. In July 1820 he wrote to Fanny Brawne that he was "marking the most beautiful passages in Spenser, intending it for you," and when he left England for Italy he gave her some of his annotated books, notably a folio Shakespeare.[29] Like Hester Piozzi, he occasionally made presents to people of books that he had initially marked just for himself, a well-traveled example being the copy of the chivalric romance *Palmerin of England* in Southey's translation that he gave to one of the Hunt children.[30] In other ways, however, Keats's case is exceptional. It might be said to provide the supreme justification for every student who has ever gone to work with a yellow highlighter, for most of his marginalia are only highlighting, and yet his relatively small body of marginalia has had more attention—and *better,* more fruitful attention—from biographers and critics than any other (Fig. 23). This special status he owes partly to his own talent; partly to the intensely literary circle of his friends, who provided models, incentive, and publicity; and partly to literary scholarship.[31]

Several of the extant books with Keats's notes and markings actually belonged to other people—a Spenser to George Keats, for instance, and a Chaucer to Charles Cowden Clarke. But the owners, who also had the marking habit, encouraged him to write in their books. (George Keats marked "I Stood Tiptoe Upon a Little Hill" in his presentation copy in the same way as his brother marked his books, singling out especially fine passages [Lowell, 2:574–75]. The Chaucer, now in the British Library, contains Clarke's marks of approval as well as Keats's, and a penciled note that is evidence of shared reading: "Is not this perfectly beautiful dear Charles?" [11:148].) In other cases, friends made gifts to Keats of books with notes in them or added notes when the books came to them from him, so several contain the record of successive owners. The copy of Shakespeare's *Poetical Works* that Keats took with him to Italy had belonged to John Hamilton Reynolds, who had marked favorite passages and written a sonnet of his own composition at the back of the first volume. Keats contributed a version of "Bright Star," and Severn a third sonnet (Owings, 53). Keats's notes in the Milton that he gave to Maria Dilke were transcribed into at least two other copies (Lau, 15). In short, Keats's closest associates—his brother George, Hunt, Reynolds, Bailey, Brown, Clarke, Woodhouse, Lamb, Dilke, Severn—all valued good marginalia, routinely wrote in books themselves, and expected others to do the same.

The two most common practices in the group were the marking of fine passages and the introduction of original compositions. With as bookish a poet as Keats, these activities are of special interest. Biographers and biographical critics seeking to trace the sources of his inspiration have been active scrutinizing and analyzing the marked passages and reflecting on the creative process as they find parallels in Keats's own work. Original composition sparked by reading is an even more exciting phenomenon, but manuscript evidence in books has to be treated with some caution. In the context of sociable Romantic use of

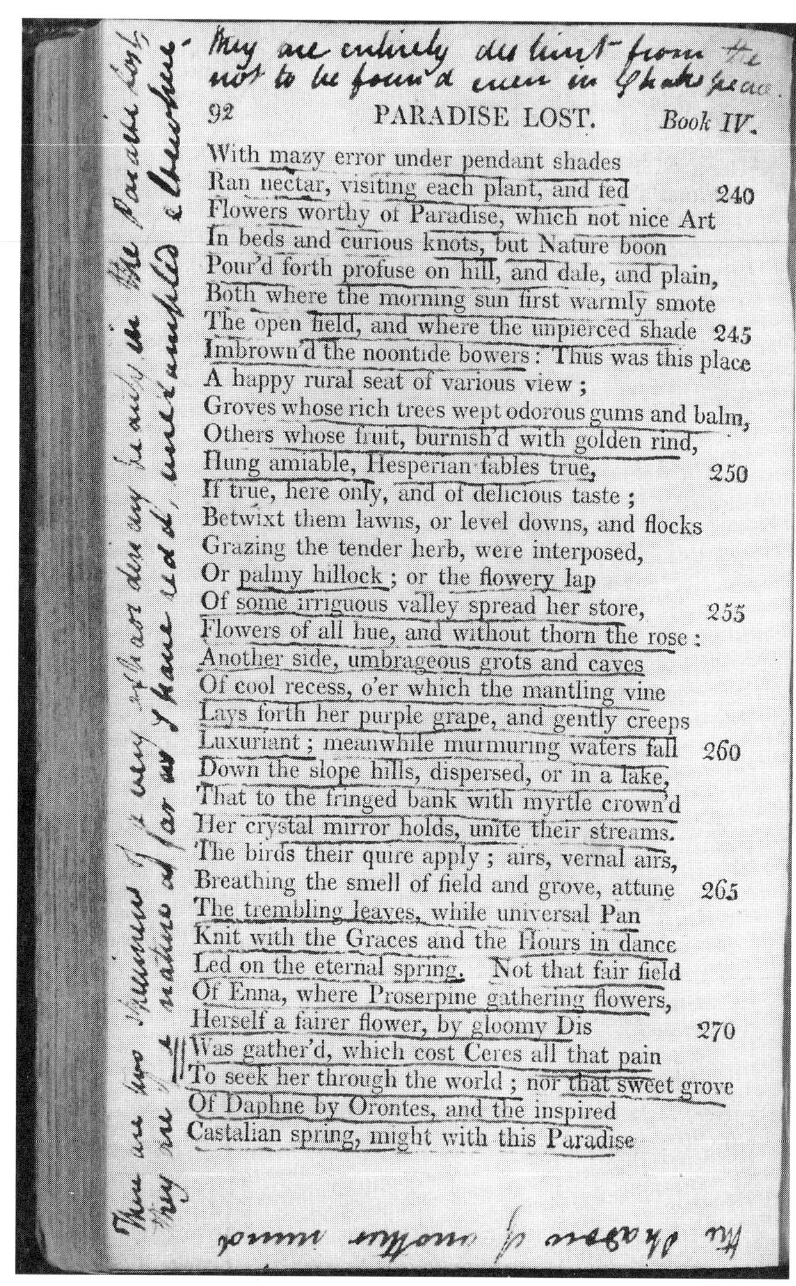

They are entirely distinct from the
not to be foun'd even in Shakespeare.

92 PARADISE LOST. Book IV.

With mazy error under pendant shades
Ran nectar, visiting each plant, and fed
Flowers worthy of Paradise, which not nice Art
In beds and curious knots, but Nature boon
Pour'd forth profuse on hill, and dale, and plain,
Both where the morning sun first warmly smote
The open field, and where the unpierced shade
Imbrown'd the noontide bowers: Thus was this place
A happy rural seat of various view;
Groves whose rich trees wept odorous gums and balm,
Others whose fruit, burnish'd with golden rind,
Hung amiable, Hesperian fables true,
If true, here only, and of delicious taste;
Betwixt them lawns, or level downs, and flocks
Grazing the tender herb, were interposed,
Or palmy hillock; or the flowery lap
Of some irriguous valley spread her store,
Flowers of all hue, and without thorn the rose:
Another side, umbrageous grots and caves
Of cool recess, o'er which the mantling vine
Lays forth her purple grape, and gently creeps
Luxuriant; meanwhile murmuring waters fall
Down the slope hills, dispersed, or in a lake,
That to the fringed bank with myrtle crown'd
Her crystal mirror holds, unite their streams.
The birds their quire apply; airs, vernal airs,
Breathing the smell of field and grove, attune
The trembling leaves, while universal Pan
Knit with the Graces and the Hours in dance
Led on the eternal spring. Not that fair field
Of Enna, where Proserpine gathering flowers,
Herself a fairer flower, by gloomy Dis
Was gather'd, which cost Ceres all that pain
To seek her through the world; nor that sweet grove
Of Daphne by Orontes, and the inspired
Castalian spring, might with this Paradise

FIG. 23 Notes and underlining by Keats in Milton's *Paradise Lost* (1807). By permission of the Corporation of London: London Metropolitan Archives, reference number K/BK/1/13.

brief pathos of Dante - and they are
- they are all according to the great

Book IV. PARADISE LOST. 93

Of Eden strive; nor that Nyseian isle,
Girt with the river Triton, where old Cham,
Whom Gentiles Ammon call, and Lybian Jove,
Hid Amalthea and her florid son
Young Bacchus, from his stepdame Rhea's eye;
Nor where Abassin kings their issue guard,
Mount Amara, though this by some supposed
True Paradise under the Ethiop line
By Nilus' head, inclosed with shining rock,
A whole day's journey high, but wide remote
From this Assyrian garden, where the fiend
Saw undelighted all delight, all kind
Of living creatures, new to sight and strange.
Two of far nobler shape, erect and tall,
Godlike erect, with native honour clad,
In naked majesty seem'd lords of all;
And worthy seem'd; for in their looks divine
The image of their glorious Maker shone,
Truth, wisdom, sanctitude severe and pure,
(Severe, but in true filial freedom placed),
Whence true authority in men; though both
Not equal, as their sex not equal seem'd;
For contemplation he and valour form'd,
For softness she, and sweet attractive grace;
He for God only, she for God in him.
His fair large front and eye sublime declared
Absolute rule; and hyacinthine locks
Round from his parted forelock manly hung
Clustering, but not beneath his shoulders broad:
She, as a veil, down to the slender waist
Her unadorned golden tresses wore
Dishevell'd, but in wanton ringlets waved
As the vine curls her tendrils, which implied
Subjection, but required with gentle sway,
And by her yielded, by him best received,
Yielded with coy submission, modest pride,

books, the introduction of poems in manuscript may be a poetic tribute inspired by the book and made to appear as impromptu as possible, or simply the sort of "filing" described in Chapter 1, where like text attracts like extract—or something in between, the filing of a tribute composed or discovered elsewhere. The verse tribute was a recognized minor genre, a species of society verse and a staple of the newspapers and magazines under such titles as "Lines written in a copy of ——" or "On Reading——." Collective editions often included them by way of introduction, as we print extracts from favorable reviews as puffs. The Hunt circle turned out many poems of this kind, tributes to favorite authors and to one another. Woodhouse wrote the draft of a sonnet "To Apollo—written after reading Sleep & Poetry" in one of his volumes of Keats. Keats himself wrote a fair copy of a sonnet about "The Flower and the Leaf," a medieval dream allegory then attributed to Chaucer, in Clarke's book, signing it with his initials and dating it February 1817 (12:104–5). It was published in Hunt's *Examiner* on March 16, prompting Reynolds to compose a sonnet of his own, "To Keats—On Reading his Sonnet written in Chaucer" (Lowell, 1:267). Besides the Chaucer, two Shakespeares, a Milton, a Dante, a pocket-book, and an edition of plays by Beaumont and Fletcher all contain original poems by Keats in manuscript.[32] As an instance of "filing," the Dante also contains a transcription of Keats's "Bright Star" in the hand of Fanny Brawne.

Whether or not composed on the spot where they are written—some probably were, some certainly were not—Keats's verse tributes are psychologically and aesthetically revealing, for they show the indebtedness of one author to another (in both directions—Shakespeare owes Keats for "On Sitting Down to Read *King Lear* Once More") and provide direct evidence of the relationship between reading and new writing. But Keats's poems have been studied very thoroughly; so having noted their presence in some of his books, I wish to turn to other kinds of marginalia and their uses. The chief of these is criticism.

The Romantic period was an age of critics, chiefly on account of the example of the competitive periodical reviews. Southey put the vulnerable author's case most forcibly: "I look upon the invention of reviews to be the worst injury which literature has received since its revival. . . . Every body is a critic, that is, every reader imagines himself to be superior to the author, and reads his book that he may censure it, not that he may improve by it" (2:276–77). To protect themselves against the cruel pens of anonymous critics, writers may have come to take more care about work in progress and have been more inclined to solicit critical advice from friends before venturing into print. John Wilson Croker once asked John Murray to try out his *Stories for Children, from the History of England* on his little boy before publishing them: "Perhaps you or Mrs. Murray would be so kind as to make a mark over against such words as he may not have understood, and to favour me with any criticism the child may have made, for on this occasion I should prefer a critic of 6 years old to one of 60" (Smiles, 1:340). Croker's assumption, like Southey's, was that criticism is fault-finding. But there was also a tradition of appreciative commentary, associated more with editions and periodical essays than with reviews: the classic examples were Addison's *Spectator* papers on *Paradise Lost* and Pope's edition of Shakespeare with the fine passages and fine scenes marked typographically for the reader. Though the members of the Hunt circle both wrote and suffered their share of "bad" reviews, their critical approach was typically of the booster variety.

Keats's annotated books make frequent use of the underlining and lines in the margin that were meant to draw attention to especially fine passages. These conventional marks record a favorable first impression, suggest a (slight) desire to single out a part of the work to be mentally registered, and guarantee further attention on later reading.[33] Double lines in the margin are common; treble do occur. His friend Reynolds, using the same system, rose to four lines in the copy of Shakespeare that they shared. Keats marked Hazlitt's essay on *King Lear* in *Characters of Shakespeare's Plays* quite heavily, indicating general approval, but only one passage called for three lines: "That poetry is an interesting study, for this reason, that it relates to whatever is most interesting in human life. Whoever therefore has a contempt for poetry, has a contempt for himself and humanity" (177). With Keats's marginalia as more transparently with Hunt's, the impulse behind a note or mark is often personal application—he picked out statements that he could endorse—and this affirmation of the centrality of poetry obviously appealed to him as a poet.

Once in a while in his annotations Keats expresses personal feeling independent of any professional motive. When Burton, in the *Anatomy of Melancholy*, describes how jewels and precious stones "have excellent vertues to pacifie the affections of the mind," he wryly observes, "Precious stones are certainly a remedy against Melancholy: a valuable diamond would effectually cure mine" (2:99). A long first-person note in the same book, at the beginning of the section on love-melancholy, reflects bitterly on the "horrid relationship" between lust and the "abstract adoration" of women (2:166–67). A particularly poignant example is his underlining of Edgar's refrain "poore *Tom*" in *King Lear* (III iv 41) in the folio Shakespeare, with the date of 4 October 1818, to commemorate the fact that he was rereading the play at the bedside of his dying brother. Two years later he gave that copy to Fanny Brawne.

His notes are not normally as directly revealing as these, however, nor as detached from his identity as a poet and critic. For the most part, his annotated books may be thought of as working books, the author's stock in trade, with the complication that they could be shared by other people. The marking of good bits and bad bits, with just an occasional word of clarification, would have been sufficient for his own needs, but if others were to make sense of his marks, something more was needed. The basic system of lines and crosses had to be adapted. The *Anatomy of Melancholy* is a case in point.[34] Only one volume survives, of two. The book was a gift from Brown and contains a few brief penciled notes in his hand. Keats's contribution consists of the usual underlining and marginal lines, a manuscript "index" or list of topics at the back (but the page reference for the story of Lamia, which Keats used later, is out of sequence and not in his hand), and a number of notes serving a variety of purposes. There are the personal notes mentioned earlier, some of which are cynical in tone, and I think not expected to be strictly private. The note on lust poses questions which might have been rhetorical or actually looking for answers: "is the love of God and the Love of women express'd by the same word in greek?" (2:166–67). Keats perhaps had Brown in mind as his audience: there are also a few notes indicating contemporary parallels to Burton's text that Brown would have appreciated, for instance allusions to the famous beauties "Mary of Buttermere, Knighton Sally" (2:225) and to "Parson Malthus" (2:409), besides a little list of the bald men Keats knew, which begins with Brown (2:440).

Most of the notes are literary, though. They link Burton with other writers—Sterne, who was known to have made use of the *Anatomy* in *Tristram Shandy* (2:14, 99); Shakespeare (2:26, 264, 302); Milton (2:222); Jonson (2:297); and Massinger (2:404, 444). Keats makes the connections economically with a name or, more commonly, a quotation. When Burton, for example, writes about the role of clothes as more effective than nakedness in exciting lust, Keats responds with a line from *Lear:* "Beware of the rustling of silks and the creaking of shoes" (2:242). This sort of note may be interesting to us as a revelation of the way Keats's mind worked while he was reading, one text instantly recalling another stored in memory, but it was not a particularly unusual procedure to take note of parallel wording and parallel ideas, as we have seen in books annotated by Burney, Ferrers, Woodhouse, and Horseman, as well as in editions of major authors. The recording of parallels tended to confirm the rightness of the text (for Shakespeare says the same sort of thing) and at the same time to make a place for it in the general mass of the reader's knowledge. Brown would have understood and approved of what Keats was doing.

Toward Shakespeare himself Keats's attitude was uniformly worshipful, but Shakespeare's commentators were his rivals. A little group of critical texts shows a more competitive side to Keats's use of books; here he behaves like some of the readers discussed earlier in this chapter, talking back to his peers. Keats knew and liked Hazlitt and admired him as a critic; nevertheless, his copy of *Characters of Shakespeare's Plays* has crosses as well as lines in it, and now and then Keats ventures to disagree. Hazlitt for instance praises the "well-timed levity" of the Fool in *Lear* which "comes in to break the continuity of feeling when it can no longer be borne, and to bring into play again the fibres of the heart just as they are growing rigid from over-strained excitement" (158).

In a detailed note Keats questions this interpretation, tentatively putting forward, instead, the idea that the Fool maintains and may even heighten the continuity of feeling:

> This is almost the last observation from Mr. Hazlitt. And is it really thus? Or as it has appeared to me? Does not the Fool by his very levity—nay it is not levity—give a finishing touch to the pathos; making what without him would be within our heart-reach nearly unfathomable. The Fool's words are merely the simplest translation of Poetry high as Lears—
>
> > "Since my young Ladies going into France
> > Sir, the Fool hath much pined away."

Here one sensitive critic challenges another on his own ground, assessing the emotional effect of the scene by subjective experience.

Keats responded to the editors and textual critics of Shakespeare less favorably than to Hazlitt. Zachariah Jackson's proposed emendations of Shakespeare's lines, under the title *Shakespeare's Genius Justified*, contains no marginal lines of approval. Keats enters into the debate about Shakespeare's diction, as other readers of his time (and of this volume) did, by rejecting Jackson's alternatives and explanations and offering a few of his own. The idea that Cleopatra should have said that Antony's "reared arm *clefted*" the world (as opposed to "crested"), for example, gets a cross and a mild rebuke, "Doltish—'tis a glorious simile from heraldry," with a little drawing of an heraldic raised arm (313). Jackson, however, was easy to dismiss; Samuel Johnson less so. In the tiny volumes of the 1814 set of Shakespeare that Keats bought in 1817 and took with him to Italy, there is no room for textual notes and very little for editorial apparatus of any kind, but the publishers did include the final judgment of Johnson or Steevens, extracted from their comprehensive edition, at the end of each play.[35] There is likewise little room for manuscript notes by a reader, except for whatever blank space there might be following their brief statements. In these little volumes, besides making a handful of brief and conventional remarks about the text, Keats did a curious thing. In response to Johnson's or Steevens's verdicts on nine plays, he wrote not his own opinion in his own words but a line or two from the play, turning Shakespeare's words against the critic. (The one exception is *Titus Andronicus,* defended with a line from *Julius Caesar.*) In most cases he also roughly crossed out the objectionable criticism. This game is not entirely fair, for the editors were often defending Shakespeare against still harsher judgments, but their remarks were too cautiously balanced for Keats, and in any case the game is amusing. Keats may have added quotations as he reread each play, building up a little collection: the four quotations from *A Midsummer Night's Dream,* for instance, are not in the order in which they appear in the text of the play. Sometimes he had to adapt a line to make it work, so "Such tricks hath strong imagination" in that play is converted to "Such tricks hath weak imagination," and Audrey's question in *As You Like It* III iii, "I do not know what 'poetical' is: is it honest in deed and word? is it a true thing?" becomes "Is Criticism a true thing?"—an allusion rather than a quotation—in Keats's note. The selection is subtle: Keats does not pick out casual abuse but makes a clever application of dialogue. For *Antony and Cleopatra,* for example, he chooses Charmian's lines from V ii: "Your Crown's awry/I'll mend it." Keats eventually gave these volumes to Severn, who could be counted on to appreciate the whimsy of the notes; and Severn later felt free to use them in his own way, adding bibliographical memoranda of his own in Vol. 1—a little list of sources for information about King Arthur.

Marks of agreement and disagreement, brief expansions of those marks, and wittily applied quotations may be interesting in their own way, where the annotator was Keats, but serious critical commentary from him is rare, and the only two surviving works containing such notes stand out from the other annotated books. Both were given as gifts to women, the folio Shakespeare to Fanny Brawne and the pocket copy of *Paradise Lost* to Maria Dilke. If the extended notes were not written expressly for them (as I am inclined to believe some of them were), at least Keats must have thought the notes would be suitable.

Though they are exceptional in quality, they are the same type of note that others in his circle—indeed many contemporaries—were writing in their own books.[36] Keats and his kind were not playing at being editors or commentators; they were not committing themselves to sustained literary analysis; but they were pausing occasionally over striking words and taking the time to think about and articulate what it was that made them so striking. This fitful exercise of the critical faculty is suggestive in that it shows what kind of reading they valued and what their conversation over books must have sounded like. The annotating reader attempts to articulate his appreciation of a particular passage. When the books are passed on, the new owner reads as though in the presence and under the stimulus of the earlier one (in "co-perusal," as Hunt called it). All Keats's notes in these books are in ink: he meant them to be permanent.

The folio Shakespeare is an unusual book, a reprint of the Folio of 1623 produced in London about 1807 or 1808. It is thick, heavy, and unwieldy, but it has wide margins and might have been expected to make a good copy to study and annotate. It has no editorial apparatus; Keats's few notes make it clear, however, that he was either consulting another edition that did have textual notes, or more likely remembering some specific cruxes in the text. He corrects a few press errors and comments on the absurdity of two or three conventional emendations. What is most unusual, though, is the fact that Keats did so little with this imposing book. He marked only five plays, most of them not all the way through, and wrote just a handful of notes in the whole volume before giving it to Fanny Brawne. He may have been marking it for her, as he did the Spenser mentioned in his letter, and have taken it up for that purpose on several occasions; but if so, he did not get very far with it. He marked only one *opening*, two pages, in *Midsummer Night's Dream* part of *1 Henry IV*, and (surprisingly under the circumstances) only a few pages of *Romeo and Juliet*, but the whole of *King Lear* and *Troilus and Cressida*.

The few notes in this copy of Shakespeare are not overtly personal, but they have something of the instructional tone that we have found other lovers adopting. Keats uses the longer note to explain his reasoning and to show how a particular word or phrase, properly understood, displays Shakespeare's genius. His defense of the Folio reading of a line in *Troilus* against the eighteenth-century (and modern) editors is a case in point. Troilus says, "I have (as when the Sunne doth light a-scorne) / Buried this sigh, in wrinkle of a smile" (I i 38). From other editions Keats knew that "a-scorne" was commonly emended to "a storm." His note acknowledges the problem of typographical errors in the Folio but considers the text justified here:

> I have not read this copy much and yet have had time to find many faults—however 'tis certain that the Commentators have contrived to mistake many beautiful passages into common places as they have done with respect to "a scorn" which they have hocus pocus'd in "a storm" thereby destroying the depth of the simile—taking away all the surrounding Atmosphere of Imagery and leaving a bare and unapt picture. Now however beautiful a Comparison may be for a bare aptness—Shakespeare is seldom guilty of one—he could not be content to "the sun lighting a storm," but he gives us Apollo in the act of drawing back his head and forcing a smile upon the world—"the Sun doth light a scorn"

Whether he is right or not about the reading, this is masterful criticism. It gives Shakespeare the benefit of the doubt at a time when critics like Zachariah Jackson were striving to make names for themselves by correcting him. It focuses on detail without losing sight of the larger significance of the detail. It also exhibits a quality that has often been noticed and admired in Keats's criticism, in his letters especially—the physical or kinaesthetic response to words, so that "a-scorn" leads him to imagine the sun-god "in the act of drawing back his head" just as "blown up" later in the play brings him to say "One's very breath while leaning over these Pages is held for fear of blowing this line away" (I iii 317). The impression overall is of intense sympathetic engagement with the author, whose lines Keats protectively expounds as though they had been his own and he was proud of them.

His notes to Milton are similar in some ways, and have the same air of sharing an enthusiasm, holding the text up for admiration. But in other ways the books are quite different. The two volumes of *Paradise Lost* are so small as almost to defy annotation, unlike the vast inviting Shakespeare; and yet the whole of the text is marked and there are about twenty notes, most of them long and involved. Keats must have worked with this Milton over several months, reading it through carefully and returning to some parts repeatedly.[37] It is quite likely that the marking was done first, the extended note-writing later. For part of the time Keats and Dilke studied Milton together; Dilke had a marked and annotated copy of his own. The note to the beginning of Book Four in Keats's copy appears to refer to him—"A friend of mine says this Book has the finest opening of any—the point of time is gigantically critical"—though in a curiously oblique, perhaps coy way, given that the book was eventually presented to Mrs. Dilke and became part of their family library.

Partly on account of constraints of space, the Milton notes tend to be excitedly elliptical and impressionistic. Nevertheless it seems to me that most if not all of them were written for the sake of other readers, to *communicate* Keats's enthusiasm. Several are written in the first person plural as though including others, and the set of notes at the beginning of the first volume, where there was a bit of space to be expansive in, serve the customary purpose of introducing the work by outlining the nature of Milton's genius—something Keats had little reason to spell out for himself. The essence of it, he says, lies in "*the Magnitude of Contrast*" (1:[2]). Here he is breathlessly summarizing the contents of a single page the whole of which he had underlined (1:18), but quoting also from an apposite later Book:

> The light and shade—the sort of black brightness—the ebon diamonding—the ethiop Immortality—the sorrow, the pain, the sad-sweet Melody—the P[h]alanges of Spirits so depressed as to be "uplifted beyond hope"—the short mitigation of Misery—the thousand Melancholies and Magnificences of this Page—leaves no room for any thing to be said thereon, but "so it is"—

Keats's literary opinions were admired in his circle, and apart from the interest of this note in revealing how he might for himself have digested Milton's lines, it shows off his skills, seeming to get at the essence of the text even as it declares it to be beyond criticism.

Another epitomizing note occurs at the beginning of Book Three, where Keats invokes his favorite Apollo again, as in the comment to *Troilus and Cressida,* and quotes a phrase that he had marked and remarked upon earlier. This note, too, has the signs of performance or at least of a consciousness of shared experience about it, in its use of "we" (1:62–63):

> The management of this Poem is Apollonian—Satan first "throws round his baleful eyes" the[n] awakes his legions, he consu[l]ts, he sets forward on his voyage—and just as he is getting to the end of it we see the Great God and our first parent, and that same satan all brough[t] in one's vision—we have the invocation to light before we mount to heaven—we breathe more freely—we feel the great Author's consolations coming thick upon him at a time when he complains most—we are getting ripe for diversity—the immediate topic of the Poem opens with a grand Perspective of all concerned.

Apollo is invoked less as sun-god than as god of poetry, Keats seeking figures to convey his admiration for Milton's achievement. To some extent it is the admiration of an apprentice trying to work out how such great effects may be brought about; but surely it is also the admiration of a reader carried away and speaking for (and to) other readers who have the same experience. Specifically, Keats is addressing himself to a literary coterie comfortable in its shared values. Keats's marginalia have long been admired and quoted as expressions of his critical standards and as evidence of his creative processes, but our focus on the individual writer has tended to obscure the social context that nurtured his note-making. The individual in this case is also representing a collective practice, not perhaps saying *what* his set thought about a given work but revealing *how* they were disposed to think about literature in general.

Though we think of reading now as a solitary and private experience, marginalia of the Romantic period prove that it was not always and is not necessarily so. Books were annotated for an anticipated audience, usually friends and familiars, thus performing complex social functions and being governed more by social than by literary conventions. When Walter Scott returned to Joanna Baillie a copy of a book of hers with marginal remarks in pencil, he assured her in the accompanying letter that his observations were made "frankly" but not "dogmatically," for "in communicating our sentiments to our friends as in stating our opinions in society we may expect a hearing from their candour but should never presume to demand acquiescence" (*Letters* 4:524). Even when the reader really was alone with the book with no reason to expect that his or her notes would be seen by anyone else, the attitude expressed in the notes is typically personal: the book is approached as someone to be talked to. To the more neutral techniques of extracting, linking, and supplementing, sociable readers added elements that brought personality to the fore, identifying passages especially relevant to themselves, freely declaring their agreement and disagreement with the text, and deploying distinctive personal styles. Marginalia of this type give us access now to opinions on all manner of subjects, many of them the views of readers who were not writers and therefore had no outlet in print. Confidently expressed, not without inhibitions of a kind, but without the inhibitions of formal composition, these marginalia provide a source of occasional, unofficial criticism that shows not only how a particular reader responded to a particular book, but also how that reader was accustomed to talk about books in congenial company, as the Keats circle evidently discussed their feelings about specific words, phrases, and fine passages. They serve, in a way, as correspondence does, by allowing us to hear the conversational tones of the period and to reinforce our sense of the individual voice. Scott's son-in-law Lockhart described sharing Scott's library as tantamount to having his company: "So many of the volumes were enriched with anecdotes or comments in his own hand, that to look over his books was in some degree conversing with him. And sometimes this occupation was pleasantly interrupted by a snatch of actual conversation with himself, when he entered from his own room, to consult or take away a book" (8:218).

The marginalia of this chapter are communicative on a spectrum from one-to-one intimacy through the familiarity of groups of three (author, reader, and reader's friend) or more (author, reader, and reader's friends) to the semi-public dissemination of ideas. The next chapter turns to marginalia that aimed to be even more public and more permanent.

Custodians to Posterity

Romantic readers were hunter-gatherers by training and necessity. They sought out and assembled useful bits of writing even if they could only transcribe and not own them; some of the poorest among them cherished chapbooks and broadsides and salvaged odd volumes. Even the Cheap Repository Tracts that were often distributed free were advertised as collectible items. The activity of these readers is partially registered in the books they wrote in. To us who follow, those books all appear as artefacts, though some were and are more obviously artefactual than others. This chapter deals with the deliberate marking and adapting of books for show, especially with a view to posterity, and so we shift from the world of informal socializing to the competitive sphere of the collector—which itself expanded significantly between 1790 and 1820.

HORACE WALPOLE

Horace Walpole, fourth Earl of Orford, was in both admirable and risible ways the epitome of the eighteenth-century English collector and a pattern for those who came later. His example continued to be influential after he died in 1797, by virtue of collections that had been itemized and visited as well as by writings published during his lifetime and the posthumous publications that established his reputation as a commentator on his era: his *Works,* edited by Mary Berry (5 vols., 1798); *Walpoliana,* collected by the Scottish antiquarian John Pinkerton (1799); *Reminiscences* (1805); letters to various correspondents (from 1818); and *Memoires of the Last Ten Years of the Reign of George the Second* (1822). His name also appeared regularly in gossip columns, verse satires, and contemporary memoirs. The youngest son of the powerful Whig prime minister, wealthy and privileged, the product (like his father) of Eton and King's, holder of pocket boroughs and sinecure appointments, Walpole rather defensively described himself as "the first antiquary of my race" (quoted in Lewis, 1:lxxi).[1] He chose to lead the life of a dilettante and did it very well, filling his house, Strawberry Hill, with curiosities and knickknacks; running a private press there; traveling; entertaining; and writing (besides thousands of letters) catalogues, bibliographies, editions and translations, periodical essays, poems, plays, and *The Castle of Otranto.* His unconventional but considerable achievements are easy to disparage as the pastimes of an amateur; Walpole of course led the way and judged himself—in a mood that went beyond aristocratic sprezzatura—as only a "middling" writer who ought never to have published (*Correspondence* 33:574).

His library, which amounted in the end to about 7,000 titles and still included some of the books he had bought as a child, favored English history, genealogy, antiquities, and topography, together with French novels and memoirs. For all the grandeur of his position, Walpole's budget was not unlimited and he bought rather carefully. Pinkerton maintained that for most of his life, until he succeeded to his earldom, he had "about five thousand pounds a year, a mere pittance for a person of his birth and rank" (*Walpoliana,* xxxviii). For his own publishing projects he collected the works of royal and noble authors as well as tracts, plays, and poems of the reigns of George I and II. He had a room full of books of prints and indulged in the fashionable hobby of extra-illustration. Writing in books was for him a lifelong custom and a pleasure. Commentators regularly mention his love of writing notes and observe that annotations occur in two-thirds of the books in his reconstituted library.[2] Substantial quantities of his marginalia have by now found their way into print.

It is possible, however, to misconstrue and overestimate the extent of Walpole's annotating activity. This is not to say that commentators have been deliberately misleading, only that the experience of the published marginalia and of appreciative critical attention may cause us to expect more than we should. The majority of Walpole's books contain either no notes (one-third of the collection) or only routine and pedestrian annotation. He used unobtrusive marks to indicate approval and disapproval: his short horizontal line and his cross, indicating degrees of favorable attention, appear in a copy of Thomson's *Seasons* dating from his schooldays just as they do in books that he read at the end of the century. By way of collection management, in dealing with tracts and ephemera Walpole tried regularly to add the name of the author (if suppressed or concealed) and the month of publication to the title page, but most of these tracts have no further marginalia, and in some cases even those details may have been the work of the bookseller (Hazen, 1:x). He kept separate notebooks for extracts and therefore did not need to be diligent about cross-referencing or copying from one book to another. Besides marks and bibliographical details, the commonest form of note in his books is the identification of a person unnamed or whose name is disguised in the text: "HW's copy with his identifications" is a regular refrain in Hazen's catalogue. But even the business of identification occupied Walpole only fitfully, and he is not entirely reliable. A book with Walpole's annotations may prove disappointing.

If we also subtract the books he annotated for work in progress, as part of the Strawberry Hill production line, such as the copy of Anthony Hamilton's *Mémoires du comte de Grammont* that he used as the basis for an edition of 1772 (translating his own marginalia into French), the body of marginalia appears considerably diminished. Furthermore, most of his marginalia fall outside the period with which I am concerned; he was in his seventies by the time of the Revolution in France. All the same, Walpole's was and remains an important example, his practice was consistent, and there are books available with notes dating from 1789 and later that clearly demonstrate his goals and his strengths. An interesting case is a favorite Voltaire, the *Essay sur l'histoire générale et sur les moeurs et l'esprit des nations depuis Charlemagne jusqu'à nos jours* in seven volumes, very heavily marked in every volume with signs of approbation and of occasional disagreement, but with only a few notes. These are interesting for two reasons, first because most of them are in French, in keeping with Walpole's usual practice—he wrote and presumably thought in French when reading in that language—and second because they must have been written on different occasions between 1756 or so and the 1790s, and yet are uniform in spirit, talking back to the book in a corrective but appreciative way. He told Lady Ossory that he was rereading this book in November 1789 (*Correspondence*, 34:79) and at least one of his longer notes in it (5:55) confirms that statement: to Voltaire's account of disturbances in Paris in 1651, when he observes that "Les Chefs de parti furent peu cruels, & les peuples peu furieux; car ce n'était pas une guerre de Religion" ("The leaders were not very cruel nor the people very violent, for it was not a religious war"), Walpole responds by offering a counterexample, "Le Peuple de Paris etait bien furieux en 1789, & ce n'ètait pas une guerre de Religion" ("The people of Paris were quite violent in 1789, and that was not a religious war").

Earlier in 1789, Walpole had reported to Pinkerton that he was making slow progress with Pinkerton's newly published *Inquiry into the History of Scotland*. What he has to say about his experience of reading, in this apology to the author, is revealing. He has been slow, he says, because "I do not care a straw about your subjects, with whom I am no more acquainted than with the ancient inhabitants of Otaheite"; he cannot rouse himself to be interested in "savage manners, unassisted by individual characters"; and "the novelty, to me at least, requires some helps to connect it with the memory" (*Correspondence*, 16:302–5). "Many years ago," he confesses, "when my faculties were much less impaired, I was forced to quit Dow's *History of Indostan*, because the Indian names made so little impression on me, that I went backward instead of forward, and was every minute reverting to the former page to find out about whom I was reading" (306). This disarming self-analysis is probably true enough, and not peculiar to Walpole. Speaking for himself but presuming that Pinkerton will understand the general principles, Walpole, who normally read to pursue his own interests, explains that interest and knowledge reinforce one another. We are likely to be interested by subjects we already know something about; as we know more, our interest grows and we find it easier to remember what we learn, connecting new materials to the structures of memory. His realm is that of polished manners and "individual characters," as his works and his marginalia repeatedly demonstrate.

One of the engaging features of eighteenth-century antiquarianism is the generous way in which enthusiasts assisted one another. If Walpole was struggling with Pinkerton's unappealing book in order to be able to offer constructive criticism for a second edition, that would be altogether typical. Antiquarians networked just as naturalists did, presumably for similar reasons: they needed one another to further individual and collective projects, and collaboration produced camaraderie. Walpole had met Pinkerton only in 1785, but he cooperated with him when he was preparing a second edition of his *Essay on Medals* (1789), which includes references to Walpole's collection and is dedicated to him. Walpole's copy of that work is marked in typical fashion: crosses and lines in pencil throughout, with a few longer notes in pencil or ink, one identifying Walpole's old friend Gray as the author of an unattributed quotation, a few others supplementing the text with further technical information, and one adding the sort of anecdotal evidence that Walpole particularly relished. Pinkerton mentions that "In 1670 current half-pence and farthings began to be struck at the Tower" (2:84). Walpole improves on this information, noting that from a collector's point of view the less valuable farthings are harder to come by: "farthings not very common, owing, it is said, to beggars flinging them away, that nobody may give them less than a half penny." This is the sort of dubious though colorful—dubious *because* colorful?—story that did stick in his memory and that flavors his letters and marginalia. It is characteristic of him that he does not cite textual authority as someone like Hargrave would have done, but gives the information on his own authority, based ultimately on oral sources that a more rigorous historian might dismiss as gossip, rumor, or vulgar error but that may be worth preserving all the same, if only because they reflect the common beliefs of a certain era.

In July 1790, laid up with gout, Walpole spent a few days writing notes in Thomas Pennant's new book *Of London.* As he explained to Mary Berry, he had once thought of writing such a book himself and had been "collecting notices" for it, so when Pennnant told him about the project he had given him "such hints as I recollected—but as he is more impetuous than digestive, I had not looked out my memorandums, and he has made such a bungling use of those I gave him (for instance, calling the Duchess of Tirconnell *the white milliner* instead of *the white widow*) that I am glad I furnished him with no more" (*Correspondence,* 11:94–95). The book, now at Farmington, corroborates Walpole's letter. A later owner pasted in prints depicting Walpole and Strawberry Hill, but it was Walpole himself who filled the book with notes in ink and added to the title page "with MSS notes by Mr Horace Walpole" (he did not succeed to the earldom till 1791). Having gone back to his "memorandums," he was able to add 17 pages of facts about London sights, alphabetically arranged from Albemarle Street to Whitehall, together with miscellaneous information about the city, which are bound in at the back.[3] His notes in the text, some of them very long, are quite different from the compilation at the back, having been written on the spot from memory, a process that makes them less predictable and more conversational.

In these notes, Walpole is naturally at pains to correct the stories derived from himself, such as the business of the white widow, which he had, he says, from his mother (135); but he also responds at particular points where he has something to say, and it is not always to correct or disagree. Pennant, for example, describing Westminster Abbey under Mary Tudor, observes that "She with great zeal restored it to the ancient conventual state; collected many of the rich habits and insignia of that splendid worship" (75–76). Walpole adds, "three sumptuous Copes are still preserved in Westminster-abbey. I saw them worn by 3 Prebendaries at the funeral of George 2$^{d.}$ Some remain in a few other cathedrals, as Durham &c." More often than not, though, his notes point out Pennant's errors of fact or opinion. Walpole splutters vehemently about

Henry Chichely, a "worthy" man by Pennant's standard whom Walpole considers "never sufficiently stigmatized by Historians" (19), and he expresses his frustration over Pennant's persistence in misattributing portraits said to have been of the Countess of Desmond (119). He even goes to some trouble to provide circumstantial detail in challenging Pennant's account of the death of Count Königsmark (by Pennant spelled "Koningsmark" and by Walpole "Konismark") in Germany in 1686: rather comically for one so fond of salacious anecdotes himself, he seems to have objected to its sensationalism as well as to its inaccuracy. Pennant had said that Königsmark, an adventurer responsible for the murder of a rival named Thynne, had "attempted an intrigue . . . with a lady of distinguished rank," whereupon he was waylaid at the order of the lady's husband and "was literally cut to pieces, and his remains flung into a privy, which was instantly bricked up" (125). Walpole first identifies the lady, and then goes on to refute Pennant's version of the story.

> *the wife of K. George 1st. Konismark was not cut to pieces nor buried as is said here. When George 2d on his first journey to Hanover made some alterations in the palace, the Count's body, who had probably been strangled, was found under the floor of the Electress's dressing-room, where he had been murdered by order of the old Elector, father of George 1st., who was then absent at the army.

Walpole's version of this ancient scandal is more accurate than Pennant's—significantly exculpating the future George I—though still flawed from the point of view of later historians, who tell us that the date was 1694 and that Königsmark disappeared, no body having ever been recovered. One of Walpole's contemporaries, relying on different sources, maintained in another annotated copy that the man who murdered Thynne was not this Königsmark, Philip, but his brother Charles.[4] So little by little false reports might be corrected, Walpole's strength as a historian of his own time, following the model of Burnet, being his candid contemporary perspective backed up by extensive if not deep reading.

Of greater interest to readers today is Walpole's copy of the first edition of Boswell's *Life of Johnson,* with many marked passages as usual and a few notes, most of them in pencil and all rather milder than one might have expected given Walpole's disdainful attitude toward Johnson while he was alive. There are occasional identifications, some not known to modern editors, for instance Lady—— —— "who was a wonderful mimick"; according to Walpole this was Lady Emily Hervey (1:357). There are some corrections to Boswell's grammar and to his French, though not many. Once in a while Walpole shows resistance to Boswell's argument, as when Boswell defends Johnson against Hawkins's accusation of "emnity against Milton," quoting Johnson's praise for *Paradise Lost* and demanding, rhetorically, "Is this the language of one who wished to blast the laurels of Milton?" (1:127). Walpole singled out this passage with an exclamation mark and shrewdly enough commented, "not the laurels, but the character." And he countered Boswell's complaints about Mrs. Thrale's publication of Johnson's parody of Burke by pointing out that Boswell had done worse himself: "he has committed numberless things to writing that do no honour to D[r] Johnson's temper or philosophy" (2:515). Dismissing Boswell's speculation that Walpole's "prejudice" against Johnson might have arisen from his having heard a report of Johnson's boast that in his parliamentary reporting he always "took care to put Sir Robert Walpole in the wrong," Walpole simply says "I never heard it till now" (2:515). But he does not expand on this statement, nor does he allow himself to be drawn on Boswell's other statements about him or even object to being referred to very familiarly in print as "Horry Walpole." Since his marginalia were not unguarded comments but contributions to a potentially public record, Walpole was careful to exercise restraint.

A final example is Walpole's copy of Archibald Robertson's *Topographical Survey of the Great Road from London to Bath and Bristol* (1792), which describes Strawberry Hill as worth visiting for its "singularity" and its "fine collections" (1:34–35). Once again Walpole declared his contribution on the title page: "With additions & corrections. MSS by H. W. Earl of Orford." Only the first volume is annotated, the second straying too far, presumably, from London. Having read the book fresh from the publisher and still in boards, as usual, Walpole on a flyleaf directed that "If this book ever be bound, care should be taken not to cut the margins of the leaves, as notes are written on some to the bottom" (1:—2). Some notes too long for the margins were written on separate pieces of paper and tipped in. In the text itself, we see the same process carried on as in Pennant: corrections of fact or of emphasis, and supplementary information. Of Richmond Park, which Robertson describes as having been made "in the reign of King Charles II.," Walpole says, "This is a great mistake; it was a charge against Charles the first that he usurped private property to inclose in his new-made park" (1:29). Of course he is most interesting and authoritative on Strawberry Hill itself, not being content with Robertson's description, according to which "The house is of Gothic architecture, and in its appearance resembles an ancient priory: the same idea prevails within, the apartments being arranged and fitted up in the style of a religious house" (1:34). Not so, Walpole points out; the interior decoration is not in the same style as the exterior: "It is a mixture of the cathedral & castle styles; but is not fitted up in that manner, tho with furniture meant to resemble the supposed residence of ancient nobility." And to Robertson's praise of its "large museum of antiquities; some valuable sculpture; and other extraordinary pieces of art" he adds, "particularly many in sculpture by Mrs Damer, & in water colours by Lady Diana Beauclerc, Miss Agnes Berry & Lady Lucan" (1:34).

Walpole's compliment to these living female artists who were among his close friends is a useful clue to the purpose of his most extensively annotated books. What we find out about his library on close examination is that while some of his books were simply marked as a way of keeping track of a collection, some contain only reading marks and sketchy notes (usually desultory identifications), and others were used as drafts for his own press or as a record of revisions for a new edition, the most deliberately annotated were books destined to circulate among Walpole's friends and antiquarian colleagues during his lifetime and after that to assist posterity—as they have done. It was not a project of his declining years; there are similar examples from earlier in the century, including Dodsley (1748–58), Collins (1752), an anonymous *Lon-*

don and its Environs published by Dodsley (1761), Chesterfield (1777), Mason (annotated 1779), and Dodington (1784).

Walpole realized early on that if it was to detach itself from the stigma of triviality and to be taken seriously by nonpractitioners, antiquarianism had to contribute to the writing of history. He would have subscribed to the mission statement, as he did to the publication, of Francis Grose's periodical *The Antiquarian Miscellany* (1775–84), which handsomely published original essays, extracts from very scarce books, and prints of previously unpublished subjects.[5] The introduction to the first number regretfully acknowledged that antiquaries had to some extent brought upon themselves the reputation of being "humdrum, plodding fellows, who wanting genius for nobler studies, busied themselves in heaping up illegible Manuscrips, mutilated Statues, obliterated Coins, and broken Pipkins" (iii), and it set out a program for the rehabilitation of their study:

> In cultivating the study of Antiquities, care must be taken not to fall into an error, into which many have been seduced, I mean that of making collections of things which have no other merit than that of being old, or having belonged to some eminent person, and are not illustrative of any point of history. Such is the Scull of Oliver Cromwell, preserved in the Ashmolean Museum at Oxford, and pieces of the Royal Oak, hoarded by many loyal old ladies. That Oliver had a scull and brains too would have been allowed without this proof; and those who have considered the Royal Oak do not, I believe, find it essentially different from the wood of a common kitchen table. These must be rather stiled Reliques than Pieces of Antiquity, and it is such trumpery that is gibed at by the Ridiculers of Antiquity. (vii)

Walpole shared Grose's hopes for their subject, that it should justify itself as what we now call material history. The term they would have used—that Grose does use in this passage—was "illustrative." Walpole found his own way of working in that direction by "illustrating" and improving some of his books with relevant information that he himself could vouch for, such as the preservation of Tudor copes in

Westminster Abbey. He went a step farther than Grose and his allies by aiming to make history itself less dull, and so incorporating vivid anecdotes and "individual characters," the absence of which he complained about to Pinkerton. While any book annotated in this way by Walpole has a distinctively Walpolian character, his procedure was not out of line with that of his contemporaries, many of whom can be seen "illustrating" their books with marginal comments (Piozzi, Horseman, and Hemans, for example), behaving like editors as we shall see shortly (Thompson, Woodhouse), circulating their marginalia within a private circle (Hunt, Keats), and using the vehicle of the printed book as an alternative to publication (Lidwill, Blake). These were accepted practices from the top to the bottom of the social scale.

BIBLIOMANIA

Walpole's library was the work of a collector but not of a bibliophile, as Lewis has pointed out (lxii). Walpole did not care what edition he read and did not seek out very old and rare books. In a letter written to Lady Ossory in 1787 which incidentally suggests that he thought of reading and writing (or at least marking) in the margins as aspects of the same activity, he even complained about the high prices given for his Strawberry Hill editions, observing that they commanded such prices only because they were scarce, "and a collector who pays extravagantly for a rare book, will never read *in* it, or allow anybody else, for the virgin purity of the margin is as sacred with him as the text" (*Correspondence*, 33:573). The other kind of collector, the one who prizes rarity, was a familiar enough figure in Walpole's day, however. Within a few years of his death, the bibliophile enjoyed a brief dominance.

British bibliomania is often treated as an isolated episode in the history of collecting, a temporary insanity or frenzy that took hold early in the nineteenth century, came to a head at the Roxburghe Sale of 1812, and was finished a decade or so later, when even the prodigious "book-collecting ardour" of one of the leaders of the movement, Earl Spencer, is said to have flagged (Lister, 91). Traditionally, its bookends are Thomas Frognall Dibdin's first version of *Bibliomania* (1809) and his *Bibliophobia* (1832), the latter with the subtitle "Remarks on the Present Languid and Depressed State of Literature and the Book Trade."[6] (Dibdin's lavish *Bibliographical Decameron* of 1817, dispensing friendly advice about typography, bindings, illumination, and like topics, sits somewhere in the middle of the shelf.) And it is true that the excesses of wealthy collectors, vying with one another for a scrap of early printing or fine printing, or for a luxury binding no matter what the contents, were staple subjects, usually of ridicule, in the periodical press throughout the first quarter of the century, an era that one commentator calls "the now fabulous world of early nineteenth-century book-collecting" (O'Dwyer, 7). Most of the English words beginning "biblio-," generally derived from Greek via French, were introduced then, including "bibliographer" (in the sense of "one who writes about books, a copyist"), "bibliography," and "bibliophile," besides many more absurd and less durable compounds.[7] (This is not to say that the science of bibliography was unknown to earlier generations: Dibdin himself produced a new edition of Ames's 1749 *Typographical Antiquities.*) The enthusiasts who preemptively and defiantly claimed for themselves the name of "bibliomane," "bibliomaniac," or sufferer from "bibliomania" flourished especially during the Regency, when establishing or enlarging a private library must have presented itself as a more practicable, secure, and positively virtuous way of spending money than such traditional status symbols as new buildings or Old Masters. To Lady Louisa Stuart, currently in the process of weeding books from a library, Scott gave some half-playful advice in 1825:

> Dread, my dear Lady Louisa that in preferring some comely quarto to a shabby duodecimo your Ladyship may be rejecting the *editio princeps.* Consider that in banishing some antiquated piece of polissonerie you may destroy the very work for which the author lost his ears two centuries since and which has become almost introuvable. Then there are so many reasons for not parting with duplicates for they may have a value in being tall or a value in being short or

perhaps in having the leaves uncut or some peculiar and interesting misprint in a particular passage that there is no end to the risque of selection. So much for Bibliomania— (*Letters*, 9:12).

But bibliomania needs to be seen in a larger context, and to be taken seriously. More needs to be done in the way of investigation of its French roots and models—the literary chitchat of the anas en masse, as well as specific titles like Bollioud de Mermet's *De la bibliomanie* (1761) and Peignot's *Dictionnaire raisonné de la bibliologie* (1802).[8] Did British essayists and bibliographers step in to fill a gap caused by the suspension of trade during the war years? Were they merely naturalizing a successful foreign article? Was there reciprocal influence? Philip Connell has recently analyzed the role of bibliomania in cultural history as an aspect of the emerging awareness of a national literary heritage. Here I can only emphasize its status as the crest of a commercial wave and its effect on the practice of readerly annotation.

The market for books grew steadily in the second half of the eighteenth century, that pattern of growth accelerating in the 1790s; but it grew partly by extending itself to new areas in society, hence to individuals and families with little previous experience of book ownership. Thus there arose opportunities for guidance of various kinds: how to read, what to read, what to look for, what to collect. Dibdin and Goodhugh at one end of the scale advising the gentry and Isaac Taylor at the other addressing teenaged apprentices have been mentioned before.[9] In 1807, some years before they made their appearance, Southey had foreseen the marketability of such advice and proposed to Longman a critical catalogue of British books: "None but those who have libraries will buy it; and all those may be calculated upon. There will also be some sale for it abroad, more than is usual for English books" (*Life*, 3:109). He meant to enlist Dibdin, but nothing came of the proposal. In the meantime other contenders appeared. Egerton Brydges's *British Bibliographer*, building on the success of his articles about "old English books" in *Censura Literaria* (1805–9), started to appear in 1810 and was completed in four volumes, with the assistance of Joseph Haslewood, in 1814.[10] In 1818 in Glasgow, Robert Watt brought out proposals for a subscription edition of *Bibliotheca Britannica; or, a General Index to the Literature of Great Britain and Ireland,* which he duly produced in a four-volume set (1824) that is still a valuable work of reference. The emphasis on British books, especially on Elizabethan literature, which grew in prestige as interest in classical and Italian literature waned, may have owed something to the educational limitations of a new class of collectors as well as to patriotism. In 1800 Hester Piozzi remarked upon the taste for books among local businessmen: "Here has Mr Giles laid out a Thousand Pounds (no less) in books for our Library, and Mr Gillon grieves when a secondhand Shakespear slips from his hand at an Auction, for want of Courage to give 20 Guineas for it" (*Letters,* 3:240).

The vogue for book collecting was also supported and stimulated by memoirs of writers and publishers, and by collections of literary anecdotes—most of which were extensively reported and extracted in reviews and magazines, thus reinforcing the trend. Isaac D'Israeli's *Curiosities of Literature,* which started as a single volume in 1791 (when it already included an article on "The Bibliomania" or "the collecting an enormous heap of books"), had grown to six volumes by 1834 and was frequently reprinted. D'Israeli capitalized on its success with further collections—*An Essay on the Literary Character* (1795), *Miscellanies, or Literary Recollections* (1796), *Calamities of Authors* (1812–13), *Quarrels of Authors* (1814)—and others followed suit, for example Adam Clarke in his *Bibliographical Dictionary . . . with Biographical Anecdotes* (1802–4); William Beloe in *Anecdotes of Literature and Scarce Books* (6 vols., 1806–12); John Nichols in *Literary Anecdotes of the Eighteenth Century* (1812–15, an expansion of memoirs of Bowyer published thirty years earlier); William Davis in *An Olio of Bibliographical and Literary Anecdotes* (1814); and Joseph Spence in his celebrated, posthumously published *Observations, Anecdotes, and Characters, of Books and Men* (1820), which retailed the personalities and gossip of the age of Pope.[11] Brydges, Beloe, and Dibdin, like Lackington and Trusler, also wrote autobiographies.

I realize that I am jumbling together the scholar's sacred and profane by bundling the likes of Watt with Dibdin's energetic but slapdash propagandizing, but all these books about books and their producers contributed to the fashion for book collecting and fanned the flames of obsession. In their time they generated institutional gatherings of the like-minded in the form of clubs, printing societies, and private presses on the model of Strawberry Hill, so their influence continued to be felt long after "The Bibliomania" was said to have been over.

COLLECTION MANAGEMENT: JOHN MITFORD

What did collectors do with the books they assembled; specifically, what did they write in them? Their most characteristic procedures fall under the general category of collection management. Like their predecessors and successors, they tended to use the front flyleaves of their books as the place to store essential information, which for them meant factual matters of ownership, provenance, and market value. To their personal inscriptions or bookplates they would systematically add details of the date and place where they had acquired the book together with what they knew about distinguished former owners (the pedigree) and the special features of their copy. This practice is so commonplace that it hardly needs to be documented, but brief examples may serve as representative. R. D. Shackleford, observing the traces of former owners—"from the Author," "Bp. of Ely's Sale Nov. 1808," and a presentation inscription of December 1808 from someone named Inglis "To Dr Gossett"—proudly traced his copy of a pamphlet by Francis Wollaston, *The Secret History of a Private Man,* from Wollaston to Dr. Yorke, the Bishop of Ely, and thence to Inglis and so to Isaac Gosset at whose sale in 1813 he himself had bought it, noting further that it was "extremely scarce" since it had been printed for distribution to friends and not actually published. Sarah Sophia Banks, who collected among other things books about archery, noted in a damaged copy of Ascham's *Toxophilus* (1545) that she had acquired it in 1808 and that a previous owner was responsible for the replacement pages in manuscript facsimile: "this imperfect copy more than 20 years past was purchased by the late Mr Dodd of Drury Lane Theatre for £1. 1.—bound up with Shottrell's Archery revived—it was a curious item in his library and reserved from the sale of it—". Francis Douce's folio Aesop includes his note on a flyleaf: "I purchased this beautiful copy at the sale of my worthy friend George Isted's books, who had devoted much time and expense in making it up from various copies from which he selected the best impressions of the engravings." These are conventional ways of recording matters of fact important to collectors, for which later owners and booksellers often have reason to be grateful.

Many collectors of the period went further, adding to the front flyleaves of some or all of their books biographical evidence about the author, references to earlier or later editions, and extracts from criticism in reviews or commentaries. Philip MacDermott's hard-used little Spenser has essential critical cross-references squeezed into its front flyleaves: "See Critiques on Fairy Queen & other Poems in Craik's Book on Spenser" (−3), "See Southey's Eulogy on Spenser—in Biographies of Poets—National School Book" (Dedication page). Francis Douce, a great collector who bequeathed most of his estate, including 19,000 books, to the Bodleian Library—and £500 to his friend Dibdin—often added a few pages to his books to take notes and clippings of this kind. The first volume of his Boswell, for instance, contains a pasted-in portrait of Boswell and a facsimile engraving of Johnson's handwriting, along with manuscript extracts from reviews and other references assembled over the course of several years—notably a harsh line from the *Monthly Magazine* of 1800 in which Johnson is described as a "carnivorous kraken of literature" (−4). Humphry Davy's secondhand copy of Vince's *Elements of the Conic Sections* includes a note about the author, his parentage, education, and death-date (1821), together with a list of his other publications and reference to another edition of this one (−2). Much but not necessarily all of this sort of material would have been collected from secondary sources. One unidentified owner of the egregious Theophilus Swift's *Touchstone of Truth* laboriously copied onto the flyleaves of the book factual information about Swift and other players in his story "from a note in Dr. Barret's copy, written with his own hand"—that is, adopting information that was circulating through marginalia—before adding a long note about Swift on his own authority, which included detailed evidence to prove that Swift, who had bigamously courted Emma Dobbin, "was not a person for a young female to fall in love with." (This book has further biographical information about Swift and the Dobbins on a flyleaf at the back.) Words could be, often were, combined with graphic elements. Without marring the pages of the text, Dawson Turner gave Dibdin's enlarged *Bibliomania* of 1811 the full collector's treatment—a fine binding, a fore-edge painting of Strawberry Hill, a manuscript "key" to the characters in the story, a pasted-in autograph, annotated clippings dating between 1812 and 1819 to demonstrate the rise and fall of prices in the rare-book trade, and an engraving of Dibdin made in 1821 by Mrs. Turner (Fig. 24).

To turn to a particularly well documented example, John Mitford (1781–1859), Vicar of Benhall near Saxmundham in Suffolk, represents the comfortable collector and man of letters of the time. He was ordering books from Lackington's catalogue as early as 1804 when he was still an Oxford undergraduate.[12] After he took orders and settled at Benhall, though he also maintained lodgings in London and traveled extensively, the process continued, so that over time he accumulated an enviable library, especially strong in classical and British literature. The auctions of this books in 1859–60 included just over 6,000 lots and raised £4,029; manuscripts were dealt with separately. As the sale catalogue pointed out, "Many of the Volumes forming this valuable collection possess on the fly leaves Critical Remarks, References, and Extracts, by the late Rev. John Mitford."[13] What it meant was not that they contained original critical remarks but that Mitford had assembled appropriate bibliographical references and copied or pasted them in at the front. Scores of Mitford's books are readily available in public and institutional libraries, so it is easy to trace the development of his habits in handling books. As a student he collected variant readings and parallel passages that he entered directly on the pages of texts such as his Horace, but he soon abandoned that practice, leaving the text clear (apart from occasional check-marks in pencil, indicating approval) and focusing his attention on the front flyleaves where he gathered references, and to a lesser extent on the back ones where he sometimes made a list of page references or other reading notes.

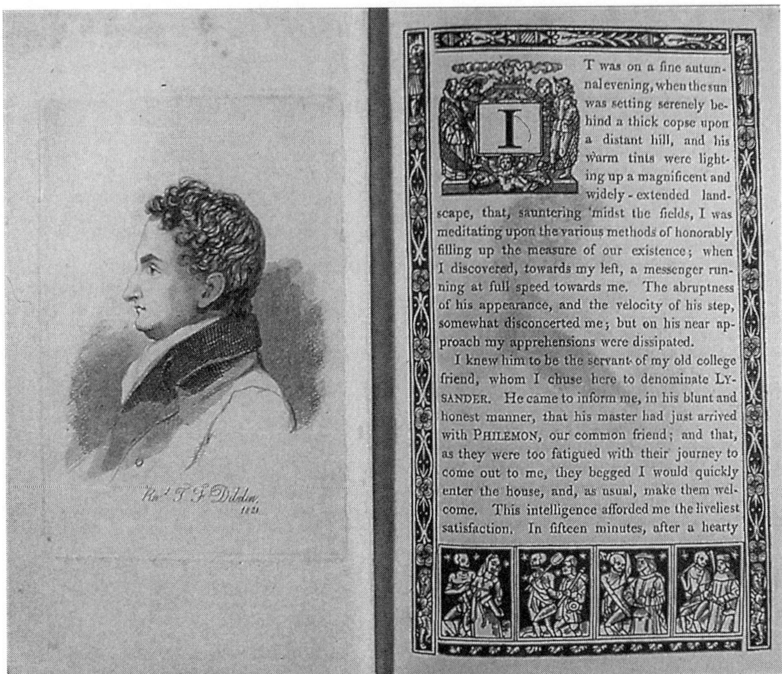

IT was on a fine autumnal evening, when the sun was setting serenely behind a thick copse upon a distant hill, and his warm tints were lighting up a magnificent and widely-extended landscape, that, sauntering 'midst the fields, I was meditating upon the various methods of honorably filling up the measure of our existence; when I discovered, towards my left, a messenger running at full speed towards me. The abruptness of his appearance, and the velocity of his step, somewhat disconcerted me; but on his near approach my apprehensions were dissipated.

I knew him to be the servant of my old college friend, whom I chuse here to denominate LYSANDER. He came to inform me, in his blunt and honest manner, that his master had just arrived with PHILEMON, our common friend; and that, as they were too fatigued with their journey to come out to me, they begged I would quickly enter the house, and, as usual, make them welcome. This intelligence afforded me the liveliest satisfaction. In fifteen minutes, after a hearty

FIG. 24 The decorative first page of T. F. Dibdin's *Bibliomania* (1811) with an engraved portrait of the author (1821) by Mary Turner, wife of Dawson Turner. Courtesy of the Lewis Walpole Library, Yale University.

Mitford was eminently methodical. In every book he put his name and the year of acquisition. Sometimes there is a later date recording a specific reading: so his Brydone has "J. Mitford. 1816" and in pencil, "Nov$^{r.}$ 1816," and his copy of the memoirs of the duchesse de Montpensier has "Mitford. 1826." and "March. 1829." There follow tidy notes about the special features of the copy, as for instance in his copy of Hamilton's *Memoirs of the Life of the Count de Grammont* "(With MS. Notes by Isaac Reed.) In this Copy all the blanks for names are filled up"; and then assorted references having to do with the reception and reputation. Some of these lists, incorporating clippings from magazines and booksellers' catalogues as well as extracts in Mitford's tiny hand, fill a page; most are scantier than that. The full set of entries in his copy of Sir William Waller's *Divine Meditations* is a case in point:

J. Mitford. 1816.

See an account of S^r. W^m. Waller and his works, in Beloe's Anecd: vol: vi. 305. This is called the least common of his works.

S^r. W^m. Waller's Vindication of himself from taking arms against the King, republished in 1793. by Lord Roslyn, then L^d. Chancellor, from an original MS. See a curious account of the book, and Author, in British Critic: vol: ii. p. 32.

I believe there is also the Diary of S^r. W^m. Waller published, at the end of some Poems by Mr Greatheed, or one of the La Crusca School. J. M.

Mitford was not cross-referencing this book to others in his own collection: the Beloe he must have owned, but not the Roslyn, for which his evidence is at second hand through a periodical, and certainly not the final item, for which he is relying on memory and doing not badly—the exact reference would be to Waller's "Recollections," printed in one of the Della Cruscan volumes, *The Poetry of Anna Matilda*, of 1788.

Some of Mitford's books show the desultory work of many years. As new information came in, he entered it in the appropriate volumes. The notes in the Brydone that he read in 1816 include a clipping announcing the author's death in 1818, a reference to an obituary of 1820, and comments on Brydone's work by other travelers, such as those contained in an extract from "Duppa's Trav. in Italy p. 183," published in 1828, which accused Brydone of having fabricated some of his best sights: "when he arrived at the top, there was so damp a vapor, that he could hardly see his Hand. This I was told by Mr Richd Glover who was with him" (−2). In his copy of George Tooke's very rare pamphlet *Annae-dicata*, which he bought in 1816 and looked into again in 1826, Mitford's notes record the existence of an effigy and a portrait of Tooke, the sale of a copy of his poems for five guineas, and evidence about him in extracts from Evelyn's diary and Pepys's memoirs. He also pasted in clippings from booksellers' catalogues and the entire text of an article about Tooke in the *Gentleman's Magazine* for November 1839. Although he tended to confine his own contributions to the flyleaves and endpapers of his books, Mitford was not averse to marginalia of other kinds: the title page of the sale catalogue of his library makes a point of the "valuable manuscript notes & emendations by . . . erudite scholars of critical celebrity" in the Greek and Latin texts, and as his notes about Reed's additions to the *Memoirs of the Count of Grammont* indicate, he was glad to have books containing notes by English authorities too. He owned Walpole's annotated copies of works by John Nichols, Joseph Warton, and Edward Young, purchased at the famous Strawberry Hill sale of 1842.

ATTRIBUTIONS AND IDENTIFICATIONS

It must be evident, however, that Mitford was not following Walpole's example. He neither mended the historical record nor identified unnamed characters (filling up the blanks, as he observed of Reed). He did not even attempt, as Walpole did, to record attributions for works published by unnamed or pseudonymous authors. And yet this was a practice, common among serious collectors, that has proved a boon to generations of cataloguers and bibliographers, since to have any name to attach to an ephemeral or insecure or libelous book or pamphlet lifts it out from the hordes of the anonymous. Of course the attributions vary in reliability as they do in their sources of authority. George Canning's complete set of original numbers of *The Anti-Jacobin*, to which he was one of the chief contributors, is invaluable for its revelation of secret authorship, as it assigns the paper on "Finance" (27 and 30 Nov. 1797) to Pitt, "Neutral Navigation" (19 Feb. 1798) to Liverpool, and the "Letter from a Lady . . . exactly as it has come to our hands" (18 Dec. 1797) to himself. Of similarly high insider authority are the attributions in a privately circulated *Picture of the Changes of Fashion* by "D. S. M.," who is identified as Mrs. Mackie by her brother John Chamier, and in a presentation copy "from the Author" of the third edition of *The Patriot Wolves: A Fable. By a Scotch Episcopal Clergyman*, where the owner to whom it had been presented names

"Rev^{d.} Mr. Robb." Nearly as authoritative are the attributions of experts, as in the case of the Oxford fellow Philip Bliss, who worked for many years on an edition of selections from the diaries of Thomas Hearne and whose interleaved copy of Hearne's *Life* of himself punctiliously identifies the editors (−4): "Mr William Huddesford of Trinity was the Editor of this Volume, as of the Lives of Leland and Wood printed with it, and whereas in the preface p. iv he speaks of 'the editors', it may well be understood that Thomas Warton the Historian of English Poetry is the other person alluded to, who probably suggested the publication, but as was his wont, took but small trouble in its execution."

Often, however, the owner of the book is not specially qualified, and the attribution seems to have come by the grapevine, which may or may not be dependable. British Library copies affirm that the author of *Hints, &c., submitted to the Attention of the Clergy,* described as "A Layman" on the title page, was Augustus Henry Fitzroy, the Duke of Grafton; that "Viator," who published a pamphlet on *The Policy of England and France,* was a Mr Henry; and that *A Summary of the Duties of Citizenship,* which led to the prosecution of the booksellers, was written by "Iliff a dissenter, who prepared it to be printed, and without consulting the booksellers whose names he placed before it, is s^d to have made y^{m.} responsible for the publication." All these attributions are now accepted, the second seemingly on the basis of the manuscript note alone. But if proof were needed that the grapevine might be wrong, there is the counterexample of the spoof edition of *Macbeth,* allegedly by "Harry Rowe, Trumpet-Major to the High Sheriffs of Yorkshire," a real figure but clearly a front for someone else. In a note in his copy, F. G. Waldron, an actor with Garrick who became an editor and bookseller, attributed it to Andrew Hunter, M.D., of York, as did Isaac Reed in a copy in the Boston Public Library; nevertheless, the *DNB* which cites the Boston copy disagrees with them and attributes the work to John Croft of York, who had been a benefactor of Rowe's in other ways.

Writers chose to leave their names off the title pages of their works for, of course, a variety of reasons: discretion, on their own behalf of someone else's; fear of publicity, if they were respectable; fear of failure; fear of prosecution. Southey, we recall, advised a budding poet first to publish anonymously in the newspapers, then if successful to seek payment for further contributions, then to issue a volume, and finally—if *that* were successful—to acknowledge authorship. A familiar feature of eighteenth-century publishing, the option of publishing anonymously or pseudonymously carried over into the Romantic period, when it was brilliantly exploited by Scott and his publishers on behalf of the Waverley novels. All this is well known. What has not been much investigated is the way in which readers reacted to this situation, nor the way in which anonymity in authorship was one of several guessing games played by publisher and reader. Secrecy naturally arouses curiosity; concealment courts disclosure. A closed door may represent a challenge rather than an impossibility. Though names were routinely withheld in the text as well as on the title page, marginalia amply document the efforts of readers to discover what had pointedly been hidden from them. Again, circumstances vary; nevertheless it is possible to describe the commonest forms of disguise or concealment and the persistent will to know among Romantic readers.

The same devices prevail in serious and satiric works, on a spectrum of provocation. Names may be left unmentioned without being deliberately concealed. In histories and memoirs, for example, minor figures may be identified only by their role: a young lady, a neighbor, a clergyman. For someone more important who is not to be named, the author may adopt a fictitious name like Lysander or Chloe, or give a hint by using initials: Lady H., Lieut. D., Madame C. The last method especially provokes the reader to try to penetrate the disguise, since the writer (or publisher) has already gone partway toward providing the supposedly suppressed name. Taking the process a step farther still, one or more letters of the name may be provided with blanks or asterisks in place of the missing letters, as in "Lord L---," "Mr. D--d-s," "D**ns." These are the sorts of occasions that spurred Walpole to action, along with many of his contemporaries eager to prove that they were in the know. For whose benefit were they doing it? For their own pleasure in the first instance, presumably, since it is gratifying to know things and to prove that you do. For a later reading, when the events of the day might be dimmer to memory. For a circle of friends discussing the same work, perhaps, or circulating the book informally among themselves, so that they should feel less in the dark and be encouraged to make their own contributions. For future readers at a greater distance from the events described.

It does seem that in this form of engagement with the text, readers colluded with publishers much as they do in the modern crossword puzzle, exercising their information and their wits with the help of carefully planted clues. In two typical cases of alleged fraud, for instance, Mrs. Gunning's *Letter to the Duke of Argyll* and Mrs. M.W.'s *Narrative of Insidious Transactions,* readers gleefully identify Lord B—— and Lord L—— in the first case as Lords Blandford and Lorne, and Lieut. S—— and Dr. C—— in the second as Lieut. Scot and Dr. Callanan of Cork. Someone who annotated *The Sexagenarian,* William Beloe's posthumously published memoirs, made dozens of circumstantial identifications, going back even to Beloe's schooldays, when "The master predicted I should be a feather in his cap," and this apparent insider is able to gloss "master" with "Mr Raine father of Matthew Raine late Master of the Charter House" (1:10). In a flurry of name-dropping, the same reader identifies the man "of some literary pretentions" who so tormented the great classical scholar Porson that he was driven to declare his "contempt for you, Mr. ***" (1:231): "M^{r} D'Israeli at the table of Mr Hill in Henrietta St Covent Garden. Mr Morris, Mr Kemble, M^{r} Du Bois Mr Fillingham and the late Mr Perry were present. In return for these expressions of severity M^{r} D'Israeli retorted on the Professor in a severe and illnatured note in his Novel of 'Flim Flams'."

Notes like these do not necessarily—not even normally—reflect private information. The readers of Mrs. W.'s and Mrs. Gunning's pamphlets might have been drawing on newspaper reports, and even the knowledgeable owner of *The Sexagenarian* could have been collating Beloe's with other volumes of literary recollections. (On the other hand, he could have been a close acquaintance, a relative, or Thomas Rennell, the editor of Beloe's work, wanting to leave a more detailed record for posterity.) In some cases, "keys" circulated in print or in manuscript, enabling readers to fill in the blanks: for instance, Dawson

Turner's copy of Dibdin's *Bibliomania* contains, as previously noted, a manuscript key to the real-life originals of the thinly fictionalized characters. Hester Piozzi mentions a key to Lady Caroline Lamb's roman-à-clef *Glenarvon* that was passing from hand to hand in her circle in 1816 (*Letters,* 5:527). This traditional reader's aid, like the solution to the crossword puzzles of today, was ideally reserved as a crutch to turn to for correction or confirmation when the reader's own resources had been exhausted, though some purchasers must have simply completed their own copies of the work by adding the names from the key when it came their way.

Books that once belonged to Sir William Musgrave usefully represent the continuity of tradition in such identifications. Musgrave had been a trustee of the British Museum and his significant collection of manuscripts went to the Museum in 1799 after his death, along with a large number of printed books, several of which belong to the genres that rely most heavily on teasing half-concealment, political satires and "secret histories" or lightly veiled scandal. All have identifying notes, usually by Musgrave, occasionally by an earlier owner. His set of *Poems on Affairs of State* (1703–7) is a classic case. The topical references were no longer obvious, and Musgrave approached the works as a historical exercise, with only sporadic success. Assisted by the letters that are supplied and by the rhyme, for instance, when the poem says "Here Painter draw our Politician B--le, / That fawning Arse-worm with his cringing Smile," Musgrave can write in the missing letters to make "Boyle." He doesn't bother with the next puzzle, though (because it's obvious, or because it's indecorous?), as the verse continues, "Relations, Country, Court do all despise him, / He's grown so low ev'n B--g-ry can't rise him." But he carefully identifies "Boyle" in a separate note: "Hen. Boyle M. P. for Cambridge afterw$^{ds.}$ L$^{d.}$ Carleton" (2:431). Likewise in a group of works by Delarivier Manley—*Secret Memoirs and Manners of Several Persons of Quality, The Adventures of Rivella, Memoirs of the Life of Mrs. Manley,* and *The Secret History of Queen Zarah*—Musgrave identifies Zarah as Sarah, Duchess of Marlborough, "Sir Charles Lovemore" as "Lieut$^{t.}$ Gen$^{l.}$ John Tidcomb" (*Adventures,* 1), and a "Lady of Worth and Honour" who came with "a very large

Joynture" as "Marg$^{t.}$ dau.$^{r.}$ & coheir of Geo. L$^{d.}$ Candois and Relict of W$^{m.}$ Brownlow of Humby in Lincoln--" (*Adventures*, 46). In some cases he had the aid of printed keys included in the volumes, but he frequently improves on them. These books remind us that the custom of half concealing and half revealing names was well established in British publishing and that readers took pleasure in literally filling in the blanks; the way the words were printed actively invited the reader's pen (Fig. 25).

When readers today encounter fictitious names and blanks in satires and political allegories of the Romantic period they tend to assume that these devices were dictated by prudence, that the writer and publisher would have been at risk (challenge, prosecution, retaliation) if they had named names. But with very few exceptions, the names are so badly hidden that they might as well not have been hidden at all, and the laws were so seldom enforced that they were generally disregarded. If the authorities were out to get particular publishers or authors, no amount of discretion would save them anyway, so the producers of Pigott's *Jockey Club*, with satirical portraits of the P----e of W---s, D--e of Y--k, and Mr. F-x, could enjoy the revenues of at least six editions in 1792, revel in poetic controversy, and publish a sequel, *The Female Jockey Club*, two years later. If initials, rhymes, and rhythm were not enough, the publishers might offer more clues in printed footnotes. In Charles Stewart's "The Regicide," for example, the couplet "All press'd some tribute of respect to bring, / B---, B---, B---, B---, B---, B---" is attached to a footnote: "To fill up all the blanks, see a list of the opposition of the day" (11). (Though about as well informed on the topic of contemporary politics as a reader could be, William Hone filled in only the rhyming final name "Byng" in his copy.) John Gifford's *Orange, a Political Rhapsody* gets the reader started by means of printed footnotes such as the one glossing "L-------e" in "Yet Popish L-------e, or more Popish B----e": "This gentleman is an ingenious poet and Baronet, being the author of Catholic Emancipation, and several copies of obscene verses, which he handeth about amongst the young ladies of his acquaintance.—" With this help the reader was able to identify "Sir Hercules Langrishe" (14).

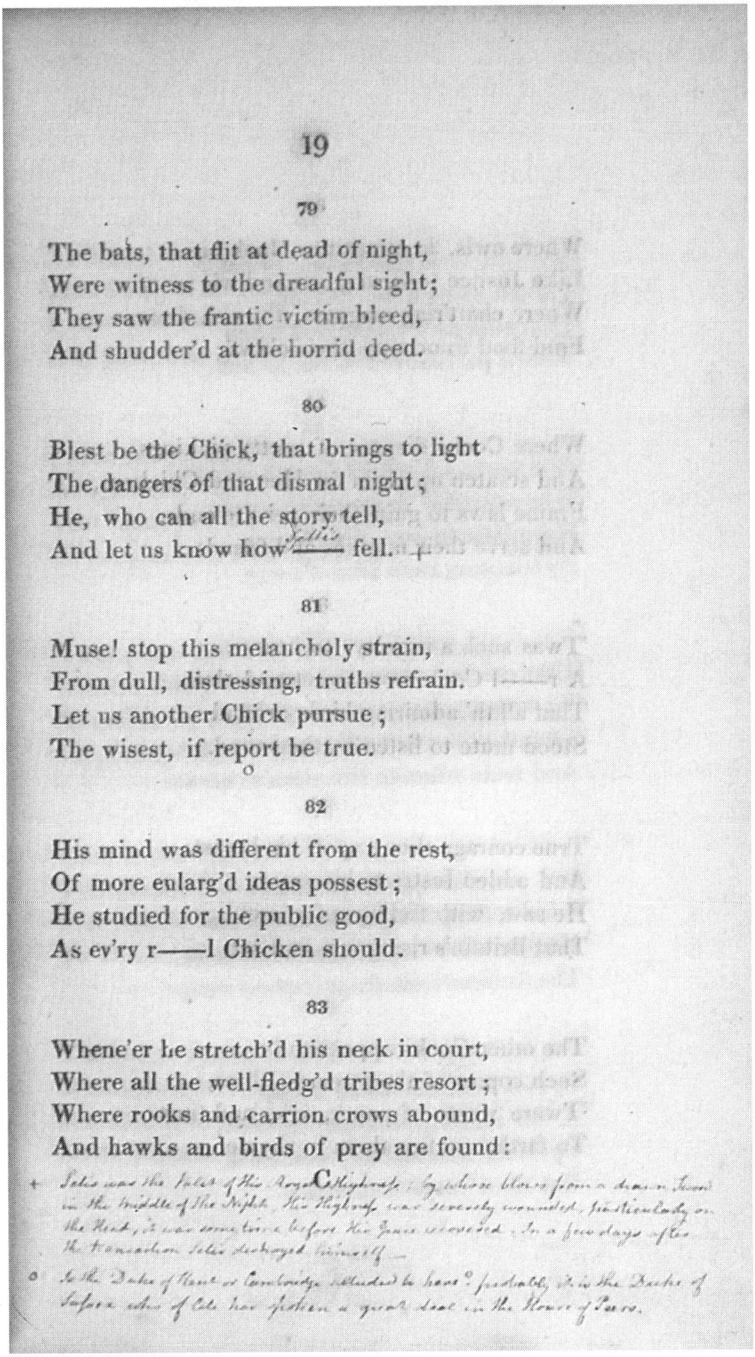

19

79

The bats, that flit at dead of night,
Were witness to the dreadful sight;
They saw the frantic victim bleed,
And shudder'd at the horrid deed.

80

Blest be the Chick, that brings to light
The dangers of that dismal night;
He, who can all the story tell,
And let us know how ——[Sellis] fell. +

81

Muse! stop this melancholy strain,
From dull, distressing, truths refrain.
Let us another Chick pursue;
The wisest, if report be true. o

82

His mind was different from the rest,
Of more enlarg'd ideas possest;
He studied for the public good,
As ev'ry r——l Chicken should.

83

Whene'er he stretch'd his neck in court,
Where all the well-fledg'd tribes resort;
Where rooks and carrion crows abound,
And hawks and birds of prey are found:

C

\+ Sellis was the valet of His Royal Highness, by whose blows from a drawn Sword in the middle of the Night, His Highness was severely wounded, particularly on the Head, it was some time before His Grace recovered. In a few days after the transaction Sellis destroyed himself—

o Is the Duke of Kent or Cambridge alluded to here? probably it is the Duke of Sussex who of late has spoken a great deal in the House of Peers.

FIG. 25 A page from *The R---l Brood*, 15th edition (1814), by "Peter Pindar, Jun.," with notes by an unidentified reader. By permission of the British Library.

The guessing game had a social side, as readers argued about concealed identities or helped one another out. Byron made a present of the identification of "Joannes! best and dearest of my friends" ("Lord Clare, Harrow") when he gave a lady a copy of his *Poems on Various Occasions* (112). On the other hand, disagreement and uncertainty are also revealed in marginalia, even between the boards of a single book, as when a later owner of the copy of Pigott's *Jockey Club* now in the British Library complained on a flyleaf, "The names are often filled up very incorrectly" (−2). At least one copy of *A Town Eclogue,* the talk of Edinburgh in 1804, offers two readers' different guesses about an unnamed reviewer, a barrister who would harangue the very whores in a brothel about "the necessity of pushing vigorous measures at home" (10): one thought it was Jeffrey, the other thought Brougham.[14] More commonly, debate is reflected in multiple copies of a work with differing identifications. The National Library of Scotland holds four annotated copies of this *Town Eclogue,* published anonymously by George William Auriol Hay-Drummond, a clergyman, brother to the Earl of Kinnoul. The authorship appears to have been an open secret, but annotators differ about other details. Is "H*******" in the line "How H******* din'd, and how the Duchess dress'd" Hamilton, which matches the asterisks, or Huntly, which scans (22)? A copy in the British Library which claims the authority of a key furnished by "the late G. Drummond Hay—cousin of the Writer" (6) has some but not all of the answers. It endorses "Hamilton." It also contains on an interleaf a tongue-in-cheek biography of the author, "a Man of the most profligate habits [who] . . . went to Ireland and in returning from thence was to the great consolation of all his friends—drowned."

AN AGE OF EDITORS

The common practice of filling up blanks and adding corroborative detail shades easily into various kinds of editorial activity. The eighteenth century had seen a great increase in the number of annotated editions of vernacular literature, the traditions of humanist scholarship being brought to bear on works written in or translated into English.[15]

As with the classical editions described earlier, the eighteenth-century editors of Shakespeare, Milton, Butler, Swift, Pope, and others divided their attention between text and commentary: in some cases where the texts were obscure or corrupt much effort might go into seeking manuscript versions or early, authoritative printings, but in others the editors' time went to clarification of the meanings of words and images by means of paraphrase or parallel passages. A commentary might even be published without the text, to accompany whatever version the reader already owned: the publisher Jonathan Richardson and his son (also Jonathan) thus produced their massive *Explanatory Notes and Remarks on Milton's Paradise Lost* in 1734. These editions and commentaries were not, as they might be today, the preserve of academics; the work had not yet been professionalized. The copyright decision of 1774, coupled with a demand for literature of all kinds in English, made the growing market very inviting to editors, commentators, and compilers, with the result that by 1804, when Southey sent Longman a proposal for an edition of the works of Sidney, he felt obliged to advise him, "If you approve the scheme, it may be well to announce it, as we may very probably be forestalled, for this is the age of editors" (*Life*, 2:307).

The editorlike behavior of many readers of the period could be said to be overdetermined: they had all sorts of incentives. At a very basic level, there was the pressure of economy. The reader who could afford only one copy of White's *Selborne* or Cowper's poems could build on that, incorporating in manuscript what seemed like suitable materials from later editions and other sources, and thus making up a unique customized edition. Then there was the model of the great editions, particularly the variorum editions of the Bible, Shakespeare, and Milton, with notes culled from various commentators implicitly urging readers to judge between them and if they could, to add their mite to the collection. As in natural history, no professional qualification was required and readers were not automatically excluded from what Marcus Walsh calls the "community of commentary" that the editions represented (95). At a psychological level, there was the sense of participation that most readers feel when they read, which can be made concrete in a contribution to the text; once started, the work of contributing can become a regular pastime, a project, and the reader a lieutenant to the author. Finally there was the possibility of publication, either through print or through manuscript circulation.

A remarkable example in the biblical tradition is the work of William George Thompson, a follower of the prophetess Joanna Southcott (1750–1814) who claimed to be the "woman clothed with the sun" of Revelation 12. Many of Southcott's prophecies were published in tracts that were then collected by and shared among believers, gathering manuscript commentary as they went. Some existing annotated copies contain merely expressions of admiration and attention; others have corrections, improvements, and questions. In the British Library, one owner of Southcott's *Copies and Parts of Copies of Letters* points out passages that are "Striking" (6, 7, 40) or "Wonderfull" (8), and enjoins other readers to "Attend to this" (9), while another unknown annotator of *The Third Book of Wonders* takes up doctrinal matters and carefully explains that he or she has "made these remarks concidering who's to read this book" (6). The sect evidently took the publication and dissemination of its beliefs as a serious responsibility. Thompson joined Southcott's sect at Easter, April 14, in 1811; the date is commemorated in an inscription in the first volume of his collection of tracts by and about Southcott. He prepared these works carefully for circulation: a note at the end of the first volume explains that he would lend them out "provided their return'd safe," and that if one did not prove persuasive, the borrower could have another. His friends, he says, may think him a "deluded Youth," but he believes, and sets out to prove, that Southcott's prophecies were "indicted, by the same Spirit, that inspired those men that wrote the old and new Testament" (+1).

Thompson's work remains incomplete—he probably stopped when Southcott died without delivering the promised Shiloh—but its direction is clear. His method was to annotate these tracts in imitation of editions of the Old and New Testaments. Following much controversy, the 1611 King James version of the Bible had been authorized on condition that it appear without interpretative commentary, glosses being restricted to explanations of obscure Hebrew and Greek terms, and internal cross-references. Although commentary inevitably crept back in, the basic minimum for the dominant English Bible continued to be an apparatus of marginal references showing the recurrence of the same phrases in the two Testaments. Thompson studied Southcott's texts as though they were new books of the Bible and demonstrated their inspired composition by dressing them in the familiar garb: to every phrase that echoed or alluded to a verse in the Bible he gave a little italic superscript letter, generally in red ink, keyed to the margin where the corresponding biblical texts were cited. The first volume (of five extant) also contains running heads in manuscript and cross-references for the set of tracts itself—that is, besides references to the Bible, notes indicating where else in her prophecies Southcott makes the same point, for instance, "as Christ took his Trial for Man, Satan must now take his—1.1.175, 176 | 1.2.11, 98 | 6.2.32 | 6.3.84, 87, 106, 115."[16] The references indicate volume, part, and page in Thompson's arrangement. This note incidentally suggests that there were once six volumes or more in the collection. He organized the pamphlets into volumes and wrote tables of contents for the first two volumes before having them all bound in sober black, like Bibles, with the title "Joanna Southcott Prophecies" gold-tooled on the spine and his own name at the base of it. Only the first volume has this kind of cross-reference, however; at some point Thompson gave up his task. But while it lasted it was undoubtedly a work of devotion and self-discipline.

Some of the annotated books of this period that look like editions must actually be drafts that were never published, or work in progress like Thompson's. But many others, especially works that already contain editorial apparatus, merely show readers disagreeing with the printed notes or adding notes of their own. Apart from one interleaved set in which he composed his lecture notes, Coleridge's Shakespeares—indeed almost everybody's Shakespeares—are like that. He expresses a preference for one editor's speculative emendation over another's, grumbles about editors who dwell on the obvious and overlook a crying need ("A note explanatory on Pigromitus &c would have been more acceptable"), and entertains bright ideas as they come to him, for instance the notion that Shakespeare must really have named the prostitute in *Henry IV Part 2* Doll Tear-street, Tear-sheet being an apparent corruption of the text.[17] Readers like him became involved in the collective project of fully explaining Shakespeare. And yet the tone of his notes shows that he was responding to and refining the work of the editors, not aiming to displace them with an edition of his own.

New work, as opposed to titles of proven worth, presents other opportunities to the editorial mindset. Marginal annotation is particularly suited to the sort of minute verbal criticism that textual editors specialized in, but scholarly editors did not normally practice on their contemporaries. In the absence of official press readers and copyeditors, authors got advice, both solicited and unsolicited, from readers through the medium of marginalia. Boswell acknowledged the contributions of a friend who had sent him an annotated copy of the *Life of Johnson* when he was preparing the second edition, and we know of at least one other that he received anonymously but chose not to make use of.[18] John Clare suffered the well-meaning advice of socially superior patrons, conveyed in notes to his manuscripts and printed texts.[19] James Browne of Edinburgh advised George Goldie in his dispute with James Hogg by recommending revisions to his *Letter to a Friend in London*, marking up what may be a prepublication copy for that purpose.

In another case of prepublication printing, Sir James Bland Burges tested the waters of reader response by having a handful of copies of his Spenserian poem *Richard the First* printed for distribution to friends for their advice. The British Library holds three of these annotated copies together with a fourth into which Burges entered the suggestions he had decided to accept from a total of seven readers. It is altogether a remarkable example not only of collaborative revision but also of the expectations and standards of the time, and it worked—at least, the poem was a fashionable success when it appeared in 1801. Some of Burges's friendly critics attacked the poem line by line, recommending changes to the sense or rhythm. Most of them also made general observations about the plan and style. The most assiduous reader, William Boscawen, rolled up his sleeves and started in on the very first lines: "The lines do not appear (upon the whole) as good as they ought to be; particularly ye two first & ye sixth. The 7th too is rather equivocal in meaning: &, as this Poem coincides with our own Theology, I would not invoke the Muse 'from the Aonian Mount'" ([1]). John Anstey, on the other hand, tried to save time with a thumbs-up / thumbs-down method of marking that left the author to figure out what might be wrong:

> NB. For the sake of convenience & dispatch & to avoid repetition in commenting upon the Poem the following method is adopted—a Qy is set against such lines & expressions as appear defective in poetical Spirit or Rhythm or in short are supposed to be in any way incorrect or exceptionable—an X is annexed to such passages as appear to be remarkable for justness of Expression or imagery & excel generally in any of the Properties of good poetical Composition ([1])

The three readers whose work survives did not often coincide in their criticism. With the natural ingratitude of an author, Burges appears to have accepted some specific verbal improvements but rejected others, and to have ignored general suggestions altogether. The whole group of copies nevertheless deserves closer study and comparison for what it might reveal about practical critical standards in the period.

In contrast to the friendly advice of Burges's readers, hostile readers sometimes also expressed their opinions in editorial form. I have described elsewhere Samuel Parr's heartless treatment of the poems of Mrs. Pickering, following his emendation of the title page to include "notes explanatory and ornamental by Philononsensicus."[20] About 1830, Brackstone Baker wrote numbered footnotes to his copy of James Ingram's admittedly rather sanctimonious volume of poems about love and piety, *The First Sabbath, and Other Poems.* Like regular editors he observes parallel passages in other poets, but with the apparent intent of disparagement rather than elucidation: Ingram is shown to be silently indebted to Byron and Hemans. Like Lidwill, Baker glosses the text in such a way as to translate Ingram's words. But his aim is to expose the pretensions of the author, who seems to have been a grocer. Baker's notes are cynical and snobbish, but shrewd. "My lonely lattice tower" is glossed as "Garret Window—in Maryport St" (1); "My Native Vale" as a laundry in Maryport Alley (20). To the lines "One flower of heavenly birth still blooms/To gild your darkened horoscope" Baker objects, "How can a flower gild a horoscope, 3 very discordant images" (43). In a love poem, Baker questions the social as well as literary correctness of an image but makes a suggestion that would be even more ludicrous. Ingram's lines are "So droops that gentle form till I,/The sun to the sweet flower, am by" (130). Baker's response: "Unconscionable assurance—to call yourself a Sun in Heaven, & the Lady a poor drooping Plant on Earth—The image might be reversed with more propriety—."

An earlier instance of the mocking mock edition is a presentation copy of Thomas Smith's *Poems*, published in Manchester in 1797 and described in the "Advertisement" as a collection of poems produced for a writing group got together "to relieve the languor of a secluded situation." It was a gift from the author to a fellow poet, William Hampson, who either assembled or invented a group of friends of his own to criticize it in a dozen or so manuscript footnotes, written under several names (as in a variorum edition) but in the same hand. They combine to make fun of particular lines, for example, "The strain'd eye, pacing o'er the dewy lawn" (52):

> i.e. on its Palfrey—Wm Hampson
> It evidently means the eye pacing over the lawn in Pattens. J. Bardsley
> I think it means the eye walking slowly & in its Night Gown & Slippers. J. Kenworthy

"The latent sources of the moral power" must be an "error of the press again | he means the moral Pose" (81). Finally, when something is said to "Melt into mist, and swim before the sight" (90), the annotators comment, "Of this Author we can only say that his Imagery and meaning 'Melt into mist & swim before the sight['] Monthly Review." In cases like these the critical tools of the editor and reviewer are combined to damn the author, and we may be painfully reminded of the kind of close scrutiny writers had to expect from their readers. Thanking a friend for a detailed critique, Byron once remarked in a letter, "I need not remind you, how few of the *best poems* in our Language, will stand the Test of *minute*, or *verbal* Criticism" (*Letters*, 1:111).

The most touching case of a reader of the time behaving like an editor is that of Keats's close friend Richard Woodhouse, who carefully assembled a collection of "Keatsiana" that he left to Keats's publisher John Taylor on his death in 1834. Interleaved and annotated copies of Keats's *Poems* (1817) and *Endymion* (1818) are at the core of a set of papers—letters, albums, scrapbooks, and commonplace-books—that constitute such an important contemporary archive that most of them have now been published in transcription or facsimile.[21] Woodhouse's training as a lawyer may have made him a careful reader, a tireless transcriber, and the efficient manager of a system of record-keeping, but what is most impressive about these annotated books is not the industry they represent but the loyal faith that led Woodhouse to treat the works of his young friend as though they were already in the class of Shakespeare and Milton. Woodhouse's notes are not a record of private reading but a collection of bits and pieces of information by which he aims to guide other readers. Since he had privileged access to Keats, his notes bear unusual authority. At several points he is able to say, "So explained by the author to me," or the equivalent.[22] Although the two volumes are interleaved and annotated in similar ways, the front flyleaves being used for tributes and epigraphs, the text for variant readings and explanatory notes (some of them in shorthand), and the back flyleaves for longer extracts and transcriptions, the *Poems* gives more the impression of work done to satisfy personal interest, and *Endymion* that of an incomplete draft edition geared for eventual publication. The *Poems* contains some quite intimate revelations, for instance an indication of Keats's sensitivity about his height; *Endymion* does not.[23] *Endymion* has more formal and expansive notes—or gestures toward them—, particularly on mythology, as when a reference to the Argonauts leads Woodhouse to write, "The Allusion is to a circumstance told by Apollonius Rhodius in his Argonautic Expedition. The following extract from the translation of this Work will make these lines more intelligible."[24] (But no extract follows.)

Woodhouse's work is no doubt most valuable for having preserved information not available through other sources. It has a secondary interest, however, as a record of what one contemporary reader thought other contemporary readers would be interested in knowing—that is, as evidence of shared critical standards. Most of his assumptions are perfectly conventional. Like other literary editors, Woodhouse records variant readings and proposes emendations to the text; the distinction between these two kinds of note is not always as clear as we might like it to be. He traces allusions and quotes sources, finding the "dimpled hand . . . some wonder out of fairy land" in "Calidore," for example, in the "white wonder of Juliet's hand" in *Romeo and Juliet*.[25] He uses parallel passages for sources and to illustrate usage, and paraphrase to clarify obscure meanings. "Why so sad a moan" in "Sleep and Poetry," for instance, is first scanned and then glossed "yet why look on life in such sad colours?"[26]

Like the friendly critics of Burges's work, however, Woodhouse devotes most of his attention to fine points of diction and meter; in doing so he is very much of his time, for diction and meter, on the evidence of marginalia, are what readers chiefly attended to. The notes to *Endymion*, if they were intended to make up a new edition some day, are incomplete. At certain points Woodhouse merely indicates what he wants to know, what as yet eludes his understanding. Of "my crystalline dominions / Half lost," he says, "Q[uery] half? why?"[27] Letters and other records of the period tend to confirm this focus on detail among readers of verse. Crabb Robinson recalls one occasion when he read Wordsworth aloud and there was general discussion of what he could have meant by "seeing Jehovah unalarmed," also an evening with Wordsworth at the Lambs' in 1815, when the news about his work was that "He has substituted *ebullient* for fiery, speaking of the nightingale, and *jocund* for laughing, applied to the daffodils" (1:465, 482). Meter, likewise, was a matter of practical concern if poetry was to be read in company, and as we have seen, even charity children were taught about patterns of emphasis. Woodhouse himself wrote poetry, though apparently not for publication: there is a draft of a sonnet "To Apollo—written after reading Sleep & Poetry" at the back of the *Poems*. Some of his metrical analyses look odd by modern standards, but he knew what he was doing and he lays the system out plainly, with illustrative quotations, at the beginning of the *Poems,* so perhaps there is something to be learned about contemporary practice from his example.[28] His overt critical pronouncements seem lame enough to modern readers; nevertheless they are consistent with the standards of criticism of the time when, apart from declared allegories, overall meaning seems to have been taken for granted but local meaning—words and phrases—debated. Of the Indian Maiden's song in Book Four of *Endymion* he merely observes, "The poetical power shewn in this ode cannot be described"; of lines about the role of poesy as "a friend / To soothe the care, and lift the thoughts of man," in "Sleep and Poetry," he says, "beautiful representation of the true subject of poetry."[29]

Woodhouse is an outstanding contemporary witness to the way poetry was read during the period, in a combination of traditional and newly emerging approaches. As far as criticism and the history of criticism are concerned, the great originality and value of his annotated copies of Keats lie in his deliberate application of biographical information to the interpretation of the poems. Eighteenth-century readers might have liked to hear about the lives of the writers whose work they admired, but in the first place not much information was available for writers of earlier ages, and in the second place, with the exception of occasional verse editors tended to keep the lives and the works separate. Biographical memoirs might appear at the front of an edition of somebody's works, but the works were not usually glossed with reference to the life. Johnson's "Prefaces," which set the standard for a century or more after they appeared in 1779–81, not only came to be published apart from the edition to which they first contributed, but were usually internally divided into two distinct parts, one a narrative of the life and the other a critical commentary on the work, piece by piece. After a few very successful literary biographies of the 1790s and early 1800s, however—works such as Boswell's *Life of Johnson* and Hayley's *Cowper*—the two tended to merge, especially after 1802 under the influence of reviews on the *Edinburgh* model which discussed the work and the author almost interchangeably. In 1820, writing in fact about Keats, John Clare observed that "every body is anxious to know something about an author & woud even buy the book to satisfy that curosity" (*Letters*, 17).

Woodhouse was quite clear about his intentions for the collection as a whole:

> There is a great deal of reality about all that Keats writes: and there must be many allusions to particular Circumstances, in his poems: which would add to their beauty & Interest, if properly understood.—To arrest some few of these circumstances, & bring them to view in connexion with the poetic notice of them, is one of the objects of this collection—and of the observations—as it is of the notes in the interleaved copies of his published Works.[30]

He goes on to say, in a remark that may suggest that he was aware that what he was doing represented a special kind of approach to literature at large, "How valuable would such notes be to Shakespeares Sonnets, which teem with allusions to his life, & its circumstances, his age, his loves, his patrons &c—." Woodhouse correctly assumes that other readers of the time (after 1818, before 1834) think along the same lines, and so his mission is to do for Keats what can never be done for Shakespeare, that is, to record biographical evidence relevant to the work, as in the idea that Keats's personal insecurity about his height lay behind "Had I a man's fair form." He accordingly takes pains to describe the circumstances surrounding the composition of particular poems and to identify the real-life people whose names had been concealed. He mentions Keats's guide to the interpretation of the opening of Book Three of *Endymion:* "It will be easily seen what I think of the present Ministers by the beginning of the 3^d. Book."[31] He records, but in pencil and in shorthand, so it might be that he was not sure that he should use it, Keats's emotional response to lines about the charm of a fickle woman, "like a milk-white lamb that bleats / For man's protection": "When K had written these lines he burst into tears overpowered by the tenderness of his own imagination."[32] This is a revelation that has nothing to do with the sense or diction or meter of the lines but a lot to say, or rather to suggest, about personal significance.

Even without Thompson's or Woodhouse's sense of mission, collectors of the time liked to work with their books and many of them, methodically minded, turned special books into long-term projects. The British Library copy of Hay-Drummond's *Town Eclogue* is a good example of a seemingly ephemeral publication's having become such a project for its owner, James Maidment, who had extra pages bound in to take notes and clippings. Bit by bit, he turned it into a fragment of local history. In the same spirit but on a larger scale, an unidentified annotator worked for years on a collection called "Pindaric Poems," also now in the British Library.[33]

"Pindaric Poems" is the collector's name for a set of 140 poems published between 1809 and 1821, each about 30 pages long, many of them presented under one version or another of the "Peter Pindar" pseudonym. By 1809 the original Peter Pindar, John Wolcot, was no longer producing his lively, lucrative topical satires and so imitators sprang up, especially between 1812 and 1820, the years of the "Whig vendetta" against the Prince Regent (George, xxii). The only thing that is certain about the second-generation "Peter Pindar" and his alter egos "P---- P-----," "Peter Pindar Jun.," "Peter Pindar Minimus," "The Real Peter Pindar," etc. is that he was no single writer. George Daniel and John Agg are known to have used the name, but so did others. Nor did "he" have a single publisher: Fairburn and Johnston both advertised multiple titles suitable for collecting (Fig. 26), and half a dozen other publishers were responsible for particular titles. Groups of these poems, gathered in one volume or in several, are not uncommon today, for purchasers would soon have found they had the makings of a collection even without the encouragement of the publishers. The British Library's "Pindaric Poems" are as a set neither pure nor complete: they do not include all the Pindar poems of the Regency and they do admit satires of the same style published anonymously and under other pseudonyms: "Humphrey Hedgehog," "Beelzebub Junior," "Syntax Sidrophel," "Zachary Zealoushead," and so forth. They are arranged in approximately chronological order, with manuscript tables of contents

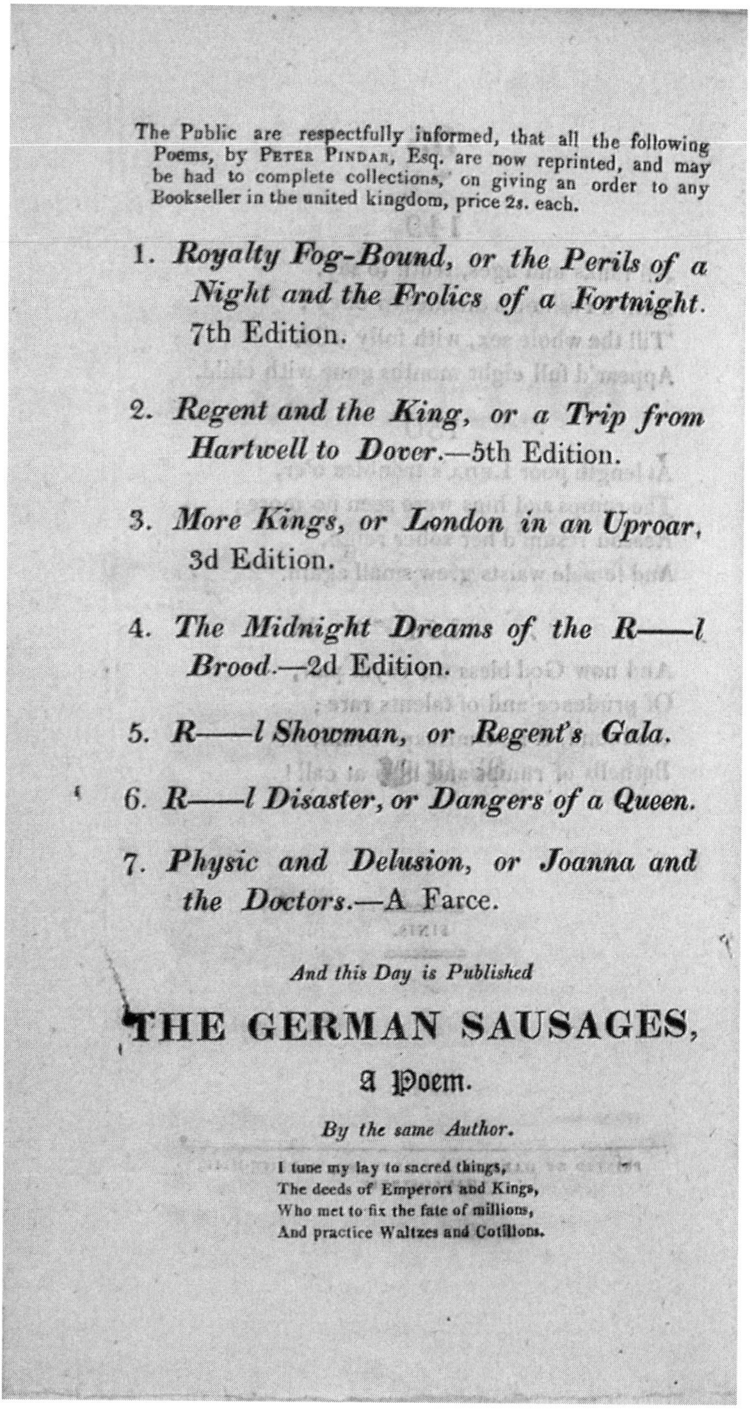

The Public are respectfully informed, that all the following Poems, by PETER PINDAR, Esq. are now reprinted, and may be had to complete collections, on giving an order to any Bookseller in the united kingdom, price 2s. each.

1. *Royalty Fog-Bound, or the Perils of a Night and the Frolics of a Fortnight.* 7th Edition.

2. *Regent and the King, or a Trip from Hartwell to Dover.*—5th Edition.

3. *More Kings, or London in an Uproar,* 3d Edition.

4. *The Midnight Dreams of the R——l Brood.*—2d Edition.

5. *R——l Showman, or Regent's Gala.*

6. *R——l Disaster, or Dangers of a Queen.*

7. *Physic and Delusion, or Joanna and the Doctors.*—A Farce.

And this Day is Published

THE GERMAN SAUSAGES,

A Poem.

By the same Author.

I tune my lay to sacred things,
The deeds of Emperors and Kings,
Who met to fix the fate of millions,
And practice Waltzes and Cotillons.

FIG. 26 Publisher's advertisement in a copy of *The Cork Rump, or Queen and Maids of Honour* (1815). By permission of the British Museum.

FIG. 27 *John Bull Mad with Joy!* (1814). © The Trustees of The British Library.

that must have been late additions. The owner began the process of annotation when the poems first came out, but continued to tinker at it: the earliest dated notes are from 1816, the last datable allusion is 1842 or later. He wrote most of his notes in pencil so that he could correct and improve them over time, but at a certain point he began to trace them over neatly in ink, a task he never finished.

The Pindars of the Regency and their ilk offered amusing, irreverent commentary on the news of the day. Before Peterloo they could hardly be called radical. (Hone and his associates, after Peterloo, are another story; a few of their poems are included toward the end of this collection.[34]) They were the verbal counterpart of the better known satirical prints, which cost about the same amount, a shilling or two, and which usually also contained verbal elements, including half-hidden names to be filled in by the owner, as in Fig. 27. (The Jubilee which is the subject of this print was the occasion of several Pindar poems, including *The R----t's Fair, The R----t's Fleet, The P----e's Jubilee, The R---l Showman,* and *The Temple Knock'd Down; or, R---l Auction!! The Last Day of the Jubilee,* all included in the third volume of the British Library collection.)

The owner of these Pindars, perhaps surprisingly, seldom speculates about authorship.[35] Nor does he express decided political opinions, though he seems to have been cautiously whiggish. His attention goes first to filling in the names and then, by an extension of that exercise, to glossing more covert allusions to persons and events. Fig. 25, for example, represents a page from *The R---l Brood*, which surveyed the royal dukes one by one under the guise of a barnyard allegory as the "chicks" of "Farmer" George the Third. The blank in stanza 80, where the subject is the cruelty of a particularly "ferocious Cock" identified earlier as the Duke of Cumberland, is filled up with the name "Sellis"; then a footnote explains,

> Selis was the Valet of His Royal Highness; by whose Blows from a drawn Sword in the middle of the Night, His Highness was severely wounded, particularly on the Head, it was some time before His Grace recovered. In a few days after the transaction Selis destroyed himself—

As proof that the owner was drawing on his own information and not on a key, the following note, seeking to identify the "wisest" of the chicks "if report be true" is uncertain: "Is the Duke of Kent or Cambridge alluded to here? probably it is the Duke of Sussex who of late has spoken a great deal in the House of Peers."[36] In this case the game of filling in the blanks developed into something more like a running commentary, though there is no sign of any intention to publish.

This annotator's historical facts are not absolutely reliable, and since the Pindaric poems themselves are no longer read it probably doesn't matter, but his thousands of notes constitute an interesting record of common preoccupations of the time and of the mental habits of readers of this kind of work. They have also the incidental charm of casual reference to local customs long since lost, as when the poet reflects on the Regent's taking over the Serpentine for the model ships enacting a naval battle at the Jubilee:

No more, upon thy verdant banks,
Shall wanton urchins' early pranks
Offend thee, e'er Sol's ruddy beam
Has shone upon thy silent stream.

The annotator explains, "Permission is given to Bathe in the Serpentine before 8 °Clock in the Morning, but not after that hour."[37]

The annotator of these little pamphlet-poems may have been keeping records to assist his own memory, but he clearly also expected that his notes would be useful to other readers sooner or later. And so they have been, though it is increasingly likely that efforts like his will be primarily of interest as historically conditioned exercises rather than as sources of information. The same is true of many such projects, including some that have been described under other headings here, for instance the Bible that Hester Piozzi annotated for Susanna Rudd, creating an heirloom; John Horseman's extensively "illustrated" copies of books by and about literary women; and the Southcott pamphlets carefully prepared for circulation by Thompson. Among the categories of works that quite often turn up with decades-worth of readerly contributions are Bibles and prayer books, specialist catalogues (for instance, of coins or prints), and county histories. But a collector could turn almost any kind of book to account. Richard Warner's *Antiquitates Culinariae; or Curious Tracts relating to the Culinary Affairs of the Old English* (1791), acquired by Sarah Sophia Banks in 1811, was steadily improved with notes that display her lively interest in historical, culinary, gustatory, and linguistic aspects of the subject. Warner, for example, declares that the Roman diet was disgusting, "for surely it would be esteemed preferable, to suffer something from hunger, than to load the stomach, with *dormice*, *polypi*, *hedge-hogs*, and *cuttle-fish*" (viii); but Banks disagrees, pointing out that polypi and cuttle-fish are still eaten in Southern Europe and considered "Savory & Wholsome Food." A recipe for "grewel forced" with a footnote explaining that "forced" means "enriched with flesh" draws from her the remark "The word forced, is probably derived from Vorst, Germ: a Sausage filld with meat ground small in a mortar our Forcemeat balls are clearly similar to sausage meat" (4). From the presence of a recipe involving cherries she infers that cherries must have been grown in England earlier than had been thought (13). And she cites other authorities, not holding back her own opinions: in a section on rice, she observes, "Gervase Markham speaking of Rice says 'altho it grow not much in our kingdom' Farewell to Husbandry Book 2. Ch. 19. I doubt" (5). An alert and informed reader, she systematically introduces new information, better references, and contrary opinions.

John Lawrence, the son of a brewer who appears to have worked breeding animals and managing estates and eventually became a writer on husbandry, also wrote for periodicals and was known as an advocate for the prevention of cruelty to animals. He collected materials for a history of his own time and is said by the *DNB* to have been "unable to restrain a too facile pen." These last qualities are rather improbably on display in his copy of Anthony Robinson's antiwar tract of 1798, *A View of the Causes and Consequences of English Wars.* Lawrence presents himself as a collaborator in this book, with his name in manuscript under the author's on the title page: "With M.S. Notes by J. L." Lawrence approached the book methodically: penciled notes at the front keep track of the dates of major events; notes in ink at the back trace topics page by page and constitute a summary of the work. The text is marked in ink with lines and underlining and occasional marginal notes, but most of Lawrence's contributions appear in the form of neat footnotes wherever he had something to add. Once in a while he corrects a fact or challenges an opinion, but on the whole he supports Robinson's democratic argument that Parliament should be reformed in order to allow the people to make their views count, since if the governments of Europe had listened to the populations of their countries most of these devastating wars would not have happened. Though more than thirty years had passed since Robinson published the book—Lawrence's ownership inscription is dated 1831—reform was still a matter of great concern. Since the book takes a long perspective on English wars and Lawrence's interest was chiefly in the politics of his own time, the number of notes increases as the history comes closer to the present. Lawrence, like Walpole, retails anecdote and does not hesitate to include his own opinions and experience in these notes. For example, when Robinson mentions that certain alleged Jacobite conspirators had been severely punished on very slight evidence, Lawrence adds (166): "These Conspirators were detained in prison throughout their lives, an especial Act (I believe) being necessary & passed in every successive Parliament for that purpose. A son of one of them, an artificial feather-maker lived in Catharine Street, Strand, at the period when the present writer was about thirty years of age—about 1783." Lawrence's often extensive notes look back over the issues and events of his adult life, reflecting on the outcome of the wars which were still in progress when Robinson reluctantly lent his voice to the war against France though "Every friend of humanity weeps to find that this is necessary, and wishes for peace" (240n). "Peace at length came," notes Lawrence, "& with it the renovation of ancient tyranny, which needed & produced in due time, a second revolution in France." In the project of commenting on Robinson, Lawrence found an outlet for his own views and experience.

CORRECTING THE PUBLIC RECORD

Being able to write notes in the margins of books created an opportunity not only for collectors and the well-to-do but for all owners and some (indulged, uninhibited, or unscrupulous) borrowers to display their knowledge or expertise and do good at the same time by correcting the public record. Books annotated in this way for show and for posterity deserve to be recognized as historical resources since they represent an alternative contemporary voice and often call into question a received view. This function is especially conspicuous in memoirs and biographies, as the examples of Walpole and Piozzi (and of Thelwall to come) suggest: their notes in the margins serve various purposes but reminiscence about people they had known tends to make them expansive, and since they well knew that their books would circulate and their notes would be copied, the notes amount to public or semi-public statements.

A struggling painter and occasional writer, Benjamin Robert Haydon deliberately signed many of the notes in his books. His copy of Williams's *Life and Correspondence of Sir Thomas Lawrence*, for instance, annotated in 1833, disputes Williams's presentation of the fashionable portraitist at point after point, starting with the frontispiece self-portrait: "how the eyes beam with an intelligence the brain possesses not," Haydon observes, "Ah Lawrence, handsome Lawrence, thou wast made for the Time & the Time for thee!" Haydon was talking back to the book as we have seen others do, but unlike them he pointedly adds his name or initials to strong expressions of opinion ("Not a fact. BRH" [1:347]) and to debunking anecdotes such as ones about Lawrence's arrangement with a bailiff named Radford and his scheming to have a picture of his own better hung while that of "a brother artist" was demoted (1:131, 2:50). On the other hand, he praises Lawrence's testimony on the Elgin Marbles: "Lawrence's evidence on the Elgin Marbles will remain, when the meretriciousness of his art has been found out & despised—B.R.H." (1:405). For Haydon as for that other neglected, impoverished, embittered artist, Blake, the margins of books provided an outlet and potentially publicity for his views.

It was not only in matters of personal acquaintance that readers chose to set the record straight by way of marginalia. Any significant event—a battle, an expedition, an execution—of which they had firsthand knowledge invited comment. Eyewitness marginalia, especially, add detail to the public record and may represent otherwise unheard points of view. They were surely composed with the idea that they might some day be called on. For example, a series of penciled notes, some of them signed, in Heriot's account of the 1781 siege of Gibraltar contributes the impressions and recollections of an officer, W. Booth, who had been in charge of working parties on the day that the British forces made an unexpected and strategically risky sortie. The anonymous *Account of the Conquest of Mauritius* attracted notes on such petty points that they can only have been written by someone who was there. The owner, T. Hardwicke—perhaps Thomas Hardwicke, who later published on India—disputes, for instance, the author's account of the way the expedition crossed a river, the troops being said to have passed "over the beams [of an improvised bridge] without any other inconvenience" (14). Hardwicke proposes an addition: they passed without any other inconvenience "than obliging the Artillery to drag their Guns over the River thro a narrow but rapid Current—and rendered difficult from the Number of fragments of Rock scattered through the whole bed of the River." In the same spirit of mild grievance, Nicholas Revett annotated copies of Richard Chandler's *Travels in Greece* and *Travels in Asia Minor*, seemingly over a period of years, first composing his notes in pencil and then carefully tracing them over in ink, so as to correct and supplement the account of travels in which he had been a participant. Revett died in 1804, and in 1811 the new owner, recognizing the value of his notes, presented the volumes to the British Museum.

Another pair of works presented to the Museum was John Whitaker's *History of Manchester* and *The Ancient Cathedral of Cornwall Historically Surveyed*. This was not a case of mild grievance but a calculated act of revenge. The owner, Francis Douce, left his books to the Bodleian Library as noted earlier, but he made a specific exception in his will for "my commented copies of the blockhead Whitaker's History of Manchester, and his Cornwall Cathedral" (*Douce Legacy*, 13). (The same will left two hundred pounds to the surgeon Sir Anthony Carlisle "requesting him either to sever my head or extract the heart from my body, so as to prevent any possibility of the return of vitality.") Douce was certainly an eccentric man, but the Museum accepted the bequest and, as we have seen, he was not alone in choosing the medium of marginalia to make his contrary views known. It was in fact a shrewd decision. If he had published a review, article, or pamphlet against Whitaker, who had carelessly misrepresented him on a point about the names of chess pieces, it might have reached a few contemporaries before vanishing from sight, but as it is, every reader using the British Library copies of Whitaker's books has been obliged for almost two centuries now to take Douce's hundreds of outraged corrections along with them.

Douce worked over these books for years, starting in 1804 when the offending *Cornwall* appeared. In the front flyleaves of *Manchester* he gathered authorities to support his ill opinion of it, and on its title pages he produced mocking epigraphs taken from the text itself: "Erudition, running wild in the mazes of folly" (quoting 1:8) and "Nothing but the dreams of fancy, and the visions of wildness" (quoting 2:519). His running commentary—a sort of adversarial editing—in both works, sometimes framed in sarcastic footnotes, attacks Whitaker's evidence, arguments, and style. Having objected to the use of the conjunctions "and" and "but" as the first word in a sentence, for instance, Douce systematically underlined every instance of that practice in *Manchester*. He also objected to the speculative "must" (as in, such a thing *must* have been so) and underlined a host of examples, observing, "For a single fact there are twenty conjectures in this fanciful work, which might punningly be called a musty work" (1:—2). He knew that he was being spiteful, but considered that it was in self-defense (2:—2): "It must be conceded that the marginal remarks in these volumes savour much of Ritsonian acrimony and sarcasm; but let it be remembered that they are levelled against a man who, in the midst of his Self-conceit and intolerable arrogance, shewed no mercy whatever to others."

Douce in his scholarly way was accustomed to use his books as storehouses for information, especially when—as in the case of Thomas Warton's *History of English Poetry*—they were connected with projects of his own. Such books he crammed full of manuscript supplements and amendments; they became collections in themselves. He adopted the same technique in the Whitakers, though they represent a project of a different kind, a project of destruction. Point by point, Douce questions, contradicts, ridicules, or demolishes the words of his enemy. In *Cornwall* he complains bitterly of "that precipitate manner of reading that W. must have been accustomed to from his innumerable blunders & misconceptions" (2:391). Annotating these volumes as he did was practically guaranteed to keep Douce from the same fault. Nothing seems to have escaped him. Whitaker for example describes a "charnel chapel" or "carnary" as "the repository of a saint's bones" (*Cornwall*, 1:42). Douce splutters in response, "Notwithstanding this wordy and conceited argument, a carnary is simply a charnel house, and not a repository for sanctified bones: as might easily be proved by numerous authorities." But having been slowed down and forced to read carefully, he has also sometimes to acknowledge that his adversary is not all bad and that others might be still worse: "The animadversions on Gildas are the very best part of Whitaker's work. That writer is scarcely ever to be understood; or, when understood, to be believed. He is at once defective, obscure, and fanatical" (*Manchester*, 2:535). By his methodical annotation of Whitaker's books, Douce aimed to set the record straight with regard both to Whitaker's subjects and to his claims to authority.

Douce's strategy was unusual, but his goals and methods were commonplace. Antiquaries as a group collected facts and quotations on the flyleaves and in the margins of their books, with the view of contributing to the general fund of knowledge. Readers of all kinds teased, disputed with, or approved the writers whose works they were reading; if they had access to supplementary or contradictory information, they were likely to put it in for the benefit of future users. It is not always clear from the form of the record whether they wrote from firsthand experience or from a secondary written record; eyewitness evidence, when it emerges, is naturally of special value. For example, executions were still public in Britain and the process leading up to an execution—reports of the crime, the arrest, the trial, appeals for clemency or pardon, the conviction, the gallows statement—generated a literature of its own. Pamphlets about such cases may contain a reader's note on the outcome, as in the case of a man charged with leading a riot in 1796. *John Hartland, tried at Kingstown* offers a copy of the brief for the case and heads of a sermon preached about it. On the back wrapper, the owner noted, "This poor Man was executed on Monday the 4 April 96—on Kennington Common, & declared himself Innocent—to the last." Was the owner, possibly John Craven, there to see Hartland hanged? He might have had this information from a newspaper, but the tone of compassion suggests an unusual level of involvement. There can be no doubt about Walter Scott's attendance at the trial of a murderer in December of the same year. In his *Memoirs*, Lockhart published Scott's detailed account of his visit to the cell of the condemned man, taken from a long note on "his copy of the 'Life of James Mackean, executed 25th January 1797.' " Scott explains the circumstances of the visit, describes the prisoner's appearance ("a good-looking elderly man, having a thin face and clear grey eye: such a man as may be ordinarily seen beside a collection-plate at a seceding meeting-house, a post which the said Mackean had occupied in his day"), weighs his protestations of irresistible impulse against the contradictory evidence of premeditation, and concludes that "All Mackean's account of the murder is apocryphal" (1:291–92).

Such memorable experiences called for a record of some kind, and the margins of a book where the subject had been introduced were an attractive option for Romantic readers. An unidentified reader who must have been part of the Fourth Regiment at the time of the recapture of Almeida in 1811, objecting to the account of that event given by George Elliott in his 1816 *Life of Wellington*, wrote a few notes to sort it out. (Only that section of the book contains extensive notes.) Some have to do with minor details: the officer named as Lieutenant-General Paget was actually "Major Gen[l] Sir Ed[w] Paget, & brother to the Earl of Uxbridge" (267). But others contest the portioning out of blame. According to Elliott, the Fourth Regiment had missed its road and as a consequence part of the garrison escaped. The reader protests that she only mistake was the author's, and writes a long note to exculpate the regiment (362–63).

A more impressive example of the same impulse appears in a similarly restricted set of notes to Helen Maria Williams's *Sketches of . . . the French Republic:* the occasion was the revolution at Naples in 1798–99, and the annotator Horatio Nelson. Williams devotes six "letters" to this controversial episode. She is scathingly sarcastic about Lady Hamilton, and while she avoids direct condemnation she makes it clear that she considered Nelson chiefly responsible for the betrayal and execution of Admiral Caracciolo and other "illustrious martyrs of liberty" (1:222). But Nelson may not have got that far in his reading. His notes appear in only a few pages of the first letter, which is concerned with events prior to the revolution itself. (He was presumably guided to the Naples section by the Table of Contents; there are no marks or notes before then.) There he pointedly underlined Williams's statement that "it is no easy task to distinguish between the simple truth of historical fact, and the exaggerated features of an heated imagination," implying that her account was indeed exaggerated (1:122–23). He made a single attempt to justify the hostility of the court of Naples to the French ambassador

Garat, observing that "this man read the sentence of death to the Queens sister, & was sent as the most obnoxious person they could find" (1:127). But after that his response is confined to contradicting Williams on such trivial matters of fact as whether the British fleet had to have a pilot or not in the Bay of Naples, and it soon comes to an end. He may have set out to correct the record but have realized that in so polemical and inaccurate an account there was not much point. In this case the reader's reserve is itself telling.

CONCLUSION

As the last few examples and others earlier in this book demonstrate, it was not collectors only who entrusted their memories to the margins and flyleaves of their books. The practices of collectors overlapped with those of more casual readers who talked back to their books, filed scraps of information and extracts in them, or approached them as though they (the readers) were editors. The difference is two- or perhaps threefold. Whatever the collector's practice, it was typically systematic, not to say fanatical, in a way that is foreign to the desultory reader. Walpole routinely had the month of publication added to the title pages of his pamphlets. Mitford invariably noted the dates of acquisition and reading on a front flyleaf or title page, and assembled factual information there. Douce underlined every "and" or "but" standing at the beginning of a sentence in the unfortunate Whitaker's history. Beckford (introduced in Chapter 1) habitually copied extracts onto the flyleaves in orderly sequence. The Pindar annotator attempted to fill in every blank in his collection of poems. Then too the collectors' notes, amassed over time, constituted collections in themselves. As they mounted up, Beckford thought of having some of his extracts published. Mitford and Douce aimed at comprehensiveness in their citations and cross-references. James Maidment gradually turned his copy of *A Town Eclogue* into a gallery of Edinburgh characters circa 1804. Nicholas Revett painstakingly gathered the evidence of later authorities in order to undermine the work of Richard Chandler. Finally, in every case the annotator's sights were fixed on posterity, or at least on the unknown future owner.

Walpole would settle down to spend a few days or evenings deliberately composing notes to selected volumes—his Boswell, his Pennant, his Robertson—when he thought he had something worthwhile to contribute. Douce, as we have seen, made a special project of the Whitakers. Beckford, Mitford, and Dawson Turner, in different ways, knew their manuscript additions would be an asset in the auction room.

In the art of annotation, collectors belong to one of two traditions. As Walpole observed, the severe bibliophile bans marginalia altogether. This negative tradition may have contributed to the prohibition against writing in books after 1830, though I doubt that it played a major part. The other, more positive tradition associated with collectors of the time is a discipline of order: the reader's notes are confined to flyleaves or at least rigorously controlled, being all of one kind, contributing to one end, and uniform throughout a collection, as opposed to the informal mixed use practiced by readers like Piozzi, Keats, Sussex, and even the professional Hargrave.

chapter four

The Reading Mind

Earlier chapters aimed to establish the common environment of readers in Britain in the Romantic period and to lay out the evidence of their marginalia. The time has come to bring that evidence to bear on the question we started with: what can we learn or infer from these marginalia about the experience of reading at the time? But the question itself is open to so many objections that it might appear to be hardly worth raising. Perhaps the way to begin is briefly to consider obvious objections and attempt to clarify the issues. Then the question might be reformulated in a more useful way.

The question presumes uniformity where it is not to be found: "readers" are not all of a kind, "Britain" was not all of a piece, and the "Romantic period" however it is defined saw profound changes in politics, society, and culture. How can any meaningful generalization be made that would be equally valid for a weaver in Belfast in 1792 and a schoolmistress in Bath in 1830? Then the terms of the question are fuzzy to a degree. Chapters 1–3 may have created the impression of a large part of the adult population scribbling away in books for one purpose or another, but what has that activity to do with reading? What we usually have in mind when we talk about "the experience of reading" is something more internal and subjective: we want to know the psychology of it, what goes on in readers' minds when they are engaged with books. Then, what is "reading"? What is meant by "experience"? If our aim is to understand a mental process, it might be argued that the situation in which a reader takes up a book with the intent of writing notes is different from that in which a reader just reads; the annotating frame of mind changes the conditions of reading and subtly alters the experience. The readers who are called to witness here would then have to be considered as constituting a special class within the literate population; they might not be typical. Of that special class, furthermore, only about two thousand exemplars are included, from the subset of those whose books by deliberate effort or by chance washed up in rare book collections, so the sample is small and not necessarily representative.

But to acknowledge limitations is not to say that empirical study on this scale is pointless. We might just as easily, perhaps more profitably, question the criteria of typicality and representativeness. As James Secord says, "To learn what is really important about reading, the limited and partial evidence of the situated case . . . remains vital even when audiences number in the millions" (519). In the absence of a complete and perfect documentary record, whatever that would look like, we just deal with what we have. The primary sources here might not meet a statistician's standards of range and inclusivity, but they are real. There may be no ideal Belfast weaver or Bath schoolmistress, but there is Philip MacDermott along with Hester Piozzi, the Duke of Sussex, Eliza Hawtrey, William Blake, and hundreds of their contemporaries. Our "Romantic Readers" were individuals operating within the confines of common social, educational, and literary customs. On the basis of their practice it becomes possible to detect patterns both in the individuals and in the larger collective—not uniformity but patterns of use and ways of thinking. So we might rephrase the original question in more pragmatic terms: what patterns of use can we discover in these marginalia, and what implications are there for the history of reading? This chapter will draw on evidence already laid down, revisit some notable cases, and introduce new ones in order to describe aspects of the experience of readers between 1790 and 1830. It moves broadly from the outside in, or from the thicker to the thinner ice, and from the general to the particular, starting with the solid, familiar features of everyday routine and working toward the ever-elusive holy grail of the historian of reading, the mental experience of the individual reader.

ROUTINE USE

As things have evolved, we nowadays assume that readers who write notes in their books are a tiny minority of all readers, and that they do it out of habit—bad habit. I have come to believe that in the Romantic period, on the contrary, almost all readers fortunate enough to own books wrote in them, but that they did it only now and then for specific purposes, not as a matter of habit. I do not know of any figure whose books we have traced who did not at some point write in some of them. On the other hand, even the most notorious writers of marginalia—Walpole, Piozzi, Blake, Coleridge, and Keats—left behind books that they had owned and read but had *not* annotated. The only one who seems to have made an invariable habit of writing in his books is Beckford, and because of the history of the dispersal of his collections we cannot know whether or not he had done it all his life. Even with Beckford, the word "habit" with its modern pejorative connotations may be unfair, and "system" more appropriate. Beckford's routine of making extracts on the flyleaves of his books saved him the trouble of rereading by offering a capsule summary of the original experience whenever he might want it.

Whether or not annotating readers were in the majority, we know that writing in books was tacitly sanctioned throughout the period and that it had a place in the educational system. A traditional practice that spread with increased ownership, it had manifest benefits and few drawbacks. Before 1830, little was said against it, and such criticism as did begin to emerge was almost invariably in the context of complaints about circulating libraries and their users, complaints tainted by class and gender prejudice and—at least at first—irrelevant to the private practice of book owners. Edward Mangin's *Essay on Light Reading* (1808), for instance, aimed to shame the mainly female customers of the circulating libraries by what the author probably thought of as affectionate teasing; he imagines his own book subjected to the "flattering marks" of their attention, "viz. a leaf or two torn out, scratches of pins, scorings of thumbnails, and divers marginal illustrations, executed by means of a crow-quill, or a black-lead pencil" (3). The general atmosphere, however, was permissive and even encouraging, both for the disciplined kind of note-making associated with learning and scholarship, and for the freer recreational kind associated with personal opinions and critical response.

Many readers had been deliberately trained to mark and annotate books using techniques that in themselves reveal prevalent attitudes toward books and reading. In important ways, these attitudes reinforced conventional wisdom and worked against what we now think of as distinctively Romantic doctrines. For instance, although we associate Romanticism with the idea of organic unity, marginalia reflect the common-sense assumption that books do not grow, but are made; that they are constructed from separate parts that can be dismantled and used again somewhere else, and that they are susceptible of improvement. The underlining and taking of extracts promotes the notion that some parts are better than others and that they can be enjoyed in isolation. Heads and summaries mark the movement from one portion of a narrative or argument to another—again reminding the reader that it is assembled from parts—and may eventually supplant the words of the original text. Corrections and additions show the work to be flawed and subject to decay, not perfect or timeless, whatever Coleridge's old schoolmaster, and Coleridge after him, had to say about the peculiar fitness of every word to its proper place in great writing.[1] Even Shakespeare, whose works were beginning to be venerated, was subject to such processes. These methods were applied equally to poetry and prose, to informative and creative works; if novels were generally spared it is more likely to be because they were not thought worth the trouble, being books to be read only once, than because they were thought of differently. Nor does originality fare well. One of the most common forms of annotation, as we have seen, was the supplying of parallel passages, a technique that emphasizes tradition. Another was the personal application, in which readers confirm and endorse (or deny and reject) the writer's words by referring to their own experience—still stressing common ground rather than singularity. These readers implicitly approved of work that had a bearing on their own lives, reminded them of other things they'd read, and supported their understanding of the way the world works. They would not have known what to make of a book without precedent, if that is what is meant by "originality."

From the common foundation of general attitudes we can turn to broad patterns of use. Even everyday use, even the briefest and most impersonal supplement to a work of reference, can tell us something about the state of mind of the reader who wrote it, especially when the note occurs in the context of other evidence about that owner's use of the book, and when it is multiplied many times over in the comparable practice of other readers. One general truth about sets of readers' notes of the period is that they are seldom single-minded; even if written on a single occasion (a first reading, for example) or at a single sitting, they are likely to adopt varied attitudes and serve a variety of functions. But they are more likely to have been written on several occasions. Few people owned so many books that they could afford to neglect or forget about them. They were constantly in sight and regularly reread or dipped into, but at different stages in the owner's life and under varying circumstances, meeting different needs on different occasions as time passed, and consequently attracting notes of more than one kind. Not many readers would have had the luxury, had they even wanted it, of reserving separate copies of a work for separate purposes; so annotation tends to be multipurpose, mixed-use. Keats, as we have seen, marked a Shakespeare as he studied the plays with a view to improving his own writing, but he also wrote notes in it for Fanny Brawne, besides the touching anomalous memorandum of his brother's illness. In 1824 Charles Augustus Tulk, a wealthy businessman and student of Swedenborg, interrupted his philosophical commentary on Swedenborg's *Arcana Caelestia* to record in the margin the death of his wife Susannah, adding, "A heavy day for me; but I trust in the Lord of Life and Mercy, that it may prove a happy one for my soul" (Hume, 5). As diligent and methodical a professional as Francis Hargrave admitted some personal observations into the margins of his law books along with new citations and editorial improvements.

Often multipurpose, readers' annotation of books in the period was at the same time fitful. This characteristic is also associated with private use as opposed to preparation for publication. A professional commentator is obliged to find something to say on every page, a professional editor to do thorough collations; but private users are free to concentrate on the parts of a work that interest them. Even study notes and techniques for assimilation such as heads and summaries reflect a reader's vacillating attention. That is one reason for saying that even the most impersonal note may reveal something of the state of mind of the reader: it shows which parts of the book engaged him or her enough to warrant the contribution of a note, and by the same token, which parts did not. The Duke of Sussex was, as we recall, such a methodical annotator once he started in that we can be pretty sure that if a large section of a book is completely free of marks it is because he didn't read it. Besides the negative evidence of blank spaces, the level of uniformity in the notes may be significant. An impersonal note in the context of other similar ones suggests a disciplined frame of mind in the reader, while changes of tone may reveal fluctuating moods. A very ordinary marked copy of Richard Duppa's *Travels in Italy, Sicily, and the Lipari Islands* (1828), for instance, that seems to have belonged to a student, perhaps an adult student like Isaac Taylor's working "Teens," contains a lot of dutiful underlining, heads at the tops of the pages, and corrections, but once in a while the reader was moved to independent comment, notably on encountering the translation of a love letter attributed to Henry VIII (42): "Henry the 8$^{\underline{th}}$ was a treacherous tyrant—a brutal and bloody beast—a rotten-hearted ruffian—who never had any love, but lust for women—& chopped off their heads when he was tired of them—". This is a passionate outburst, not the earnest contribution of an antiquarian, but it does constitute a kind of correction to the text and it clearly displays the reader's train of thought. The fact that notes of this kind are rare in the volume testifies to the reader's normal docility.

These are small illustrations of the kind of observations we can make about the ways readers used their books, which in turn shed light on the ways they were reading. Was their reading, then, also multipurpose and desultory? I should think so, though I do not mean to suggest an exact correlation between level of attention and quantity of marginalia. Marginalia simply provide black-and-white evidence of something we knew or suspected already, the variability of reading experiences—indeed the variability *within* any given reading experience. It has become customary among historians and psychologists of reading to talk about modes or styles of reading: Roger Chartier has even declared that he favors "a history of modes of reading" over the less definable "history of reading" (134). Whether we reflect on our own experience or investigate the reading practices of particular figures of the past, it soon becomes clear that beyond the mechanics of passing the eye over written characters there is no uniform "reading experience."[2] (Even the mechanics are subject to exceptions, as with Braille for the blind.) We adopt different modes of reading—different frames of mind—depending upon such external factors as purpose (work, debate, hobby?), genre (sermon, travels, romance?), and site (coffeehouse, riverside, bedroom?) and such internal ones as stage of life, reading ability, motivation, and mood. In the length of time that it takes to read an extended work some of these factors are more than likely to change. There are so many variables to consider that some reputable historians have argued against even attempting to recover or reconstruct reading experiences of the past.[3] But we may go some distance toward that goal by coming to understand the circumstances of particular readers and observing them at work summarizing, correcting, and quarreling with their books, even if we cannot describe every twist and turn of the dynamics of the process. *That* we cannot do even for ourselves; how could we ever have imagined it might be possible to do it for a reader of two hundred years ago? Did we ever imagine such a thing?

THE GENERAL NOTE

A common form of routine annotation not yet described here is the general note, the one that usually appears at the front of a book on a flyleaf or title page. It falls about the middle of the spectrum of usage between the impersonal extreme of a cross-reference and the personal extreme of an indiscretion. Not strictly factual like the kind of compilation made in the interest of collection management that is described in Chapter 3, it sums up a reader's assessment of the book and serves as a reminder (a) that it had been read before and (b) of how worthwhile it seemed at that time. Though it comes first in the series of marginalia it will have been written last; usually it passes over the hesitations and ambivalence of the earlier notes so as to make an unambiguous statement. To a later reader it may provide a helpful introduction or warning, but its primary value is as a memorandum to the owner. Montaigne had recommended this kind of note, though he put it at the back of the book himself (*Essais,* 2:89). Ranging from a simple thumbs-up or thumbs-down to a complex critical assessment, general notes of this kind in books of the period have for us the incidental benefit of revealing the reader's original expectations as well as his or her final judgment.

Endorsements and their opposites constitute the most basic kind of general note. A simple example is the copy of a technical *Treatise on Practical Navigation and Seamanship* by William Nichelson, published in 1796 and owned by B. W. Page, whose bookplate indicates that he was a captain in the Navy; eventually he became an admiral. His notes in the text occasionally amplify or correct it, but mostly indicate approval ("good," "very good," "very very true"). His considered opinion, at the front, is that "These most excellent Remarks & Advice are deserving a Reprint and should be issued with the Naval Instructions to all HM Ships as much good &c such must instill into the mind" (title page). When it was passed on, one way or another, this book from Page's library would go with his solid recommendation. The general note by an unknown reader in a copy of Hazlitt's *Letter to William Gifford,* on the other hand, declares, "These Heroes [Hazlitt and Gifford] are equally scurrilous: & this man in the unabashed avowal of his Principles, prodigal of Infamy. As a Critic I hold the other thoroughly contemptible—pert, ignorant, empty. This man tho more brisk & lively, has a congenial claim to many of these qualities" (title page). The one note registers admiration, the other disgust—although with a certain relish too. The standard by which a practical treatise was to be judged perhaps does not need to be spelled out, but in Hazlitt's tract the reader, in keeping with its polemical mode, casts his evaluation in terms of character as revealed by prose style. He evidently prizes liveliness and, since he deplores scurrility, etc., it seems he had hoped to find one opponent more honorable, dignified, and refined than the other and so to be able to take a side in the dispute, but had failed. (Hazlitt's attack on Gifford begins, "Sir, You have an ugly trick of saying what is not true of any one you do not like; and it will be the object of this letter to cure you of it.")

Some readers aim to record a more balanced appraisal by describing both good and bad features. As a young man in Ireland fascinated by the recent history of the French Revolution, John Wilson Croker acquired a copy of Mercier's *New Picture of Paris* in two volumes, with short chapters on a great variety of subjects—"Powdered Heads," for instance. Croker gradually assembled an impressive collection of French pamphlets concerned with the Revolution and a comprehensive knowledge of its events and development. He worked with Mercier's book over many years, adding details, marking passages, correcting matters of fact. One of his notes telling what was done to the body of Mme de Lamballe is in Latin, perhaps to protect any woman who might happen upon it (1:41). At some point he committed himself to a general note (title page):

> Mercier had considerable cleverness, or rather smartness—a lively & epigrammatic style—but he was a paradoxical enthusiast & personally, as well as in his writings, more than half crazy—but his work contains many valuable hints & anecdotes relative to the Revolution. Its most remarkable feature is the inconsistency of the Author & his opinions are worth nothing—but the facts which he records are exceedingly curious.

Croker in his maturity was a reviewer for the *Quarterly* as well as an important statesman. His judiciousness shows in this brief statement in which, unlike the reader of Hazlitt, he is careful to separate the character from the work, dismissing Mercier's opinions while commending his information and implying that he himself is in a position to vouch for the accuracy of his facts.

A final, colorful example is a copy of Lady Mary Wortley Montagu's *Letters* annotated by Byron's friend and executor John Cam Hobhouse. The *Letters* were famous especially for their account of society in Turkey early in the eighteenth century, when the Montagus had spent a year on an embassy to Constantinople. Nearly a hundred years later, Hobhouse had been there too; when he acquired his copy of the *Letters* in 1813 he was in a position to challenge some of Lady Mary's facts, as he proceeded to do in a few marginal notes. He also wrote a disproportionately long general note of about four hundred words, covering the high reputation of the letters, the unreliability of those facts about Turkey that Hobhouse had been able to investigate, his suspicion that Lady Mary exaggerated out of vanity, and the rumors, based on malicious reports by Pope and Walpole, of her dirtiness and "habitual nastiness." In this note he declares that "what a man who has seen Turkey can controvert, I am myself capable of proving to be unfounded." There is, however, a discrepancy between the marginal notes and the general note. The corrections in the margins are either petty, or inconclusive because the differences he encountered might be accounted for by the passage of time. Lady Mary comments on the outward "appearance of subjection" among the Turks, observing that "a minister of state is not spoke to, but upon the knee," to which Hobhouse objects "not without a low reverence but not on the knee" (75). She writes of the difficulty of getting into Saint Sophia when other mosques are no problem; he says the reverse is the case: "any one may see Sta Sophia, but the other moschs are not to be seen but with an order from the Pasha" (135). She describes the dance of the "dervises" as lasting "above an hour"; he says, "10 minutes" (139). These trivial objections hardly justify the extended personal attack on Lady Mary in the general note; indeed, some of Hobhouse's notes *agree* with her views about the Turks. In this case the general note appears to be separate from the marginal notes and may have been added much later. Hobhouse's overt criterion is accuracy of information, but his implied criterion is character; unlike Croker, he does not attempt to separate the two and assumes that if one is bad, both must be. His book is like the others, though, in that the notes in it reveal the reader's mental progress away from the particular details of the text toward a synthetic view of the whole, and thus from engagement to detachment.

SELF-DEFINITION

Written at the end of a period of close attachment, the general note distances the reader from the text. It also tends to reverse the relationship between them as the reader emerges from a phase of pupillage to assert him- or herself, putting the text in its place. The reader implicitly declares a measure of superiority by venturing to judge the work, even when the judgment is admiring, as in Page's case. Furthermore the whole process of arriving at a judgment by partly yielding and partly resisting was, in the larger scheme of things, also a process of self-definition for the reader. Self-image, if not identity, was always involved in the fact of reading, as some articulate readers of the period clearly realized. This awareness is acute in readers who write while reading. Blake and Hunt, whose marginalia were described earlier, represent two extremes in their attitudes toward this process, but both alike acknowledge it. At the submissive end, Hunt liked to be able to admire the writers whose works he read and aspired to be as good as they were. He believed the reader must keep growing, and he recommended writing marginalia partly as a check on one's development, "to see what progress he [the reader] makes with his own mind, and how it grows up towards the stature of its exalter." For Blake who, as we have seen, defined himself by opposition, writing notes was a test of stability and integrity, not of growth: scoffing at Sir Joshua Reynolds for being "full of Contradictions" is another way of affirming the value of consistency for himself, as he also does when he looks back at the marginalia of his youth.

The process can of course be seen to be working even where there is no general note and where readers show less self-awareness than Blake and Hunt possessed. A modest example is a devotional book of writings by W. J. Brook, who gave up his fashionable Brighton living in the Church of England on doctrinal grounds, ministered occasionally to other congregations, and died in 1811 at the age of thirty-six. The posthumously published volume consists of *Letters* addressed to those congregations or to individuals within them, and a poem, *Traces of Providence.* The annotator, Mary Bowles, acquired it in 1817. (There is a second owner's name in it, Mary Bigg, 1827, but all the notes belong to the first Mary.) Clearly a devoted admirer of the author, whom she may or may not have known personally, she worked on it in a number of conventional ways. The text contains considerable marking, bracketing, and underlining, mostly in pencil. The front and back flyleaves are taken up with biographical information about Brook, in ink, most of it copied from a letter by someone who had known him well. An engraved portrait is pasted in as a frontispiece, together with a newspaper clipping about the death of Brook's daughter, which occurred before 1819. Some of the unnamed addressees of the letters are identified in manuscript. On a few occasions in 1818, 1819, and 1820, Bowles was moved to add her initials and the date, in pencil, by way of special endorsement, to sentences she had underlined: "I am at present beset on every side, with neither power nor counsel of mine own to carry me through" (27); "The Lord is teaching me some useful lessons, but it is in a school that is not pleasant" (40); "I am indebted to none for their love and favour" (61); and "I am more and more disposed to cleave to the best of friends"—that is, to Christ (71). The book was evidently a resource in times of spiritual trouble and discouragement, particularly when it seemed to the owner to be speaking *for her.* She demurs only once. "The light, the faith of Abel—of Noah—of Abraham—of Moses—of David—of the Prophets—of Paul," says Brook, "will not do for me; I must have more than they had" (85). "I cannot subscribe to this nor do I think Brooke had more light than the Prophets and Apostles who went before him," is the response, signed "M. Bowles." Bowles was reading carefully. Much as she admired Brook, reverential though her attitude was as a rule, and even while she accorded him as much light as the prophets and apostles, here she thought he had gone too far. Her sense of sympathy and identification lapse for a moment as she asserts her separate identity. But acquiescence and resistance together define the way she sees and presents herself.

Insofar as marginalia are expressive, they must express the character of the reader who composed them. The writing of any note marks a moment of self-assertion. Particular notes affirm particular views; sets of notes reveal and reinforce habitual ways of thinking. All are generated in relation to the text and within the limits of convention, and yet with scope for individual variations. Looking back at the content of previous chapters we can see self-definition as an element in notes of all kinds. The annotators of Chapter 1 see themselves as laborers in one intellectual area or another: the Plotinus annotator as a novice philosopher reformulating ancient arguments in his own terms; Charles Burney as a classical scholar of a certain type; Philip MacDermott as a well-rounded man with a special interest in Irish affairs. The naturalists claim their places in the community of naturalists, the collators and commentators in the school of editors. It is as much their technique as the content of their notes that defines them and discloses their states of mind. Index-making suggests a focused search, hunting and discarding, whereas cross-reference and the illustration of one author by another, exercising the powers of memory and association, indicate a different mindset. The socializing annotators of Chapter 2 characterize themselves through their familiar relationship to the text first of all, and second through their relationship to the addressee, the one for whom they are putting on their engaging performance. Blake and Tooke do it mostly by opposition, Hunt by identification; Piozzi vis-à-vis a particular friend, Keats in the context of his circle. The memoirists and collectors of Chapter 3 by their activity declare themselves serious contributors, experts, and patrons in their various ways. In all these situations books serve as vehicles for self-definition and to some extent—but in adult readers it is usually a negligible extent—as instruments of it.

CASES FOR COMPARISON

What we observe in marginalia of the Romantic period is a range of responses and styles of response that are at once liberated and limited by convention. The whole of this book is devoted to displaying the versatility of readers writing notes, but it has hitherto described individual cases without much attempt at comparison. At this point comparisons may serve to show how different styles of annotation reflect different mindsets in the individuals concerned.

Walter Savage Landor (1775–1864) and William Wordsworth (1770–1850) were roughly of an age, came from provincial backgrounds, were university-educated, expressed strongly Jacobin opinions in their youth, published poetry in a Miltonic style, and tried country living. In the course of time their differences easily outweighed their similarities, but they started off with a good deal in common. In both cases there exist just a few books with marginal notes, none of them very interesting or revealing in themselves but illuminating for the contrast they expose. Several of the extant Landor books are editions of classical authors in which he typically takes note of technical details about text and meter—but not rigorously—and makes brief evaluative remarks. His reading of Catullus, for example, halts briefly over a suspected textual error: "Aut ne is not Latin—it must be neve or neu" (6). He judges one poem as "bad" (6) and one as "best" (7), objects that another has the "same idea as in V" (7) and that a fourth is "a rambling poem—unworthy of him" (65). Landor was not reading Catullus for the first time, and he appears to have been reading recreationally, not for any project nor to gratify any other reader. His penciled notes are scarce and sketchy; they would not slow him down much. Still they indicate his frame of mind. He was paying attention to language and technique, and ranking the poems against one another. His is a trained, practiced, somewhat weary literary response, and other books annotated by him are like this one. Wordsworth's copy of John Davis's *Travels . . . in the United States of America*, also read recreationally and idly, likewise exhibits a literary response—more surprisingly, given the character of the book—but the approach is different.[4] There are only five notes in all, four of them in one section of twenty-five pages so probably made at a sitting. One is a sarcastic remark (possibly not Wordsworth's, not that he was incapable of sarcasm) about the improbable speed with which a student learnt French; all the others are brief jottings to note connections with other writers. The description of a girl's lip, looking "as if some bee had newly stung it" gets "Suckling's ballad on a wedding" (354); at a line about not measuring happiness by the standards of other people, Wordsworth notes "Horace" and quotes a few words of the Latin parallel (363); a comment about philosophers who could not "bear the tooth-ache patiently" is recognized as an echo of Shakespeare (378); and an observation about the futility of traveling to escape unhappiness is traced again to "Horace" (451). What this tiny but telling sample indicates is that Wordsworth's mind was so stocked with poetry that even a book of travels led him to think automatically of literary parallels. Most of the book is unannotated, and these notes were not part of a program of any kind, but Wordsworth's habit of mind led him to associate what he was reading with the works of the poets. This response is unlike Landor's. It is not critical or evaluative, it merely makes connections. But it is just as conventional, and we have seen plenty of other readers doing the same thing. Most of Lamb's books also have brief references of just this kind. Wordsworth and Landor, exercising different options from the array of possibilities available, took different approaches to books and presumably had different experiences in reading.

When two readers go to work on the same book one after the other, such differences are all the more apparent. Not being the first reader is bound to complicate the situation. Do second readers respond to the first? Identify with the first? Seek to differentiate themselves? Ignore the other's notes altogether? More generally, what is the relationship between one set of notes and the other? An interesting case is the copy of William Godwin's *Enquiry concerning Political Justice* annotated by P. B. Shelley and Margaret King Moore, Lady Mount Cashell, once a pupil of Mary Wollstonecraft's.[5] The two quarto volumes of the first edition (1793) contain ample evidence of use: dozens of passages marked in pencil with the usual lines, crosses, asterisks and so on, and the two sets of notes, also in pencil. Shelley wrote only eight notes, all in the first volume (he may have borrowed only the one); Lady Mount Cashell wrote fifty-five, spread equally through the two volumes. No page contains notes by both of them. The book belonged to Lady Mount Cashell, who had probably already read it and left her notes long before Shelley borrowed it in March 1822. He had it for less than two weeks and does not seem to have paid it much attention: he was reading other things besides, and since this was not his first reading of *Political Justice* he was rather renewing his acquaintance and looking for help with a current project of his own than entertaining new ideas. Lady Mount Cashell's notes, on the other hand, record the reactions of an intelligent, sympathetic first-time reader, working right through the book, excited and provoked but increasingly doubtful about the practicality of Godwin's program for the human race.

She does what we have seen many other readers do. She agrees, disagrees, and expresses doubt: "this certainly is not true" (1:266), "I am not sure of that" (1:354), "I cannot agree in this opinion" (2:709), "indeed I think so" (2:854). "The love of fame is no doubt a delusion," says Godwin sternly, and she agrees but softens his statement: "but the most agreeable of delusions" (2:826). She cites another writer in support of Godwin's ideas: "This is very much the opinion of Hume on the same subject" (1:61). And she adds specific examples to support general maxims, such as Godwin's view of the hazards of ministerial dependence on the monarch. Godwin points out that small daily compromises can lead to serious consequences, as when "he that began perhaps only with the preference of an unworthy candidate for distinction ends with the most atrocious political guilt," and Lady Mount Cashell produces a topical instance, "N.B. The Duke of York appointed Commander in chief of the troops on the continent," alluding to an appointment made in 1798 in spite of the Duke's unsuccessful campaigns of 1793–95 (2:447). Many of her notes are more expansive than this, raising questions or reflecting on issues. She is a respectful but independent reader of a kind Godwin would surely have welcomed. His spare prose and remorseless argument invite counterexamples and provoke reflection, though they do not make it easy. On the definition of punishment, she seems to have caught him out in an uncharacteristically mystical moment when he observes (2:688–89):

> Punishment is generally used to signify the voluntary infliction of evil upon a vicious being, not merely because the public advantage demands it, but because there is apprehended to be a certain fitness

> and propriety in the nature of things, that render suffering, abstractedly from the benefit to result, the suitable concomitant of vice.

To which she responds,

> I do not think this a good definition of the word punishment—It has sometimes been explained——An infliction of ill on a vicious person to prevent a continuance of actions detrimental to mankind and as an example to deter others by terror from a similar conduct—

There is no reference to a dictionary or other writer, though she does not claim the definition as her own. She was not preparing a commentary on Godwin. But she did spot a weakness in his armor and address it in an appropriate way, matching definition with definition. That is typical of her. On the whole she accepts what he has to say, but now and then she replaces his rigorous analyses and proposals with more pragmatic human ones. "The Author of this Work seems to forget," she says, "how much vice there is in the world—every man does not weigh his own & the publick benefit so impartially" (1:358).

She was also a self-conscious reader. A particularly interesting note is the one she wrote in response to Godwin's enquiry "Whether the mind can ever have more than one thought at any one time" (1:325).

> I think it certainly may, or else how is it possible for us to read for several hours without remembering any thing we have read, and recollect a train of thought foreign to the subject that took place in the mind at the time of reading? this has often happened to me when obliged to read aloud & I have been informed that notwithstanding this inattention, I read as well as usual—

Having a pen or pencil in hand for note-making is a way of enforcing attention, and Lady Mount Cashell was certainly alert while she was reading *Political Justice*. (It is not clear whether the inattention she describes was something she experienced in silent reading as well as in public performance. Were people ever required to read aloud for "several" hours at a time?) Her attitude toward the book, to judge by the notes, was consistently engaged but not blindly admiring. She dissents, qualifies, challenges. Her thinking, guided by the text, leads to questions, reflections, and new solutions. If her mind wandered in the way she describes, there is naturally no record; we see the evidence only of focused attention.

Shelley's notes at first appear quite different: less sustained, less consistent, less positive, and of course fewer. They occur sporadically in the first volume. His frame of mind was undoubtedly different because his circumstances were different. His reading may not have been continuous; he may have been dipping. It was not a first reading, he did not have the book for long, and he was not on good terms with his troublesome father-in-law, the author. Four of his eight notes express objections to the conduct of the argument. One, on the paste-down at the back of the volume, consists of a very brief memorandum of topics that Shelley might have planned to pursue, based on particular chapters: "Fear | Fraud | Violence | Happiness is the end, & all [. . .] merely the means. Let us not mistake the means for the end nor the end for the means | What Happiness is." Two are expressions of approval: "Admirable—" (1:185) and "how true!" (1:370).

When we turn to the text to see what it was that Shelley found admirable and true—so admirable and true as to merit appreciative notes when 376 other pages failed—we find, first, a philosophical position with which he was bound to agree, "By its very nature political institution has a tendency to suspend the elasticity, and put an end to the advancement of mind. Every scheme for embodying perfection must be injurious." (Shelley marked the second sentence.) More obscurely, on p. 370 Godwin observes that even morally excellent people may not achieve in their lifetimes the recognition they deserve, because of relatively minor weaknesses: "Prudential and timid virtues . . . triumph only for a day: but that they are transitory is of little avail, while those who are most worthy of lasting esteem, wantonly barter it for gratifications, contemptible in themselves, and fatally important in their effects." What can Shelley have been thinking of when he wrote "how true!" next to this line? Was he thinking of his own situation? Godwin's? Byron's? If he had been marking the book for Lady Mount Cashell to see, he might have explained himself, but he was not, and we cannot be sure. I suspect immediate personal relevance, however, given that the one remaining note is of that kind. In Chapter Four of Book Three, which is about political authority, Godwin discusses the delegation of authority as a general good, since the authority goes to a more capable body. "It is of no consequence," he points out, "that I am the parent of a child, when it has once been ascertained that the child will receive greater benefit by living under the superintendance of a stranger." Shelley, whose own children by his first wife were in that situation, bitterly remarks, "The Chancery proceeds upon this doctrine—" (1:161).

Shelley's response to Godwin on this reading, though less well documented, can be said to be more various than the reaction of Lady Mount Cashell, who does not register personal applications. The two of them must have approached the book, as I have said before, in different frames of mind. And yet the mental *activity* demonstrated in their notes is not dissimilar, because it is guided by the text. Shelley too follows Godwin's words and expresses resistance in the philosophical, propositional style they represent. On the matter of laws, for example, Godwin maintains that they should be judged by their reasonableness and not by the way they came about: "no measure is to be resisted on account of the irregularity of its derivation. If it be just, it is entitled both to my chearful submission and my zealous support. So far as it is deficient in justice, I am bound to resist" (1:162). Shelley resists in just the way we have seen Lady Mount Cashell do, starting with "but": "But the justice of a measure is composed of the circumstances from which it is derived & the object to which it tends. For the former modify the latter, by promoting for instance a submission to the authority from which the measure proceeds." This copy of *Political Justice*, then, documents two different reading experiences with a substratum of kinship: readers in different circumstances, with different moods, taking note of different passages, but both alike accommodating their minds to the author's topics and terms of reference.

Sometimes it is possible to compare the experience of the same reader with different books or, even better, with the same book, to try to define that reader's personal style—of annotation, if not actually of reading. More books survive annotated by Coleridge than by any other reader of this period as far as we are aware, and all the known marginalia have been published, so he offers many such opportunities. The trouble with Coleridge is the embarrassment of riches, which makes it possible and necessary to choose but at the same time introduces complications. He owned multiple copies of Scott's novels, but they are all annotated in the same way. He owned or had the loan of multiple copies of Shakespeare, likewise much of a kind except for the set in which he drafted his lectures; and of Leighton, but with notes written under such radically different circumstances that there is scarcely any basis for comparison left. And all of these cases are so extensive and complex as to require much more space than I can afford here. All might, furthermore, be considered compromised by the conditions under which they were written, whether it was for the sake of a literary project of some sort, or for a friend whom Coleridge wanted to please. They seldom reveal him in mental isolation, communing with the book alone. But the same could be said of every one of Coleridge's annotated books: he knew they would circulate sooner or later, and it is rare to find him so forgetting himself as to address the text without the slightest consciousness of a prospective other reader. Even when he seems to have done so, we cannot be sure. Among the most anguished and seemingly intensely personal notes that he ever wrote, castigating himself as "S. T. C., sinful tormented culprit," were those written in pencil in a copy of Leighton borrowed from a casual acquaintance and returned to the owner with the notes untouched (*Marginalia*, 3: 512, 507–8). Was Coleridge punishing himself, or seeking exposure? Did he hope, by his sorry example, to save the owner from errors of the same kind? Was he just forgetful? Or, like a person carrying on an intimate conversation on a cellphone in a public space, did he not much care whether he was overheard or not?

Coleridge's marginalia deserve more scholarly and critical attention than they have had. They contain enough matter for a full-scale study on their own, and they could play a strong supporting role in new accounts of his life and thought. Coleridge's relationship with Leighton, as with several other writers whose works occupied his time off and on for many years, is well documented in the marginalia and was as important to Coleridge as most of his "real" human relationships. His reading of Luther, among others, was an event in his life comparable to some of the physical exploits that routinely receive more notice. For my purposes here I have decided to take for comparison two books representing different stages of his career as an annotator. To simplify the task I have chosen books written in English, not obviously relevant to any of Coleridge's current publishing projects, and not copiously annotated. The idea is briefly to illustrate the way Coleridge's marginalia evolved, to describe their characteristic features, and to reflect on what they may reveal about his experience of the reading process—not *what* he read, but how.

In marginalia and elsewhere, Coleridge wrote well about the experience of reading. His cardinal rule was "geniality" or reading as far as possible in the same spirit as that in which the work had been composed, that is, strongly identifying oneself with the author. The principle is both psychological and mystical, suggesting that the critical reader is open to inspiration just like the creative writer. "Every Book worthy of being read at all," he said, "must be read in and by the same Spirit, as that by which it was written. Who does not do this, reads a Dial by Moonshine" (*Marginalia,* 2:561). And in another place, "The man who reads a work meant for immediate effect on one age, with the notions & feelings of another, may be a refined gentleman, but must be a sorry Critic" (*Marginalia,* 2:969). In practical terms, "genial" reading means exercising historical imagination: suspending contemporary prejudices to the best of one's ability and making an effort to judge a work in relation to others of its own time. Of all the critical axioms with which Coleridge has been associated, this is the one he most consistently adhered to in his own practice. His marginalia prove him to have been an exceptionally charitable reader—which is not to say he did not sometimes noisily lose his temper.

Although he himself described writing marginalia as a habit "indulged" by his friends (*Marginalia* 3:373), Coleridge was not what we would normally think of as a habitual annotator: he did not begin regularly to write in books until he was in his thirties, and like most of the annotating book-owners described here, he did not do it to all his books, only to particular books under special circumstances. Since he always kept notebooks as well, he did not need to make remarks in the margins of the books; if he chose to do so, he generally had a reason for it. The first occasion on which Coleridge appears systematically to have written notes in a set of books was in the summer of 1807, when he visited his old friend Thomas Poole in Nether Stowey and was given the run of Poole's library, with an invitation to write comments in the books. About a dozen annotated books survive from this extended visit, a mixed bag of political, scientific, literary, and theological works, with a strong seventeenth-century component (*Marginalia*, 2:966–67, 4:84, 199). One was a recent travel book, Robert Percival's *Account of the Island of Ceylon* (1803). In this spacious quarto of 420 pages, Coleridge wrote just twelve notes, in ink, signing a few with his name or initials. Given that he was reading the book for the first time and apparently straight through, it is rather surprising that his first note does not appear until p. 152, but it is worth waiting for, and is in significant ways typical of the set. Percival describes the use of mild intoxicants, betel and "bang" (also spelled "bhang" or "bangue"), among the Ceylonese, and warns about the effects of over-indulgence in bang, which he inaccurately describes as "a species of opium":

> I have frequently seen these people, after having chewed too large a portion of this noxious drug, lying speechless on the ground with their eyes fixed in a ghastly stare. Yet, such is the effect of habit, that they get completely infatuated with fondness for this drug, and absolutely cannot do without it.

Coleridge responds with further information based on personal experience, correcting and supplementing Percival (*Marginalia*, 4:84–85):

> *The Bang* is the powder from the dried Leaves of the Cannabis Indica, or Indian Hemp / It is commonly blended with opium; & in Turkey and Barbary with Saffron & Spices. It is either chewed in large Pills, or smoked in the Powder. I have both smoked & taken the Powder / so did my ever-honoured ever-lamented Benefactor, T. Wedgewood: the effects in both were the same, merely narcotic, with a painful weight from the flatulence of stifled gas, occasioned by the morbid action on the coats of the Stomach. In others however it had produced, as we were informed by Sir J. Banks, almost frantic exhilaration. We took it in the powder, and as much as would lie on a Shilling. Probably, if we had combined it with opium and some of the most powerful essential Oils, to stimulate & heat the stomach, it might have acted more pleasantly. On the coast of Barbary the charitable Mahometans give it to poor Criminals, previous to the amputation of their Limbs; and it inspires a complete insensibility to suffering, and in these circumstances does not commonly disturb the understanding. Tippoo Saib gave to each of his Horse soldiers a pipe immediately before the engagement—likewise to those sent to storm forts. S. T. Coleridge.

Coleridge's other notes are about the loyalty of the Roman Catholic population to their priests, however venal (he confirms Percival's observations by citing his own experience in Sicily), about the plausibility of Percival's accounts of animal and vegetable life (buffalo, ichneumon, honey-bird, white ant, mango, plantain), and about his careless use of language. Coleridge corroborates Percival's description of the activity of the ants by referring to the abridged version of the *Philosophical Transactions* of the Royal Society that he had just been reading in Poole's collection, but he considers some of his other evidence as showing too credulous an acceptance of travelers' tall tales. When Percival makes the claim that "no one mango resembles another plucked from the same tree in taste or flavour," Coleridge challenges him: "not even *resemble?*" (*Marginalia*, 4:88).

"Throughout this work I have noticed with pain the apparent

unthinkingness of the Writer," Coleridge declares at p. 315 (*Marginalia*, 4:88). With such a level of critical disapproval, Coleridge might be thought to have violated his own rule of geniality, but geniality has to do with fairness, not kindness. It does not preclude correction. As a contemporary writer, Percival had to be held to contemporary standards, and that is what Coleridge did in writing about him. These notes are interesting in a number of ways—for their content, because of course we are interested in the history of Coleridge's addiction to opium; but also for their character and consistency. Written in the first person and including personal testimony as marginalia often do, they are nevertheless strikingly impersonal. The author conveys information and Coleridge responds in kind, providing more facts, more scrupulously documented: here is the proper botanical name for "bang"; here is the way it is prepared in different countries; here are the names of important people who can vouch for my own part in the experiment; this is the amount I took and the way I took it, and this is all I felt; my conclusion is as follows. He repeatedly cites other eyewitnesses or published authorities to reinforce his own testimony. When he is skeptical of Percival's evidence or methods, he takes pains to indicate how they might have been improved and made more rigorous. Unlike Wordsworth, who could read a book of travels and take note only of literary parallels, Coleridge's approach is scientific. The crucial difference in their ways of reading is perhaps the fact that the book Coleridge was annotating belonged to Poole. His mode of reading is thus conditioned partly by the character of the book itself, partly by personal relevance (he stops at "bang" because he knows something about it that not everybody knows), and partly by the scientific interests of his friend, who will keep the book when he himself is gone, and will be reminded of him as he reads it.

The set of notes Coleridge wrote in Poole's copy of Percival is a relatively uncomplicated example of his practice early on. As time passed, that practice evolved to become more complex and distinctive, although even the Percival notes show signs of their authorship, notably in the length and slightly rambling quality of the first one. Coleridge was relatively uninhibited about the length of his notes: in general, he carried on writing for as long as it took to finish the train of thought the text had started. But now and again he apologizes for their length, and in this book he does not actually exceed the space available in the margins. Twelve years later, his behavior was markedly different.

The Displaying of Supposed Witchcraft (1677) by the Nonconformist John Webster was the kind of unfashionable, antiquated, seventeenth-century work that Coleridge especially relished, and that was enjoying a revival in the anti-Enlightenment, anti-French climate of the British book trade in the early nineteenth century. (Coleridge faced competition for his proposed edition of "beauties" from Leighton's work, and eventually produced *Aids to Reflection* instead. Editions of Shakespeare and Milton, but also of major prose writers such as the four Bs—Bacon, Burton, Bunyan, and Browne—were doing well.) Webster had been engaged in learned controversy with Joseph Glanvill and Meric Casaubon on the question of the existence of witches, he arguing that testimony about witches could be accounted for by delusion (madness) or imposture, that there never had been any such thing as a witch, and specifically, that the Devil never made pacts with witches, sucked on their bodies, copulated with them, or enabled them to do magic. This might have seemed a dead issue by the time Coleridge read the book, but it involved and addressed still urgent questions about law, pathology, and church doctrine. The record of Coleridge's response to Webster clearly displays his excitement as he read, assimilated, and tried to work out the lessons of Webster's work.

Coleridge probably acquired the book in 1819, and his first thorough reading of it appears to belong to late October of that year. Its attractions are obvious. It dealt with the supernatural, a subject in which Coleridge had both a poetical and a philosophical investment; he had lectured on witches and magic in 1818. It belonged to a lost world of arcane learning and ornate prose associated with Milton and his contemporaries, men such as Jeremy Taylor, the Cambridge Platonists, and Sir Thomas Browne, whose works Coleridge knew well. And it was the product of a crucial period in the history of the Church, the period of Baxter and Leighton. Since the book had never gone into a second edition, Coleridge's copy was the original tall thin folio edition of 346 pages, in this case containing some marginalia by an earlier reader, probably made before 1700 (Fig. 28). These are interesting in themselves, since they provide contrary evidence and arguments and sometimes run on for several pages; but Coleridge appears to have ignored them.

Coleridge wrote one set of notes in the margins of the book and another, at the same time, in his notebooks.[6] The sequence of the notebook entries proves that he went from beginning to end on this first reading. Later on he returned to the book and added more notes: on internal evidence, at least one must have been written after 1820 and another after 1823, perhaps both of them on a single occasion after 1823. The first run seems to have been consecutive and private—that is, the initial series of notes does not appear to have been written under a social motivation or with a special friend in mind. There are some signs, however, of the book's having been lent out later. Coleridge wrote and signed a note at the front of the book as a way of summing up his judgment of Webster and asking another reader to be "genial" and make allowances for him—something he regularly did for his old-fashioned favorites. "One good thing I have derived from my fondness for Old Books," he begins, "that I estimate Men and Authors by qualities, that have the same worth & value, or the Contrary, in all ages; but which are more creditable to the Individual in proportion to the weaknesses and ignorance which he partakes of with his Age." For this reason, he says, he prizes Webster's "good Sense" and "sound Judgement" all the more for his bad science, which he could hardly help, being dependent on the information available at the time. This statement, the sum of his marginal observations and obviously written after them, offers a personal assessment of the merits and weaknesses of the work according to the conventions of the general note described earlier in this chapter.

The other material piece of evidence proving that Coleridge lent this book out with his notes in it is the response to one of them, written on a folded sheet of paper now pasted in at the relevant page, signed by Charles Augustus Tulk. Coleridge and Tulk had met two years earlier and had been exchanging books. Tulk, a businessman and by that time

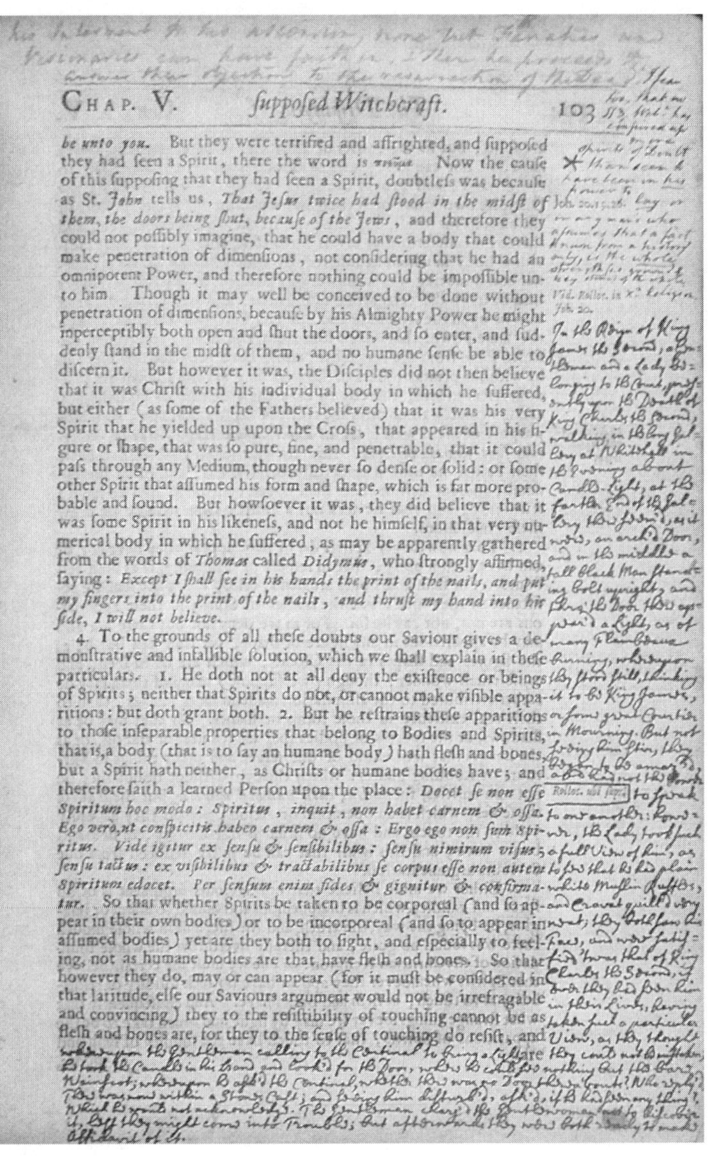

CHAP. V. ſuppoſed Witchcraft. 103

be unto you. But they were terrified and affrighted, and ſuppoſed they had ſeen a Spirit, there the word is πνεῦμα. Now the cauſe of this ſuppoſing that they had ſeen a Spirit, doubtleſs was becauſe as St. *John* tells us, *That Jeſus twice had ſtood in the midſt of them, the doors being ſhut, becauſe of the Jews*, and therefore they could not poſſibly imagine, that he could have a body that could make penetration of dimenſions, not conſidering that he had an omnipotent Power, and therefore nothing could be impoſſible unto him. Though it may well be conceived to be done without penetration of dimenſions, becauſe by his Almighty Power he might inperceptibly both open and ſhut the doors, and ſo enter, and ſuddenly ſtand in the midſt of them, and no humane ſenſe be able to diſcern it. But however it was, the Diſciples did not then believe that it was Chriſt with his individual body in which he ſuffered, but either (as ſome of the Fathers believed) that it was his very Spirit that he yielded up upon the Croſs, that appeared in his figure or ſhape, that was ſo pure, fine, and penetrable, that it could paſs through any Medium, though never ſo denſe or ſolid: or ſome other Spirit that aſſumed his form and ſhape, which is far more probable and ſound. But howſoever it was, they did believe that it was ſome Spirit in his likeneſs, and not he himſelf, in that very numerical body in which he ſuffered, as may be apparently gathered from the words of *Thomas* called *Didymus*, who ſtrongly affirmed, ſaying: *Except I ſhall ſee in his hands the print of the nails, and put my fingers into the print of the nails, and thruſt my hand into his ſide, I will not believe.*

Joh. 20.19.26.

Vid. Rollot. in 20. Johan. Joh. 20.

4. To the grounds of all theſe doubts our Saviour gives a demonſtrative and infallible ſolution, which we ſhall explain in theſe particulars. 1. He doth not at all deny the exiſtence or beings of Spirits; neither that Spirits do not, or cannot make viſible apparitions: but doth grant both. 2. But he reſtrains theſe apparitions to thoſe inſeparable properties that belong to Bodies and Spirits, that is, a body (that is to ſay an humane body) hath fleſh and bones, but a Spirit hath neither, as Chriſts or humane bodies have; and therefore ſaith a learned Perſon upon the place: *Docet ſe non eſſe Spiritum hoc modo: Spiritus, inquit, non habet carnem & oſſa. Ego vero, ut conſpicitis habeo carnem & oſſa: Ergo ego non ſum Spiritus. Vide igitur ex ſenſu & ſenſibilibus: ſenſu nimirum viſus; ſenſu tactus: ex viſibilibus & tractabilibus ſe corpus eſſe non autem Spiritum edocet. Per ſenſum enim fides & gignitur & confirmatur.* So that whether Spirits be taken to be corporeal (and ſo appear in their own bodies) or to be incorporeal (and ſo to appear in aſſumed bodies) yet are they both to ſight, and eſpecially to feeling, not as humane bodies are that have fleſh and bones. So that however they do, may or can appear (for it muſt be conſidered in that latitude, elſe our Saviours argument would not be irrefragable and convincing) they to the reſiſtibility of touching cannot be as fleſh and bones are, for they to the ſenſe of touching do reſiſt, and

Rollot. ubi ſupra.

FIG. 28 Notes by Coleridge and a predecessor in Webster's *Displaying of Supposed Witchcraft* (1677). By permission of the British Library.

also a Member of Parliament, chaired a society dedicated to publishing the works of Swedenborg though he was not a member of the Swedenborgian "New Church"—Swedenborg himself had never left the established church of his own country. He had just begun to give Coleridge the writings of Swedenborg to read, so Swedenborg's accounts of visions came to Coleridge's mind as he read the testimony about witches and spirits in Webster, and he speculated about the possible causes of such visions in sane and honorable people.

Coleridge's note is a splendid example of his way of thinking, though Tulk did not like it. The process began with Webster's account, taken from Johannes Baptista Porta, of a witch who rubbed herself with an ointment that put her into such a deep sleep that she did not react even to being beaten by the onlookers, but when she woke she gave a vivid description of the travels and adventures she had just experienced. Coleridge immediately made a connection between this case and ancient reports of magic potions and unguents, on the one hand, and the latest medical documentation of patients in the trance of mesmerism or "animal magnetism," on the other. The mesmerized—we would say hypnotized—patients spoke and performed actions during their trances, but had no recollection of it on waking. Coleridge would have liked to believe that the new theories of animal magnetism could explain the long history of such delusions, and that the witches of the seventeenth century might have experienced some sort of autohypnosis before the phenomenon was properly recognized or understood, but he realized that the witches, unlike the patients of Mesmer, *did* claim to remember what had happened while they were entranced. He aired some ideas about ways in which the discrepancy might be resolved, and then ended his long note as follows (*Marginalia*, 6:100):

> That Self-magnetism is in certain conditions, those indeed of the rarest occurrence, possible, has been rendered highly probable, at least. The cases of Behmen, Helmont, Swedenborg, and the assertions of Philo Judaeus of himself, and of Porphyry both of Plotinus and of himself might at all events receive a natural solution from the hypothesis. Indeed, the best service which mesmerism or zoomagne-

tism has yet done is that it enables us to explain the Oracles & a score other superstitions without recourse either to downright Self-conscious Lying and Imposture on the one side, or to the Devil and his Works on the other—reducing the whole of Demonology and Diabolography to Neuro-pathology.

Tulk cannot have been happy to see Swedenborg lumped together with witches and pagans; however, his note, which he must have included with the book when he returned it, merely objects in a general way to the leveling of diverse kinds of spiritual experience to the single state of zoomagnetism, and warns Coleridge that by embracing this physiological explanation he "degrades all those facts of a supernatural kind which are recorded in the Holy Scripture."

Neither Coleridge nor Webster was unaware of the hazards of proposing natural explanations for the supposedly supernatural activities of witches, since the Bible was often invoked as an authority on witchcraft, demonic possession, and the work of the Devil. The miracles of Christ themselves were feared to be vulnerable to the arguments used in exposing the "superstitions" about witches. Webster devoted a large part of his book to examining the Hebrew and Greek texts of the Old and New Testaments to make a philological case against the witch-mongers. Where their false tenets could not be traced to mistranslation, Webster declared misinterpretation, his own principles demanding literal interpretation unless literalism produced absurdity, in which case he would allow a metaphorical reading (139). Tackling the problem from the vantage point of his own period after over a century more of textual scholarship devoted to the Bible, Coleridge found himself articulating the influential distinction between allegorical and symbolical interpretations of the Bible that he eventually published in *Aids to Reflection* in 1825. The margins of Webster seem to have been a useful place for him to try these ideas out as recklessly as he liked. Of 53 notes in this copy, 22 are concerned directly with the interpretation of the Bible, either by proposing interpretations of particular verses and incidents, or by working out a rationale for his method. He observed of his own gloss on a verse from Job that it had the potential to solve the vexed theological issues of creation and free will—"and thus do Scripture & true Philosophy reciprocally confirm each other" (*Marginalia*, 6:113). He could not very well parade this sense of triumph in print or even in letters to his friends, but he could record it to spur himself on in a promising line of thought.

Coleridge's use of a notebook along with the margins of Webster for recording his thoughts while reading is a good example of his normal practice at that stage of his life. Though there is a certain overlapping of functions, by and large the margins are for rapid response and the notebooks are for storing up materials for future use. The notebooks take in extracts and serve the purpose of a commonplace-book without imposing the usual alphabetical organization. The first Webster entry in the notebooks, for example, contains quotations from pages 2 to 20—passages by Webster himself together with his quotations from the Bible and other authorities—in some cases with the sketch of the argument they might be used in (*Notebooks*, 4:4611). Then it goes on to a full-scale version of Coleridge's interpretation of the "Miracle of the Blind Man, whose Eyes our Lord anointed with Clay," which had exercised Webster and drawn a marginal comment from Coleridge already. He switched to the notebooks either because he could see that he would need a lot of space or because he hoped to use the longer note as a draft for further development. Later there is a short series of marginal notes copied into the notebooks—again, presumably because they looked like promising material for future use.[7]

How and why do the notes in Webster differ from those in Poole's copy of Percival? There are more of them and they address a greater variety of subjects, but that might be because Webster's is a book of controversy, not an account of travels, and Coleridge had more to say on intellectual issues. (There are a few factual notes, specifically a series about remarkable stomach-contents, quite like the notes to Percival: Coleridge cites his own observation to suggest that Webster's improbable-sounding anecdotes could be true.) Or it might be because the book belonged to Coleridge himself, who could therefore write with reference exclusively to his own concerns, not thinking of any third party; could make his notes in a more leisurely way; and could expect to keep the book, return to, and reread it as he liked. These are all significant factors. But there is a qualitative difference in the notes as well, which might be illustrated by one further example, on a topic that was not so close to Coleridge's heart as the meaning of scripture.

Webster is attempting to answer the objection that giving up belief in witches entails discrediting many reputable figures of the past, specifically the judge and juries that condemned the witches to death. The alleged witches had been tried, he says,

> before Judges that were accounted wise, grave, and learned, and by Juries of honesty and understanding: were there therefore no true Martyrs, and were they all justly condemned and put to death? or is it absurd to be guilty of such incredulity, as to think and hold, that so many grave and wise Judges, and knowing Juries, were deceived, and did unjustly? (73)

Coleridge's long and thoughtful note introduces some of the moral complexities that Webster, as an advocate, has had to ignore. He begins by acknowledging that in many cases the accused witches *had* in "malignant and devilish" ways injured their neighbors, "tho' through the medium of their own imagination." He supposes himself in his own time in the position of a witch who had succeeded in frightening someone to death: certainly he would deserve to die, and his guilt would be all the greater if he had done it believing "that the person, who had taught me these tricks, had learnt them from the accursed Spirit and enemy of God and Man," yet still had sought out this knowledge in order to inflict harm. But then his thinking takes a surprising turn:

> Whether the making especial Laws for this particular mode of poisoning was wise or no, and whether such Laws did not & must not multiply the crime, they meant to prevent, by confirming the imaginations of the people in the previous state, requisite both for Witching and being bewitched, is another Question of easy solution; but which Judge & Jury were not concerned with. (*Marginalia*, 6:101).

Laws, that is, may perpetuate if they do not create false belief. Coleridge's note as a whole makes a rather oblique response to Webster, and the abrupt opening out of the problem at the end to include large social forces goes far beyond him. There is no such radical departure from the subject in the Percival notes, but it is quite common in Coleridge's evolved practice, where notes start out from the text but then take on a life of their own.

The improvisational technique of Coleridge's later years, especially when he was writing in an uninhibited way and not directly addressing another reader, must have helped him to think, to join things up as they occurred to him, without having to stop for second thoughts and exceptions to the rule. Not all his marginalia are of this kind, but those that were formed part of a creative process such as we have seen in similar though isolated examples of opinion-forming and self-definition by other readers. It was just about the time that he annotated Webster that Coleridge began deliberately to exploit the intellectual capital that had been gradually building up in his annotated books. In November 1819, extracts from his marginalia were published, probably at his suggestion, in *Blackwood's Magazine* (*Marginalia*, 1:795–97). In January 1820, he wrote to Tulk about the frustrations of his writing life, incidentally revealing the role his books now played in the process of composition: "Of three great Works I have all the materials in bonâ fide mss Existence, that require little more than transcription from the various slips & scraps & pocket-books and Book-margins (to be done unhappily by myself alone) and the putting them together; and instead of this I am doomed to write or rather to attempt writing *popular* reading for Magazines"—such as, presumably, the marginalia contributed to *Blackwood's* (*Letters*, 5:18).

Under these circumstances, if by this time practically all his reading was geared toward publication, and if he expected to mine the marginalia as he did the notebooks, how reliable are Coleridge's marginalia as a guide to the way he read? Of course it depends on what we mean by "the way he read." Like anyone else, he commanded a variety of ways of reading and adapted himself automatically to circumstances when he picked up a book. Reading for use, looking out for good bits, is itself a common mode. In the annotated Webster we can see that Coleridge's attention was drawn to parts of the work that could be made relevant to topics in which he already had a special interest, particularly the interpretation of the Bible and the physiology of dreams and visions; he was also interested in assessing Webster in relation to eminent writers of his time. But the general approach, whatever it is, may yield to a lapse of attention or to the impulse of a moment. Some of Coleridge's notes are jocular, some quite remote from his major concerns. Like most of his fellow annotators, he is not rigorous or single-minded in his reading: the marginalia show that for the most part he read along in a receptive and accepting spirit until something caught his eye—an error, a flaw, a personal association—whereupon he took time out to make a note of it, correct it, ruminate on it. Or until reading the text somehow generated an interesting idea, in which case he would try to get the idea down.[8] Why some points rather than others caught his eye and how a new idea might be generated are questions that Coleridge himself could not have answered definitively. Though his marginalia cannot tell us the whole content of his mind—they are not stream-of-consciousness exercises, let alone stream-of-unconsciousness—they do show the stop-and-start progression of his reading and reveal his train of thought at the moment of writing.

For all their differences and in spite of what I have said about the greater freedom and sophistication of his established practice, there is a good deal of continuity between Coleridge's early notes on Percival and the later ones on Webster. Both sets of notes are unmistakably Coleridgean, just as Blake's, Piozzi's, and Walpole's marginalia bear the stamp of their personalities. The impression of a personal style has to do to some extent with content, with the subjects chosen for comment and the revelations of personal experience, as when Coleridge describes the experiment with "bang" or Piozzi tells stories of her childhood. It depends even more, however, on the distinctive "voice" that a writer creates by choices of language and syntax, range of tone, and characteristic patterns of thought. As a familiar mode of address, marginalia often adopt the informal manner of personal correspondence, which in turn has traditionally been supposed to sound like the writer's way of talking. (This is one reason for Lockhart's feeling that reading Scott's books was like having a conversation with him, or rather listening to him converse.) It is in the longer notes especially that we "hear" Coleridge's voice, because the personal stamp appears chiefly in the rapid movement from one idea to another, and that movement, though often surprising, can usually be seen to have a thread of connection running through it. In the example last cited, though Coleridge's remark about the moral responsibility of the law-makers emerges abruptly after the imaginary case against himself, it is linked to the original passage in the text, which treated of judges and juries, so there is an intellectual progression and the note circles back to its source (which is the way his contemporaries sometimes described Coleridge's conversation).[9] By contrast, Piozzi's notes, which also often use the text as a springboard for reflection, are more closely controlled in their movement: a word or anecdote in the text triggers an association which leads to a personal memory or a like anecdote, or both, and then the note comes to an end. It is for example typical of Piozzi's reminiscent style that when Pegge discusses the Cockney phrase "the musick" and proposes that it should really be plural—"the musicks" comprising sharps and flats as well as the "natural keys"—she remarks, "Dr. Burney Senr told me that when he was made Organist of Lynn in Norfolk & felt desirous to shew off both his Instrument & his Skill—one of the Aldermen in the Church said to the Other—This is a fine young Fellow, Faith,—and makes excellent Music; when will he come to the flats and Sharps?" (146). It is hard to see how this note could be mistaken for anyone else's. Neither Piozzi nor Coleridge *characteristically* composes notes like Blake's, aggressively contrary and epigrammatic, nor did they write letters like his. Their distinctive styles express different attitudes toward books and ways of thinking while reading—though not so different as to be mutually incomprehensible.

THELWALL READS COLERIDGE

John Thelwall's annotated copy of Coleridge's *Biographia Literaria* provides a particularly well documented opportunity to study the reading mind through marginalia.[10] Thelwall is an attractive case partly because of his outsider status: he was never a member of any Establishment—social, political, or literary—so what can be said of him that can also be seen to be true of many of his more comfortable contemporaries seems likely to have wider relevance.

Eight years older than Coleridge and the son of a silk mercer in Covent Garden, Thelwall was removed from school at thirteen to work in the family business, but he rebelled against the shop. He was apprenticed for a time to a tailor and then to an attorney; finding neither suit him, like many others in the publishing boom of the 1780s he tried with moderate success to earn a living by writing for the periodicals. Though he lacked Trusler's advantages in formal education, he too made himself into a polymath capable of writing about anything. Like Trusler again, either compulsively or out of necessity he turned practically everything he did into copy for the press. In his twenties, he became involved with the debating societies and with politics, and made friends with Horne Tooke; he also embarked on the study of medicine and published an essay on biology. The turning point in his life was his arrest for treason along with Hardy and Horne Tooke in 1794. All three were acquitted to public applause: Thelwall published *Poems Written in Close Confinement in the Tower and Newgate* in 1795. But he then left London and traveled as a lecturer in the provinces until 1798, when he retired from political activism for a time and tried farming in Wales.

It was in the period after his release, when he was stirring up the country towns and looking for a place to settle with his family, that he made the acquaintance of those other young democrats Coleridge and Wordsworth. He and Coleridge had a lively exchange of letters, sparring about politics and poetry, before they met in person. Thelwall was a declared atheist and materialist. The tone he adopted in his letters seems to have been pretty blunt, but Coleridge responded with affectionate teasing. Accused by Thelwall of displaying "the furious prejudices of the conventicle" and of offering in his poems "Visions fit for Slobberers" and "Morals for the Magdalen and Botany Bay," Coleridge remarked that it seemed they had "different *creeds* in poetry as well as religion. N'importe."[11] On one occasion he assured Thelwall that he had enjoyed a particular poem and only parenthetically hinted at reservations about it: "Your sonnet—(as you call it—& being a free-born Briton who shall prevent you from calling 25 blank verse lines a Sonnet, if you have taken a bloody resolution so to do)—your Sonnet I am much pleased with" (*Letters*, 1:351). Thelwall hoped to settle near Coleridge at Nether Stowey and visited him and Wordsworth there in 1797, but the plan fell through, apparently because the neighborhood would not tolerate three dangerous radicals at once. Coleridge and Wordsworth went to see him in Wales briefly before they left for Germany in 1798. Then the correspondence petered out. The vast differences in their views about religion and philosophy, which had at first seemed irrelevant or even piquant, began to look more like "a chasm of utter dissimilitude," as Coleridge was forced to admit (*Letters*, 2:273). In 1803 Thelwall paid a visit to Keswick, where he renewed his acquaintance with Coleridge and Wordsworth and met Southey, but that is the last close contact they are known to have had.

Thelwall returned to London in 1804 and enjoyed a profitable career as a lecturer and a teacher of elocution. A pioneer in what we would now call speech therapy, he was at the height of his prosperity, running an institution for the cure of speech impediments in fashionable Lincoln's Inn Fields, when Coleridge brought out his *Biographia Literaria* in July 1817. Thelwall read it straight away, apparently from cover to cover and only once—at all events making notes only on the first reading. His neat underlining, marks, and annotation, in ink, begin about the end of the third chapter and continue with occasional gaps of thirty or forty pages to the very end. He was as free an annotator as Coleridge, taking all the time he needed over his notes, some of which are very brief while others spill over from one page to the next. He does not seem to have been writing for a specific purpose or for another reader, though some of his notes are of the memoirist kind and he did eventually exploit the notes in his journalism, as we shall see. He was at the time "just reading" and leaving a record of what he thought. In the following attempt to reconstruct his experience as it unfolded I shall be describing the notes in sequence as they occur (but selectively) rather than grouping them by kind.

The *Biographia* is a notoriously eccentric book. Although it develops in a broadly chronological way, starting with Coleridge's school days and ending in the present, and although it circles round and round a set of closely related subjects—poetry, philosophy, criticism, imagination—it is rambling and digressive and unpredictable. The reader never knows what's coming next. Thelwall seems not to have minded; he read on, responding when he felt like it. Passing silently over Coleridge's account of his schooling, his suffering at the hands of anonymous reviewers, and the early poetry of Southey and Wordsworth, Thelwall first stops to make a note at the point at which Coleridge outlines the process of reflection that led to the germ of his distinction between imagination and fancy. He had come to suspect, Coleridge says, that they were two quite different mental faculties, not the same thing or merely varying degrees of the same thing. Thelwall underlined this passage and wrote in the margin,

> True: but why all this pompous display of metaphysical analysis about a discovery which the mere consideration of the passages quoted by the blundering obtuseness of the anti-etimological Johnson under the word Fancy might sufficiently have evinced. The distinction has during the last ten of fifteen years been a favorite topic of my public Lectures—and many a hard rap has the surly lexicographer had from me for his throng of ignorant interpretions of these words. (1:86–87)

Thelwall's remark was triggered by personal interest, as marginalia often are. He agrees with Coleridge about fancy and imagination, but simple underlining would have indicated that without significantly interrupting his reading. He chooses, however, to make an issue of the fact that he was accustomed to making the same distinction in his lectures, exposing the inadequacy of Johnson's *Dictionary* in the process. He does not suggest that Coleridge got the idea from him—it was in the air and Coleridge himself cites a few predecessors—though he does make some claim to priority and sounds irritable both about Johnson and about Coleridge's "metaphysical analysis."

The point about the importance of discriminating between synonyms, which Coleridge pursues in a long footnote on the same page and the next, elicits further notes, one merely correcting a press error and one an infelicitous phrase of Coleridge's own, one approving an analogy as "particularly happy—& original," one noting a debt to Horne Tooke, and one expanding on another good image. I do not propose to give a blow-by-blow account of every note and marked passage in the two volumes (there are 127 altogether) but these early notes establish an attitude and merit close attention. The echo of Horne Tooke is very slight: in a list of examples Coleridge includes "if" and "give" which Tooke had covered in his *Diversions of Purley*. But Thelwall seizes upon it in a note that suggests that he might after all have felt a bit possessive about imagination-fancy:

> It is curious to observe how freely persons of a certain cast of mind will borrow from those they affect to despise. What reader acquainted with the Diversions of Purley will fail to discover that the fountain of all this reasoning is in that book—which indeed has given a new impulse to the grammatical speculations of mankind. Yet Coleridge in his conversations affects an utter contempt for Tooke & his grammatical philosophy, & scrupled not to apply to him in some discussions we had upon these subjects, with all the bitterness of rooted scorn, the epithet of Charletan.

Whether or not it was prompted by a sense of personal grievance, Thelwall's defence of Tooke—his even detecting Tooke as a source for the passage, on the basis of two words, and his general point about Coleridge's unacknowledged indebtedness—is shrewd. Coleridge had at one time been very excited by Tooke's work, and though he deliberately rejected it later, he did not shake off its influence. This note is the first of many in which Thelwall invokes firsthand recollections to challenge Coleridge's representation of his life and thought. He must as he read have found himself regularly revisiting and reassessing the past.

His attitude, while challenging, was not hostile. He "talks" to the book in a familiar way. His very next note approves of and improves on

Coleridge's observation that the distinction of fancy from imagination might perhaps be "no less grounded in nature, than that of delirium from mania" (1:88). Here Coleridge was touching on a subject Thelwall had given some thought to already, and Thelwall's note expresses excitement over the new idea that Coleridge's analogy had generated in his mind, the possibility that the difference between imagination and fancy might offer a means of accounting for different forms of madness. He gave the passage three exclamation marks and wrote,

> This is perhaps even a better illustration than the writer himself perceived—for delirium displays itself in distempered fancy, or incoherency of mind—*Mania* is distempered imagination intensely coherent to the fantom of its creation; so that present realities cannot divert it from its imaginative object, & things the most dissimilar are converted to its likeness—windmills become giants & flocks of sheep are armies—because the distempered sees with the eyes of his imagination instead of the eyes of sense.

Here Thelwall is setting out an idea prompted by his reading, as Coleridge would do a year or two later in some of his notes on Webster.

After this flurry of activity, Thelwall let thirty pages go by without comment, pages in which Coleridge lays the foundation for his philosophical discrimination of imagination from fancy by way of the doctrine of association, which he traces from Aristotle through Descartes to Hartley and Mackintosh. When Thelwall felt moved to make a note again, however, he made his feelings about the uncommented section plain. Coleridge declares that "no errors of the understanding can be morally arraigned unless they have proceeded from the heart" (1:122). Thelwall underlined the words, adding an observation that sounds like a sigh of relief: "This one moral axiom is worth all the metaphysics the author either vents or combats." But he had not skipped over the argument, and his very next note, a few pages later, shows that he was quite alert enough to take Coleridge's own stated premises to an opposite conclusion: if body and spirit are legitimately considered opposite modes of a common substance, as Coleridge says they are, both may be alike *material.* Thelwall sketched out this counterargument and put his initials to it (1:128–29). Coleridge presses on making his own case and disparaging materialism; the dogmatic materialist unable to defend his position, he says, is liable "to affect the mysterious, and declare the whole process a revelation *given,* and not to be *understood,* which it would be prophane to examine too closely" (1:132–33). Thelwall could hardly believe his eyes. He underlined the passage quoted and wrote in the inner margin "! ! ! Ha! Ha! Mr S. T. C. ! ! !" Here was Coleridge, he must have thought, calling the kettle black, accusing his philosophical opponents of just the kind of behavior he himself was much more likely to be guilty of. While this mocking note may hark back to twenty-year-old disputes between the protagonists, it is also the kind of thing we have seen on other occasions where the reader talks back to the book without any special knowledge of the author; Thelwall had complained before, in his very first note, about superfluous "metaphysical analysis."

Thelwall's remaining notes to this chapter continue to demonstrate his engagement and fair-mindedness. He disputes Coleridge's absolutist view of conscience and rejects an argument founded on an analogy, but he likes the distinction Coleridge makes between eternity and infinitude. He hints at Coleridge's weaknesses of drunkenness, indolence, and love of orthodoxy, but is interested by an observation about common-sense objections to scientific truth, and uses the margin for speculation much as Coleridge did with Webster (1:133–35). The next cluster of notes comes thirty pages later, when Coleridge in autobiographical mode plays down his early political radicalism. Here Thelwall becomes indignant at what he perceived as apostasy and hypocritical denial. He does not just mark the text with crosses and exclamation marks, he spells out his disagreement. An evasive phrase sets him off when Coleridge describes his *Watchman* of 1795 as having been published every eighth day to avoid the newspaper tax and "contribute as little as possible to the supposed guilt of a war against freedom" (1:167). Coleridge was trying to indicate that in those days he had opposed the war against France as a war against freedom, but that he no longer considers it in that light.

> And was it only supposed? Does Mr C. really now believe that no part of the bloodshed in France, the twenty years of groans & slaughters—the temporary agrandisement of France beyond all limits—the subjugation of Europe to the domination of one man, & finally the present degraded & perillous state of the civilised world, is to be attributed to the guilt of that war—or is hostility against freedom no longer guiltly in the orthodox creed of Mr C.?

In the pages following, in several long notes, Thelwall queries Coleridge's account of his younger self and, citing his visits to Stowey and Keswick, calls on personal recollection to witness that Coleridge had been "a down right zealous leveller & . . . a man of blood" though he now denies having ever been activated by Jacobin or democratic principles (1:175). The tone of these notes is combative, but even here Thelwall takes care to spell out his position, carefully disentangling different meanings of the term "Jacobin" from one another. He quotes nine lines of an unpublished sonnet to himself as further proof of Coleridge's formerly radical sympathies (1:177–78).[12] These examples of eyewitness testimony may be the most interesting of Thelwall's notes from the point of view of the Coleridge specialist or the literary historian, but to the historian of reading they represent only one of several phases in Thelwall's progress through the book.

The second volume of the *Biographia* is more consistently literary than the first, and new topics attract Thelwall's attention. The annotation is heavier; themes begin to emerge. Thelwall expresses admiration for Coleridge's discussion of the nature of poetry and especially for the analysis of Shakespeare that follows in Chapter 15, of which he says that "sometimes the very illustrations & language seem as if they were but the echo of those I have so long & so frequently enforced in my Lectures" (2:22). He might again be suspected of raising the possibility of plagiarism, but it seems more likely that he is showing pleasure at having his own thoughts reinforced and validated in this way; later on he mentions having made the same case as Coleridge is making in a discussion with a relative, as a boy—an event Coleridge could not have known about (2:51). Like other readers, Mary Bowles for example,

Thelwall registers his impression that the author is speaking for him, expressing ideas that he has also entertained and feelings with which he strongly identifies himself. In these pages Thelwall also begins to mark some of the quoted poetry to indicate phrasing for reading aloud, or possibly to scan it by a system of his own something like bars in music: "And | Peace pro | claims | olives of | endless | age" for instance, where the stresses come at the beginning of the "bars" but iambic measures are ignored (2:19). In the reference to the lectures and the practice of the scansion (if that is what it is), he is asserting his authority in a small way: as a man who regularly gives lectures and teaches elocution, he has an interest in these subjects and a contribution to make.

Thelwall's notes may be less entertaining to a later reader when he finds himself basically in agreement with Coleridge, but like the notes of the social readers I considered in Chapter 2 they are helpful reminders of common concerns of the time that we may have lost sight of. Coleridge praises the polished rhythms of poets of the fifteenth and sixteenth centuries in contrast to "new metres, such as have been attempted of late" which introduce such an "overpowering tune" that the reader, reading aloud, has to let sense give way to it with "an effect not unlike that of galloping over a paved road in a German stage-waggon without springs" (2:28–29). Thelwall, underlining this passage, wholeheartedly concurs; his long note cites several recent offenders (Moore, Campbell, Beattie, Southey) and shows his relish for Coleridge's metaphor. Southey, he notes in conclusion, "gives us plenty of the German Waggon in his new old measures (his Sapphics & his Dactylics)—In Thalaba & Kehama his wheels are frequently light enough & his springs sufficiently elastic; but he carries us thro roads so soft & so unequal that we are frequently slough'd up to the axle, & thrown fairly out by the jerk." When it comes to the survey and analysis of Wordsworth's poetry, however, Thelwall goes into a dissenting mode again, not having as high an opinion of it as Coleridge has. In "The Idiot Boy," he says grumpily, "I can find nothing that is poetical—To me it is perfect drivelling" (2:44–5). And when Coleridge acknowledges that some readers are made uneasy by "sudden and unpleasant sinkings" in "The Thorn," Thelwall notes a change of attitude: "I am amused by these concessions. Some years ago, when C. and I had much talk about this poem in particular I could not wring from him any accordance with me upon the subject. The thorn was then an object of unqualified panegyric to him" (2:47). Again the text is tested against memory and Thelwall is "amused" to find that Coleridge has changed his tune. The subject was evidently an old quarrel, on the whole a friendly one, but Thelwall is pleased to find that while Coleridge has come round some way toward his own position (just as Coleridge has changed his political allegiances, though in the opposite direction), he himself has stood firm.

Some incidental remarks in a footnote, having to do with the way children are taught to read, provoke one of Thelwall's longest and most interesting notes (2:60–61). The reason is obvious: Coleridge was trespassing on Thelwall's turf, indeed invading it. Reading aloud, Coleridge says, "ought to differ from talking"; and then he uses the footnote to attack the common misconception of teachers to the contrary and to deplore the way children are punished for "singing" as they read. Thelwall reacts as a thoughtful professional who had trained many public readers. "Reading (generally speaking) must differ from talking," he begins, "because we talk with a communicant feeling, we read with a recipient feeling—that is to say with the sensation not of a speaker but a hearer." But he makes the case for trying to bring the two closer together. In *recitation* at least, "a man should pronounce (the subject & the mode of treating it considered) as he would speak. He should have made the composition (passion sentiment & character) his own; & deliver it as from himself—unless indeed when he quotes for the purpose of shewing his admiration of the passage itself when a sort of emphasis & tone of admiration may properly be superadded." In a more ad hominem spirit, he observes that Coleridge himself was not a particularly good model: "The very rhythmus of C's poetry is frequently contaminated by his own abominable singsong drawl of delivery." This is one subject on which Thelwall had strong feelings and well-developed views; like other confident readers he debates the issue with the author. It would be good to know whether he thought of silent reading in the same way as reading aloud, from a psychological point of view: did the silent reader also feel "recipient" (which is not to say passive) and have the impression he was "a hearer" of the text? On the evidence of his argumentative marginalia, Thelwall did. He listened and then responded to the text.

As Coleridge carries on with his detailed criticism of Wordsworth, Thelwall marks many passages, disputing some but accepting most of them. The culmination of this phase in his reading comes when Coleridge writes about Wordsworth's particular excellence of "just and original reflection" and quotes among other passages the lines from "Simon Lee" (2:164; Fig. 29):

> O Reader! had you in your mind
> Such stores as silent thought can bring,
> O gentle Reader! you would find
> A tale in every thing.

Thelwall in response quotes a few lines of his own:

> Thus to reflections sober train
> Each plant a useful lesson gives—
> A moralizer on the plain
> Each turf & lowly blossom lives. Thelwall's (early) Poems.

He makes no further comment on the conjunction here, but his example is surely meant to contest Coleridge's praise of "original reflection," since he can prove that another poet (himself) had had the same thought He is not laying charges of plagiarism; he would have been aware that the idea was not original with him either.

Coleridge's summing up toward the end of Chapter 22 leads Thelwall to some general observations of his own. At one point Coleridge turns to figurative language to convey his sense of the freshness and fidelity of Wordsworth's representations of nature: "Like a green field reflected in a calm and perfectly transparent lake, the image is distinguished from the reality only by its greater softness and lustre. Like the moisture or polish on a pebble, genius neither distorts nor false-colours

164

myself to find *more* exceptions, than in those of Wordsworth. Quotations or specimens would here be wholly out of place, and must be left for the critic who doubts and would invalidate the justice of this eulogy so applied.

The second characteristic excellence of Mr. W's works is: a correspondent weight and sanity of the Thoughts and Sentiments,—won, not from books; but—from the poets' own meditative observation. They are *fresh* and have the dew upon them. His muse, at least when in her strength of wing, and when she hovers aloft in her proper element,

Makes audible a linked lay of truth,
Of truth profound a sweet continuous lay,
Not learnt, but native, her own natural notes!
S. T. C.

Even throughout his smaller poems there is scarcely one, which is not rendered valuable by some just and original reflection.

See page 25, vol. 2nd: or the two following passages in one of his humblest compositions.

" O Reader! had you in your mind
Such stores as silent thought can bring,
O gentle Reader! you would find
A tale in every thing." ×

and

" I have heard of hearts unkind, kind deeds
With coldness still returning:
Alas! the gratitude of men
Has oftener left *me* mourning."

165

or in a still higher strain the six beautiful quatrains, page 134.

" Thus fares it still in our decay:
And yet the wiser mind
Mourns less for what age takes away
Than what it leaves behind.

The Blackbird in the summer trees,
The Lark upon the hill,
Let loose their carols when they please,
Are quiet when they will.

With nature never do *they* wage
A foolish strife; they see
A happy youth, and their old age
Is beautiful and free!

But we are pressed by heavy laws;
And often, glad no more,
We wear a face of joy, because
We have been glad of yore.

If there is one, who need bemoan
His kindred laid in earth,
The household hearts that were his own,
It is the man of mirth.

My days, my Friend, are almost gone,
My life has been approved,
And many love me; but by none
Am I enough beloved."

or the sonnet on Buonaparte, page 202, vol. 2; or finally (for a volume would scarce suffice to exhaust the instances,) the last stanza of the poem on the withered Celandine, vol. 2, p. 212.

FIG. 29 Notes by John Thelwall in Coleridge's *Biographia Literaria* (1817). By permission of The Fales Library and Special Collections, New York University.

its objects . . . " (2:168–69). Thelwall underlines this passage but instead of praising or pursuing the imagery as he had done before, he remarks, "The similies of Coleridge are frequently much more luminous & logical than his arguments." This astute observation is the product of the reading process: having repeatedly found himself approving of Coleridge's metaphors, he now discovers the pattern both of his own observations and of Coleridge's technique—and incidentally disparages Coleridge's method of argument again. At this stage he is ready to try out a general position about Wordsworth as well: "In main matter or substance—in subject & in manner Wordsworth is original but in detached parts & individual passages, he is frequently a borrower—a paraphrast rather than an imitator" (2:172). This is not a statement triggered directly by a particular sentence in the text but the result of a process of thought stimulated by Coleridge's criticism.

Further notes in the second volume follow the practice now established: Thelwall underlines, marks, briefly offers encouragement or takes exception, and occasionally comments expansively on some of the now familiar topics—meter, metaphysics, Christianity, and Jacobinism—incidentally revealing details of his and Coleridge's past lives, such as efforts of his own on behalf of Kant in England (2:246). One very long note, taking off from Coleridge's phrase "the modern jacobinical drama," considers the damage done by "unmeaning, but yet popular cant nick names," objects very strongly to Coleridge's attaching the epithet "jacobinical" to fashionable melodrama, but temperately agrees with him about the drama itself (2:271–72). He meets Coleridge's pleas on behalf of Christianity in the final chapter with skepticism but good humor. Coleridge proposes that an awareness of spiritual incompleteness is the proper "foundation" of Christian faith: "the sense, the inward feeling, in the soul of each Believer . . . the experience, that he *needs* something, joined with the strong Foretokening, that the Redemption and the Graces propounded to us in Christ are *what* he needs" may serve to lead him to Christ. Thelwall dismisses this argument with a ludicrous illustration and a last stab at Coleridge's "metaphysics" (2:305):

> To him, therefore who hath no such sense, feeling, experience & foretokening, it hath no foundation at all. Now to some cold reasoners these inward feelings & longings may appear but very ambiguous arguments—"I feel a sudden pain across my breast", says K. Arthur in Tom Thumb, "nor can I say if this proceeds from Love, or only the wind collic." Mr C.'s metaphysics perhaps might have solved the difficulty & put an end to the monarch's scepticism. As for the latter half of this p. if it be not the rant & cant of the conventicle, what is it?

The word "conventicle" harks back to Thelwall's correspondence with Coleridge twenty years earlier, showing that Thelwall's opinion of

Coleridge was not substantially changed by the *Biographia* and suggesting that in many of the notes he may be revisiting old quarrels, as we have seen memoirists seeking to settle old scores. No doubt Thelwall's reading of Coleridge was conducted under exceptional circumstances. Readers are not often personally acquainted with the author of their books. Nor do they generally publish their notes. But Thelwall could not afford to let his reading go to waste, and in any case he had been shocked by Coleridge's public apostasy. Late in 1818 he bought the *Champion*, a weekly paper to which he had been an occasional contributor; the issue of 3 January 1819 first announced that he was the new editor and proprietor. On 21 December 1818, under the initials "A. S." the *Champion* included his report of Coleridge's latest lecture on Shakespeare. Though he praised the lecture and recommended both of the series of lectures upon which Coleridge was then embarked, he began his report with some reservations about the mental capacity of the lecturer. What are we to think, he asked, about someone who misremembers the past? And he cited one of the anti-Jacobin passages in the *Biographia*, quoting the still unpublished sonnet to contradict Coleridge's recollection of his youthful enthusiasm. "Alas! poor Coleridge!" was his comment, "a seraph! and a worm!"[13]

Every reading takes place in the context of some such set of circumstances, however, and there is no reason to suppose that Thelwall read the *Biographia* in a fundamentally different way from any other book that might have crossed his path, or that his reading of it was psychologically anomalous. He was not reading it for review; the opportunity to make use of his notes came later, and he picked out only one note of many. What we observe when we track his reading through his marginalia is a relatively unguarded process of response. Though acquainted with Coleridge, he did not set out with a firm position for or against him. On the whole he was receptive in a positive sense (the reader is "recipient" as he says), ready to take in what was offered. He reacts point by point, here pleased enough to underline, there leaving marks of surprise or doubt or denial, and from time to time moved to write more extensively about a faulty argument or an opinion with which he does not concur. He is especially eloquent about matters in which he has a pre-established personal stake—memories of the past, theories of poetry, methods of reading aloud, and political principle. But he also registers discoveries as he reads, especially new ideas that are generated by interaction with the text; and he seems gradually to take the measure of the book and to move toward a settled view of his relationship to it and its author. Recognizing the power of Coleridge's similes and, about the same time, the limitations of his assessment of Wordsworth, he is left in the end with an informed position, the qualified respect that he later expressed in his report in the *Champion*.

Thelwall was already in his fifties when he read the *Biographia*. His self-image was well established, and I am not aware that anyone ever singled him out for his modesty. Most of his longer notes cite his own experience or his publications. But self-referentiality is a built-in feature of reading; all readers want to know how a book is relevant to their lives. As readers go, Thelwall does not seem unusually egocentric. As often as they draw attention to himself, his notes in the *Biographia* indicate a suspension of thoughts of self, as though he were experiencing double or alternating consciousness, now his own and now the writer's. In those sections in which there are no notes, or where underlining or annotations show Thelwall appreciatively recognizing thoughts he could adopt or had already indistinctly entertained, identification with the author is dominant; in those where he breaks in and objects, resisting identification, it is subordinate. The same could be said of most of the readers whose marginalia are described in this book, and some of them said it of themselves.

CONCLUSION

Using words that have been echoed by later readers as well as by modern theorists and phenomenologists such as Barthes, Poulet, Holland, Ingarden, and Iser, several of the self-conscious readers of the time wrote about the experience of reading as a kind of benign possession. They may all be proven wrong one day by the neurologists, but until then, there is some comfort in the general endorsement of the intuitive view that reading involves an oscillation between text and reader, a vacillation between surrender and self-assertion. It is by consensus a matter of proportion and predominance, not a system of alternative existence in which when the text is on, the reader must be off, and vice versa. As in psychological accounts of dramatic illusion and in Coleridge's related doctrine of poetic faith—"that willing suspension of disbelief for the moment"—awareness of the real world and consciousness of fiction do not go away when the audience puts itself in the hands of the playwright or poet. They are only more or less in abeyance. Lady Mount Cashell discovered that in reading she could entertain two trains of ideas at once, her own and the author's. This is the repeated theme of readers reflecting on the subject throughout the period, perhaps because it was the conventional thing to say but surely also because it corresponded to their own experience. Wordsworth described that temporary oblivion, the loss of self-consciousness that comes with absorbed reading, as a positively voluptuous experience: "Reading is now become a kind of luxury to me. When I do not read I am absolutely consumed by thinking and feeling and bodily exertions of voice or limbs, the consequence of those feelings" (*Letters,* 236). Lamb, similarly, said that he loved to "lose" himself "in other men's minds" (2:172). Godwin wrote about reading as a doubling of existence and declared that when he read Thomson he became Thomson (140, 33). With characteristic boldness, Coleridge speculated that oneness with God might feel something like reading the words of a powerful writer (his example is Leighton) and so identifying oneself with the author that "his thoughts become my thoughts" (*Marginalia,* 3:523).

In the mortal world, the agreeable form of possession or rather the state of being possessed to which these readers bear witness is always provisional and temporary, fluctuating with their moods and circumstances, and subject to moments of rupture, when the self breaks in again. Marginalia record some of those moments and generally document the reader's relation to the text. They bring us about as close as we can reasonably expect ever to get to the reader's processes of thought, and what they tend to show is that while the reader's regular habits of mind may be suspended in the course of reading, they are not fundamentally altered. Coleridge goes on thinking the way he thinks, as do

Thelwall, Piozzi, Blake, and Walpole, though for a time all more or less defer—mentally, willingly—to the books they are reading. Questions remain. How typical are such readers? The ones named here are atypical in that they became famous, but in other ways they seem much the same as their contemporaries. Under circumstances peculiar to themselves they exercised the common skills of reading and the common behavior of writing notes to record some of the thoughts that occurred to them while they were doing it. Did not the practice of note-making itself contaminate the process? Since without notes there is no record, we cannot be sure, but we know that Thelwall, Coleridge, Piozzi, and the others read many books without leaving notes, and it is hard to imagine that their mental experience was radically different under those circumstances. They had all learned to read in an environment that countenanced writing in conjunction with reading and provided a broad range of models to follow, so that ways of approaching and thinking about books were common to those who did and those who did not choose to write in them. Reading with pen in hand may have enhanced the process that it recorded, sharpening the reader's responses, but the basic business of reception, association, assimilation, and judgment would also go on without it, such difference as there was being a matter of degree, not of kind.

Conclusion

Let us return to the questions with which this study began. What does the evidence of marginalia have to contribute to the history of reading in Britain? Though the response must be as provisional as the survey was limited, it is possible to sketch out some answers by approaching the question from three different angles. What does the evidence reveal about the history of marginalia? About actual readers? About the history of reading in general?

In the English-speaking world of the early twenty-first century, writing notes in books is almost universally condemned as a selfish and messy business, so unless professional duties absolutely require it (as in the case of authorial and editorial revision, and of reviewing), readers are accustomed to feel guilty about it, and to do it secretly. Schools and libraries forbid the marking of books and make such an issue of it that by the time students emerge from the education process they have generally internalized the prohibition. If they choose to write in books anyway, their notes tend to be written for only themselves to see, and to reflect purely personal concerns. Like any guilty pleasure, writing marginalia is liable to become addictive: if a reader indulges, it is probably with all books indiscriminately and habitually. In Britain in the Romantic period, on the other hand, the practice was well established and its value was only beginning to be questioned. Society as a whole accepted this form of readerly intervention. Educators encouraged it. There *were* no public libraries (in the sense of free libraries open to all) to raise the alarm, though the circulating libraries had made a start. In such a permissive environment, it was normal for readers to write in books where they found it advantageous to do so, but they appear to have done it opportunistically and occasionally, not habitually. Since books had to be shared, the owners always knew, at some level of consciousness, that their notes would one day be seen by somebody else, so they did not use their freedom to commune with themselves: their notes tend to be either objective and utilitarian or subjective but interpersonal, a form of communication with the imagined author or with another reader.

The behavior of annotating readers circa 1800 and indeed their attitudes toward their books in general had more in common with the behavior and attitudes of their counterparts two hundred years earlier than with ours two centuries later. They continued to use traditional techniques of assimilation (glosses, heads, cross-references) and enrichment (correction, supplement, commentary) that had been carried over from manuscript to print culture, while they increased the proportion of original and personal note-making and enthusiastically adopted the social possibilities of annotation. These latter trends, which had been gaining strength throughout the eighteenth century, reached a high-water mark in the Romantic period. But then, with the exposure in the periodical press of what had previously been only a semi-public form of writing, marginalia were suddenly on a par with personal letters, susceptible of exploitation. Under these new conditions, readers' notes were bound to become either more guarded or better protected. The annotating reader went into retreat. The advent of mass publishing in the 1830s and '40s made it easier to keep books and the notes in them to oneself; good models faded from view; and public libraries and compulsory education joined forces to discourage note-making. Though it did not quite die out, this common custom came to be stigmatized as antisocial.

But the change was gradual and late-coming. Between 1790 and 1830, as far as marginalia are concerned, the situation was quite stable.

Readers continued to interact with their books as they had been doing for generations, whether at a first encounter or in long-term association: improving them with relevant extracts and facts gathered from elsewhere; haranguing them; preparing them to be shared with friends. Their marginalia show how they took control of their books and made them serve their needs.

Metaphors of control and mastery have unpleasantly fascist, even sadistic, connotations nowadays. Individually and collectively, however, Romantic readers are attractive figures, and after all the subject is books and not human relations. Even when they quarrel with their books these readers do it engagingly. Circumstances conspired to make them attentive, articulate, self-assertive. Major figures like Blake, Keats, and Coleridge prove more winning in their informal reflections on books than in some of their strenuous published writings; the voices we hear in their marginalia are like the ones we hear in their letters, only speaking on less predictable topics. Minor literary figures like Walpole, Seward, Beckford, Piozzi, Woodhouse, and Thelwall also appear to advantage as annotators, warmer and more candid than we might have expected, as do others whom we hardly know as writers at all—Hargrave, Sussex, Douce, MacDermott—as well as hundreds of other unnamed contemporaries. The reason is that marginalia were not then the almost wholly unregulated things they have become, but exercises in a known mode, destined sooner or later to be seen by other eyes than the writer's. There were tacit incentives to perform well. The high status of books, assisted perhaps by the high price of paper during the war years, made the social exchange of books especially popular, and thus accounts for the quantity of charming personal marginalia that survive. There may even have been an element of competitiveness involved. De Quincey at one point grumbled that Wordsworth's marginalia did not "illustrate his intellectual superiority. The comments were such as might have been made by anybody" (2:314). His casual remark seems to imply that intelligence and talent ought to be on display even in this minor genre.

The history of marginalia is naturally related to the history of reading but also, less obviously, to the history of writing and production.

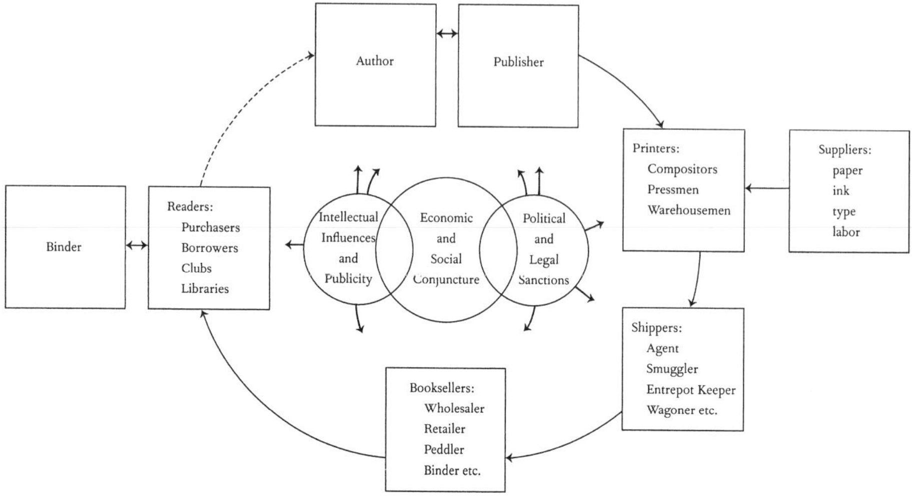

FIG. 30 "The Communications Circuit," from *The Kiss of Lamourette* by Robert Darnton. © 1990 by Robert Darnton; used by permission of W. W. Norton & Company, Inc.

When writing in books is normal behavior and readers have incentives to act as contributors or editors, they may easily come to conceive of themselves as equal or superior to the author. From there it is a short step to authorship on one's own account. Robert Darnton's diagram of the "Communications Circuit" that shows knowledge passing from the author through the publisher through distribution systems to the reader notoriously has a dotted line, meaning "process unknown," between the reader and new writing (Fig. 30). In the marginalia of many Romantic readers we seem to see the gap closing, the dots being joined up.

Some other aspects of the print culture of the period lend support to the idea that marginalia constituted a form of writing-practice. Clifford Siskin, for instance, has argued that the conditions of the time made readers into writers because "unprecedented numbers of people learned both the skills *and*—that crucial component of modern literacy—the belief in their transformative power" (6). Jon Klancher has pointed out that the evolution of the periodical press meant that for a few decades, magazines and newspapers relied on contributions from their readers—another form of "writing in." He describes readers and writers as "interchangeable participants" in the periodicals before 1830, but sees that "communal exchange of reading and writing" as a casualty of mass-market consumerism after then (*Making*, 39, 45).

As far as actual readers are concerned, I should hope that the examples of marginalia presented in this book, many of them by "common readers" (according to Jonathan Rose's handy definition, "any reader who did not read books for a living" [51]), will make historians aware of hitherto neglected resources and provide a context for particular cases. While the range of practices on exhibit is wide, there are many recurring features: the perceived value of extracts, the construction of networks of information by systems of cross-reference, and the revealing license to "illustrate" more or less ad lib. These are habits we have for the most part abandoned. On the other hand, we have developed habits unknown to Romantic readers. For example, though their reading was naturally self-referential, they hardly ever used marginalia for self-analysis, not even Coleridge, whereas self-analysis and self-promotion are common features of marginalia today. The options available to annotating readers of the time included citing personal experiences to corroborate or contradict the text, but not dwelling on private concerns. When Lady Mount Cashell noticed that she was capable of thinking about two things at once, for instance, it was to reject a specific assertion of Godwin's. And though readers of the Romantic period regularly passed judgment on their books, they did not analyze *them* either. That is to say, they might analyze in the sense of breaking down an argument into its major and minor parts, or providing heads to keep track of the development of a narrative, but they rarely propose an interpretation. With the significant exceptions of the Bible and allegory, they take meaning to be self-evident. They do not "translate" or paraphrase the text section by section, nor do they summarize works, literary or not, in terms significantly different from their (the works') own. Instead, they argue with the author, or with members of their social circle, about fine points of style and reasoning: this is an effect of the close attention that reading to make notes induces. And they argue about overall merit, as we see conspicuously in the "general note."

The last and biggest question has to do with the history of reading in general. Darnton's challenge, quoted in my Preface, was to discover whether marginalia could be employed in the interests of the history of reading to reveal "the mental processes by which readers appropriated texts." Given the cultural conditions under which they were written, the marginalia of this period are only moderately revealing. Because they are plentiful, writing in books having been routine everyday practice, they give us insight into both the reading experiences of particular individuals and the common mindset of the time. Because they were so often composed to be read by a circle of intimates, they tend to be more expansive than notes written only for oneself, and therefore provide more material to work with than we generally find in earlier and later periods. But for the same reason, they are more or less removed from the immediate encounter with the text. They give us what readers were prepared to tell their friends about the experience they were having; beyond that we are in the realm of inference. Under the right circumstances, as with Hargrave's Blackstone or Coleridge's Webster, we can with some confidence reconstitute the mental processes readers went through; in such cases, marginalia bring us very close to the original experience. Darnton, a realist, would probably ask no more than that: as he has said elsewhere, we "hardly know what it [reading] is when it takes place under our nose" (*Forbidden*, 85), and readers of two centuries ago were even less likely than we are to think of interrogating themselves about an experience as they went through it. With a small group of readers on particular occasions we can get close; with many others we have some glimpses and can put those glimpses together to construct plausible generalizations.

But the history of reading need not be confined to the reconstruction of mental processes, as Darnton's phrase perhaps unintentionally implies it is. Scholars have yet to agree on the meaning of "history of reading" and are hardly in a hurry to do so, since it makes a convenient umbrella for a mix of materials and approaches, from the external trappings of library furniture through the statistics of auction catalogues, lending records, and best-seller lists to theories of reading, hermeneutics, and phenomenology. James Secord's inclusive definition—"all the diverse ways that books and other forms of printed works are appropriated and used" (3)—serves my purposes well because it folds the history of marginalia into the history of reading. Marginalia of the Romantic period may be only moderately revealing about mental processes, but they provide plenty of solid evidence about use. They show how by a range of methods and in accordance with common codes, books and pamphlets were appropriated by individuals and put to use intellectually, professionally, and socially. In part because books were hard to get, new ones being expensive and even cheap old ones requiring informed effort, they were made to earn their keep. Readers who invested money and time and attention in this way, sometimes over the course of years, express attitudes toward books and conceptions of themselves as readers that are no longer common.

I do not wish to end, however, by appearing to represent Romantic readers as the happy inhabitants of a lost Golden Age. The concept of reading that would magnify the differences between them and us is itself flawed. Because we take it for granted that reading is one of the most subjective of acts, intensely private, personal, and mysterious, and because we treat our own notes in books as secret if not shameful, we are surprised to find Romantic readers exposing their thoughts in an interpersonal and semi-public way. But perhaps our assumptions are mistaken. Reading has always had both social and solitary aspects to it; emphasizing one does not eliminate the other. We retain many of the social customs and institutions that encouraged readers two hundred years ago—libraries, book clubs, literary chitchat. Our motives for reading are as often as not socially driven: we choose one book or magazine rather than another in order to bolster a sense of community and to be able to participate in certain kinds of conversations. It is time to adjust not only our ideas about marginalia but our ideas about reading, and the witness of Romantic readers can help us on both counts.

Notes

Introduction

1. An early historian of publishing in the period, J. G. Lockhart, described Constable's vision of an audience of millions as having led the way "in one of the greatest revolutions that literary history will ever have to record" (7:130). The language persists. Clifford Siskin's *The Work of Writing* claims that "the new technology of writing" by which he means "the entire configuration of writing, print, and silent reading" produced a revolution in "society's ways of knowing and working" between 1780 and 1830 (2). Kathryn Sutherland before him described a revolution in printing that had occurred "by the 1830s" (3) accompanied by "something amounting to a revolution in consciousness" (43). Brewer and McCalman also document what they refer to as a "publishing revolution" in the period (206).
2. Lackington, *Memoirs,* 254–55; quoted in Steinberg (239), Irwin (256), Brewer and McCalman (197), and Mayo (220, skeptically).
3. Godwin, *Enquiry,* 364; Coleridge, in a diatribe against the "reading public" in *Biographia Literaria* (1817), e.g. 1:48–49, and privately in marginalia to the novels of Scott, where he deplores the turn to recreational reading as a consequence of the fact that "every man is now a Reader" (*Marginalia* 4:610). Government measures to subdue the radical press included successive increases in the stamp tax on newspapers and fitful crack-downs on blasphemous, treasonous, or seditious libel, notably in the trials of Leigh and John Hunt (1812), William Hone (acquitted, 1817), and Richard Carlile (1817–19).
4. The prolonged attack on women's reading has been the subject of many studies: a comprehensive recent example is Jacqueline Pearson's *Women's Reading in Britain, 1750–1835.*

5. K. Sutherland, 6. Deane and Cole estimate the population of the United Kingdom (i.e., adding Ireland to the figures for Great Britain) as 13 million in 1781 and 24.135 million in 1831 (Table 3). Marshall (8–10) shows the breakdown for England and Wales (together), Scotland, and Ireland.
6. For different reasons, both the Anglicans and the Methodists had decided to teach the poor to read but not to write: Rule, 147–48; K. Sutherland, 5. Lackington describes his own situation in *Memoirs.* As an apprentice he paid his master's son to teach him one hour a week. He claims to have read Plato, Plutarch, Seneca, and Epictetus at the age of twenty-two, but it was after that that he taught himself to write by copying bits of manuscript (97, 102–3). Even allowing for self-aggrandizement in Lackington's account, and for the self-serving desire to sell books, there seems no reason to doubt the *sequence* of events.
7. Maxted's Table (xxxi) gives "rough counts" of annual book production from 1700 to 1836. Plant doubts "whether the number of volumes had risen in the same proportion" (462)—that is, an increase in the number of new titles might signify greater variety without greater quantity.
8. Henry Thornton, M.P., in a report included in a volume of the tracts in the British Library, shelf-mark 4418.e.70.
9. Thrale, *Thraliana,* 1:355, cited in Pearson, 186.
10. Southey and his son Cuthbert, for example, looking back on the state of "The Great Trade" circa 1830 (*Life,* 6:173). Altick more plausibly speculates that in the absence of cheap publications, working-class readership declined "after the Jacobin fever wore off" (72).
11. Steinberg points out that whereas a hand press printed about 300 sheets an hour, the steam model of 1814 printed 1,100 and the model of 1828 printed 4,000 (279).
12. Twyman, *Breaking the Mould,* 24.
13. For further details about these developments see Coleman, Glaister, Steinberg, K. Sutherland, and Twyman.
14. Brewer's *Pleasures of the Imagination,* Raven's *Judging New Wealth,* and the collection of essays edited by Raven, Small, and Tadmor provide vivid accounts of the reading environment of the eighteenth century.
15. In 1822, Lord John Russell gave the figure of 23,600,000 for the number of newspapers sold throughout the country in the previous year: quoted in *Monthly Magazine* 54 (1822): 59.
16. On top of this established nationwide system, there were special-interest networks created by philanthropic organizations to distribute pamphlets. They typically worked through local branches of a church or society. Marcus Wood explains how the movement for the abolition of the slave trade after 1780 made use of existing Quaker networks. Paine's notorious *Rights of Man* was taken up by Constitutional Societies that reprinted, abridged, and distributed it (Goodwin, 177–78). The Cheap Repository (1795), the Religious Tract Society (1799), and the British and Foreign Bible Society (1804)—the last fully

documented by Leslie Howsam—depended on the activity of committees across the country. House-to-house traveling salesmen were a later commercial development reported as a novelty by the *Monthly Magazine* in 1815 (39:550).

17. In 1806, in a letter to Murray, Constable was eloquent about the advantages of "the continued advertisement of a book *long* previous to publication": it made country readers keen and caused country booksellers to place orders even before reviews appeared (1:348). A meeting of London booksellers in 1815 estimated that advertising accounted for almost a quarter of the cost of "a single octavo volume": *Monthly Magazine* 39:549.
18. Feather, 98–100, Brewer, *Pleasures*, 132–39, Brewer and McCalman, 197. Feather is particularly good at explaining the way the system grew up. The agents seem often to have carried medicines in their shops as well as print. They might also be responsible for postal service: in *Sir Thomas More* (1829) Southey mentions the "postwoman" of Keswick who has just arrived with letters and newspapers (1:1). Of course the success of the network of agents depended upon good transport, recently improved by the introduction of Palmer's mail-coaches in 1784. The postal system did not change significantly till Aaron Hill's system was introduced in 1840, nor transport till the advent of the railway network in the 1840s.
19. Roper, 25–26. Roper cites circulation figures of 1797 which he considers plausible: *Monthly Review*, 5,000; *Critical Review*, 3,500; *British Critic*, 3,500; *Analytical Review*, 1,500 (24).
20. Klancher, "Vocation," 301.
21. Rule, *Albion's People;* Gayer et al., *Growth and Fluctuation.*
22. Twyman, *Printing*, 5.
23. Eliot, *Some Patterns*, 83–84.
24. On restrictive trade practices see Pollard; Gaskell 180–81; and Brewer, *Pleasures*, 132–39. On some of the implications of the decision in Donaldson *v.* Becket, see Mark Rose, 92–112.
25. *DNB* (More, Hannah; Scott, Sir Walter); Jack, 33; Roberts, 2:170; K. Sutherland, 38; McClary, 41. For other best-sellers see also Steinberg, 337–43.
26. Southey, *Life* 1:283, 3:122, 3:125; *DNB* "Jeffrey, Francis."
27. Lackington, not in the first edition of his *Memoirs* but in expanded later editions, e.g., in the 7th ed of 1794 (under the slightly revised title *Memoirs of the Forty-Five First Years*), 222–24. A letter of Southey's from 1796 seems to confirm Lackington's statement. Southey had published *Joan of Arc* in Bristol; though the book was available for sale in London, he wished it had gone through the London publishers in the first place: "they can put off an edition of a book however stupid; and without great exertions in its favour no book, however excellent, will sell. The sale of Joan of Arc in London has been very slow indeed. Six weeks ago Cadell had sold only three copies" (*Life*, 1:291).
28. Trusler, MS memoirs, 211–12.

29. Coleridge, *Letters* 1:206. Though it has been suggested that Coleridge was interested in Rumford's plan for a garden city, the context of the proposal and his account of Rumford's *Essays* in his periodical *The Watchman* a few days later make the scheme for poor relief a likelier candidate: *Watchman* 177–78. In the *Biographia Literaria* of 1817, Coleridge's advice to young authors was always to prefer an outright sale of copyright: "fifty pounds and ease of mind are of more real advantage to a literary man, than the *chance* of five hundred with the *certainty* of insult and degrading anxieties" (1:176).
30. Jane Millgate, "Scott and Copyright," keynote address at the International Scott Conference, University of Oregon, July 1999.
31. Blake, letter of 2 July 1800, quoted by Bentley, 267. A magazine circle of 1807 gives an interesting analysis of the reasons for the increase in booksellers, emphasizing the "diffusion of printed priced catalogues" and auction catalogues priced in manuscript since 1743 that "has set all the world agog to sell books": "Memoirs of Henry Lemoine," 2237.
32. The big houses tended to have diverse investments outside publishing as well, a fact that may have contributed to their difficulties in 1826. An economic analysis of that year cited "large speculations in hops, land, houses, &c.": *Monthly Magazine* n.s. 2 (1826):17.
33. On Johnson's dinners see also Tyson, 118.
34. E.g. Smiles, 1:264; and for dinner-parties, Smiles *passim*.
35. Title page and advertisement in British Library copy, shelf-mark T.882.(4.).
36. Knott, 7–8. Wilson includes "Tobacco and snuffs" in the list of goods that can easily be combined with the management of a small circulating library in *The Use of Circulating Libraries Considered* (1797), a pamphlet reprinted as an appendix in Varma, 193–203.
37. Twyman, *Printing*, 7.
38. Printers were accustomed to working fast and accommodating the writer's schedule. Edmond Malone, publishing with Cadell and Davies, left the following note in his own copy of his *Inquiry into the Authenticity of certain Miscellaneous Papers . . . attributed to Shakespeare . . .* (1796), showing how the press set type close on the writer's heels: "Begun to be written about the 10th of Jany. Begun to be printed about the 20th of Jany—finished at the press Monday March 28—published March 31. 1796. 500 Copies sold on that day and the next."
39. Coleridge, *Poetical Works*, ed. Mays, 1:480.
40. Coleridge, *Biographia Literaria*, 1:15.
41. Most of the biographical information in this paragraph is from the *DNB* and the anonymous "Memoirs" published in the *Wonderful Museum* during his lifetime.
42. Like its rivals, the *Wonderful Magazine* puffed the book trade by carrying profiles and poems about it: a print representing "Dr. Ve-d—n, a remarkable Walking Bookseller Quack Doctor &c &c" (1:facing 406: this was "Dr. Ver-

dion," actually a woman); "Anecdotes of J. Lackington" (3:119–22); "An Account" of John Love of Weymouth, a bookseller and one of the most corpulent men in England (4:222); and a series of imagined street cries, in verse, by workers associated with the *Magazine*—publisher, printer, binder, designer, retail bookseller, and stationer (5:279–84).

43. "A List of Books, published by the Rev. Dr. Trusler, at the Literary-Press, No. 62, Wardour-Street, Soho. 1790." Catalogue attached to *The Honours of the Table* (1788), Lewis Walpole Library copy, shelf-mark 53 T77 788. Though Trusler describes the sermons as engraved, surviving copies appear simply to be printed in a script-like font. In 1790 Trusler advertised 150 different sermons, by a variety of authors, available at a shilling apiece, with a discount for bulk purchase; he said the print run was 400. His own *Twelve Sermons* (1796) illustrated in Fig. 6 appears to be a subset of the 150.
44. Ms memoirs, 216.
45. Ms memoirs, 240.
46. Ms memoirs, 211.
47. Trusler, "A List of Books." After he moved to Bath c. 1795, his books were handled by a printer there. A four-page "Advertisement" promoting his publications, including the *Memoirs* of 1806, issued by Smith of New Bond St., Bath, is included in a British Library copy of Trusler's *Proverbs in Verse*, shelf-mark 12201.h.3.(2.) The *Proverbs* were also available as a set of images printed on "playing cards" to whet the curiosity of the preschool set.
48. Ms memoirs 343–46. James Raven comments on and provides a context for Trusler's views on working-class education in "From Promotion to Proscription," 192–93.
49. Ms memoirs, 346.
50. An advertisement in the British Library copy of Trusler's novel *Life* (shelf-mark N 1889) promotes this periodical with the subtitle "Cheap and Interesting Magazine." It cost fourpence, was distributed by newsmen, and promised to contain "every thing worth attention, adapted to all readers from the scholar to the farmer."
51. "But books are no longer solely respected for their insides since they have been honourd with admission into the drawing room which although a very pleasing & sensible transition from the stiffness of ancient manners when every guest was obliged to sit with hands across & listen to the prosing of such as could prose, has nevertheless contributed greatly to render Books expensive as elegant pieces of furniture": letter to Anna Seward, 13 Jan. 1807 (*Letters*, 1:346).
52. Austen, *Letters*, 304.
53. Though the figures here, based on a small sampling, are less reliable for new fiction than those recorded in Garside et al., they fall within the same general range and follow the same trajectory.
54. This was the conclusion also of an economic analysis of 1807 in the *Monthly*

Magazine (24:274–75). While deploring "the luxurious taste of the times" which drove up production costs, the writer pointed out "that books have not risen in price more than other articles, and that they are much cheaper, *caeteris paribus,* than in any other country in Europe, and at half the price at which they can be produced in America."

55. Mathias, 36n.
56. Advertisement in *Morning Chronicle,* 6 May 1795.
57. Advertised in the *Morning Chronicle,* 1 May 1795.
58. For example, Mary Russell Mitford's copy of the *Literary Pocket-Book* (1819) contained printed lists of useful addresses, remarks about the seasons, exchange rates, and samples of poetry and anecdotes even before she filled every blank space with memoranda and diary entries. Daines Barrington published a *Naturalist's Diary* in a convenient oblong quarto format that was in use from 1767 well into the 1790s: it provided headings and the reader added details, in columns. A particularly charming copy of *A New Common-place Book* (1788) was used in an Irish parish between about 1785 and 1828 mainly for useful quotations and recipes—"Black Ink," "For the Scab in Sheep," etc.
59. Coleridge, *Biographia Literaria,* 2:176. Addison in *Spectator* #85 claims to have "once met with a Page of Mr. *Baxter* under a *Christmas* Pye."
60. The quotation is from one of Southey's letters of 1799 (*Life,* 2:14); Lamb's essay is his "Detached Thoughts on Books and Reading" of 1822 (*Works,* 2:172–76).
61. Piozzi, *Letters,* 3:282. On the whole "tract system" (515) and the Cheap Repository Tracts in particular, see Gilmartin.
62. *DNB* "Fitzroy, Augustus Frederick."
63. Some apprentices of course read on the job. Stower's manual *The Printer's Price Book* (1814), which introduces fonts and enables jobbing printers to work out how much to charge per page, amazingly uses the full texts of Milton's *Areopagitica* and Locke's treatise on education as printing samples.
64. Wiles traces the development of part-publication from 1678 to 1750, recording prodigious profits especially in the 1730s and 1740s, and adding detailed accounts for Smollett's commissioned *History of England,* which was published in weekly parts 1758–60 (5–6).
65. Wordsworth, *Letters: The Early Years,* 1:359. As a point of comparison, an agricultural laborer at the time would have been earning about £30 a year; a carpenter or a skilled cotton-spinner in a factory about £60: rough calculations based on Cole and Postgate 125, 140, 205–6.
66. This point was made even of the Cheap Repository Tracts, an advertisement for which promises that "Some good Book, fit for Sunday Reading, will be sold every Month price a Halfpenny or a Penny. As all these Books will be neatly printed in the same Size, they will soon make a valuable Volume when stitched together": in vol. 2 of a British Library set, 4418.e.70. I have not been

able to verify a reader's claim that Volney's *Ruins* was once sold in "penny slips": John Lawrence in Robinson's *View of the Causes* . . . , xiii.

67. Coleridge, *Letters,* 1:455. His account is confirmed by the Wordsworth letters: William and Dorothy in 1799 wanted to rent "near a good library, and if possible in a pleasant country." They seem to have had in mind the collection of Sir Frederick Vane-Fletcher (1:266 and n).
68. *European Magazine and London Review* 17 (1790):329; *Blackwood's Edinburgh Magazine* 6 (1819):197–98.
69. Ms note in Pegge, 255.
70. Lamb, *Letters,* 3:210: "I have not bound the poems yet. I wait till People have done borrowing them. I think I shall get a chain and chain them to my shelves More Bodleiano & people may come & read them at chains length. For of those who borrow, some read slow, some mean to read but dont read, and some neither read nor meant to read, but borrow to leave you an opinion of their sagacity."
71. Cited, with the list of titles of books expelled, in Jackson, *Marginalia,* 78.
72. Kaufman, "English Book Clubs." Peter Clark's *British Clubs and Societies,* especially 109–11, sees the book clubs and book societies as part of a larger pattern of voluntary association.
73. See Hamlyn, Irwin, Kaufman, Raven ("From Promotion to Proscription"), and Varma for detailed histories. Robin Alston's Library History database at http:///www.ralston.co.uk/contents.htm is an ongoing resource for library history up to 1850.
74. *The Times,* 8 May 1800.
75. In its extreme anti-Jacobin form, the case against novels and circulating libraries (which went together like horse and carriage) accused novels of advocating adultery: see for example Hannah More, "Unprofitable Reading."
76. Austen, *Works,* 2:30, 238. Erickson has an excellent chapter on Austen and the circulating libraries.
77. Cobbett, *Life and Adventures of Peter Porcupine,* 25.
78. Crabb Robinson describes one memorable introduction effected by such a review: "I have a distinct recollection of reading in the *Monthly Review* a notice of the first volume of Coleridge's poems before I went abroad in 1800, and of the delight the extracts gave me" (1:266).
79. *Gentleman's Magazine* 2nd ser. 70:935–37, 1053–54.
80. Austen, *Letters,* 111; cf., on the sale of his books and study furniture, Tomalin, 170, 299.
81. *A Catalogue of the Entire Library of the late Granville Sharp, Esq.* (London: Leigh and Sotheby, 1813).
82. *A Catalogue of the Genuine Library, Prints, and Books of Prints, of an Illustrious Personage, lately Deceased* (1819): priced copy, BL 123.f.16.
83. De Quincey, *Works,* 3:340–41. Ships' captains were specifically targeted in

booksellers' catalogues and advertisements, perhaps because they were expected to provide recreational reading for passengers.

84. Lamb, *Works,* 1:272–74.
85. On the evolution of social codes during the eighteenth century see Barker-Benfield, who is not at all dismissive.
86. Cobbett, *History,* para 173. The book was printed but suppressed by Spencer Perceval in 1807; his copy of the original edition, with his note on the cover, "Most secret & Confidential," together with instructions for security, is in the BL, shelf-mark B.P. 8/3.
87. Barnard, *Bibliothecae Regiae Catalogus;* Barnard publishes the letter of advice that he received from Samuel Johnson in 1768 when he first set out to buy books for the King on the Continent. The Queen's collection is itemized in the sale catalogue of 1819, *Catalogue of the Genuine Library.* It includes half a dozen of her extra-illustrated books, some listed among the books and others among the books of prints. On the Queen's interests, see Burney, e.g. *Journals and Letters* 1:11, 149. Walpole bought "from the Widow of Scott the Printer, who taught her Majesty how to print" a broadside consisting of nine lines of verse "Printed by Queen Charlotte at Buckingham-House": ms note by Walpole ("Broadside").
88. See for example Brewer "Reconstructing," 241–42; Pearson, 171–74; Newlyn, 333–71.
89. Clairmont, *Journals,* 116.
90. Seward, *Letters,* 4:287.
91. King, 111; Coleridge, *Letters,* 1:48; Mitford, *Recollections,* 180–81.
92. Robinson, *Diary,* 1:299, 2:10, 2:228.
93. See the index to Coleridge's *Marginalia* for books lent and notes preserved by Robinson; and on the copy of Wordsworth annotated by Blake, Blake's *Writings,* 2:1752, and Robinson's *Diary,* 2:381–82. Though he does not appear to have written notes in his own books, Robinson was interested in marginalia. Touring in Milan, he mentions being shown a famous copy of Virgil with a note in it by Petrarch (*Diary,* 2:183).
94. Roberts, *Memoirs,* 1:422; Dibdin, *Reminiscences,* 1:510; Moore, *Journal,* 3:1040–41; Robinson, *Diary,* 2:216–17.
95. Hobhouse, *Recollections,* 1:321. The book was *The Substance of Some Letters written . . . during the Last Reign of the Emperor Napoleon* (1816).

Chapter 2

1. Alan Richardson's *Literature, Education, and Romanticism* gives a full account of the debate about goals and methods in education.
2. Erasmus, "On the Method of Study," 670; *Correspondence* 1:58.
3. An arresting fictional example of the power of the parental pencil occurs in Mary Brunton's novel *Discipline* (1814): the redemption of the heroine begins

when she notices a "slight mark" against a particular verse in her dead mother's Bible (260–61). Maria Edgeworth herself is known to have written notes in some of her books, including a copy of Austen's *Persuasion* which is described by Claudia Johnson (160).

4. The 1818 and 1819 editions of Wakefield's work included Sarah Hoare's poem "The Pleasures of Botanical Pursuits," but Fenn's extracts are different. On women's contributions to botany, see Shteir, *Cultivating Women.*
5. Quoted from Derwent Coleridge's edition of Hartley's poems in Hartley Coleridge, *Letters,* 208.
6. These men are identified by their initials in the footnotes and are named in the Preface as W. H. Herbert, Robert Sweet, and James Rennie. Herbert was a clergyman, Sweet a horticulturalist, and Rennie the Professor of Natural History at King's College.
7. The annotations in Linnaeus's books are described by Savage, "Synopsis of the Annotations."
8. Blackwood, 1172. The book itself is in the Library of The Wordsworth Trust, Grasmere, and is included in the annotated catalogue by Duncan Wu.
9. This copy is described, with colored plates, by Enid Slatter in her article "From the Archives."
10. *Dictionary of Quotations, in Most Frequent Use* (1799); and MacDonnel, *Dictionary of Quotations* (1811), neither of them paginated.
11. E.g. BL CT.107.(1–7), Cup.407.ff.34.(1–9), 01838.dd.50.(1–8). One collection that includes pamphlets owned by Bentham, some of them annotated but not so recorded, is BL 8285.ff.12. (1–10).
12. Books from Beckford's library were sold off in a series of auctions (1804, 1808, 1817, 1823, 1882–83) and are now to be found all over Britain and North America. For descriptions of his collection and handling of books, see the works by Babb, Beckford (17–20), Gemmett, Melville (271–76), and Rosebery in the bibliography of secondary sources. The largest cache in public hands is that in the National Library of Scotland, in two collections (Rosebery and Durdans) donated by the fifth Earl of Rosebery and his daughter Lady Sibyl Grant. Many of these books also contain notes by Rosebery on Beckford's model.
13. Beckford, *The Consummate Collector,* 19.
14. As for example in *The Sacred Books of the New Testament . . . Illustrated with Critical and Explanatory Annotations, Carefully Compiled from the Commentaries. . . . Embellished with Ornamental and Useful Representations . . . Engraven on Copper* (1739), and *The Plays of King Lear and Cymbeline, with Notes and Illustrations, selected from the Various Commentators* (1801). Byron's friend Hobhouse published *Historical Illustrations of the Fourth Canto of Childe Harold* (2nd ed., 1818), and Robert Chambers produced a companion to the Waverley novels in 1822 (enlarged 2nd ed., 1825), citing historical precedents for

incidents in Scott's fiction, as *Illustrations of the Author of Waverley*. The English use of the word descends from humanist editions, as in the Virgil mentioned earlier in this chapter.

15. The Godwin volume is described in detail in Jackson, *Marginalia*, 200–203.
16. Boswell, *Life*, 2:449.
17. In a volume of such plays in the Bodleian Library, Vet. A5 e. 1839.
18. Biographical and bibliographical information systematically added to their books by collectors will be discussed separately in Chapter 3.
19. The pamphlets, BL 1570/1158, are listed in the bibliography under Fox; the Boswell is described in Jackson, *Marginalia*, 171.
20. *Hansard* 26 (1813) cols. 617, 1005. The plan at the time was to have the collection housed at Lincoln's Inn, but in the end it went to the British Museum. A catalogue of the manuscripts, roughly 500 entries including transcripts made by Hargrave as well as more ancient and valuable materials, was prepared by Sir Henry Ellis and published in 1818. The first such "parliamentary acquisition" had been the Lansdowne manuscripts in 1805; the third would be the Burney collection in 1818 (Edwards, 434–46).
21. *Journals of the House of Commons* 68 (1813):944–45.
22. *Journals of the House of Commons* 68 (1813):944.
23. The elder, Edward Robert Hargrave, is not mentioned in the proceedings but his marriage to a Miss French is reported in *Gentleman's Magazine* 72 (1802):781. The younger, Francis Hargrave Junior, was called to the bar in 1809: Lincoln's Inn *Records* 4:245.
24. Hargrave was in the news again, appositely if peripherally, 180 years later. In 1990 three portraits, two by Gainsborough and one by Reynolds, were stolen from Lincoln's Inn. When two of them turned up again in 1993 the innocent purchaser claimed ownership under the twelfth-century law of *market overt*, notoriously a "thieves' charter," which was subsequently abolished. The Reynolds portrait was of Hargrave. *Sunday Times*, 7 March 1993 (1:5a) and 21 March 1993 (1:8), *Times* 25 July 1994 (1:5).
25. *DNB;* Lemmings, 256; Lincoln's Inn *Records*, 4:91, 115, 118, 121, 130, 132. The *DNB* entry (by Charles William Sutton) on Hargrave is mistaken at several points about the chronology of his career.
26. Holdsworth, 12:410. Hargrave urged the court to resist the introduction of a new form of slavery from the colonies as English courts had successfully suppressed their own ancient form of it, saying, "there is now no slavery, which can be lawful in England, until the Legislature shall interpose its authority to make it so" (Hargrave, *Argument*, 45).
27. He published the pamphlets himself, paying the costs and hoping to break even. It seems unlikely that there was money in the family, so Hargrave would have depended on professional income. There is some evidence of difficulty before the crash of 1813: in 1783 he sought a patronage appointment for

his father Christopher, without success; and in 1794 he tried to get an advance from his publisher Cadell (British Library Add MSS 38309 fol. 81[v], 34846 fol. 10).

28. An unexpected tribute to "Hargrave's State Trials," as it came to be known, from an unexpected quarter, is Mary Russell Mitford's. She loved collections of documents and so relished the drama of the courtroom reflected in these volumes that she was oblivious to the discomfort of handling them, though "between the size of the books and my own short-sightedness, I well remember that I was compelled to move the reading-desk twice in the course of every double-columned page" (2:236–37).
29. Hargrave, "Address," n.p. This statement is generally included in copies of the Hargrave-Butler edition, e.g., in the 18th ed., 2 vols., 1823.
30. Coventry thus justifies his edition: "The text [of Littleton] and commentary [of Coke]—unique and intelligible in themselves—have nevertheless been so overloaded with excellent though incongruous notes and references, that the formidable appearance, of the whole and the still more enormous price, have deterred many an aspiring tyro from entering on the perusal of so laboured a performance" (v).

Chapter 2

1. A counterillustration, however, is provided by the distinctly hostile notes in Richard Underwood's copy of *Reflections upon Some Persons and Things in Ireland,* by Sir William Petty. The work was originally published in 1660; Underwood's edition is dated 1790 with an ownership inscription of 1807. Underwood held a grudge against Petty and his descendants for the property Petty had secured in Ireland. Over a period of years, probably, Underwood dismantled the arguments Petty gave in self-defense, responding in the margins in green, brown, black and red ink: "you certainly must have known where the best Lands lay," "which I most firmly believe you certainly did to the utmost Extent your Cunning and Means would admit" (18), etc.
2. *A Catalogue of the Valuable Library, late the property of John Horne Tooke, Esq.* (London: King and Lochée, 1813).
3. Robinson, 3:187–88. Rogers's justification was, "He who gives money for things, values them. Put in a museum, nobody sees them."
4. For example, a copy of Virgil translated into Scottish verse, now in the Houghton Library at Harvard, which John Horne acquired in 1774 and read out of an interest in the Scottish vocabulary, contains his sardonic response to the translator's worldly success. He—the translator—is reported in the attached "Life" as having retained his position as Warden of the East and Middle Arches "even when his friends were in the worst Circumstances" (1). Horne's comment: "A Scotch Virtue and a Scotch Encomium."
5. *European Magazine* 58 (1810):21, 78 (1820):210.

6. Qoted in Le Faye, 224.
7. This is the epithet attached to him in *The Royal Humbugs* (or rather *The R---l H-mb-gs*) by "Peter Pindar," 1818.
8. These figures come from the introduction to the catalogue by his librarian, Thomas Pettigrew.
9. The BL copies of the priced catalogues are at S.C.E.69.(1–6.). The auctioneer was Evans, and the sales took place 1844–45.
10. Plumb describes him as a foolish but warm-hearted man (150); Hibbert, noting the history of mental illness in the family, suggests that in the case of Sussex there may not have been "all that much intellect to derange" (372).
11. Collective editions of Swift published his generally caustic marginalia as "Remarks" upon this or that book throughout the eighteenth century, and Scott maintained the tradition in his new edition of 1814. De Quincey is the first known to have published marginalia by Coleridge, in the *Westmorland Gazette* in August 1819; Coleridge himself was almost certainly behind the publication of his "Marginalia" to Browne in *Blackwood's* three months later: Coleridge, *Marginalia,* 1:795–97, 6:290. Two volumes of Coleridge's *Literary Remains* consist of marginalia (often spliced with notebook material), and more appeared gradually in Victorian editions prepared by members of the family.
12. There are records of fourteen books annotated by Blake. In most cases the books themselves survive, but in a few cases the marginalia are known only through transcriptions. Keynes, Bentley, and Erdman all included Blake's marginalia in their editions of his collected works. Valuable recent scholarly supplements to these print versions are facsimile editions of his notes to Watson and to Lavater, listed in the Bibliography of Secondary Sources under Blake and Lavater respectively, which are my sources for marginalia in those works; otherwise I cite the originals.
13. Bentley's *Blake Books* gives evidence of his ownership of 49 titles (681–702).
14. Bentley, *Blake Books,* 691n., 701; and Robinson, 2:381.
15. This volume is awkwardly paginated. It uses roman numerals for the Dedication and prelims but then starts again with a new series of roman numerals before the Discourses. In quotations of Blake's words, punctuation and capitalization are complicated by the fact that many of the notes were written in pencil and then overtraced in ink.
16. There is no surviving evidence of Shelley's having used *annotated* books in courtship. The manuscript notes in his books, several sets of them now published in the volumes of *Shelley and His Circle,* are usually sketchy reading notes and marks. The most interesting case—a copy of Godwin's *Political Justice* that also contains notes by Lady Mount Cashell—will be discussed in Chapter 4.
17. Coleridge, *Letters,* 1:27–29, 57–58, 60.

18. A copy of Taylor's *Holy Living and Holy Dying* later passed on to their eldest child Hartley may be a relic of that period (*Marginalia,* 5:488–89).
19. For surveys of Coleridge's career as a writer of marginalia see George Whalley's Introduction to the edition of Coleridge's *Marginalia* (1:lvii–lxxxii) and Jackson, *Marginalia,* 150–65.
20. Coleridge, *Marginalia,* 1:226–27, 740–99; 2:1117–28; 4:282–93.
21. Coleridge described his set of Scott's novels as "my ever circulating Copy" when he addressed a note explicitly to its "young Readers"—a group that might have included boys but certainly teenaged girls: *Marginalia,* 4:612. The Index to the *Marginalia* makes it possible to trace books annotated specifically for other women friends.
22. E.g. *Marginalia,* 1:768, 4:694, 719.
23. Byron, *Letters and Journals,* 6:215–16, and Byron in *Shelley Circle,* 8:1107–21.
24. Without naming him, but in such a way as to make clear to whom he was referring, Isaac D'Israeli cited Byron's marginalia in an earlier edition as an incentive to him to prepare a new edition of *The Literary Character* (Preface to the 1818 edition, iv). Byron protested to Murray at the "breach of confidence": *Letters and Journals* 6:84.
25. Attention has hitherto focused on what she had to say about Johnson and Boswell, notably in a 1938 edition of Boswell's *Life of Johnson* with her notes from two annotated copies; but see also Allison, Brownell, Ewing, Lyell, and Nicolson in the Bibliography of Secondary Sources for notes on other kinds of works. Jackson, *Marginalia,* 102–12, provides a case study of a copy of Johnson's *Rasselas* annotated by Piozzi for a young actor.
26. Jackson, *Marginalia,* 102–3.
27. Johnson, *Rasselas,* 113.
28. At the time of his death he had fewer than a hundred books (titles, not volumes), and some of those were on loan: Owings, ix. About 25 are known to survive, 16 of them with Keats's marks or annotations over and above the ownership inscription. Owings's catalogue gives current locations, the two major collections belonging to Harvard and to Keats House. The Keats House books once owned by Keats are now housed in the London Metropolitan Archives. All quotations from the marginalia have been checked against the originals.
29. Keats, *Letters,* 2:302, quoted by Lau, 14; and Owings, x.
30. Owings, 23. This book was lent or given to Keats by his publisher Hessey; Keats gave it to Thornton Hunt; it was somehow reclaimed and returned to Hessey on Keats's death; Hazlitt acquired it (it contains his ownership signature); then Leigh Hunt found it at a bookstall, recognized it, and bought it to give to his son again, first inking over Keats's penciled lines to preserve them and adding a note of his own about the book's history. It is now in the Keats collection at Harvard.

31. Keats's marginalia consist to a great extent of markings; the number of discursive notes is surprisingly small. Literary scholarship began making the *notes* available quite early on, selections being published by H. Buxton Forman as early as 1883 (the best edition is 1938–39) and typographic facsimiles of marked passages as well as notes being produced by Amy Lowell in her biography of 1925 and by Caroline Spurgeon in her critical study of the little seven-volume Shakespeare in 1928. Beth Lau's edition of Keats's notes and markings in the 1807 Milton, with a thorough introduction which surveys previous work and reflects on the purpose of all the marginalia, is the latest contribution to this tradition. Twentieth-century biographies and critical studies of Keats—notably Finney, Gittings, and Ward—make good use of these materials.
32. Owings, 21, 31, 35, 45, 53, 55.
33. Marking to indicate approval seems to have been all but universal, the default system, though Charles James Fox is on record as having marked a copy of the *Aeneid* so as to single out passages he did *not* like, either out of perversity or because there would be fewer of them (*Memoirs*, 3:212).
34. Owings, 17. Forman prints the marginalia (5:306–20) and Gittings, in *John Keats: The Living Year* (215–23), lists parallels between the *Anatomy* and Keats's poems and letters.
35. Spurgeon publishes most of the marks and notes in this edition with her commentary, superseding Forman.
36. An instance of the kind of critical reflection already present in one of Keats's books is Reynolds's observation on "Venus and Adonis" in the copy of Shakespeare's *Poetical Works,* against a stanza where Venus pleads with Adonis, "Upon the earth's increase why should'st thou feed," etc.: "Venus' reasoning powers are here most curiously put forth. They are something like the metaphysics of the passion" (7). It has been pointed out (Lau, 25–26) that Dilke's own heavily marked and annotated copy of Milton contains a note at the beginning of Book Four of *Paradise Lost* that closely resembles Keats's note at the same point, presumably reflecting their conversation.
37. Lau goes over the evidence and arguments about the dating of the notes and concludes that the process probably began in the spring of 1818 and continued through to the summer of 1819 (23–35).

Chapter 3

1. In his study of Walpole as an art collector, *The Prime Minister of Taste,* Brownell disputes the label and describes Walpole instead as "a courtesy book gentleman posing as virtuoso and antiquarian" (17).
2. Notably Lewis, very engagingly, 1:lxii–lxvii.
3. The complete entry for Southampton Row, as a sample, is as follows. (Pennant does not mention it at all.) "Southampton row | at the end to the north is a large House built by the last Calvert Ld Baltimore where for a pretended rape

on Miss Woodcock he was tried for his life at Kingston, but acquitted. Henry Duke of Bolton has since bought the House."

4. Pennant, *Of London*, Lewis Walpole Library copy 53 P37 790.
5. Walpole's copy, with marks and a few notes, is at Farmington: LWL 49 3850.
6. E.g. K. Sutherland, 9, 45. Dibdin took the idea of his first *Bibliomania* from John Ferriar's poetic jeu d'esprit of the same title (1809) and subsequently rewrote it as a "bibliographical romance" (1811), greatly enlarging it in the process. Both *Bibliomania*s were dedicated to the legendary collector Richard Heber, whose collection at his death in 1833 has been calculated as having contained 146,827 volumes, not including pamphlets (*DNB;* Basbanes, a more recent source, offers other estimates between 150,000 and 300,000 [110]). During a twentieth-century resurgence of the spirit of bibliomania, Holbrook Jackson followed in Dibdin's footsteps by producing *The Anatomy of Bibliomania* (1931), *The Fear of Books* (1932), and *The Reading of Books* (1947)—all, interestingly, reissued in 2001.
7. For the following words the *OED* has an example from 1800 or later as its earliest, with a high proportion from between 1810 and 1832, and a high proportion of *those* attributable to Dibdin. As the editors point out, many of the coinages are "ponderously humorous" in the jocular style of self-conscious enthusiasm: "biblioclasm," "bibliognost," "bibliogony," "bibliograph," "bibliographer," "bibliographic," "bibliographically," "bibliographize," "bibliography," "biblioklept," "bibliology," "bibliomane," "bibliomaniac," "bibliomaniacal," "bibliomanian," "bibliomanism," "bibliopegia," "bibliopegically," "bibliopegy," "bibliophagist," "bibliophile," "bibliophobia," "bibliopoesy," "bibliotaph," "bibliotheca," "bibliothecal," "bibliothecarial," "bibliotherapy," "bibliothetic." "Bibliosophia" (book-wisdom), the title of a work published anonymously in 1810 by James Beresford, capitalizing on the success of Dibdin's *Bibliomania,* is not included.
8. Neil Kenny's article on French bibliomania is a thought-provoking model though strictly French.
9. The periodicals also dispensed advice to their particular constituencies. A correspondent calling himself "An English Scholar" in the Unitarian *Monthly Repository* of May 1815 (10:297) sought guidance on "such English books as are proper for a serviceable library, in the departments of theology and general literature, to occupy the shelves of one who, though engaged in trade, has yet some time and taste for reading, and who desires above all things to train up his family in habits of reading and thinking." He cites as a model the "catalogue of a *Cheap and Useful Library*" already available in the columns of the *Christian Reformer.* The *Monthly Magazine* for years carried news about the establishment of book clubs, reading societies, and subscription libraries, to encourage by example.
10. *Censura Literaria* itself filled ten volumes and went into a second edition in 1815.

11. In 1807 Hester Piozzi claimed the credit for starting the vogue for literary anecdotes with her 1786 *Anecdotes of Johnson: Letters,* 4:147.
12. BL Add MS 28654 fols 47–52 are letters between Mitford and various London booksellers, ranging in date from 1804 to 1820.
13. Sotheby and Wilkinson, *Catalogue* (17 Dec. 1859), 1.
14. Hay-Drummond, *A Town Eclogue,* National Library of Scotland copy 1961.24.(2).
15. Walsh provides a thoughtful and thorough account of the editing of Shakespeare and Milton in the eighteenth century.
16. Southcott, *A Continuation of Prophecies* (1807), 167:BL 699.h.22.(2.)
17. Coleridge, *Marginalia,* 4:703, 713–14, 759, 803.
18. Boswell, 1:13. The unsolicited copy heavily annotated by Fulke Greville is described in Jackson, *Marginalia,* 123–37.
19. He had to instruct his publisher to ignore Lord Radstock's "pencelings in the 'Peasant Boy' " (*Letters,* 40); Eliza Emmerson's copy of his 1820 *Poems,* inscribed to Radstock, proposes better wording and some excisions.
20. Jackson, *Marginalia,* 220–22.
21. Stuart Sperry provides a transcription of the annotated *Poems.* The facsimiles were issued in Donald Reiman's Garland series *The Manuscripts of the Younger Romantics,* the Keats volumes being edited by Jack Stillinger: see Keats in the Bibliography of Secondary Sources.
22. Keats, *Endymion,* interleaf facing 72.
23. Keats, *Poems,* interleaf facing 80.
24. Keats, *Endymion,* interleaf facing 20.
25. Keats, *Poems,* interleaf facing 24.
26. Keats, *Poems,* 104 and interleaf.
27. Keats, *Endymion,* interleaf facing 90.
28. Sperry decided to leave the scansion out of his transcription, but he discusses some of Woodhouse's concerns about prosody (126–27).
29. Keats, *Endymion,* interleaf facing 166; *Poems,* interleaf facing 112.
30. Woodhouse's "Scrapbook," quoted by Sperry, 106–7.
31. Keats, *Endymion,* facing [105].
32. Keats, *Poems,* interleaf facing 49, as transcribed in Keats, *Manuscripts,* 1:248. Sperry (109) frankly describes these as "some of the worst lines he ever composed."
33. The annotator may have been T. Crofton Croker (1798–1854), who made his name as a collector of Irish folklore: Jackson, "England's Populist Pindars," 18. This article gives a fuller account of the collection and of the Pindar phenomenon at large; it also addresses the issue of authorship, many of these works having been attributed to "C. F. Lawler" on very tenuous evidence.
34. Diana Donald sees the amiable ironies and chiefly West End market of the familiar Regency prints as incompatible with Hone's serious political activism and targeting of lower-class audiences. Though her subject is satiric prints

(which gave way to Hone's woodcuts) the point is applicable to the poems as well. Some printers produced and some dealers handled both prints and poems.

35. He does in one late note correctly attribute the suppressed *R---l Stripes* (1812) to George Daniel, on the printed authority of Daniel's memoirs: "Pindaric Poems" C.131.d.2.(4), title page verso.
36. "Pindaric Poems" C.131.d.2.(1), 19.
37. Stanza 21 of *The R----t's Fleet; or, John Bull at the Serpentine:* "Pindaric Poems" C.131.d.3.(1).

Chapter 4

1. Coleridge, *Biographia Literaria,* 1:9: "I learnt from him, that Poetry, even that of the loftiest, and, seemingly, that of the wildest odes, had a logic of its own, as severe as that of science. . . . I was wont boldly to affirm, that it would scarcely be more difficult to push a stone out from the pyramids with the bare hand, than to alter a word, or the position of a word, in Milton or Shakspeare, (in their most important works at least) without making the author say something else, or something worse, than he does say" (1:9, 23).
2. Important case studies make this point repeatedly, of readers from the sixteenth century onwards, for example Grafton on Budé, Sherman on Dee, DeMaria on Johnson, Brewer on Larpent, Secord on Darwin (428–29).
3. E.g., Kintgen and Machor, quoted in Jackson, *Marginalia,* 252–55. D. R. Woolf rejects the counsel of despair though he admits that the task is difficult, since "The contexts of history reading are nearly as variable as the number of readers" (101) and—he might have added—the more fine-grained the study, the more variables there are, so that in the end there might be said to be even more variables than there are readers. He detects a shift in the way history books were read in Britain between 1475 and 1730, moving from a disciplined humanist mode to a more informal, personal one.
4. The existence of these notes was brought to my attention by Carolyn Moss's article in *PBSA;* transcriptions are from the original. Wordsworth must have acquired the book at second hand: the title page has the ownership inscription "J Butler 1804."
5. This copy is described, and the notes are published, in *Shelley and His Circle* 8:897–915, but I cite the original here.
6. Coleridge, *Notebooks,* 4:4611, 4612, 4617–22.
7. *Marginalia,* 6:110, 118, corresponding to *Notebooks,* 4:4618 f17^{v}, 4:4621.
8. Scott's diary for 24 Feb. 1829, has an interesting observation about using books as a stimulus to creative thinking, though he does not appear to have relied on margins for recording his ideas: "I can very seldom think to purpose by lying perfectly idle, but when I take an idle book, or a walk, my mind strays back to its task, out of contradiction as it were; the things I read become mingled with those I have been writing, and something is concocted. I cannot

compare this process of the mind to any thing save that of a woman to whom the mechanical operation of spinning serves as a running bass to the songs she sings, or the course of ideas she pursues" (Lockhart, 7:179).

9. E.g., in Armour and Howes, ed., *Coleridge the Talker.*
10. The book is in the Fales Library of New York University. All transcriptions are from that copy directly, ignoring cancellations but leaving signs of haste such as slips of the pen. There is a convenient published transcription by Pollin.
11. Coleridge, *Letters,* 1:212, 281, 282, 258.
12. The editor of the standard edition of Coleridge's poems plausibly suggests that Coleridge may have included the sonnet as a presentation inscription in the copy of his *Poems* sent to Thelwall in 1796: Coleridge, *Poetical Works,* 1:264.
13. Coleridge, *Lectures 1808–1819,* 2:275–76; also *Poetical Works,* 2:257–58.

Bibliography of Books with Manuscript Notes

BL = British Library

Account of the Conquest of Mauritius . . . by an Officer, who Served on the Expedition. London: Egerton, 1811. BL T.1550.(8). Annotated by T. Hardwicke.

Aesop. *Fables.* Trans. John Ogilby. London: Roycroft, 1665. Bodleian Library: Douce A subt. 85. Annotated by Francis Douce.

Albin, Eleazar. *Insectorum Angliae Naturalis Historia.* London: Innys, 1731. BL 445.f.24. Annotator unknown.

Almon, John. *Anecdotes of the Life of the Right Hon. William Pitt, Earl of Chatham.* 7th ed. 3 vols. London: Longman, 1810. BL C.28.g.13–14. Annotated by Augustus Frederick, Duke of Sussex.

Anti-Jacobin. See Canning.

Antoninus, Marcus Aurelius. *Meditations.* Glasgow: Foulis, 1749. Berg Collection, New York Public Library. Annotated by Leigh Hunt.

Ascham, Roger. *Toxophilus.* London, 1545. BL C.31.e.29. Annotated by S. S. Banks.

Ayliffe, John. *Parergon Juris Canonici Anglicani: or, A Commentary, by way of supplement to the Canons and Constitutions of the Church of England.* 2nd ed. London: Osborne, 1734. BL 515.1.14. Annotated by Francis Hargrave.

Bacon, Francis. *Essays Moral, Economical, and Political.* London: Edwards, 1798. Dept. of Rare Books, Cambridge University Library: Keynes.U.4.20. Annotated by William Blake.

Beloe, William. *The Sexagenarian; or, the Recollections of a Literary Life.* 2nd ed. 2 vols. London: Rivington, 1818. BL 1203.c.3. Annotator unknown.

Bentham, Jeremy. *Plan of Parliamentary Reform, in the Form of a Catechism.* London: R. Hunter, 1817. BL C.193.b.60. Annotated by Sir James Mackintosh.

Bentley, Richard. *Richardi Bentleii et Doctorum Virorum Epistolae, partim mutuae.* Ed. Charles Burney. London, 1807. BL 829.m.6. Annotated by Charles Burney.

Berkeley, George. *Siris.* Dublin: R. Greene, 1744. Wren Library, Trinity College, Cambridge. Annotated by William Blake.

Black, John. *Life of Torquato Tasso.* 2 vols. Edinburgh and London: Murray, 1810. Annotated by Leigh Hunt.

Blackstone, William. *Commentaries on the Laws of England.* 4 vols. Oxford: Clarendon Press, 1765–69. BL 507.f.7–10. Annotated by Francis Hargrave.

Booth, George. *The Nature and Practice of Real Actions.* London, 1701. BL 509.h.5. Annotated by Francis Hargrave.

Boswell, James. *Life of Samuel Johnson LL.D.* 2 vols. London: Dilly, 1791. National Art Library, Victoria and Albert Museum: Dyce T 4° 1274. Annotated by Horace Walpole.

Boswell, James. *Life of Samuel Johnson, LL.D.* 2nd ed. 3 vols. London: Dilly, 1793. Bodleian Library: Douce B 459–461. Annotated by Francis Douce.

Boswell, James. *The Life of Samuel Johnson, LL.D.* 2nd ed. 3 vols. London: Dilly, 1793. National Library of Scotland F.7.b.4. Annotator unknown.

Broadside. [Nine lines of verse beginning "Firendship [*sic*], adieu thou dear deceitful good."] BL 558*.g.19.(2.). Annotated by Horace Walpole.

Brook, W.J. *Letters written by W. J. Brook, Addressed to the Several Churches and Individuals Among Whom He Occasionally Ministered. Traces of Providence, in a Tour from Brighton Through the Isle of Wight in October, 1808.* Brighton, 1812. BL 4905.bb.48. Annotated by Mary Bowles.

Brydone, Patrick. *A Tour through Sicily and Malta.* 2 vols. Paris, 1780. BL 10151.a.32. Annotated by John Mitford.

Burges, James Bland. "Richard the First: A Poem." Pre-publication copies, 1800. BL C.128.h.9–12. The first three copies annotated by William Boscawen, Richard Cumberland, and John Anstey respectively; the fourth a collation of revisions by Burges.

Burke, Edmund. *Reflections on the Revolution in France.* London: Dodsley, 1790. Houghton Library, Harvard University: *EC75 B9177 790raa (A). Annotated by John Horne Tooke.

Burke, Edmund. *A Speech . . . On Presenting to the House of Commons (on the 11th of February, 1780) a Plan for the Better Security of the Independence of Parliament.* 3rd ed. London: Dodsley, 1780. BL 08138.dd.50.(4.). Annotated by Jeremy Bentham.

Burton, J., ed. *ΠΕΝΤΑΛΟΓΙΑ.* 2nd ed. 2 vols. Oxford, 1779. BL 995.e.18. Annotated by Charles Burney.

Burton, Robert. *The Anatomy of Melancholy.* 11th ed. Vol. 2 (of 2). London: Walker et al., 1813. Corporation of London, from the Keats House Collection: K / BK / 01 / 015. Annotated by Charles Brown and John Keats.

Byron, George Gordon, Lord. *Childe Harold's Pilgrimage: A Romaunt*. London, 1827. BL 11642.a.51. Annotated by Philip MacDermott.

Byron, George Gordon, Lord. *Poems on Various Occasions*. Newark, 1807. BL C.28.b.9. Annotated by Byron.

Canning, George, et al. *The Anti-Jacobin*. 20 Nov. 1797–9 Jul. 1798. BL C.40.1.2. Annotated by George Canning.

Cases in Equity during the Time of the Late Lord Chancellor Talbot. London, 1741. BL 510.i.11. Annotated by Francis Hargrave.

Castiglioni, Luigi. *Viaggio negli Stati Uniti dell'America Settentrionale fatto negli anni 1785, 1786, e 1787*. 2 vols. Milan, 1790. Library of the Royal Institution of Great Britain. Annotated by Benjamin, Count Rumford.

Catullus, Tibullus, and Propertius. *Opera*. London, 1822. BL C.134.e.33. Annotated by Walter Savage Landor.

Cebes. *ΚΕΒΗΤΟΣ ΘΗΒΑΙΟΥ ΠΙΝΑΣ. Cebetis Thebani Tabula*. Ed. Thomas Nugent. London: Davidson, 1745. BL 715.c.1. Annotated by Charles Burney.

Chandler, Richard. *Travels in Asia Minor*. Oxford: Clarendon Press, 1775. BL 1782.b.17. Annotated by Nicholas Revett.

Chandler, Richard. *Travels in Greece*. Oxford: Clarendon Press, 1776. BL 1783.a.23. Annotated by Nicholas Revett.

Chaucer, Geoffrey. *Poetical Works*. Bell's Edition. 14 vols. London and Edinburgh, 1762–82. BL Add. MS 33516. Annotated by John Keats and Charles Cowden Clarke.

Chesterfield, Philip Dormer Stanhope. *Miscellaneous Works*. Ed. M. Maty. 2 vols. London: Dilly, 1777. BL C.60.o.4. Annotated by Horace Walpole.

Cicero. *Opera quae supersunt omnia*. 20 vols. Mannheim, 1783–87. BL 833.b.6-25. Annotated by Augustus Frederick, Duke of Sussex.

Clare, John. *Poems Descriptive of Rural Life and Scenery*. London: Taylor and Hessey, 1820. Berg Collection, New York Public Library. Annotated by Eliza Louisa Emmerson.

Coleridge, S. T. *Biographia Literaria*. 2 vols. London: Rest Fenner, 1817. Fales Library, New York University: PR 4476.A1 1817. Annotated by John Thelwall.

Collins, Arthur. *Historical Collections of the Noble Families of Cavendishe, Holles, Vere, Harley, and Ogle, with the Lives of the Most Remarkable Persons*. London: Withers, 1752. BL 1322.ff.8. Annotated by Horace Walpole.

Collins, Arthur. *Proceedings, Precedents, and Arguments, or Claims and Controversies, concerning Baronies by Writ, and other Honours*. London, 1734. BL 516.m.1. Annotated by Francis Hargrave.

Conyers, J.D. *Tables of Weights, for Reducing English Weight into Factory and Bazar Weight and the Contrary*. Calcutta, 1812. BL 8229.aaaa.18. Annotated by P. Foster.

Cowley, Abraham. *Works*. 12th ed. 2 vols. London, 1721. Berg Collection, New York Public Library. Annotated by Leigh Hunt.

Cowper, William. *The Task*. London: Johnson, 1785. BL C.71.c.22. Annotated by Anna Seward.

Croker, John Wilson. *A Sketch of the State of Ireland, Past and Present.* London: James Carpenter, 1808. BL 8145.dd.48. Annotator unknown; possibly R. E. Coote.

Davis, John. *Travels of Four Years and a Half in the United States of America During 1798, 1799, 1800, 1801, and 1802.* London: R. Edwards, 1803. BL 10411.d.4. Annotated by William Wordsworth.

Dibdin, T. F. *Bibliomania; or Book Madness: a Bibliographical Romance.* London, 1811. Lewis Walpole Library, Farmington CT: 485 811 D54. Annotated by Dawson Turner.

Dictionary of Quotations, in Most Frequent Use. 3rd ed. rev. London: Robinson, 1799. BL 012305.g.43. Annotator unknown.

Dixon, Joshua. *The Literary Life of William Brownrigg, M.D. F.R.S.* London, Dublin, Edinburgh and Whitehaven: Longman et al., 1801. BL 1453.g.5. Annotated by John Sherwen.

Doddridge, Philip. *The Rise and Progress of Religion in the Soul.* Birmingham: Beilby and Knotts, 1817. Trinity College Dublin OLS B-6-341. Annotated by Hannah Hutton.

Dodington, George Bubb. *Diary.* Ed. Henry Penruddocke Wyndham. Salisbury: Easton, 1784. Wren Library, Trinity College, Cambridge. Annotated by Horace Walpole.

Dodsley, R., ed. *A Collection of Poems . . . by Several Hands.* 6 vols. London: Dodsley, 1748–58. BL C.117.aa.16. Annotated by Horace Walpole.

Drinkwater, Samuel. *Every Man His Own Farrier.* Hereford, 1796. BL 1509/910. Annotator unknown.

Dunlop, John. *The History of Fiction.* 3 vols. London: Longman, 1814. Berg Collection, New York Public Library. Annotated by Leigh Hunt.

Duppa, Richard. *Travels in Italy, Sicily, and the Lipari Islands.* London, 1828. BL 10130.cc.12. Annotator unknown.

Edgeworth, Maria. *Letters for Literary Ladies.* 2nd ed. rev. London: Johnson, 1799. Trinity College Dublin OLS B-1-784. Annotated by John Horseman.

The Elements of Logic. Dublin, 1816. BL 8466.aaa.15. Inscribed but not annotated by Philip MacDermott.

Elliott, George. *The Life of . . . Wellington . . . down to the Battle of Waterloo, and his Invasion of France in 1815.* 2nd ed. London: Sherwood, Neely, and Jones, 1816. BL 1452.h.8. Annotator unknown.

Eton, William. *Authentic Materials for a History of the People of Malta.* London: Cadell and Davies, 1802–7. BL 1196.d.28. Annotated by Augustus Frederick, Duke of Sussex.

Facts and Observations relating to the Temple Church, and the Monuments contained in it. London, 1811. BL 577.k.21.(6.) Annotated by Francis Hargrave.

Field, Barron. *An Analysis of Blackstone's Commentaries on the Laws of England.* London: Cadell and Davies, 1811. BL 6145.aaa.12. Annotator unknown.

Fitzherbert, Anthony. *The New Natura Brevium*. London, 1730. BL 508.e.2. Annotated by Francis Hargrave.

Fitzroy, Augustus Henry. *Hints, &c. submitted to the Clergy . . . by a Layman*. 2nd ed. London, 1789. BL 3477.cc.20. Annotator unknown.

Forbes, William. *An Account of the Life and Writings of James Beattie, LL.D. . . . Including Many of his Original Letters*. 2nd ed. 3 vols. Edinburgh: Constable, 1807. BL 10856.ee.9. Annotated by Hester Piozzi.

Fox, C. J. A collection of five pamphlets, 1782–1809. BL 1570/1158. Annotator unknown.

Franklin, Benjamin. *Memoirs*. Ed. William Temple Franklin. 3 vols. London: Colburn, 1818. BL 1341.n.3. Annotated by Augustus Frederick, Duke of Sussex.

General Abridgment of Cases in Equity. 4th ed. London, 1756. BL 509.i.16. Annotated by Francis Hargrave.

Gifford, John. *Orange, a Political Rhapsody. In Three Cantos*. 9th ed. Dublin: Milliken, 1798. BL 11633.cc.11. Annotated by Sir John Russell?

Gisborne, Thomas. *A Familiar Survey of the Christian Religion, and of History as connected with the Introduction of Christianity, and its Progress to the Present Time. Intended Primarily for the Use of Young Persons of Either Sex, during the course of Public or Private Education*. London: Cadell and Davies, 1799. BL 3558.bb.13. Annotated by Eliza Hawtrey.

Gleanings from Books, on Agriculture, and Gardening. 2nd ed. rev. London: Samuel Bagster, 1802. BL 1146.k.7. Annotator unknown.

Godwin, William. *An Enquiry concerning Political Justice*. 2 vols. London: G. G. J. and J. Robinson, 1793. Pforzheimer Collection, New York Public Library. Annotated by Margaret King Moore (Lady Mount Cashell) and P. B. Shelley.

Godwin, William. *Memoirs of the Author of A Vindication of the Rights of Woman*. London: Johnson, 1798. Pforzheimer Collection, New York Public Library. Annotated by John Horseman.

Goldie, George. *A Letter to a Friend in London; containing Observations on the Memoir of Himself, written by James Hogg, the Ettrick Shepherd, and Prefixed to a Late Edition of the "Mountain Bard."* [Edinburgh, 1821]. National Library of Scotland MS.3369. Annotated by James Browne.

Goldsmith, Oliver. *Essays, Poems, and Plays*. London, 1826. BL 12271.aa.7. Annotated by Philip MacDermott.

Grose, Francis, et al., eds. *The Antiquarian Repertory: A Miscellany, Intended to Preserve and Illustrate Several Valuable Remains of Old Times. Adorned with Elegant Sculptures*. London, 1775–84. Lewis Walpole Library, Farmington CT: 49 4850. Annotated by Horace Walpole.

Gunning, Mrs. *A Letter . . . to the Duke of Argyll*. 2nd ed. Dublin: Wogan, 1791. BL 10864.s.11. Annotator unknown.

Hall, Basil. *Extracts from a Journal, written on the Coasts of Chili, Peru, and Mexico, in the Years 1820, 1821, 1822.* 2 vols. Edinburgh: Constable, 1824. National Library of Scotland: Dur. 534. Annotated by William Beckford.

Hall, Robert. *An Apology for the Freedom of the Press, and for General Liberty.* London: Robinson, 1793. BL 1389.g.20. Annotated by Augustus Frederick, Duke of Sussex.

Hamilton, Anthony, Count. *Mémoires du comte de Grammont.* Paris: Pissot, 1746. Lewis Walpole Library, Farmington CT: 49 2389. Annotated by Horace Walpole.

Hamilton, Anthony. *Memoirs of the Count of Grammont.* London, 1714. BL 10660.bb.8. Annotated by John Mitford.

Harvest: General Weeding of the Earth; or, An Address to the Professors of Christianity, Heathen, and All Others, the Inhabitants of the World: with Observations on the Resurrection of Dry Bones, or, Restoration of Israel. By a Labourer. Dublin, 1799. BL 1609/5411. Annotated by John Lidwill.

Harwood, Busick. *A Synopsis of a Course of Lectures on the Philosophy of Natural History and the Comparative Structure of Plants and Animals.* Cambridge, 1812. BL 458.b.1. Annotated by Robert Smith.

Haworth, A. H. *Miscellanea naturalia.* London: J. Taylor, 1803. Library of the Royal Botanical Gardens, Kew. Annotated by W. J. Hooker.

Hay-Drummond, George William Auriol. *A Town Eclogue.* Edinburgh: For the Author, 1804. National Library of Scotland: Ry.1.4.196. Annotator unknown.

Hay-Drummond, George William Auriol. *A Town Eclogue.* Edinburgh: For the Author, 1804. National Library of Scotland: 1961.24.(2). Two annotators, both unknown.

Hay-Drummond, George William Auriol. *A Town Eclogue.* Edinburgh: For the Author, 1804. BL 11645.f.9. Annotated by James Maidment and at least one other.

Hay-Drummond, George William Auriol. *A Town Eclogue.* Edinburgh: For the Author, 1804. National Library of Scotland: 1939.39.(12). Annotator unknown.

Hay-Drummond, George William Auriol. *A Town Eclogue.* Edinburgh: For the Author, 1804. National Library of Scotland: I.37/2.b. At least two annotators, unknown.

Hazlitt, William. *Characters of Shakespeare's Plays.* London: Ollier, 1817. Houghton Library, Harvard University: Keats *EC8 K2262 Zz817h. Annotated by John Keats.

Hazlitt, William. *A Letter to William Gifford, Esq.* London, 1819. BL 11724.f.34.(1.). Annotator unknown.

Hearne, Thomas. *The Life of Mr. Thomas Hearne, of St. Edmund's Hall, Oxford; From his own MS. Copy, in the Bodleian Library.* Oxford, 1722. BL C.45.e.17. Annotated by Philip Bliss.

Heriot, J. *An Historical Sketch of Gibraltar, with an Account of the Siege. . . .* London, 1792. BL 10161.e.20. Annotated by W. Booth.

Horace. *Eclogae*. Leipzig, 1788. BL 11375.c.3. Annotated by John Mitford.
Hudson, William. *Flora Anglica*. 2 vols in 1. London, 1778. Library of the Linnean Society. Annotated by J. E. Smith.
Hull. "Poll Books." BL 8132.de.6. Annotator unknown.
Huntingford, George Isaac. ΜΕΤΡΙΚΑ ΤΙΝΑ ΜΟΝΟΣΤΡΟΦΙΚΑ. *Metrica quaedam monostrophica*. London: Nichols, 1782. BL 749.a.11. Annotated by Charles Burney.
Iliff, Edward Henry. *A Summary of the Duties of Citizenship*. London, [1795]. BL 1389.d.25. Annotator unknown.
Imperial Family Bible. Stourbridge: J. Heming, 1811–14. BL C.61.f.3. Annotated by Hester Piozzi.
Ingram, James. *The First Sabbath, and Other Poems*. Bristol, 1828. BL 11644.eeee.24. Annotated by Brackstone Baker.
Iu-Kao-Li: or, The Two Fair Cousins. 2 vols. London: Hunt and Clarke, 1827. BL C.60.k.5. Annotated by Leigh Hunt and Thomas Carlyle.
Jackson, Z. *Shakespeare's Genius Justified*. London: John Major, 1819. Houghton Library, Harvard University: Keats *EC8 K2262 Zz819j. Annotated by John Keats.
Jenkinson, Charles. *A Discourse on the Conduct of the Government of Great Britain in Respect to Neutral Nations*. New edition. London: Debrett, 1801. BL 8007.e.73.(2.). Annotated by John Prinsep.
John Hartland, tried at Kingstown, March 23, 1796, for a Riot in St. George's-Fields, Southwark. London, 1796. BL 1608/2631. Annotated by John Craven?
Johnson, Samuel. *Poetrical Works*. London, 1785. BL 11633.aa.29. Annotated by Philip MacDermott.
Johnson, Samuel. *Rasselas*. London: Sharpe, 1818. Houghton Library, Harvard University: *78-1550. Annotated by Hester Piozzi.
Junius. *Letters*. London: Apollo Press, 1814. BL 8005.df.21. Annotator unknown.
Keats, John. *Endymion*. London: Taylor and Hessey, 1818. Berg Collection, New York Public Library. Annotated by Richard Woodhouse.
Keats, John. *Poems*. London: Ollier, 1817. Huntington Library, accession number 151852. Annotated by Richard Woodhouse.
Keith, Robert. *An Historical Catalogue of the Scottish Bishops, down to the year 1688*. Edinburgh, 1824. National Art Library, Victoria and Albert Museum: 266.H.22. Annotated by John Jebb.
Kentish Traveller's Companion. 3rd ed. Canterbury and Rochester, 1790. BL 579.b.2. Annotator unknown.
Key to Spelling and Introduction to the English Grammar. Designed for the Use of Charity and Sunday-Schools. London, 1788. BL 12983.b.6. Annotator unknown.
Lackington, J. *Confessions*. London: Richard Edwards, 1804. National Library of Scotland: Dur. 450. Annotated by William Beckford.

Lavater, J. C. *Aphorisms on Man.* Trans. J. H. Fuseli. London: Johnson, 1788. Huntington Library. Annotated by William Blake.

Law, Thomas. *An Answer to Mr. Prinseps's Observations on the Mocurrery System.* London: R. Faulder, 1794. BL 8022.cc.29. Annotated by John Prinsep.

Lee, James. *An Introduction to Botany . . . Extracted from the Works of Linnaeus.* Ed. C. Stewart. Edinburgh, 1806. BL 1147.e.11. Annotator unknown.

A Letter, Stating the Connection which Protestants, Dissenters, and Catholics, had with the Recent Event. . . . 4th ed. Glasgow, [1807]. BL 8135.f.28. Annotator unknown.

Letters from a Father to his Son, A Student of Divinity. Edinburgh, 1796. BL 1568/1423. Annotator unknown.

Letters from Holland, during a Tour from Harwich to Helvoetshuys, Brill . . . Amsterdam, &c. Ipswich: J. Row, 1814. Bodleian Library 20410.e.36. Annotator unknown.

Lettsom, John C. *Reflections on Religious Persecution.* London, 1799. BL T.184.(6.). Annotated by W. Davis.

Literary Pocket-Book; or, Companion for the Lover of Nature and Art. 1819. London: Ollier, 1818. BL C.60.b.7. Annotated by Mary Russell Mitford.

Locke, John. *An Essay concerning Human Understanding.* 15th ed. 2 vols. London: Browne et al., 1760. BL 528.i.20. Annotated by John Horne Tooke.

London and its Environs Described. 6 vols. London: Dodsley, 1761. Berg Collection, New York Public Library. Annotated by Horace Walpole.

MacDonnel, D. E. *A Dictionary of Quotations.* 6th ed. London: G. Wilkie and J. Robinson, 1811. BL 012305.f.73. Annotator unknown.

Mackie, Dorothea Sophia. *A Picture of the Changes of Fashion.* [1818.] BL 8409.bb.27. Annotated by John Chamier.

Magendie, F. *An Elementary Compendium of Physiology; for the Use of Students.* Trans. E. Milligan. 2nd ed. Edinburgh, 1826. BL 773.1.29. Annotated by Philip MacDermott.

Malone, Edmond. *An Inquiry into the Authenticity of certain Miscellaneous Papers . . . attributed to Shakespeare, Queen Elizabeth, and Henry, Earl of Southampton. . . .* London: Cadell and Davies, 1796. BL C.45.e.23. Annotated by Edmond Malone.

Manley, Delarivier. *The Adventures of Rivella; or, The History of the Author of the Atalantis.* London, 1714. BL 1419.f.23. Annotated by William Musgrave.

Manley, Delarivier. *Memoirs of the Life of Mrs. Manley (Author of the Atalantis).* BL 113.c.61. Annotated by William Musgrave.

Manley, Delarivier. *The Secret History of Queen Zarah.* 4th ed. London: Wilford, 1745. BL 1419.c.48. Annotated by William Musgrave.

Manley, Delarivier. *Secret Memoirs and manners of several Persons of Quality, of both Sexes. From the New Atalantis, an Island in the Mediterranean.* London: Morphew, 1709. BL 12611.dd.24. Annotated by William Musgrave.

Mason, William. A collection of five poems, 1776–1779. Houghton Library, Harvard University: *fEC75.W1654.Zz777h. Annotated by Horace Walpole.

Mawman, J. *An Excursion to the Highlands of Scotland and the English Lakes.* London: J. Mawman, 1805. Bodleian Library: Arch. H e. 18. Annotated by William Beckford.

Mercier, Louis Sébastien. *New Picture of Paris.* 2 vols. Dublin, 1800. BL C.189.d.13. Annotated by John Wilson Croker.

Milton, John. *Paradise Lost.* 2 vols. Edinburgh: W. and J. Deas, 1807. Corporation of London, from the Keats House Collection:K / BK / 1 / 013, 014. Annotated by John Keats.

Montagu, Lady Mary Wortley. *Letters of the Right Honourable Lady M--y W-----y M-----e; Written During her Travels in Europe, Asia, and Africa.* New edition. London: Taylor, 1790. BL 1477.b.29. Annotated by John Cam Hobhouse.

Montaigne, Michel de. *Works.* Ed. W. Hazlitt. London: Templeman, 1842. BL C.61.h.5. Annotated by Leigh Hunt.

Montpensier, Anne-Marie-Louise d'Orléans, duchesse de. *Mémoires.* 10 vols. Paris, 1823. BL 10662.a.15. Annotated by John Mitford.

More, Hannah. *Practical Piety.* 12th ed. 2 vols. London: Cadell, 1821. BL 1560/3250. Annotated by Henrietta Harrison.

Morton, Thomas. *A Roland for an Oliver: A Farce.* London: Miller, 1819. BL 11785.aa.16. Annotated by John Byrne.

Mudford, William. *Nubilia in Search of a Husband.* 4th ed. London: Ridgway et al., 1809. BL 12614.g.26. Annotated by A. Urquhart.

New Common-place Book. In which the Plan Recommended and Practised by John Locke, Esq. is Enlarged and Improved. 3rd ed. Cambridge, 1778. Cambridge University Library Adv.a.75.3. Annotator(s) unknown.

Nichelson, William. *Treatise on Practical Navigation and Seamanship.* London, 1796. BL 534.1.6. Annotated by B. W. Page.

Nichols, John. *Biographical Anecdotes of William Hogarth: and a Catalogue of his Works Chronologically Arranged.* London: Nichols, 1781. Lewis Walpole Library, Farmington CT: 49 2435. Annotated by Horace Walpole and John Mitford.

Paine, Thomas. *Rights of Man.* London: Johnson, 1791. BL C.115.e.3. Reading notes by J. Debenham.

Peake, Thomas. *A Compendium of the Law of Evidence.* 2nd ed. 2 pts. London: Brooke and Clarke, 1804, 1806. BL 509.c.4. Annotator unknown.

Pegge, Samuel. *Anecdotes of the English Language.* London: Nichols et al., 1803. National Library of Wales: Brynbella Piozziana Collection. Annotated by Hester Piozzi and John Broster.

Pennant, Thomas. *History of Quadrupeds.* 3rd ed. 2 vols. London: R. & J. White, 1793. National Library of Wales: MS 20745C, 20746C. Annotated by John Latham.

Pennant, Thomas. *Of London.* London: Faulder, 1790. Lewis Walpole Library, Farmington CT: 53 P37 790. Annotator unknown.

Pennant, Thomas. *Of London.* London: Faulder, 1790. Lewis Walpole Library, Farmington CT: 49 3928. Annotated by Horace Walpole.

Percival, Robert. *An Account of the Island of Ceylon*. London: C. and R. Baldwin, 1803. Victoria College, University of Toronto: Coleridge Collection. Annotated by S. T. Coleridge.

Petty, William. *Reflections upon Some Persons and Things in Ireland, by Letters to and from Dr. Petty*. Dublin, 1790. BL 1414.c.36. Annotated by Richard Underwood.

Pickbourn, James. *A Dissertation on the English Verb*. London: Robinson, 1789. BL 1477.bb.5. Annotated by John Horne Tooke.

Pickering, Priscilla, and John Morfitt. *Poems*. Ed. Joseph Weston. Birmingham, [1794]. BL 11633.bb.33. Annotated by Samuel Parr.

Pigott, Charles. *The Jockey Club, or a Sketch of the Manners of the Age*. London: H. D. Symonds, 1792. BL 785.e.14. Two annotators, both unknown.

Pindar, Peter, Jun. *See* "Pindaric Poems."

"Pindaric Poems." 13 vols. BL C.131.d.2-14. Annotated by T. Crofton Croker?

Pinkerton, John. *An Essay on Medals*. 2nd ed. 2 vols. London: J. Edwards, 1789. BL C.60.g.6. Annotated by Horace Walpole.

Pitman, T. E. *The Young Merchant's Key to a Knowledge of Marine Insurance*. Calcutta, 1813. BL 8229.aaaa.18. Annotated by P. Foster.

Pliny the Younger. *Letters*. 2 vols. London: Vaillant, 1751. BL 10902.e.1. Annotated by Leigh Hunt.

Plotinus. *Five Books of Plotinus*. Trans. Thomas Taylor. London: Edward Jeffrey, 1794. BL 8460.cc.26.(1.) Annotator unknown.

Poems on Affairs of State. 4 vols. London, 1703–7. BL 1077.1.16–19. Annotated by William Musgrave.

Preston, Richard. *A Succinct View of the Rule in Shelley's Case*. Exeter, 1794. BL 514.c.25. Annotators unknown.

Priestley, Joseph. *Disquisitions relating to Matter and Spirit*. London: Johnson, 1777. BL C.28.h.14. Annotated by John Horne Tooke.

Prinsep, John. *Strictures and Observations on the Mocurrery System of Landed Property, in Bengal*. London: Debrett, 1794. BL 8022.cc.35. Annotated by John Prinsep.

Proctor, Robert. *Narrative of a Journey across the Cordillera of the Andes, and of a Residence in Lima, and Other Parts of Peru, in the Years 1823 and 1824*. London: Constable, 1825. Bodleian Library: Arch. H e. 16. Annotated by William Beckford.

Pulteney, Richard. *Historical and Biographical Sketches of the Progress of Botany in England, from its Origin to the Introduction of the Linnaean System*. 2 vols. London: Cadell, 1790. BL 443.b.1. Annotator unknown.

Quintilian, Marcus Fabius. *Institutionum Oratoriarum libri duodecim*. 2 vols. Paris, 1760. BL 749.a.12. Annotated by Charles Burney.

Randall, Anne Frances. *A Letter to the Women of England, on the Injustice of Mental Subordination*. London: Longman, 1799. BL C.142.b.13. Annotated by Elizabeth Ross.

Report of the Committee for the Relief of the Distressed Districts in Ireland. London, 1823. BL 8285.eee.1. Annotated by William Boyd.

Reynolds, Joshua. *Works*. 3 vols. London: Cadell and Davies, 1798. BL C.45.e.18–20. The first volume annotated by William Blake.

Rivers, David. *A Sermon, preached . . . Sunday, the 17th of July, 1796*. London, 1797. BL 4475.k.11.(7.) Annotator unknown.

Robb, William. *The Patriotic Wolves: A Fable*. 3rd ed. Edinburgh, 1793. BL 11632.b.56. Annotator unknown.

Robertson, Archibald. *A Topographical Survey of the Great Road from London to Bath and Bristol*. 2 vols. London, 1792. BL C.61.c.13. Annotated by Horace Walpole.

Robinson, Anthony. *A View of the Causes and Consequences of English Wars*. London: Johnson, 1798. BL 806.c.1. Annotated by John Lawrence.

Rousseau, J. J. *A Treatise on the Social Compact*. London: Murray, 1791. BL 1608/4490. Contemporary annotator unknown.

Rundell, Maria Eliza. *A New System of Domestic Cookery*. Rev. ed. London: Murray, 1827. BL 1578/7400. Annotator unknown.

Salisbury, R. A. *The Paradisus Londinensis: containing Plants Cultivated in the Vicinity of the Metropolis*. 2 vols. London: William Hooker, 1806–8. New York Public Library, Rare Books Division. *KF 1806 (Salisbury). Annotator unknown.

Saunders, Samuel. *A Short and Easy Introduction to Scientific and Philosophic Botany*. London: White, 1792. BL 1507/817. Annotator unknown.

Schmeisser, G. *Syllabus of Lectures on Mineralogy*. London, 1794. BL 1651/1348. Annotator unknown.

Schomberg, Alexander C. *An Historical and Chronological View of Roman Law*. Oxford, 1785. BL 1127.e.7. Annotated by Francis Hargrave.

Shakespeare, William. *Comedies, Histories, and Tragedies*. London: Jaggard and Blount, [1806]. Corporation of London, from the Keats House Collection: K/BK/01/011. Annotated by John Keats.

Shakespeare, William. *Dramatic Works*. 7 vols. Chiswick: Whittingham, 1814. Houghton Library, Harvard University: Keats *EC8 K2262 Zz814s. Annotated by John Keats.

Shakespeare, William. *Henry IV Part 1*. Bodleian Library Vet. A5 e. 1839(3), in a volume of miscellaneous plays starting with Thomas Otway, *Venice Preserved* (Edinburgh, 1812). Annotator unknown.

Shakespeare, William. *Macbeth: A Tragedy. With Notes and Emendations by Harry Rowe . . . Master of a Puppet-Show*. 2nd ed. York, 1799. BL 1344.f.35. Annotated by F. G. Waldron.

Shakespeare, William. *Poetical Works*. London: Wilson, 1806. Corporation of London, from the Keats House Collection: K/BK/01/010. Annotated by John Hamilton Reynolds, John Keats, and Joseph Severn.

Sinclair, A. G. *The Critic Philosopher; or Truth Discovered.* London, 1789. From Batten's Public Library, Clapham Common. BL 8405.bb.5. Annotators unknown.

Skinner, Stephen. *Etymologicon Linguae Anglicanae.* London, 1671. BL C.45.g.2. Annotated by John Horne Tooke.

Smith, J. E. *Compendium Florae Britannicae.* London, 1800. BL 724.d.12. Annotator unknown.

Smith, James Edward. *A Compendium of the English Flora.* London: Longman et al., 1829. Library of the Royal Botanical Gardens, Kew. Annotated by John Tatham and Silvanus P. Thompson.

Smith, J. E. *Flora Britannica.* 2 vols. London, 1800. Library of the Linnean Society. Annotated by J. E. Smith.

Smith, J. E. *Flora Britannica.* 3 vols. London, 1800–1804. BL 440.f.12–14. Annotator unknown.

Smith, James Edward. *Flora Britannica.* 3 vols. in 2. London, 1800–1804. Linnean Society Library. Annotated by Richard Dreyer.

Smith, Thomas. *Poems.* Manchester, 1797. BL 11646.bbb.64. Annotated by William Hampson?

Somers, John (attributed). *The Judgment of Whole Kingdoms and Nations, concerning the Rights, Power, and Prerogatives of Kings, and the Rights, Priviledges [sic], and Properties of the People.* 8th ed. London, 1713. BL 1389.g.31. Annotated by Elizabeth Collins and Augustus Frederick, Duke of Sussex.

Songs Sung at Covent Garden. BL 11602.ff.32. and 11602.ff.32*. Annotated by William Tapsell?

Sophocles. *Tragoediae Antigone et Trachiniae.* Ed. Thomas Johnson. Oxford, 1708. BL 998.c.2. Annotated by Charles Burney.

Southcott, Joanna. [A collection of pamphlets by and about Southcott, 1802–1814. 5 vols.] BL 699.h.22–26. Annotated by William George Thompson.

Southcott, Joanna. *Copies and Parts of Copies of Letters and Communications.* [London, 1804.] BL 4377.cc.50.(3.). Annotator unknown.

Southcott, Joanna. *The Third Book of Wonders, Announcing the Coming of Shiloh; with a Call to the Hebrews.* London, 1814. BL 4139.cc.65. Annotator unknown.

Spenser, Edmund. *Poetical Works.* 2 vols. London 1819. BL 11623.aa.40, 41. Annotated by Philip MacDermott.

Stendhal, M. de. *Rome, Naples, et Florence, en 1817.* Paris: Delaunay, 1817. National Library of Scotland: Dur. 692. Annotated by William Beckford.

Sterne, Laurence. *The Life and Opinions of Tristram Shandy, Gentleman.* 9 vols. in 3. London: D. Lynch, 1760–67. BL G.13443-5. Annotated by Edmund Ferrers.

Sterne, Laurence. *A Sentimental Journey through France and Italy. By Mr. Yorick.* 2 vols. London: Becket and De Hondt, 1770. BL G.13446. Annotated by Edmund Ferrers.

Stewart, Charles. *Poetical Works in Verse.* London: J. Porter, 1816. BL 11642.d.49. Annotated by William Hone.

Stirling, John. *A System of Rhetoric.* [Together with] John Holmes. *The Art of Rhetoric Made Easy.* Dublin, 1806. BL 11825.aa.15. Annotated by Philip MacDermott.

Stock, Joseph. *A Narrative of What Passed at Killalla, in the County of Mayo, and the Parts Adjacent, during the French Invasion in the Summer of 1798.* Dublin, 1800. BL 601.h.22. Annotator unknown.

Swedenborg, Emmanuel. *The Wisdom of Angels, concerning Divine Love and Divine Wisdom.* London: Chalkin, 1788. BL C.45.e.1. Annotated by William Blake.

Swete, John. *Family Prayers for each Morning and Evening in the Week.* 4th ed. London: L. B. Seeley, 1822. BL 3456.cc.6. Annotated by William Wilberforce.

Swift, Theophilus. *The Touchstone of Truth; Uniting Mr. Swift's late Correspondence with the Rev. Dr. Dobbin, and his Family; and the Detailed Account of their subsequent Challenge and Imposture.* 3rd ed. rev. Dublin, 1811. BL 1414.e.2. Annotator unknown.

Syllabus of the Lectures on Midwifery, delivered at Guy's Hospital, and at Dr. Lowder's and Dr. Haighton's Theatre, in St. Saviour's Church-Yard, Southwark. London, 1799. BL 1175.k.45. Annotated by F. Bagnall?

Theophrastus. *Theophrasti Characteres Ethici.* Glasgow: Foulis Press, 1793. BL 8461.aa.23. Annotated by John Wordsworth.

Thomson, James. *The Seasons.* London, 1730. Lewis Walpole Library, Farmington CT: 49 66. Annotated by Horace Walpole.

Tooke, George. *Annae-dicata, or, a Miscelanie of Some Different Cansonets, Dedicated to the Memory of My Deceased, Very Dear Wife, Anna Tooke of Beere.* [n.p., n.d.] BL C.127.e.7. Annotated by John Mitford.

Townsend, Joseph. *The Physician's Vade Mecum.* London: Cox, 1794. BL 1578/2973. Annotator unknown.

Treffry, Roger. *A Dissertation on Smut-Balls amongst Wheat and Other Grain.* Haydon, 1793. BL 7076.b.61. Annotator unknown.

Trusler, John. *A Concise View of the Common and Statute Law of England.* London, n.d. [1784?] BL 6191.g.2. Annotator unknown.

Vesey, Francis, Junior. *Case upon the Will of the Late Peter Thelluson, Esq.* London, [1799]. BL T.914.(9.) Annotated by Francis Hargrave.

Viator. *The Policy of England and France.* London: Ridgway, 1822. BL 8028.b.81. Annotator unknown.

Vince, S. *The Elements of the Conic Sections, as Preparatory to the Reading of Sir I. Newton's Principia.* Cambridge, 1781. BL 8531.b.32. Annotated by Humphry Davy and an unknown reader.

Vince, S. *The Plan of a Course of Lectures on the Principles of Natural Philosophy.* Cambridge, 1793. BL 1600/1154. Annotated by Thomas Barber.

Viner, Charles. *A General Abridgment of Law and Equity.* 24 vols. Aldershot, [1742–58]. BL 506.e.1.-506.f.5. Annotated by Francis Hargrave.

Virgil. *Opera.* Ed. C. de La Rue. London, 1695. BL 1000.g.4. Annotated by Charles Burney.

Virgil. *Virgil's Aeneis, translated into Scottish Verse, by the Famous Gawin Douglas, Bishop of Dunkeld.* Edinburgh: Sympson and Freebairn, 1710. Houghton Library, Harvard University: f*EC.D7457.B710vb. Annotated by John Horne Tooke.

The Virtuoso's Guide, in Collecting Provincial Copper Coins. London: J. Hammond, 1795. BL C.125.aa.4. Annotated by T. Woodward?

Voltaire, François Marie Arouet de. *Essay sur l'histoire générale et sur les moeurs et l'esprit des nations depius Charlemagne jusqu'à nos jours.* 7 vols. Geneva, 1756. Lewis Walpole Library, Farmington CT: 49 1172. Annotated by Horace Walpole.

Voltaire, François Marie Arouet de. *Henriade.* Trans. Daniel French. London: Sancho, 1807. BL 11475.f.4. Annotated by Philip MacDermott.

W., M., Mrs. *A Narrative of the Insidious Transactions practised towards a Gentleman in the Army, in Order to Obtain his Property.* London: For the Author, 1806. BL 1132.f.75. Annotator unknown.

Wakefield, Gilbert. *In Euripidis Hecubam, Londini Nuper Publicatam, Diatribe Extemporalis.* London, 1797. BL 995.g.16. Annotated by Charles Burney.

Wakefield, Priscilla. *An Introduction to Botany, in a Series of Familiar Letters, with Illustrative Engravings.* 2nd ed. London: Newbery et al., 1798. BL 07028.k.38. Annotated by Lady Eleanor Fenn.

Walker, Joseph Cooper. *Historical Memoir on Italian Tragedy.* London: Harding, 1799. BL 11795.k.1. Annotated by R. Sarel Junior.

Waller, Sir William. *Divine Meditations upon Several Occasions.* London, 1680. BL 4406.bb.20 Annotated by John Mitford.

Warner, Richard. *Antiquitates Culinariae; or Curious Tracts relationg to the Culinary Affairs of Old England.* London: R. Blamire, 1791. BL 786.1.29. Annotated by Sarah Sophia Banks.

Warton, Joseph. *An Essay on the Writings and Genius of Pope.* London: Dodsley, 1782. BL C.60.1.14. Annotated by Horace Walpole and John Mitford.

Warton, Thomas. *The History of English Poetry.* 2nd ed. 2 vols. London: Dodsley, 1775, 1778. Bodleian Library: Douce W. Subt. 70–72. Annotated by Francis Douce.

Watson, Richard. *An Apology for the Bible; in a Series of Letters Addressed to Thomas Paine.* Kilmarnock, 1820. BL 1507/1505. Annotator unknown.

Webster, John. *The Displaying of Supposed Witchcraft.* London, 1677. BL C.126.1.10. Annotated by an unknown reader and S. T. Coleridge.

Wewitzer, Ralph. *A Theatrical Pocket Book, or Brief Dramatic Chronology.* London, 1814. BL 1343.a.13. Annotator unknown.

Whitaker, John. *The Ancient Cathedral of Cornwall Historically Surveyed.* 2 vols. in 1. London: Stockdale, 1804. BL C.28.1.8. Annotated by Francis Douce.

Whitaker, John. *The History of Manchester.* 2 vols. London: Dodsley, 1771, 1775. BL C.28.1.6,7. Annotated by Francis Douce.

Williams, D. E. *The Life and Correspondence of Sir Thomas Lawrence.* 2 vols. London: Colburn and Bentley, 1831. BL C.134.d.6. Annotated by Benjamin Robert Haydon.

Withering, William. *An Arrangement of British Plants.* 3rd ed. 4 vols. Birmingham, 1796. Library of the Linnean Society. Annotated by J. E. Smith.

Wollaston, Francis. *The Secret History of a Private Man.* London, 1795. BL 4902.dd.1. Annotated by R. D. Shackleton.

Young, Edward. *Love of Fame, the Universal Passion.* 2nd ed. rev. London: Tonson, 1728. BL C.45.c.18. Annotated by Horace Walpole and John Mitford.

Bibliography of Secondary Sources

Addison, J., and R. Steele. *The Spectator.* Ed. Donald F. Bond. 5 vols. Oxford: Clarendon Press, 1965.

Allison, James. "Mrs. Thrale's Marginalia in Joseph Warton's Essay." *Huntington Library Quarterly* 19 (1956): 155–64.

Alston, R. C. *Books with Manuscript: A Short Title Catalogue of Books with Manuscript Notes in the British Library.* London: British Library, 1994.

Altick, Richard D. *The Common Reader: A Social History of the Mass Reading Public, 1800–1900.* Chicago: University of Chicago Press, 1957.

Armour, Richard W., and Raymond F. Howes, eds. *Coleridge the Talker.* Ithaca: Cornell University Press, 1940.

Austen, Jane. *Letters to her Sister Cassandra and Others.* Ed. R. W. Chapman. 2nd ed. London: Oxford University Press, 1952; repr. 1969.

Austen, Jane. *Works.* Ed. R. W. Chapman. 5 vols. Oxford: Clarendon Press, 1923; rept. 1940.

Babb, James T. "William Beckford of Fonthill." *Yale University Library Gazette* 41 (1966):60–69.

Baker, J. H. *Introduction to English Legal History.* 3rd ed. London: Butterworths, 1990.

Barker-Benfield, B. *The Culture of Sensibility: Sex and Society in Eighteenth-Century Britain.* Chicago: University of Chicago Press, 1992.

Barnard, F. A. *Bibliothecae Regiae Catalogus.* 5 vols. London, 1820–29.

Basbanes, Nicholas A. *A Gentle Madness.* New York: Henry Holt, 1995.

Beckford, William. *The Consummate Collector: William Beckford's Letters to His Bookseller.* Ed. Robert J. Gemmett. Wilby, Norwich: Michael Russell, 2000.

Bentley, G. E., Jr. *Blake Books [with] New Preface and Post Script*. Mansfield Center, CT: Martino Publishing, 2000.

Bentley, G. E. *The Stranger from Paradise: A Biography of William Blake*. New Haven and London: Yale University Press for Paul Mellon Center for Studies in British Art, 2001.

Bewley, Christina, and David Bewley. *Gentleman Radical: A Life of John Horne Tooke, 1736–1812*. London: Tauris, 1998.

Blackwood, John. "The Wordsworths' Book of Botany." *Country Life* 74 (no. 4497: 27 Oct. 1983): 1172–73.

Blake, William. *Annotations to Richard Watson*. Ed. G. Ingli James. Cardiff: University College Cardiff Press, 1984.

Blake, William. *Writings*. Ed. G. E. Bentley, Jr. 2 vols. Oxford: Clarendon Press, 1978.

Boswell, James. *Boswell's Life of Johnson*. Ed. George Birkbeck Hill. Rev. L. F. Powell. 6 vols. Oxford: Clarendon Press, 1934–50.

Boswell, James. *The Life of Samuel Johnson, LL.D. With Marginal Comments and Markings from Two Copies Annotated by Hester Lynch Thrale Piozzi*. Ed. Edward G. Fletcher. 3 vols. London: Limited Editions Club, 1938.

Brewer, John. *The Pleasures of the Imagination: English Culture in the Eighteenth Century*. London: HarperCollins, 1997.

Brewer, John. "Reconstructing the Reader: Prescriptions, Texts, and Strategies in Anna Larpent's Reading." In *The Practice and Representation of Reading in England*, ed. James Raven, Helen Small, and Naomi Tadmor. Cambridge: Cambridge University Press, 1996. 226–45.

Brewer, John, and Iain McCalman. "Publishing." *An Oxford Companion to the Romantic Age*. Ed. Iain McCalman et al. New York and Oxford: Oxford University Press, 1999. 197–206.

Broster, John. *Collectanea Johnsoniana: Catalogue of the Library, Pictures, Prints . . . of Mrs. Hester Lynch Piozzi, Deceased*. Chester, 1823.

Brownell, Morris R. "Hester Lynch Piozzi's Marginalia." *Eighteenth-Century Life* 3 (1977): 97–100.

Brownell, Morris R. *The Prime Minister of Taste: A Portrait of Horace Walpole*. New Haven: Yale University Press, 2001.

Brunton, Mary. *Discipline*. London: Colburn and Bentley, 1832.

Brunton, Mary. *Self-Control*. 2nd ed. 2 vols. Edinburgh, 1811.

Brynbella. A Catalogue of the Valuable Paintings, Prints, Books . . . the Property of Sir John Salusbury. [n.p.], 1836.

Burney, Frances. *The Journals and Letters of Fanny Burney (Madame D'Arblay), 1791–1840*. Ed. Joyce Hemlow et al. 12 vols. Oxford: Clarendon Press, 1972–84.

Byron, George Gordon, Lord. "Holograph Marginalia in Ugo Foscolo's *Ultime lettere di Jacopo Ortis*." In *Shelley and His Circle*, ed. Donald H. Reiman. Cambridge: Harvard University Press, 1986. 8:1107–21.

Byron, George Gordon, Lord. *Letters and Journals*. Ed. L. Marchand. 12 vols. Cambridge: Belknap Press of Harvard University Press, 1973–82.

Catalogue of the Entire Library of the late Granville Sharp, Esq. London: Leigh and Sotheby, 1813.

Catalogue of the Genuine Library, Prints, and Books of Prints, of an Illustrious Personage, lately Deceased. London: Christie's, 1819. Priced BL copy: 123.f.16.

Catalogue of the Valuable Library, late the property of John Horne Tooke, Esq. London: King and Lochée, 1813.

Chartier, Roger. "Lecturers and Voyagers: From the Text to the Reader." In *Readers and Reading*, ed. Andrew Bennett. London and New York: Longman, 1995. 132–49.

Chorley, Henry. *Memorials of Mrs. Hemans*. London: Saunders and Otley, 1836.

Clairmont, Claire. *Journals*. Ed. Marion Kingston Stocking. Cambridge: Harvard University Press, 1968.

Clare, John. *Selected Letters*. Ed. Mark Storey. Oxford: Clarendon Press, 1988.

Clark, Peter. *British Clubs and Societies, 1580–1800: The Origins of an Associated World*. Oxford: Clarendon Press, 2000.

Cobbett, William. *History of the Regency and Reign of King George the Fourth*. London: Cobbett, 1830.

Cobbett, William. *The Life and Adventures of Peter Porcupine*. Philadelphia: William Cobbett, 1796.

Coke, William. *A Readable Edition of Coke upon Littleton*. Ed. Thomas Coventry. London: Saunders and Benning, 1830.

Cole, G. D. H., and Raymond Postgate. *The Common People 1746–1946*. 4th ed. London: Methuen, 1949.

Coleman, D. C. *The British Paper Industry 1495–1860*. Westport, CT: Greenwood Press, 1975.

Coleridge, Hartley. *Letters*. Ed. Evelyn Griggs and Earl Leslie Griggs. London: Oxford University Press, 1941.

Coleridge, S. T. *Biographia Literaria*. Ed. James Engell and W. Jackson Bate. 2 vols. Princeton: Princeton University Press, 1983.

Coleridge, S. T. *Collected Letters*. Ed. E. L. Griggs. 6 vols. Oxford: Clarendon Press, 1956–69.

Coleridge, S. T. *Lectures 1808–1819: On Literature*. Ed. R. A. Foakes. 2 vols. Princeton: Princeton University Press, 1987.

Coleridge, S. T. *Literary Remains*. Ed. H. N. Coleridge. 4 vols. London, 1736–39.

Coleridge, S. T. *Marginalia*. Ed. George Whalley and H. J. Jackson. 6 vols. Princeton: Princeton University Press, 1980–2001.

Coleridge, S. T. *Poetical Works*. Ed. J. C. C. Mays. 3 vols. in 6. Princeton: Princeton University Press, 2001.

Coleridge, S. T. *Table Talk*. Ed. Carl Woodring. 2 vols. Princeton: Princeton University Press, 1990.

Coleridge, S. T. *The Watchman.* Ed. Lewis Patton. Princeton: Princeton University Press, 1970.

Connell, Philip. "Bibliomania: Book Collecting, Cultural Politics, and the Rise of Literary Heritage in Romantic Britain." *Representations* 71 (2000):24–27.

Constable, Thomas. *Archibald Constable and His Literary Correspondents.* 3 vols. Edinburgh: Edmonston and Douglas, 1873.

Darnton, Robert. *The Forbidden Bestsellers of Pre-Revolutionary France.* New York: Norton, 1995.

Darnton, Robert. "Seven Bad Reasons Not to Study Manuscripts." *Harvard Library Bulletin* 4 (1993):37–42.

Darnton, Robert. "What Is the History of Books?" In *The Kiss of Lamourette: Reflections in Cultural History.* New York: Norton, 1990. 107–35.

Deane, Phyllis, and W. A. Cole. *British Economic Growth 1688–1959: Trends and Structures.* 2nd ed. Cambridge: Cambridge University Press, 1967.

DeMaria, Robert, Jr. *Samuel Johnson and the Life of Reading.* Baltimore: Johns Hopkins University Press, 1997.

De Quincey, Thomas. *Collected Writings.* Ed. David Masson. 14 vols. London: A. and C. Black, 1896–7.

Dictionary of National Biography. Ed. Leslie Stephen and Sidney Lee. 63 vols. London: Smith, Elder, 1885–1900.

Dibdin, T. F. *The Bibliographical Decameron; or, Ten Days Pleasant Discourse upon Illuminated Manuscripts, and Subjects Connected with Early Engraving, Typography, and Bibliography.* 3 vols. London: For the Author, 1817.

Dibdin, T. F. *Bibliomania or Book Madness; A Bibliographical Romance, in Six Parts.* London, 1811.

Dibdin, T. F. *Bibliophobia.* London: Henry Bohn, 1832.

Dibdin, T. F. *Reminiscences of a Literary Life.* 2 vols. London: Major, 1836.

Disraeli, Benjamin. *Vivian Grey.* Ed. Bernard N. Langdon-Davies. London: R. Brimley Johnson, 1904.

D'Israeli, Isaac. *The Literary Character, Illustrated by the History of Men of Genius.* London: Murray, 1818.

Donald, Diana. *The Age of Caricature: Satirical Prints in the Age of George III.* New Haven: Yale University Press, 1996.

The Douce Legacy: An Exhibition to Commemorate the 150th Anniversary of the Bequest of Francis Douce (1757–1834). Oxford: Bodleian Library, 1984.

Edgeworth, Maria, and R. L. Edgeworth. *Practical Education.* 2nd ed. 3 vols. London: Johnson, 1801.

Edwards, Edward. *Lives of the Founders of the British Museum.* London: Trübner, 1870.

Eliot, Simon. *Some Patterns and Trends in British Publishing, 1800–1919.* London: Bibliographical Society, 1994.

Ellis, Sir Henry. *A Catalogue of Manuscripts, formerly in the possession of Francis Hargrave, Esq*. London, 1818.

Erasmus, Desiderius. *Correspondence*, vol. 1: *Letters 1 to 141, 1484 to 1500*. Trans. R. A. B. Mynors and D. F. S. Thomson. Annotated by Wallace K. Ferguson. Toronto: University of Toronto Press, 1974.

Erasmus, Desiderius. "On the Method of Study." Trans. Brian McGregor. Ed. Craig R. Thompson. *Collected Works*, vol. 24. Toronto: University of Toronto Press, 1978. 661–91.

Erickson, Lee. *The Economy of Literary Form*. Baltimore: Johns Hopkins University Press, 1996.

Ewing, Majl. "Mrs. Piozzi Peruses Dr. Thomas Browne." *Philological Quarterly* 22 (1943): 111–18.

Feather, John. *A History of British Publishing*. London: Croom Helm, 1988.

Ferriar, John. *Illustrations of Sterne: With Other Essays and Verses*. London: Cadell and Davies, 1798.

Field, Barron. *An Analysis of Blackstone's* Commentaries on the Laws of England. London: Cadell and Davies, 1811.

Finney, Claude Lee. *The Evolution of Keats's Poetry*. 2 vols. New York: Russell and Russell, 1936; repr. 1963.

Fox, Charles James. *Memoirs and Correspondence*. Ed. Lord John Russell. 4 vols. London: Richard Bentley, 1853–57.

Garside, Peter, James Raven, and Rainer Schwörling. *The English Novel 1770–1829: A Bibliographical Survey of Prose Fiction Published in the British Isles*. 2 vols. Oxford: Oxford University Press, 2000.

Gaskell, Philip. *A New Introduction to Bibliography*. Oxford: Clarendon Press, 1972.

Gayer, Arthur D., et al. *The Growth and Fluctuation of the British Economy*. Oxford: Clarendon Press, 1953.

Gemmett, Robert J., ed. *Sale Catalogues of Libraries of Eminent Persons*, vol. 3. London: Mansell, 1972.

George, M. Dorothy. *Catalogue of Political and Personal Satires, preserved in the Department of Prints and Drawings in the British Museum*, vol. 9:1811–19. London: Trustees of the British Museum, 1949.

Gilmartin, Kevin. " 'Study to be Quiet': Hannah More and the Invention of Conservative Culture in Britain." *ELH* 70 (2003):493–540.

Gilmore, William J. *Reading Becomes a Necessity of Life: Material and Cultural Life in Rural New England, 1780–1835*. Knoxville: University of Tennessee Press, 1989.

Gittings, Robert. *John Keats*. London: Heinemann, 1968.

Gittings, Robert. *John Keats: The Living Year*. London: Heinemann, 1954; repr. 1978.

Glaister, Geoffrey Ashall. *Encyclopedia of the Book*. 2nd ed. New Castle, DE: Oak Knoll Press, 1996.

Godwin, William. *The Enquirer.* 1797. Reprints of Economic Classics. New York: Augustus M. Kelley, 1965.

Goede, C. A. G. *The Stranger in England; or, Travels in Great Britain.* 3 vols. London: Mathews and Leigh, 1807.

Goldsmith, Oliver. *Collected Works.* Ed. A. Friedman. 5 vols. Oxford: Oxford University Press, 1966.

Goodwin, Albert. *The Friends of Liberty.* London: Hutchinson, 1979.

Grafton, Anthony. *The Footnote.* Cambridge: Harvard University Press, 1997.

Grafton, Anthony. "Is the History of Reading a Marginal Enterprise? Guillaume Budé and His Books." *Papers of the Bibliographical Society of America* 91:2 (1997):139–57.

Hale, Sir Matthew. *The Jurisdiction of the Lords House, or Parliament.* Ed. F. Hargrave. London: Cadell and Davies, 1796.

Hamilton, Elizabeth. *Letters on the Elementary Principles of Education.* 2nd ed. 2 vols. Bath, 1801.

Hamlyn, Hilda M. "Eighteenth-Century Circulating Libraries in England." *The Library* n.s. 5:1 (1947):197–218.

Hargrave, Francis. "Address to the Purchasers of the New Edition, Announcing his Relinquishment of the Undertaking, and Mr. Butler's succeeding to it." Broadside, 18 Jan. 1785. British Library 1241.g.19.(7).

Hargrave, Francis. *An Argument in the Case of James Sommerset a Negro.* London, 1772.

Harris, Michael. "A Few Shillings for Small Books: The Experiences of a Flying Stationer in the 18th Century." In *Spreading the Word,* ed. Robin Myers and Michael Harris. Winchester: St. Paul's Bibliographies, 1990. 83–108.

Hazen, Allen T. *A Catalogue of Horace Walpole's Library.* 3 vols. New Haven: Yale University Press, 1969.

Hazlitt, William. *Complete Works.* Ed. P. P. Howe. 21 vols. London: Dent, 1934.

Hibbert, Christopher. *George III: A Personal History.* London: Viking, 1998.

Holdsworth, Sir William. *A History of English Law,* vol. 12. London: Methuen, 1938.

Howsam, Leslie. *Cheap Bibles: Nineteenth-Century Publishing and the British and Foreign Bible Society.* Cambridge: Cambridge University Press, 1991.

Hume, Mary C. *A Brief Sketch of the Life, Character, and Religious Opinions of the late Charles Augustus Tulk.* Boston, 1850.

Hunt, Leigh. *Autobiography.* 3 vols. London: Smith, Elder, 1850.

Hunt, Leigh. *Imagination and Fancy.* London: Smith, Elder, 1844.

Hunt, Leigh. *Selected Essays.* London: Dent, 1947.

Irwin, Raymond. *The English Library: Sources and History.* London: Allen and Unwin, 1966.

Jackson, H. J. "England's Populist Pindars." *eBLJ* (2002):1–18. www.bl.uk/collections/eblj/2002/article4.html.

Jackson, H. J. *Marginalia: Readers Writing in Books.* New Haven: Yale University Press, 2001.

Jackson, Holbrook. *The Anatomy of Bibliomania.* Urbana: University of Illinois Press, 2001.

Jackson, Holbrook. *The Fear of Books.* Urbana: University of Illinois Press, 2001.

Jackson, Holbrook. *The Reading of Books.* Urbana: University of Illinois Press, 2001.

Jackson, William. "On Literary Thievery." In *The Four Ages; together with Essays on Various Subjects.* London: Cadell and Davies, 1798. 244–57.

Johnson, Claudia L. *Jane Austen: Women, Politics, and the Novel.* Chicago: University of Chicago Press, 1988.

Journals of the House of Commons 68 (1813):944–45.

Kaufman, Paul. "English Book Clubs and Their Role in Social History." *Libri* 14 (1964–65):1–31.

Kaufman, Paul. *Libraries and their Users: Collected Papers in Library History.* London: Library Association, 1969.

Keats, John. *The Letters of John Keats 1814–1821.* Ed. Hyder Edward Rollins. 2 vols. Cambridge: Harvard University Press, 1958.

Keats, John. *The Manuscripts of the Younger Romantics: John Keats.* Ed. Jack Stillinger. 4 vols. New York: Garland, 1985.

Keats, John. *Poetical Works and Other Writings.* Ed. H. Buxton Forman. Rev. Maurice Buxton Forman. 8 vols. New York: Scribner's, 1938–39.

Kenny, Neil. "Books in Space and Time: Bibliomania and Early Modern Histories of Learning and 'Literature' in France." *MLQ* 61:2 (2000):253–86.

King, R. W. *"Parson Primrose": The Life, Work, and Friendships of Henry Francis Cary.* New York: Doran, 1925.

Klancher, Jon. *The Making of English Reading Audiences, 1790–1832.* Madison: University of Wisconsin Press, 1987.

Klancher, Jon. "The Vocation of Criticism." In *The Cambridge History of Literary Criticism,* vol. 5: *Romanticism,* ed. Marshall Brown. Cambridge: Cambridge University Press, 1989. 296–320.

Knott, D. H. "Thomas Wilson and *The Use of Circulating Libraries.*" *Library History* 4 (1976–78):2–10.

Lackington, James. *Confessions.* London, 1804.

Lackington, James. *Memoirs of the First Forty-Five Years of the Life of James Lackington.* London, 1791.

Lamb, Charles, and Mary Anne Lamb. *Letters.* Ed. Edwin J. Marrs, Jr. 3 vols. Ithaca: Cornell University Press, 1975–78.

Lamb, Charles, and Mary Lamb. *Works.* Ed. E. V. Lucas. 5 vols. London: Methuen, 1903.

Lau, Beth. *Keats's* Paradise Lost. Gainesville: University Press of Florida, 1998.

Lavater, Johann Caspar. *Aphorisms on Man (1788): A Facsimile Reproduction of*

William Blake's Copy of the First English Edition. Intro. R. J. Shroyer. Delmar, NY: Scholars' Facsimiles, 1980.

Le Faye, Deirdre. "New Marginalia in Jane Austen's Books." *Book Collector* 49 (2000):222–26.

Lemmings, David. *Professors of the Law: Barristers and English Legal Culture in the Eighteenth Century*. Oxford: Oxford University Press, 2000.

Lewis, Wilmarth Sheldon. "Horace Walpole's Library." In Allen T. Hazen, *A Catalogue of Horace Walpole's Library*. 3 vols. New Haven: Yale University Press, 1969. 1:xlvii–xc.

Lidwill, John. *History and Memoirs of John Lidwill . . . from his Birth to his Present Age of near Sixty Years*. Dublin, [c. 1800].

Lincoln's Inn. *The Records of the Honorable Society of Lincoln's Inn: The Black Books*. 4 vols. London: Lincoln's Inn, 1897–1902.

Lister, Anthony. "George John, 2nd Earl Spencer and His 'Librarian', Thomas Frognall Dibdin." In *Bibliophily*, ed. Robin Myers and Michael Harris. Cambridge and Alexandria, VA: Chadwyck-Healey, 1986. 90–120.

Locke, John. *Some Thoughts Concerning Education and The Conduct of the Understanding*. Ed. Ruth W. Grant and Nathan Tarcov. Indianapolis: Hackett, 1996.

Lockhart, J. G. *Memoirs of the Life of Sir Walter Scott, Bart*. Rev. ed. 9 vols. Boston: Houghton, 1861.

Lowell, Amy. *John Keats*. 2 vols. London: Cape, 1925.

Lyell, James P. R., ed. *Mrs. Piozzi and Isaac Watts*. London: Grafton, 1934.

Mangin, Edward. *An Essay on Light Reading*. London: Carpenter, 1808.

Mangin, Edward. *A View of the Pleasures Arising from a Love of Books: in Letters to a Lady*. London, 1814.

Marshall, B. R. *British Historical Statistics*. Cambridge: Cambridge University Press, 1988.

Mason, William. *Satirical Poems Published Anonymously by William Mason with Notes by Horace Walpole Now First Printed from his Manuscript*. Ed. Paget Toynbee. Oxford: Clarendon Press, 1926.

Mathias, T. J. *The Pursuits of Literature. A Satirical Poem in Four Dialogues. With Notes*. 5th ed. rev. London: T. Becket, 1798.

Maxted, Ian. *The London Book Trades, 1775–1800: A Preliminary Checklist of Members*. Folkestone: Dawson, 1977.

Mayo, Robert D. *The English Novel in the Magazines, 1740–1815*. Evanston: Northwestern University Press, 1962.

Melville, Lewis. *The Life and Letters of William Beckford of Fonthill*. London: Heinemann, 1910.

"Memoirs of Henry Lemoine." *Wonderful Museum* 5 (1807): 2218–40.

Miller, Edward. *That Noble Cabinet: A History of the British Museum*. London: André Deutsch, 1973.

Mitford, Mary Russell. *Recollections of a Literary Life; or, Books, Places, and People*. 3 vols. London: Bentley, 1852.

Montaigne, Michel de. "Des Livres." *Essais.* 3 vols. Paris: Garnier-Flammarion, 1979. 2:78–90.

Moore, Thomas. *Journal.* Ed. Wilfred S. Dowden. 6 vols. Newark: University of Delaware Press, 1983–91.

More, Hannah. *The Sorrows of Yamba.* London: Cheap Repository, [1795].

More, Hannah. "Unprofitable Reading." *Works.* 11 vols. London: Bohn, 1853. 11:109–14.

Moss, Carolyn J. "Wordsworth's Marginalia in John Davis's *Travels . . . in the United States.*" *PBSA* 79 (1985):539–41.

Newlyn, Lucy. *Reading, Writing, and Romanticism: The Anxiety of Reception.* Oxford: Oxford University Press, 2000.

Nicolson, Marjorie. "Thomas Paine, Edward Nares, and Mrs. Piozzi's Marginalia." *Huntington Library Bulletin* no. 10 (1936):103–33.

Oldham, John. *Compositions in Prose and Verse.* Ed. E. Thompson. 3 vols. London, 1770.

Owings, Frank N. *The Keats Library.* London: Keats-Shelley Memorial Association, [1978].

O'Dwyer, E. J. *Thomas Frognall Dibdin: Bibliographer & Bibliomaniac Extraordinary, 1776–1847.* Pinner: Private Libraries Association, 1967.

Parliamentary Debates. 1st ser. 26 (1813).

Pearson, Jacqueline. *Women's Reading in Britain, 1750–1835: A Dangerous Recreation.* Cambridge: Cambridge University Press, 1999.

Pettigrew, Thomas Joseph. *Bibliotheca Sussexiana: A Descriptive Catalogue.* 2 vols. London: Longman, 1827, 1839.

Pindar, Peter. *The R---l H-mb-gs.* London: Fairburn, [1818].

Pinkerton, John, ed. *Walpoliana.* 2 vols. London: R. Phillips, [1799].

Piozzi, Hester L. *The Piozzi Letters.* Ed. Edward Bloom and Lillian Bloom. 6 vols. Newark: University of Delaware Press, 1989–2003.

Piozzi, Hester L. *Thraliana: The Diary of Mrs. Hester Lynch Thrale (Later Mrs. Piozzi).* Ed. Katherine C. Balderston. 2 vols. Oxford: Clarendon Press, 1942.

Place, Francis. *Autobiography.* Ed. Mary Thale. Cambridge: Cambridge University Press, 1972.

Plant, Marjorie. *The English Book Trade.* 3rd ed. London: Allen & Unwin, 1974.

Plumb, J. H. *The First Four Georges.* London: Batsford, 1956.

Pollard, Graham. "The English Market for Printed Books." *Publishing History* 4 (1978):7–48.

Pollin, Burton R., with Redmond Burke. "John Thelwall's Marginalia in a Copy of Coleridge's *Biographia Literaria.*" *Bulletin of the New York Public Library* 74 (1970):73–94.

Raven, James. "From Promotion to Proscription: Arrangements for Reading and Eighteenth-Century Libraries." In *The Practice and Representation of Reading in England,* ed. James Raven, Helen Small, and Naomi Tadmor. Cambridge: Cambridge University Press, 1996. 175–201.

Raven, James. *Judging New Wealth: Popular Publishing and Responses to Commerce in England, 1750–1800*. Oxford: Clarendon Press, 1992.

Raven, James, Helen Small, and Naomi Tadmor, eds. *The Practice and Representation of Reading in England*. Cambridge: Cambridge University Press, 1996.

Richardson, Alan. *Literature, Education, and Romanticism: Reading as Social Practice, 1780–1832*. Cambridge: Cambridge University Press, 1994.

Ristine, Frank H. "Leigh Hunt's 'Horace.'" *Modern Language Notes* 66 (1951):540–43.

Rivers, Isabel, ed. *Books and Their Readers in Eighteenth-Century England*. Leicester: Leicester University Press, 1982.

Roberts, William. *Memoirs of the Life and Correspondence of Mrs. Hannah More*. 2 vols. New York: Harper, 1885.

Robinson, Henry Crabb. *Diary, Reminiscences, and Correspondence*. Ed. Thomas Sadler. 3 vols. London: Macmillan, 1869.

Roper, Derek. *Reviewing before the* Edinburgh. London: Methuen, 1978.

Rose, Jonathan. "Rereading the English Common Reader: A Preface to a History of Audiences." *Journal of the History of Ideas* 53 (1992):47–70.

Rose, Mark. *Authors and Owners: The Invention of Copyright*. Cambridge: Harvard University Press, 1993.

Rosebery, Eva. "Books from Beckford's Library Now at Barnbougle." *Book Collector* 14 (1965):324–34.

Rule, John. *Albion's People: English Society, 1714–1815*. London: Longman, 1992.

Savage, Spencer. "Synopsis of the Annotations of Linnaeus and Contemporaries in His Library of Printed Books." *Catalogue of the Manuscripts in the Library of the Linnean Society of London*. Part 3. London, 1940.

Scott, Walter. *Letters*. Ed. H. J. C. Grierson. 12 vols. London: Constable, 1932–37.

Secord, James. *Victorian Sensation: The Extraordinary Publication, Reception, and Secret Authorship of "Vestiges of the Natural History of Creation."* Chicago: University of Chicago Press, 2000.

Seward, Anna. *Letters Written Between the Years 1784 and 1807*. 6 vols. Edinburgh and London: Constable and Longman et al., 1811.

Shelley and His Circle. Ed. Kenneth Neill Cameron, Donald Reiman, et al. Cambridge: Harvard University Press, 1961–.

Shelley, Mary Wollstonecraft. *Letters*. Ed. Betty T. Bennett. 2 vols. Baltimore: Johns Hopkins University Press, 1980.

Shelley, P. B., and Margaret King Moore. "Holograph Annotations and Markings in a Copy of William Godwin's *Political Justice*." In *Shelley and His Circle*, ed. Donald H. Reiman. Cambridge: Harvard University Press, 1986. 8:897–915.

Sherman, William. *John Dee: The Politics of Reading and Writing in the Renaissance*. Amherst: University of Massachusetts Press, 1995.

Shteir, Ann B. *Cultivating Women, Cultivating Science: Flora's Daughters and Botany in England, 1760–1860*. Baltimore: Johns Hopkins University Press, 1996.

Siskin, Clifford. *The Work of Writing*. Baltimore: Johns Hopkins University Press, 1998.

Slatter, Enid. "From the Archives: The Reverend Richard Dreyer and His Illustrated Copy of Sir James Edward Smith's *Flora Britannica*, 1800–04." *The Linnean* 16 (2000):19–23.

Slights, W. W. E. *Managing Readers: Printed Marginalia in English Renaissance Books*. Ann Arbor: University of Michigan Press, 2001.

Smiles, Samuel. *A Publisher and His Friends: Memoir and Correspondence of the Late John Murray*. 2 vols. London: Murray, 1891.

Smith, J. E., and James Sowerby. *English Botany; or, Coloured Figures of British Plants, with their Essential Characters, Synonyms, and Places of Growth*. 36 vols. London, 1790–1814.

Smith, Sydney. *Letters*. Ed. C. Nowell Smith. 2 vols. Oxford: Clarendon Press, 1953.

Sotheby, S. Leigh, and John Wilkinson. *Catalogue of the Valuable Collection . . . of the Late Rev. John Mitford*. London, 1759.

Southey, Robert. *Life and Correspondence*. Ed. C. C. Southey. 6 vols. London: Longman et al., 1849.

Southey, Robert. *Sir Thomas More: or, Colloquies on the Progress and Prospects of Society*. 2 vols. London: Murray, 1829.

Sperry, Stuart. "Richard Woodhouse's Interleaved and Annotated Copy of Keats's *Poems* (1817)." *Literary Monographs* 1 (1967):101–67.

Spurgeon, Caroline F. E. *Keats's Shakespeare: A Descriptive Study Based on New Material*. London: Oxford University Press, 1928.

Steinberg, S. H. *Five Hundred Years of Printing*. 2nd ed. rev. Harmondsworth: Penguin, 1966.

Stower, Caleb. *The Printer's Price-Book*. London: Cradock and Joy, 1814.

Sutherland, John. "The British Book Trade and the Crash of 1826." *The Library* n.s. 6:9 (1987):148–61.

Sutherland, Kathryn. " 'Events . . . have made us a world of readers': Reader Relations, 1780–1830." In *The Romantic Period*, ed. David Pirie. London: Penguin, 1994. 1–48.

Taylor, Isaac. *Advice to the Teens*. 2nd ed. London: Rest Fenner, 1818.

Tomalin, Claire. *Jane Austen: A Life*. London: Viking, 1997.

"A Traveller." "Facts relative to the State of Reading Societies and Literary Institutions in the United Kingdom." *Monthly Magazine* 51 (1821):397–98.

Tribble, Evelyn E. *Margins and Marginality: The Printed Page in Early Modern Europe*. Charlottesville: University Press of Virginia, 1993.

Trusler, John. "A List of Books, published by the Rev. Dr. Trusler, at the Literary-Press, No. 62, Wardour-Street, Soho. 1790." Catalogue attached to John Trusler, *The Honours of the Table* (1788), Lewis Walpole Literary copy, shelfmark 53 T77 788.

Trusler, John. *Memoirs . . . Part I*. Bath: John Browne, 1806.

Trusler, John. "Memoirs . . . Volume Two." MS Lewis Walpole Library, Farmington, CT.

Twyman, Michael. *Breaking the Mould: The First Hundred Years of Lithography.* London: British Library, 2001.

Twyman, Michael. *Printing 1770–1970: An Illustrated History of Its Development and Uses in England.* 2nd ed. London: British Library, 1998.

Tyson, Gerald P. *Joseph Johnson: A Liberal Publisher.* Iowa City: University of Iowa Press, 1979.

Varma, Devendra P. *The Evergreen Tree of Diabolical Knowledge.* Washington, DC: Consortium Press, 1972.

Vincent, David. *The Rise of Mass Literacy: Reading and Writing in Modern Europe.* Cambridge: Polity Press, 2000.

Virgil. *Opera, locis parallelis ex antiquis scriptoribus et annotationum delectu illustrata in usum juventutis.* Oxford: Clarendon Press, 1820.

Walker, Ralph S."Charles Burney's Theft of Books at Cambridge." *Publications of the Cambridge Bibliographical Society* 3 (1959–63):313–26.

Walpole, Horace. *Correspondence.* 48 vols. New Haven: Yale University Press, 1937–83.

Walpole, Horace. *Walpoliana. See* Pinkerton.

Walsh, Marcus. *Shakespeare, Milton, and Eighteenth-Century Literary Editing.* Cambridge: Cambridge University Press, 1997.

Ward, Aileen. *John Keats: The Making of a Poet.* New York: Viking, 1963.

Watts, Isaac. *The Improvement of the Mind . . . to which is added, A Discourse on the Education of Children and Youth.* London, 1801.

White, Gilbert. *The Natural History and Antiquities of Selborne . . . with Notes by Several Eminent Naturalists.* London, [1833].

White, Gilbert. *The Natural History and Antiquities of Selborne.* Facsimile reprint of the 1789 first edition. Menston; Scolar Press, 1972.

Wiles, R. M. *Serial Publication in England before 1750.* Cambridge: Cambridge University Press, 1957.

Williams, Orlo. *Lamb's Friend the Census-Taker: Life and Letters of John Rickman.* London: Constable, 1912.

Wilson, Thomas. *An Accurate Description of Bromley, in Kent.* London: J. Hamilton and T. Wison, 1797. BL 579.a.25 includes the "Catalogue of Books."

Wollstonecraft, Mary, and William Godwin. *"A Short Residence in Sweden" and "Memoirs of the Author of 'The Rights of Woman.'"* Ed. Richard Holmes. Harmondsworth: Penguin, 1987.

Wood, Marcus. " 'The Abolition Blunderbuss': Free Publishing and British Abolition Propaganda, 1780–1838." In *Free Print and Non-Commercial Publishing since 1700,* ed. James Raven. Aldershot: Ashgate, 2000. 67–92.

Woolf, D. R. *Reading History in Early Modern England.* Cambridge: Cambridge University Press, 2000.

Wordsworth, William, and Dorothy Wordsworth. *Letters: The Early Years, 1787–1805*. Ed. Ernest De Selincourt. 2nd ed. Rev. Chester L. Shaver. Oxford: Clarendon Press, 1967.

Wu, Duncan. *Wordsworth's Reading 1800–1815*. Cambridge: Cambridge University Press, 1995.

Index

The index includes all names of persons but only selected subject categories. In long entries, passing mentions are given first, followed by subheadings for more substantive references. Peers are referred to by the name used in the text, e.g., the Duke of Sussex under Sussex, not under Augustus Frederick. Books are included in the entries for their authors and are listed individually only in the longer entries that include subheadings. Anonymous works are listed by title.

** An asterisk with the page number means that in this case the person appears as an annotator.*

† A dagger indicates a reference to an annotated book.